THE

CONQUEST OF CANADA.

BY

THE AUTHOR OF "HOCHELAGA."

IN TWO VOLUMES.

VOL. I.

NEW YORK:
HARPER & BROTHERS, PUBLISHERS,
82 CLIFF STREET.
1850.

INTRODUCTION.

England and France started in a fair race for the magnificent prize of supremacy in America. The advantages and difficulties of each were much alike, but the systems by which they improved those advantages and met those difficulties were essentially different. New France was colonized by a government, New England by a people. In Canada the men of intellect, influence, and wealth were only the agents of the mother country; they fulfilled, it is true, their colonial duties with zeal and ability, but they ever looked to France for honor and approbation, and longed for a return to her shores as their best reward. They were in the colony, but not of it. They strove vigorously to repel invasion, to improve agriculture, and to encourage commerce, for the sake of France, but not for Canada.

The mass of the population of New France were descended from settlers sent out within a short time after the first occupation of the country, and who were not selected for any peculiar qualifications. They were not led to emigrate from the spirit of adventure, disappointed ambition, or political discontent; by far the larger proportion left their native country under the pressure of extreme want or in blind obedience to the will of their superiors. They were then established in points best suited to the interests of France, not those best suited to their own. The physical condition of the humbler emigrant, however, became better than that of his countrymen in the Old World; the fertile soil repaid his labor with competence; independence fostered self-reliance, and the unchecked range of forest and prairie inspired him with thoughts of freedom. But all these elevating tendencies were fatally counteracted by the blighting influence of feudal organization. Restrictions, humiliating as well as injurious, pressed upon the person and property of the Canadian. Every avenue to wealth and influence was closed to him and thrown open to the children of Old France. He saw whole tracts of the magnificent country lavished upon the favorites and military followers of the court, and, through corrupt or capricious influences, the privilege of exclusive trade granted for the aggrandizement of strangers at his expense.

France founded a state in Canada. She established a feudal and ecclesiastical frame-work for the young nation, and into that Procrustean bed the growth of population and the proportions of society were forced. The state fixed governments at Montreal, Three Rivers, and Quebec; there towns arose. She divided the rich banks of the St. Lawrence and of the Richelieu into seigneuries; there population spread. She placed posts on the lakes and rivers of the Far West; there the fur-traders congregated. She divided the land into dioceses and parishes, and appointed bishops and curates; a portion of all produce of the soil was exacted for their support. She sent out the people at her own cost, and acknowledged no shadow of popular rights. She organized the inhabitants by an unsparing conscription, and placed over them officers either from the Old Country or from the favored class of seigneurs. She grasped a monopoly of every valuable production of the country, and yet forced upon it her own manufactures to the exclusion of all others. She squandered her resources and treasures on the colony, but violated all principles of justice in a vain endeavor to make that colony a source of wealth. She sent out the ablest and best of her officers to govern on the falsest and worst of systems. Her energy absorbed all individual energy; her perpetual and minute interference aspired to shape and direct all will and motive of her subjects. The state was every thing, the people nothing. Finally, when the power of the state was broken by a foreign foe, there remained no power of the people to supply its place. On the day that the French armies ceased to resist, Canada was a peaceful province of British America.

A few years after the French crown had founded a state in Canada, a handful of Puritan refugees founded a people in New England. They bore with them from the mother country little beside a bitter hatred of the existing government, and a stern resolve to perish or be free. One small vessel—the May-flower—held them, their wives, their children, and their scanty stores. So ignorant were they of the country of their adoption, that they sought its shores in the depth of winter, when nothing but a snowy desert met their sight. Dire hardships assailed them; many sickened and died, but those who lived still strove bravely. And bitter was their trial; the scowling sky above their heads, the frozen earth under their feet, and sorest of all, deep in their strong hearts the unacknowledged love of that venerable land which they had abandoned forever.

But brighter times soon came; the snowy desert changed into a fair scene of life and vegetation. The woods rang with the cheerful sound of the ax; the fields were tilled hopefully, the harvest gathered gratefully. Other vessels arrived bearing more settlers, men, for the most part, like those who had first landed. Their numbers swelled to hundreds, thousands, tens of thousands. They formed themselves into a community; they decreed laws, stern and quaint, but suited to their condition. They had neither rich nor poor; they admitted of no superiority save in their own gloomy estimate of merit; they persecuted all forms of faith different from that which they themselves held, and yet they would have died rather than suffer the religious interference of others. Far from seeking or accepting aid from the government of England, they patiently tolerated their nominal dependence only because they were virtually independent. For protection against the savage; for relief in pestilence or famine; for help to plenty and prosperity, they trusted alone to God in heaven, and to their own right hand on earth.

Such, in the main, were the ancestors of the men of New England, and, in spite of all subsequent admixture, such, in the main, were they themselves. In the other British colonies also, hampered though they were by charters, and proprietary rights, and alloyed by a Babel congregation of French Huguenots, Dutch, Swedes, Quakers, Nobles, Roundheads, Canadians, rogues, zealots, infidels, enthusiasts, and felons, a general prosperity had created individual self-reliance, and self-reliance had engendered the desire of self-government. Each colony contained a separate vitality within itself. They commenced under a variety of systems; more or less practicable, more or less liberal, and more or less dependent on the parent state. But the spirit of adventure, the disaffection, and the disappointed ambition which had so rapidly recruited their population, gave a general bias to their political feelings which no arbitrary authority could restrain, and no institutions counteract. They were less intolerant and morose, but at the same time, also, less industrious and moral than their Puritan neighbors. Like them, however, they resented all interference from England as far as they dared, and constantly strove for the acquisition or retention of popular rights.

The British colonists, left at first, in a great measure, to themselves, settled on the most fertile lands, built their towns upon the most convenient harbors, directed their industry to the most profitable commerce, raised the most valuable productions. The trading spirit of the mother country became almost a passion when transferred to the New World. Enterprise and industry were stimulated to incredible activity by brilliant success and ample reward. As wealth and the means of subsistence increased, so multiplied the population. Early marriages were universal; a numerous family was the riches of the parent. Thousands of immigrants, also, from year to year swelled the living flood that poured over the wilderness. In a century and a half the inhabitants of British America exceeded nearly twenty-fold the people of New France. The relative superiority of the first over the last was even greater in wealth and resources than in population. The merchant navy of the English colonies was already larger than that of many European nations, and known in almost every port in the world where men bought and sold. New France had none.

The French colonies were founded and fostered by

the state, with the real object of extending the dominion, increasing the power, and illustrating the glory of France. The ostensible object of settlement, at least that holding the most prominent place in all Acts and Charters, was to extend the true religion, and to minister to the glory of God. From the earliest time the ecclesiastical establishments of Canada were formed on a scale suited to these professed views. Not only was ample provision made for the spiritual wants of the European population, but the labors of many earnest and devoted men were directed to the enlightenment of the heathen Indians. At first the Church and the civil government leaned upon each other for mutual support and assistance, but after a time, when neither of these powers found themselves troubled with popular opposition, their union grew less intimate; their interests differed, jealousies ensued, and finally they became antagonistic orders in the community. The mass of the people, more devout than intelligent, sympathized with the priesthood; this sympathy did not, however, interfere with unqualified submission to the government.

The Canadians were trained to implicit obedience to their rulers, spiritual and temporal: these rulers ventured not to imperil their absolute authority by educating their vassals. It is true there were a few seminaries and schools under the zealous administration of the Jesuits; but even that instruction was unattainable by the general population; those who walked in the moonlight which such reflected rays afforded, were not likely to become troublesome as sectarians or politicians. Much credit for sincerity can not be given to those who professed to promote the education of the people, when no printing-press was ever permitted in Canada during the government of France.

Canada, unprovoked by Dissent, was altogether free from the stain of religious persecution: hopelessly fettered in the chains of metropolitan power, she was also undisturbed by political agitation. But this calm was more the stillness of stagnation than the tranquillity of content. Without a press, without any semblance of popular representation, there hardly remained other alternatives than tame submission or open mutiny. By hereditary habit and superstition the Canadians were trained to the first, and by weakness and want of energy they were incapacitated for the last.

Although the original charter of New England asserted the king's supremacy in matters of religion, a full understanding existed that on this head ample latitude should be allowed; ample latitude was accordingly taken. She set up a system of faith of her own, and enforced conformity. But the same spirit that had excited the colonists to dissent from the Church of England, and to sacrifice home and friends in the cause, soon raised up among them a host of dissenters from their own stern and peculiar creed. Their clergy had sacrificed much for conscience' sake, and were generally "faithful, watchful, painful, serving their flock daily with prayers and tears," some among them, also, men of high European repute. They had often, however, the mortification of seeing their congregations crowding to hear the ravings of any knave or enthusiast who broached a new doctrine. Most of these mischievous fanatics were given the advantage of that interest and sympathy which a cruel and unnecessary persecution invariably excites. All this time freedom of individual judgment was the watch-word of the persecutors. There is no doubt that strong measures were necessary to curb the furious and profane absurdities of many of the seceders, who were the very outcasts of religion. On considering the criminal laws of the time, it would also appear that not a few of the outcasts of society, also, had found their way to New England. The code of Massachusetts contained the description of the most extraordinary collection of crimes that ever defaced a statute-book, and the various punishments allotted to each.

In one grand point the pre-eminent merit of the Puritans must be acknowledged: they strove earnestly and conscientiously for what they held to be the truth. For this they endured with unshaken constancy, and persecuted with unremitting zeal.

The suicidal policy of the Stuarts had, for a time, driven all the upholders of civil liberty into the ranks of sectarianism. The advocates of the extremes of religious and political opinion flocked to America, the furthest point from kings and prelates that they could conveniently reach. Ingrafted on the stubborn temper of the Englishman, and planted in the genial soil of the West, the love of this civil and religious liberty grew up with a vigor that time only served to strengthen; that the might of armies vainly strove to overcome. Thus, ultimately, the persecution under the Stuarts was the most powerful cause ever yet employed toward the liberation of man in his path through earth to heaven.

For many years England generally refrained from interference with her American colonies in matters of local government or in religion. They taxed them selves, made their own laws, and enjoyed religious freedom in their own way. In one state only, in Virginia, was the Church of England established, and even there it was accorded very little help by the temporal authority : in a short time it ceased to receive the support of a majority of the settlers, and rapidly decayed. On one point, however, the mother country claimed and exacted the obedience of the colonists to the imperial law. In her commercial code she would not permit the slightest relaxation in their favor, whatever the peculiar circumstances of their condition might be. This short-sighted and unjust restriction was borne, partly because it could not be resisted, and partly because at that early time the practical evil was but lightly felt. Although the principle of representation was seldom specified in the earlier charters, the colonists in all cases assumed it as a matter of right: they held that their privileges as Englishmen accompanied them wherever they went, and this was generally admitted as a principle of colonial policy.

In the seventeenth century England adopted the system of transportation to the American colonies. The felons were, however, too limited in numbers to make any serious inroad upon the morals or tranquillity of the settlers. Many of the convicts were men sentenced for political crimes, but free from any social taint; the laboring population, therefore, did not regard them with contempt, nor shrink from their society. It may be held, therefore, that this partial and peculiar system of transportation introduced no distinct element into the constitution of the American nation.

The British colonization in the New World differed essentially from any before attempted by the nations of modern Europe, and has led to results of immeasurable importance to mankind. Even the magnificent empire of India sinks into insignificance, in its bearings upon the general interests of the world, by comparison with the Anglo-Saxon empire in America. The success of each, however, is unexampled in history.

In the great military and mercantile colony of the East an enormous native population is ruled by a dominant race, whose number amounts to less than a four-thousandth part of its own, but whose superiority in war and civil government is at present so decided as to reduce any efforts of opposition to the mere outbursts of hopeless petulance. In that golden land, however, even the Anglo-Saxon race can not increase and multiply; the children of English parents degenerate or perish under its fatal sun. No permanent settlement or infusion of blood takes place. Neither have we effected any serious change in the manners or customs of the East Indians; on the other hand, we have rather assimilated ours to theirs. We tolerate their various religions, and we learn their language; but in neither faith nor speech have they approached one tittle toward us. We have raised there no gigantic monument of power either in pride or for utility; no temples, canals, or roads remain to remind posterity of our conquest and dominion. Were the English rule over India suddenly cast off, in a single generation the tradition of our Eastern empire would appear a splendid but baseless dream, that of our administration an allegory, of our victories a romance.

In the great social colonies of the West, the very essence of vitality is their close resemblance to the parent state. Many of the coarser inherited elements of strength have been increased. Industry and adventure have been stimulated to an unexampled extent by the natural advantages of the country, and free institutions have been developed almost to license by general prosperity and the absence of external danger. Their stability, in some one form or another, is undoubted: it rests on the broadest possible basis—on the universal will of the nation. Our vast empire in India rests only on the narrow basis of the superiority of a handful of Englishmen; should any untoward fate shake the Atlas strength that bears the burden, the superincumbent mass must fall in ruins to the earth. With far better cause may England glory in the land of her revolted children than in that of her patient slaves: the prosperous cities and busy sea-ports of America are prouder memorials of her race than the servile splendor of Calcutta or the ruined ramparts of Seringapatam. In the earlier periods the British colonies were only the reflection of Britain; in later days their light has served to illumine the political darkness of the European Continent. The attractive example of American democracy proved the most important cause that has acted upon European society since the Reformation.

Toward the close of George II.'s reign England had reached the lowest point of national degradation recorded in her history. The disasters of her fleets and armies abroad were the natural fruits of almost universal corruption at home. The admirals and generals, chosen by a German king and a subservient ministry, proved worthy of the mode of their selection. An obsequious Parliament served but to give the apparent sanction of the people to the selfish and despotic measures of the crown. Many of the best blood and of the highest chivalry of the land still held loyal devotion to the exiled Stuarts, while the mass of the nation, disgusted by the sordid and unpatriotic acts of the existing dynasty, regarded it with sentiments of dislike but little removed from positive hostility. A sullen discontent paralyzed the vigor of England, obstructed her councils, and blunted her sword. In the cabinets of Europe, among the colonists of America, and the millions of the East alike, her once glorious name had sunk almost to a by-word of reproach. But "the darkest hour is just before the dawn:" a new disaster, more humiliating, and more inexcusable than any which had preceded, at length goaded the passive indignation of the British people into irresistible action. The spirit that animated the men who spoke at Runnymede, and those who fought on Marston Moor, was not dead, but sleeping. The free institutions which wisdom had devised, time hallowed, and blood sealed, were evaded, but not overthrown. The nation arose as one man, and with a peaceful but stern determination, demanded that these things should cease. Then, for "the hour," the hand of the All Wise supplied "the man." The light of Pitt's genius, the fire of his patriotism, like the dawn of an unclouded morning, soon chased away the chilly night which had so long darkened over the fortunes of his country.

But not even the genius of the great minister, aided as it was by the awakened spirit of the British people, would have sufficed to rend Canada from France without the concurrent action of many and various causes: the principal of these was, doubtless, the extraordinary growth of our American settlements. When the first French colonists founded their military and ecclesiastical establishments at Quebec, upheld by the favor and strengthened by the arms of the mother country, they regarded with little uneasiness the unaided efforts of their English rivals in the South. But these dangerous neighbors rose with wonderful rapidity from few to many, from weak to powerful. The cloud, which had appeared no greater than "a man's hand" on the political horizon, spread rapidly wider and wider, above and below, till at length from out its threatening gloom the storm burst forth which swept away the flag of France.

As a military event, the conquest of Canada was a matter of little or no permanent importance: it can only rank as one among the numerous scenes of blood that give an intense but morbid interest to our national annals. The surrender of Niagara and Quebec were but the acknowledgment or final symbol of the victory of English over French colonization. For three years the admirable skill of Montcalm and the valor of his troops deferred the inevitable catastrophe of the colony: then the destiny was accomplished. France had for that time played out her part in the history of the New World; during one hundred and fifty years her threatening power had served to retain the English colonies in interested loyalty to protecting England. Notwithstanding the immense material superiority of the British Americans, the fleets and armies of the mother country were indispensable to break the barrier raised up against them by the union, skill, and courage of the French.

Montcalm's far-sighted wisdom suggested consolation even in his defeat and death. In a remarkable and almost prophetic letter, which he addressed to M.

de Berryer during the siege of Quebec, he foretells that the British power in America shall be broken by success, and that when the dread of France ceases to exist, the colonists will no longer submit to European control. One generation had not passed away when his prediction was fully accomplished. England, by the conquest of Canada, breathed the breath of life into the huge Frankenstein of the American republic.

The rough schooling of French hostility was necessary for the development of those qualities among the British colonists which enabled them finally to break the bonds of pupilage and stand alone. Some degree of united action had been effected among the several and widely-different states; the local governments had learned how to raise and support armies, and to consider military movements. On many occasions the provincial militia had borne themselves with distinguished bravery in the field; several of their officers had gained honorable repute; already the name of WASHINGTON called a flush of pride upon each American cheek. The stirring events of the contest with Canada had brought men of ability and patriotism into the strong light of active life, and the eyes of their countrymen sought their guidance in trusting confidence. Through the instrumentality of such men as these the American Revolution was shaped into the dignity of a national movement, and preserved from the threatening evils of an insane democracy.

The consequences of the Canadian war furnished the cause of the quarrel which led to the separation of the great colonies from the mother country. England had incurred enormous debt in the contest; her people groaned under taxation, and the wealthy Americans had contributed in but a very small proportion to the cost of victories by which they were the principal gainers. The British Parliament devised an unhappy expedient to remedy this evil: it assumed the right of taxing the unrepresented colonies, and taxed them accordingly. Vain was the prophetic eloquence of Lord Chatham; vain were the just and earnest remonstrances of the best and wisest among the colonists: the time was come. Then followed years of stubborn and unyielding strife; the blood of the same race gave sterner determination to the quarrel. The balance of success hung equally. Once again France appeared upon the stage in the Western world, and La Fayette revenged the fall of Montcalm.

However we may regret the cause and conduct of the Revolutionary war, we can hardly regret its result. The catastrophe was inevitable: the folly or wisdom of British statesmen could only have accelerated or deferred it. The child had outlived the years of pupilage; the interests of the old and the young required a separate household. But we must ever mourn the mode of separation: a bitterness was left that three quarters of a century has hardly yet removed; and a dark page remains in our annals, that tells of a contest begun in injustice, conducted with mingled weakness and severity, and ended in defeat. The cause of human freedom, perhaps for ages, depended upon the issue of the quarrel. Even the patriot minister merged the apparent interests of England in the interests of mankind. By the light of Lord Chatham's wisdom we may read the disastrous history of that fatal war, with a resigned and tempered sorrow for the glorious inheritance rent away from us forever.

The reaction of the New World upon the Old may be distinctly traced through the past and the present, but human wisdom may not estimate its influence on the future. The lessons of freedom learned by the French army while aiding the revolted colonies against England were not forgotten. On their return to their native country, they spread abroad tidings that the new people of America had gained a treasure richer a thousand-fold than those which had gilded the triumphs of Cortes or Pizarro—the inestimable prize of liberty. Then the down-trampled millions of France arose, and with avaricious haste strove for a like treasure. They won a specious imitation, so soiled and stained, however, that many of the wisest among them could not at once detect its nature. They played with the coarse bawble for a time, then lost it in a sea of blood.

Doubtless the tempest that broke upon France had long been gathering. The rays that emanated from such false suns as Voltaire and Rousseau had already drawn up a moral miasma from the swamps of sensual ignorance: under the shade of a worthless government these noxious mists collected into the clouds from whence the desolating storm of the Revolution burst. It was, however, the example of popular success in the New World, and the republican training of a portion of the French army during the American contest, that finally accelerated the course of events. A generation before the "Declaration of Independence" the struggle between the rival systems of Canada and New England had been watched by thinking men in Europe with deep interest, and the importance to mankind of its issue was fully felt. While France mourned the defeat of her armies and the loss of her magnificent colony, the keen-sighted philosopher of Ferney gave a banquet to celebrate the British triumph at Quebec, not as the triumph of England over France, but as that of freedom over despotism.*

The overthrow of French by British power in America was not the effect of mere military superiority. The balance of general success and glory in the field is no more than shared with the conquered people. The morbid national vanity, which finds no delight but in the triumphs of the sword, will shrink from the study of this checkered story. The narrative of disastrous defeat and doubtful advantage must be endured before we arrive at that of the brilliant victory which crowned our arms with final success. We read with painful surprise of the rout and ruin of regular British regiments by a crowd of Indian savages, and of the bloody repulse of the most numerous army that had yet assembled round our standards in America before a few weak French battalions and an unfinished parapet.

For the first few years our prosecution of the Canadian war was marked by a weakness little short of imbecility. The conduct of the troops was indifferent, the tactics of the generals bad, and the schemes of the minister worse. The coarse but powerful wit of Smollett and Fielding, and the keen sarcasms of "Chrysal," convey to us no very exalted idea of the composition of the British army in those days. The service had sunk into contempt. The withering influence of a corrupt patronage had demoralized the officers; successive defeats, incurred through the inefficiency of courtly generals, had depressed the spirit of the soldiery, and, were it not for the proof shown upon the bloody fields

* See Appendix, No. I.

of La Feldt and Fontenoy, we might almost suppose that English manhood had become an empty name.

Many of the battalions shipped off to take part in the American contest were hasty levies without organization or discipline: the colonel, a man of influence, with or without other qualifications, as the case might be; the officers, his neighbors and dependents. These armed mobs found themselves suddenly landed in a country, the natural difficulty of which would of itself have proved a formidable obstacle, even though unenhanced by the presence of an active and vigilant enemy. At the same time, there devolved upon them the duties and the responsibilities of regular troops. A due consideration of these circumstances tends to diminish the surprise which a comparison of their achievements with those recorded in our later military annals might create.

Very different were the ranks of the American army from the magnificent regiments whose banners now bear the crowded records of Peninsular and Indian victory; who, within the recollection of living men, have stood as conquerors upon every hostile land, yet never once permitted a stranger to tread on England's sacred soil but as a prisoner, fugitive, or friend. In Cairo and Copenhagen; in Lisbon, Madrid, and Paris; in the ancient metropolis of China; in the capital of the young American republic, the British flag has been hailed as the symbol of a triumphant power or of a generous deliverance. Well may we cherish an honest pride in the prowess and military virtue of our soldiers, loyal alike to the crown and to the people; facing in battle, with unshaken courage, the deadly shot and sweeping charge, and, with a still loftier valor, enduring, in times of domestic troubles, the gibes and injuries of their misguided countrymen.

In the stirring interest excited by the progress and rivalry of our kindred races in America, the sad and solemn subject of the Indian people is almost forgotten. The mysterious decree of Providence which has swept them away may not be judged by human wisdom. Their existence will soon be of the past. They have left no permanent impression on the constitution of the great nation which now spreads over their country. No trace of their blood, language, or manners may be found among their haughty successors. As certainly as their magnificent forests fell before the advancing tide of civilization, they fell also. Neither the kindness nor the cruelty of the white man arrested or hastened their inevitable fate. They withered alike under the Upas-shade of European protection and before the deadly storm of European hostility. As the snow in spring they melted away, stained, tainted, trampled down.

The closing scene of French dominion in Canada was marked by circumstances of deep and peculiar interest. The pages of romance can furnish no more striking episode than the battle of Quebec. The skill and daring of the plan which brought on the combat, and the success and fortune of its execution, are unparalleled. There a broad, open plain, offering no advantages to either party, was the field of fight. The contending armies were nearly equal in military strength, if not in numbers. The chiefs of each were men already of honorable fame. France trusted firmly in the wise and chivalrous Montcalm; England trusted hopefully in the young and heroic Wolfe. The magnificent strong-hold which was staked upon the issue of the strife stood close at hand. For miles and miles around, the prospect extended over as fair a land as ever rejoiced the sight of man; mountain and valley, forest and waters, city and solitude, grouped together in forms of almost ideal beauty.

The strife was brief, but deadly. The September sun rose upon two gallant armies arrayed in unbroken pride, and noon of the same day saw the ground where they had stood strewn with the dying and the dead. Hundreds of the veterans of France had fallen in the ranks, from which they disdained to fly; the scene of his ruin faded fast from Montcalm's darkening sight, but the proud consciousness of having done his duty deprived defeat and death of their severest sting. Not more than a musket-shot away lay Wolfe; the heart that but an hour before had throbbed with great and generous impulse, now still forever. On the face of the dead there rested a triumphant smile, which the last agony had not overcast; a light of unfailing hope, that the shadows of the grave could not darken.

The portion of history here recorded is no fragment. Within a period comparatively brief, we see the birth, the growth, and the catastrophe of a nation. The flag of France is erected at Quebec by a handful of hardy adventurers; a century and a half has passed, and that flag is lowered to a foreign foe before the sorrowing eyes of a Canadian people. This example is complete as that presented in the life of an individual: we see the natural sequence of events; the education and the character, the motive and the action, the error and the punishment. Through the following records may be clearly traced combinations of causes, remote, and even apparently opposed, uniting in one result, and also the surprising fertility of one great cause in producing many different results.

Were we to read the records of history by the light of the understanding instead of by the fire of the passions, the study could be productive only of unmixed good; their examples and warnings would afford us constant guidance in the paths of public and private virtue. The narrow and unreasonable notion of exclusive national merit can not survive a fair glance over the vast map of time and space which history lays before us. We may not avert our eyes from those dark spots upon the annals of our beloved land where acts of violence and injustice stand recorded against her, nor may we suffer the blaze of military renown to dazzle our judgment. Victory may bring glory to the arms, while it brings shame to the councils of a people; for the triumphs of war are those of the general and the soldier; increase of honor, wisdom, and prosperity are the triumphs of the nation.

The citizens of Rome placed the images of their ancestors in the vestibule, to recall the virtues of the dead, and to stimulate the emulation of the living. We also should fix our thoughts upon the examples which history presents, not in a vain spirit of selfish nationality, but in earnest reverence for the great and good of all countries, and a contempt for the false, and mean, and cruel even of our own.

THE

CONQUEST OF CANADA.

CHAPTER I.

THE philosophers of remote antiquity acquired the important knowledge of the earth's spherical form; to their bold genius we are indebted for the outline of the geographical system now universally adopted. With a vigorous conception, but imperfect execution, they traced out the scheme of denoting localities by longitude and latitude: according to their teaching, the imaginary equatorial line, encompassing the earth, was divided into hours and degrees.

Even at that distant period hardy adventurers had penetrated far away into the land of the rising sun, and many a wondrous tale was told of that mysterious empire, where one third of our fellow-men still stand apart from the brotherhood of nations. Among the various and astounding exaggerations induced by the vanity of the narrators, and the ignorance of their audience, none was more ready than that of distance. The journey, the labor of a life; each league of travel a new scene; the day crowded with incident, the night a dream of terror or admiration. Then, as the fickle will of the wanderer suggested, as the difficulties or encouragement of nature, and the hostility or aid of man impelled, the devious course bent to the north or south, was hastened, hindered, or retraced.

By such vague and shadowy measurement as the speculations of these wanderers supplied, the sages of the past traced out the ideal limits of the dry land which, at the word of God, appeared from out the gathering together of the waters.*

The most eminent geographer before the time of Ptolemy places the confines of Seres—the China of to-day—at nearly two thirds of the distance round the world, from the first meridian.† Ptolemy reduces the propòrtion to one half.

* "La sphéricité de la terre étant reconnue, l'ètendue de la terre habitée en longitude déterminé, en même temps la largeur de l'Atlantique entre les côtes occidentales d'Europe et d'Afrique et les côtes orientales d'Asie par différens degrés de latitude. Eratosthène (Strabo, ii., p. 87, Cas.) évalue la circonférence de l'équateur à 252,000 stades, et la largeur de la *chlamyde* du Cap Sacrè (Cap Saint Vincent) à l'extremitè de la grande ceinture de Taurus, pres de Thinæ à 70,000 stades. En prolongeant la distance vers le sud est jusque au cap des Coliaques qui, d'après les idées de Strabon sur la configuration de l'Asie, représente notre Cap Comorin, et avance plus à l'est que la côte de Thinæ, la combinaison des données d'Eratosthène offre 74,600 et même 78,000 stades. Or, en réduisant, par la différence de latitude, le périmètre equatorial au parallèle de Rhodes, des portes Caspiennes et de Thinæ c'est à dire, au parallèle de 36° 0′ et non de 36° 21′, on trouve 203,872 stades, et pour largeur de la terre habitée, par le parallèle de Rhodes, 67,500 stades. Strabon dit par conséquence avec justesse, dans le fameux passage où il semble prédire l'existence du Nouveau Continent, en parlant de deux terres habitées dans la même zone tempérée boréale que les terres occupent plus du tiers de la circonférence du parallèle qui passe par Thinæ. Par cette supposition la distance de l'Ibèrie aux Indes est au delà de 236° à peu près 240°. Ou peut être surpris de voir que le résultat le plus ancien est aussi le plus exact de tous ceux que nous trouvons en descendant d'Eratosthène par Posidonius aux temps de Marin de Tyr et de Ptolémée. La terre habitée offre effectivement, d'aprés nos connoissances actuelles, entre les 36° et 37° 130 degrés d'étendue en longitude; il y a par conséquent des côtes de la Chine au Cap Sacré à travers l'océan de l'est à l'ouest 230 degrés. L'accord que je nommerai accidentel de cette vraie distance et de l'évaluation d'Eratosthène atteint donc dix degrés en longitude. Posidonius 'soupçonne (c'est l'expression de Strabon, lib. ii., p. 102, Cas.), que la longueur de la terre habitée laquelle est, selon lui, d'environ 70,000 stades, doit former la moitié du cercle entièr sur lequel le mesure se prend, et qu' ainsi à partir de l'extrémité occidentale de cette même terre habitée, en naviguant avec un vent d'est continuel l'espace de 70,000 autres stades, ou arriverait dans l'Inde."—Humboldt's *Géographie du Nouveau Continent.*

† "La longueur de la terre habitée comprise entre les méridiens des îles Fortunées et de Sera étoit, d'àprès Marin de Tyr (Ptol., Geogr., lib. i., cap. 11) de 15 heures ou de 225°. C'étoit avancer les côtes

Allowing for the supposed vast extent of this unknown country to the eastward, it was evident that its remotest shores approached our Western World. But, beyond the Pillars of Hercules, the dark and stormy waters of the Atlantic* forbade adventure. The giant minds of those

de la Chine jusqu'au méridien des îles Sandwich, et réduire l'espace à parcourir des îles Canaries aux côtes orientales de l'Asie à 135°, erreur de 86° en longitude. La grande extension de $23\frac{1}{2}$° que les anciens donnoient à la mer Caspienne, contribuoit également beaucoup à augmenter la largeur de l'Asie. Ptolémée a laissé intacte, dans l'évaluation de la terre habitée, selon Posidonius, la distance des îles Fortunées au passage de l'Euphrate à Hiérapolis. Les reductions de Ptolémée ne portent que sur les distances de l'Euphrate à *la Tour de Pierre* et de cette tour à la métropole des Seres. Les 225° de Marin de Tyr deviennent, selon l'Almagest (lib. ii., p. 1) 180°, selon la Géographie de Ptolémée (lib. i., p. 12) $177\frac{1}{4}$°. Les côtes des Sinæ[1] reculent donc du méridien des îles Sandwich vers celui des Carolines orientales, et l'espace à parcourir par mer en longitude n'étoit plus de 135°, mais de 180° à $182\frac{3}{4}$°. Il étoit dans les intérêts de Christophe Colomb de préférer de beaucoup les calculs de Marin de Tyr à ceux de Ptolémée et a force de conjectures Colomb parvient à restreindre l'espace de l'Océan qui lui restait à traverser des îles du cap Vert au Cathay de l'Asie orientale à 128°" (*Vida del Almirante*).—Humboldt's *Géographie du Nouveau Continent*, vol. ii., p. 364.

* That the vast waters of the Atlantic were regarded with "awe and wonder, seeming to bound the world as with a chaos," needs no greater proof than the description given of it by Xerif al Edrizi, an eminent Arabian writer, whose countrymen were the boldest navigators of the Middle Ages, and possessed all that was then known of geography. "The ocean," he observes, "encircles the ultimate bounds of the inhabited earth, and all beyond it is unknown. No one has been able to verify any thing concerning it, on account of its difficult and perilous navigation, its great obscurity, its profound depth, and frequent tempests; through fear of its mighty fishes and its haughty winds; yet there are many islands in it, some peopled, others uninhabited. There is no mariner who dares to enter into its deep waters; or if any have done so, they have merely kept along its coasts, fearful of departing from them. The waves of this ocean, though they roll as high as mountains, yet maintain themselves without breaking; for if they broke it would be impossible for ship to plow them."—*Description of Spain*, by Xerif al Edrizi: Condé's Spanish translation. Madrid, 1799.—Quoted by Washington Irving.

[1] In opposition to the opinion of Malte Brun and M. de Josselin, Mr. Hugh Murray is considered to have satisfactorily proved the correctness of Ptolemy's assertion that the Seres or Sinæ are identical with the Chinese.—See *Trans. of the Royal Society of Edinburgh*, vol. viii., p. 171.

days saw, even through the mists of ignorance and error, that the readiest course to reach this distant land must lie toward the setting sun, across the western ocean.* From over this vast watery solitude no traveler had ever brought back the story of his wanderings. The dim light of traditionary memory gave no guiding ray, the faint voice of rumor breathed not its mysterious secrets. Then poetic imagination filled the void; vast islands were conjured up out of the deep, covered with unheard-of luxuriance of vegetation, rich in mines of incalculable value, populous with a race of conquering warriors. But this magnificent vision was only created to be destroyed; a violent earthquake rent asunder in a day and a night the foundations of Atlantis, and the waters of the Western Ocean swept over the ruins of this once mighty empire.† In after ages we are told, that

* Aristotle, Strabo, Pliny, and Seneca arrived at this conclusion. The idea, however, of an intervening continent never appears to have suggested itself.—Humboldt's *Cosmos*.

† In the Atlantic Ocean, over against the Pillars of Hercules, lay an island larger than Asia and Africa taken together, and in its vicinity were other islands. The ocean in which these islands were situated was surrounded on every side by main-land; and the Mediterranean, compared with it, resembled a mere harbor or narrow entrance. Nine thousand years before the time of Plato this island of Atlantis was both thickly settled and very powerful. Its sway extended over Africa as far as Egypt, and over Europe as far as the Tyrrhenian Sea. The further progress of its conquests, however, was checked by the Athenians, who, partly with the other Greeks, partly by themselves, succeeded in defeating these powerful invaders, the natives of Atlantis. After this a violent earthquake, which lasted for the space of a day and a night, and was accompanied with inundations of the sea, caused the islands to sink; and for a long period subsequent to this, the sea in that quarter was impassable by reason of the slime and shoals.—Plato, *Tim.*, 24–29, 296; *Crit.*, 108–110, 39, 43. The learned Gessner is of opinion that the Isle of Ceres, spoken of in a poem of very high antiquity, attributed to Orpheus, was a fragment of Atlantis. Kircher, in his "Mundus Subterraneus," and Beckman, in his "History of Islands," suppose the Atlantis to have been an island extending from the Canaries to the Azores; that it was really ingulfed in one of the convulsions of the globe, and that those small islands are mere fragments of it. Gosselin, in his able research into the voyages of the ancients, supposes the Atlantis of Plato to have been nothing more nor less than one of the nearest of the Canaries, viz., Fortaventura or Lancerote. Carli and many others find America

some Phœnician vessels, impelled by a strong east wind, were driven for thirty days across the Atlantic: there they found a part of the sea where the surface was covered with rushes and sea-weed, somewhat resembling a vast inundated meadow.* The voyagers ascribed these strange appearances to some cause connected with the submerged Atlantis, and even in later years they were held by many as confirmation of Plato's marvelous story.†

In the Carthaginian annals is found the mention of a fertile and beautiful island of the distant Atlantic. Many adventurous men of that maritime people were attracted thither by the delightful climate and the riches of the soil; it was deemed of such value and importance that they proposed to transfer the seat of their republic to its shores in case of any

in the Atlantis, and adduce many plausible arguments in support of their assertion.—Carli, *Letters Amer.; Fr.* transl., ii., 180. M. Bailly, in his "Letters sur l'Atlantide de Platon," maintains the existence of the Atlantides, and their island Atlantis, by the authorities of Homer, Sanchoniathon, and Diodorus Siculus, in addition to that of Plato. Manheim maintains very strenuously that Plato's Atlantis is Sweden and Norway. M. Bailly, after citing many ancient testimonies, which concur in placing this famous isle in the north, quotes that of Plutarch, who confirms these testimonies by a circumstantial description of the Isle of Ogygia, or the Atlantis, which he represents as situated in the north of Europe. The following is the theory of Buffon: after citing the passage relating to the Atlantis, from Plato's "Timæus," he adds, "This ancient tradition is not devoid of probability. The lands swallowed up by the waters were, perhaps, those which united Ireland to the Azores, and the Azores to the Continent of America; for in Ireland there are the same fossils, the same shells, and the same sea bodies as appear in America, and some of them are found in no other part of Europe."—Buffon's *Nat. Hist.*, by Smellie, vol. i., p. 507.

* The first authentic description of the Mar di Sargasso of Aristotle is due to Columbus. It spreads out between the nineteenth and thirty-fourth degrees of north latitude. Its chief axis lies about seven degrees to the westward of the Island of Corvo. The smaller bank, on the other hand, lies between the Bermudas and Bahamas. The winds and partial currents in different years slightly affect the position and extent of these Atlantic "sea-weed meadows." No other sea in either hemisphere displays a similar extent of surface covered by plants collected in this way. These meadows of the ocean present the wonderful spectacle of a collection of plants covering a space nearly seven times as large as France.—Humboldt's *Cosmos*.

† See Appendix, No. II.

irreparable disaster at home. But at length the Senate, fearing the evils of a divided state, denounced the distant colony, and decreed the punishment of death to those who sought it for a home. If there be any truth in this ancient tale, it is probable that one of the Canary Islands was its subject.*

* See Aristotle, *De Mirab. Auscult.*, cap. lxxxiv., 84, p. 836, Bekk. This work, "A Collection of Wonderful Narratives," is attributed to Aristotle; the real compiler is unknown. According to Humboldt, it seems to have been written before the first Punic war.—Diodorus of Sicily, vol. xix. Aristotle attributes the discovery of the island to the Carthaginians; Diodorus to the Phœnicians. The occurrence is said to have taken place in the earliest times of the Tyrrhenian dominion of the sea, during the contest between the Tyrrhenian Pelasgi and the Phœnicians. The Island of the Seven Cities (see Appendix, No. II.) was identified with the island mentioned by Aristotle as having been discovered by the Carthaginians, and was inserted in the early maps under the name of Antilla. Paul Toscanelli, the celebrated physician of Florence, thus writes to Columbus: "From the Island of Antilia, which you call the Seven Cities, and of which you have some knowledge," &c. In the Middle Ages conjectures were religiously inscribed upon the maps, as is proved by Antilia, St. Borondon (see Appendix), the Hand of Satan, Green Island, Maida Island, and the exact form of vast southern regions. Humboldt refers the name of Antilia so far back as the fourteenth century. The earliest date given by Ferdinand Columbus is 1436. "Beyond the Azores, but at no great distance toward the west, occurs the Ysola de Antilia, which we may conclude, even allowing the date of the map to be genuine (in the library of St. Mark, at Venice, date 1436), to be a mere gratuitous or theoretic supposition, and to have received that strange name because the obvious and natural idea of antipodes has been anathematized by Catholic ignorance." He elsewhere says that "some Portuguese cosmographers have inserted the island described by Aristotle in maps under the name of Antilia."—*Hist. of the Discovery of America*, by Don Ferdinand Columbus, in Ker, vol. iii., p. 3–29.

The origin of the name Antilla, or Antilia, is still a matter of conjecture. Humboldt attributes to a "littérateur distingué" the solution of the enigma, from a passage in Aristotle's "De Mundo," which speaks of the probable existence of unknown lands opposite to the mass of continents which we inhabit. "These countries, be they small or great, whose shores are opposed to ours, were marked out by the word *porthornoi*, which in the Middle Ages was translated by *antinsulæ*." Humboldt says that this translation is totally incorrect; however, the idea of the "littérateur distingué" is evidently the same as Ferdinand Columbus's. The following is the hypothesis favored by Humboldt: "Peut-être même le nom d'Antilia qui paraît pour la première fois sur une carte Vénitienne de 1436 n'est il qu'une forme Portuguaise

Although the New World in the West was unknown to the ancients, there is no doubt that they entertained a suspicion of its existence ;* the romance of Plato—the prophecy of Seneca, were but the offsprings of this vague idea. Many writers tell us it was conjectured that, by sailing from the coast of Spain, the eastern shores of India might be reach-

donnée à un nom géographique des Arabes. L'étymologie que hasarde M. Buace me paraît très ingénieuse. . . La syllabe initiale me paraît la corruption de l'article Arabe. D'al Tinnin et d'Al tin on aura fait peu à peu Antinna et Antilla, comme par un déplacement analogue de consonnes, les Espagnols ont fait de crocodilo, corcodilo et cocodrilo. Le Dragon est *al Tin*, et l'Antilia est peut-être, l'île des dragons marins."—Humboldt's *Ex. Crit.*, vol. ii., 211.

Oviedo applies the relation of Aristotle to the Hesperian Islands, and asserts that they were the "India" discovered by Columbus. "Perchè egli (Colombo) conobbe come era in effetto che queste terre che egli ben ritrovava scritte, erano del tutto uscite dalla memoria degli uomin; e io per me non dubito che si sapissero, e possedessero anticamente dalli Rè de Spagna: e voglio qui dire quello che Aristotele in questo caso ne scrisse, &c. . . . io tengo che queste Indie siano quelle autiche e famose Isole Hesperide cosè dette da Hespero 12 Re di Spagna. Or come la Spagna e l'Italia tolsero il nome da Hespero 12 Re di Spagna cosi anco da questo istesso ex torsero queste isole Hesperidi, che noi diciamo, *onde senza* alcun dubbio si de tenere, che in quel tempe questo isole sotto la signoria della Spagna stessero, e sotto un medesmo Re, che fu (come Beroso dice) 1658 anni prima che il nostro Salvatore nascesse. E perchè al presente siamo nel 1535 della salute nostra, ne segue che siano ora tre milo e cento novantatre anni che la Spagna e'l suo Re Hespero signoreggiavano queste Indie o Isole Hesperidi. E come cosa sua par che abbia la divina giustizia voluto ritornargliele."—*Hist. Gen. dell' Indie de Gonzalo Fernando d'Oviedo*, in Ramusio, tom. iii., p. 80.

* "It is very possible that in the same temperate zone, and almost in the same latitude as Thinæ (or Athens ?), where it crosses the Atlantic Ocean, there are inhabited worlds, distinct from that in which we dwell."[1]—Strabo, lib. i., p. 65, and lib. ii., p. 118. It is surprising that this expression never attracted the attention of the Spanish authors, who, in the beginning of the sixteenth century, were searching every where in classical literature with the expectation of finding some traces of acquaintance with the New World.

1 "The idea of such a locality in a continuation of the long axis of the Mediterranean was connected with a grand view of the earth by Eratosthenes (generally and extensively known among the ancients), according to which the entire ancient continent, in its widest expanse from west to east, in the parallel of about thirty-six degrees, presents an almost unbroken line of elevation."—Humboldt's *Cosmos*.

ed ;* the length of the voyage, or the wonders that might lie in its course, imagination alone could measure or describe. Whatever might have been the suspicion or belief† of ancient time, we may feel assured that none then ventured to seek these distant lands, nor have we reason to suppose that any of the civilized European races gave inhabitants to the New World before the close of the fifteenth century.

To the barbarous hordes of Northeastern Asia America must have long been known as the land where many of their wanderers found a home. It is not surprising that from them no information was obtained ; but it is strange that the bold and adventurous Northmen should have visited it nearly five hundred years before the great Genoese, and have suffered their wonderful discovery to remain hidden from the world, and to become almost forgotten among themselves.‡

* " D'Anville a dit avec esprit que la plus grande des erreurs dans la géographie de Ptolémée a conduit les homnes à la plus grande découverte de terres nouvelles c'est, à dire la supposition que l'Asie s'étendait vers l'est, au delà du 180 degré de longitude."

Both Strabo and Aristotle speak of " the same sea bathing opposite shores," Strabo, lib. i., p. 103; lib. ii., p. 162. Aristotle, *De Cœlo*, lib. ii., cap. 14, p. 297. The possibility of navigating from the extremity of Europe to the eastern shores of Asia is clearly asserted by the Stagirite, and in the two celebrated passages of Strabo. Aristotle does not suppose the distance to be very great, and draws an ingenious argument in favor of his supposition from the geography of animals. Strabo sees no obstacle to passing from Iberia to India, except the immense extent of the Atlantic Ocean. It is to be remembered that Strabo, as well as Eratosthenes, extend the appellation of Atlantic Sea to every part of the ocean.—Humboldt's *Géog. du Nouveau Continent.*

† See Appendix, No. III.

‡ " Au milieu de tant de discussions acerbes qu'une curieuse malignité et le goût d'une fausse érudition classique firent naître sur le mérite de Christophe Colomb, parmi ses contemporains, personne n'a pensé aux navigations des Normands comme précurseurs des Génois. Cette idée ne se presenta que soixante quatre ans après la mort du grand homme. On savait par ces propres récits 'qu'il étoit allé à Thulé' mais alors ce voyage vers le nord ne fit naître aucun soupçon sur la priorité, de la découverte . . . . Le mérite d'avoir reconnu la première découverte de l'Amérique septentrionale par les Normands appartient indubitablement au géographe Ortelius, qui annonça cette opinion dés l'année 1570. 'Christophe Colomb, dit Ortelius, a seule-

In the year 1001 the Icelanders touched upon the American coast, and for nearly two centuries subsequent visits were repeatedly made by them and the Norwegians, for the purpose of commerce or for the gratification of curiosity. Biorn Heriolson, an Icelander, was the first discoverer: steering for Greenland, he was driven to the south by tempestuous and unfavorable winds, and saw different parts of America, without, however, touching at any of them. Attracted by the report of this voyage, Leif, son of Eric, the discoverer of Greenland, fitted out a vessel to pursue the same adventure. He passed the coast visited by Biorn, and steered southwest till he reached a strait between a large island and the main land. Finding the country fertile and pleasant, he passed the winter near this place, and gave it the name of Vinland,* from the wild vine which grew there in great

ment mis le Nouveau Monde en rapport durable de commerce et d'utilité avec l'Europe' (*Theatr. Orbis Terr.*, on p. 5, 6). Ce jugement est beaucoup trop sévère."—Humboldt's *Géog. du Nouveau Continent.*

* "Biorn first saw land in the Island of Nantucket, one degree south of Boston, then in New Scotland, and lastly in Newfoundland." —Carl Christian Rafn, *Antiquitates Americanæ*, 1845, p. 4, 421; Humboldt's *Cosmos.*

"The country called 'the good Vinland' (Vinland it goda) by Leif, included the shore between Boston and New York, and therefore parts of the present states of Massachusetts, Rhode Island, and Connecticut, between the parallels of latitude of Civita Vecchia and Terracina, where, however, the average temperature of the year is between 46° and 52° (Fahr.). This was the chief settlement of the Normans. Their active and enterprising spirit is proved by the circumstance that, after they had settled in the south as far as 41° 30′ north latitude, they erected three pillars to mark out the boundaries near the eastern coast of Baffin's Bay, in the latitude of 72° 55′, upon one of the Women Islands northwest of the present most northern Danish colony of Upernavik. The Runic inscription upon the stone, discovered in the autumn of 1824, contains, according to Rask and Finn Magnusen, the date of the year 1135. From this eastern coast of Baffin's Bay, the colonists visited, with great regularity, on account of the fishery, Lancaster Sound and a part of Barrow's Straits, and this occurred more than six centuries before the bold undertakings of Parry and Ross. The locality of the fishery is very accurately described; and Green land priests, from the diocese of Gardar, conducted the first voyage of discovery in 1266. These northwestern summer stations were called the Kroksjardar, heathen countries. Mention was early made of the

abundance.* The winter days were longer in this new country than in Greenland, and the weather was more temperate.

Leif returned to Greenland in the spring; his brother Thorvald succeeded him, and remained two winters in Vinland exploring much of the coast and country.† In the course of the third summer the natives, now called Esquimaux, were first seen; on account of their diminutive stature the adventurers gave them the name of *Skrælingar*.‡ These poor savages, irritated by an act of barbarous cruelty, attacked the Northmen with darts and arrows, and Thorvald fell a victim to their vengeance. A wealthy Icelander, named Thorfinn, established a regular colony in Vinland soon after this event; the settlers increased rapidly in numbers, and traded with the natives for furs and skins to great advantage. After three years the adventurers returned to Iceland enriched by the expedition, and reported favorably upon the new country. Little is known of this settlement after Thorfinn's departure till early in the twelfth century, when a bishop of Greenland§ went there to promulgate the Christian faith among the colonists; beyond that time scarcely a notice of its existence occurs, and the name and situation of the ancient Vinland soon passed away from the knowledge of man. Whether the adventurous colonists ever returned,

Siberian wood, which was then collected, as well as of the numerous whales, seals, walrus, and polar bears."—Rafn, *Antiq. Amer.*, p. 20, 274, 415–418, quoted by Humboldt.

* One of the objections brought forward by Robertson against the Norman discovery of America is, that the wild vine has never since been found so far north as Labrador; but modern travelers have ascertained that a species of wild vine grows even as far north as the shores of Hudson's Bay.[1] Since Robertson's time, however, the locality of the first Norman settlement has been moved further south, and into latitudes where the best species of wild vines are abundant.

† Rafn, *Antiq. Amer.*

‡ The Esquimaux were at that time spread much further south than they are at present.—Humboldt's *Cosmos*, vol. ii., p. 268.

§ Eric Upsi, a native of Iceland, and the first Greenland bishop, undertook to go to Vinland as a Christian missionary in 1121.

[1] Sir A. Mackenzie's Travels in Iceland, 1812. Preliminary Dissertation by Dr Holland, p. 46.

or became blended with the natives,* or perished by their hands, no record remains to tell.†

Discoveries such as these by the ancient Scandinavians—fruitless to the world and almost buried in oblivion—can not dim the glory of that transcendant genius to whom we owe the knowledge of a New World.

The claim of the Welsh to the first discovery of America seems to rest upon no better original authority than that of

* "The learned Grotius founds an argument for the colonization of America by the Norwegians on the similarity between the names of Norway and La Norimbègue, a district bordering on New England."—Grotius, *De Origine Gentium Americanarum*, in quarto, 1642. See, also, the Controversy between Grotius and Jean de Laët.

† Accurate information respecting the former intercourse of the Northmen with the Continent of America reaches only as far as the middle of the fourteenth century. In the year 1349 a ship was sent from Greenland to Markland (New Scotland) to collect timber and other necessaries. Upon their return from Markland, the ship was overtaken by storms, and compelled to land at Straumfjord, in the west of Iceland. This is the last account of the "Norman America," preserved for us in the ancient Scandinavian writings. The settlements upon the west coast of Greenland, which were in a very flourishing condition until the middle of the fourteenth century, gradually declined, from the fatal influence of monopoly of trade, by the invasion of the Esquimaux, by the black death which depopulated the north from the year 1347 to 1351, and also by the arrival of a hostile fleet, from what country is not known.

By means of the critical and most praiseworthy efforts of Christian Rafn, and the Royal Society for Northern Antiquities in Copenhagen, the traditions and ancient accounts of the voyage of the Normans to Helluland (Newfoundland), to Markland (the mouth of the River St. Lawrence at Nova Scotia), and at Winland (Massachusetts), have been separately printed and satisfactorily commented upon. The length of the voyage, the direction in which they sailed, the time of the rising and setting of the sun, are accurately laid down. The principal sources of information are the historical narrations of Erik the Red, Thorfinn Karlsefne, and Snorre Thorbrandson, probably written in Greenland itself, as early as the twelfth century, partly by descendants of the settlers born in Winland.—Rafn, *Antiq. Amer.*, p. 7, 14, 16. The care with which the tables of their pedigrees was kept was so great, that the table of the family of Thorfinn Karlsefne, whose son, Snorre Thorbrandson, was born in America, was kept from the year 1007 to 1811.

The name of the colonized countries is found in the ancient national songs of the natives of the Färöe Islands.—Humboldt's *Cosmos*, vol. ii., p. 268–452.

Meridith-ap-Rees, a bard who died in the year 1477. His verses only relate that Prince Madoc, wearied with dissensions at home, searched the ocean for a new kingdom. The tale of this adventurer's voyages and colonization was written one hundred years subsequent to the early Spanish discoveries, and seems to be merely a fanciful completion of his history: he probably perished in the unknown seas. It is certain that neither the ancient principality nor the world reaped any benefit from these alleged discoveries.*

In the middle of the thirteenth and the beginning of the fourteenth centuries, the Venetian Marco Polo† and the Englishman Mandeville‡ awakened the curiosity of Europe with respect to the remote parts of the earth. Wise and discerning men selected the more valuable portions of their observations; ideas were enlarged, and a desire for more perfect information excited a thirst for discovery. While this spirit was gaining strength in Europe, the wonderful powers of the magnet were revealed to the Western World.§ The invention of the mariner's compass aided and extended navigation more than all the experience and adventure of preceding ages: the light of the stars, the guidance of the sea-coast, were no longer necessary; trusting to the mysterious powers of his new friend, the sailor steered out fearlessly into the ocean, through the bewildering mists or the darkness of night.

The Spaniards were the first to profit by the bolder spirit and improved science of navigation. About the beginning of the fourteenth century, they were led to the accidental discovery of the Canary Islands,‖ and made repeated voy-

* See Appendix, No. IV. † See Appendix, No. V.

‡ See Appendix, No. VI. § See Appendix, No. VII.

‖ The numerous data which have come down to us from antiquity, and an acute examination of the local relations, especially the great vicinity of the settlements upon the African coast, which incontestably existed, lead me to believe that Phœnicians, Carthaginians, Greeks, and Romans, and probably even the Etruscans, were acquainted with the group of the Canary Islands.—Humboldt's *Cosmos*, vol. ii., p. 414.

"Porrò occidentalis navigatio, quantum etiam famâ assequi Plinius potuit, tantum ad Fortunatas Insulas cursum protendit, earumque præcipuam à multitudine canum Canariam vocatam refert."—Acosta, *De Natura Novi Orbis*, lib. i., cap. ii.

ages thither, plundering the wretched inhabitants, and carrying them off as slaves.* Pope Clement VI. conferred these countries as a kingdom upon Louis de la Cerda, of the royal race of Castile; he, however, was powerless to avail himself of the gift, and it passed to the stronger hand of John de Bethancourt, a Norman baron.† The countrymen of this bold adventurer explored the seas far to the south of the Canary Islands, and acquired some knowledge of the coast of Africa.

The glory of leading the career of systematic exploration belongs to the Portuguese:‡ their attempts were not only

Respecting the probability of the Semitic origin of the name of the Canary Islands, Pliny, in his Latinizing etymological notions, considered them to be *Dog Islands!* (Vide Credner's Biblical Representation of Paradise, in Illgen's Journal for Historical Theology, 1836, vol. vi., p. 166–186.)—Humboldt's *Cosmos*, vol. ii., p. 414.

The most fundamental, and, in a literary point of view, the most complete account of the Canary Islands, that was written in ancient times, down to the Middle Ages, was collected in a work of Joachim José da Costa de Macedo, with the title "Memoria cem que se pretende provar que os Arabes não connecerão as Canarias autes dos Portuguesques, 1844." (See, also, Viera y Clavigo, *Notic. de la Hist. de Canaria.*)—Humboldt's *Cosmos*.

* See Appendix, No. VIII.

† "Jean de Bethancourt knew that before the expedition of Alvaro Beccara, that is to say, before the end of the fourteenth century, Norman adventurers had penetrated as far as Sierra Leone (lat. 8° 30′), and he sought to follow their traces. Before the Portuguese, however, no European nation appears to have crossed the equator."—Humboldt.

"Les Normands et les Arabes sont les seules nations qui, jusqu'au commencement du douzieme siécle, aient partagé la gloire des grandes expéditions maritimes, le goût des aventures étranges, la passion du pillage et des conquêtes éphémères. Les Normands ont occupé successivement l'Islande et la Neustrie, ravagé les sanctuaires de l'Italie, conquis la Pouille sur les Grecs, inscrit leurs caractères runiques jusque sur les flancs d'un des lions que Morosini enleva au Pirée d'Athènes pour en orner l'arsenal de Venise."—Humboldt's *Géog. du Nouveau Continent*, vol. ii., p. 86.

‡ "No nation," says Southey, "has ever accomplished such great things in proportion to its means as the Portuguese." Its early maritime history does, indeed, present a striking picture of enterprise and restless energy, but the annals of Europe afford no similar instance of rapid degeneracy. There was an age when less than forty thousand armed Portuguese kept the whole coasts of the ocean in awe, from Mo-

attended with considerable success, but gave encouragement and energy to those efforts that were crowned by the discovery of a world: among them the great Genoese was trained, and their steps in advance matured the idea, and aided the execution of his design. The nations of Europe had now begun to cast aside the errors and prejudices of their ancestors. The works of the ancient Greeks and Romans were eagerly searched for information, and former discoveries brought to light.* The science of the Arabians was introduced and cultivated by the Moors and Jews, and geometry, astronomy, and geography were studied as essential to the art of navigation.

In the year 1412, the Portuguese doubled Cape Non, the limit of ancient enterprise. For upward of seventy years afterward they pursued their explorations, with more or less of vigor and success, along the African coast, and among the adjacent islands. By intercourse with the people of these countries they gradually acquired some knowledge of lands yet unvisited. Experience proved that the torrid zone was not closed to the enterprise of man.† They found that the

rocco to China; when one hundred and fifty sovereign princes paid tribute to the treasury of Lisbon. But in all their enterprises they aimed at conquest, and not at colonization. The government at home exercised little control over the arms of its piratical mariners; the mother country derived no benefit from their achievements. To the age of conquest succeeded one of effeminacy and corruption."—Merivale's *Lectures on Colonization*, vol. i., p. 44.

* See Appendix, No. IX.

† The zones were imaginary bands or circles in the heavens, producing an effect of climate on corresponding belts on the globe of the earth. The frigid zones, between the polar circles and the poles, were considered uninhabitable and unnavigable, on account of the extreme cold. The torrid zone, lying beneath the track of the sun, or rather the central part of it, immediately about the equator, was considered uninhabitable, unproductive, and impassable, on account of the excessive heat. The temperate zones, lying between the torrid and the frigid zones, were supposed to be the only parts of the globe suited to the purposes of life. Parmenides, according to Strabo, was the inventor of this theory of the five zones. Aristotle supported the same doctrine. He believed that there was habitable earth in the southern hemisphere, but that it was forever divided from the part of the world already known by the impassable zone of scorching heat at the equator. (Aristot., Met., ii., cap. v.) Pliny supported the opinion of Aris-

form of the continent contracted as it stretched southward, and that it tended toward the east. Then they brought to mind the accounts of the ancient Phœnician voyagers round Africa,* long deemed fabulous, and the hope arose that they might pursue the same career, and win for themselves the magnificent prize of Indian commerce. In the year 1486 the adventurous Bartholomew Diaz† first reached the Cape of Good Hope; soon afterward the information gained by Pedro de Covilham, in his overland journey, confirmed the consequent sanguine expectations of success. The attention of Europe was now fully aroused, and the progress of the Portuguese was watched with admiration and suspense.

totle concerning the burning zones. (Pliny, lib. i., cap. lxvi.) Strabo (lib. ii.), in mentioning this theory, gives it likewise his support; and others of the ancient philosophers, as well as the poets, might be cited, to show the general prevalence of the belief.—Cicero, *Somnium Scipionis*, cap. vi.; Geminus, cap. xiii., p. 31; ap. Petavii Opus de Doctr. Tempor. in quo Uranologium sive Systemata var. Auctorum. Amst., 1705, vol. iii.

* See Appendix, No. X.

† Barros, Dec. I., lib. iii., cap. iv., p. 190, says distinctly, "Bartholomeu Diaz, e os de sua compantica per causa dos perigos, e tormentas, que em o dobrar delle passáram che puyeram nome Tormentoso." The merit of the first circumnavigation, therefore, does not belong to Vasco de Gama, as is generally supposed. Diaz was at the Cape in May, 1487, and, therefore, almost at the same time that Pedro de Covilham and Alonzo de Payva of Barcelona commenced their expedition. As early as December, 1487, Diaz himself brought to Portugal the account of his important discovery. The mission of Pedro Covilham and Alonso de Payva, in 1487, was set on foot by King John II., in order to search for "the African priest Johannes." Believing the accounts which he had obtained from Indian and Arabian pilots in Calicut, Goa, Aden, as well as in Sofala, on the eastern coast of Africa, Covilham informed King John II., by means of two Jews from Cairo, that if the Portuguese were to continue their voyages of discovery upon the western coast in a southerly direction, they would come to the end of Africa, whence a voyage to the *Island of the Moon*, to Zanzibar, and the gold country of Sofala, would be very easy. Accounts of the Indian and Arabian trading stations upon the east coast of Africa, and of the form of the southern extremity of the Continent, may have extended to Venice, through Egypt, Abyssinia, and Arabia. The triangular form of Africa was actually delineated upon the map of Sanuto, made in 1306, and discovered in the "Portulano della Mediceo-Laurenziana," by Count Baldelli in 1351, and also in the chart of the world by Fra Mauro.—Humboldt's *Cosmos*, vol. ii., p. 290, 461.

But during this interval, while all eyes were turned with anxious interest toward the East, a little bark, leaky and tempest-tossed, sought shelter in the Tagus.* It had come from the Far West—over that stormy sea where, from the creation until then, had brooded an impenetrable mystery. It bore the richest freight† that ever lay upon the bosom of the deep—the tidings of a New World.‡

It would be but tedious to repeat here all the well-known story of Christopher Columbus;§ his early dangers and ad-

* Faria y Sousa complains that "the admiral entered Lisbon with a vain-glorious exultation, in order to make Portugal feel, by displaying the tokens of his discovery, how much she had erred in not acceding to his propositions."—*Europa Portuguesa*, t. ii., p. 402, 403.

Ruy de Pina asserts that King John was much importuned to kill Columbus on the spot, since, with his death, the prosecution of the undertaking, as far as the sovereigns of Castile were concerned, would cease, from want of a suitable person to take charge of it; but the king had too much magnanimity to adopt the iniquitous measure proposed.—Vasconcellos, *Vida del Rie Don Juan II.*, lib. vi.; Garcia de Resende, *Vide de Dom Joam II.;* Las Casas, *Hist. Ind.*, lib. i., cap. lxxiv.; MS. quoted by Prescott.

† See Appendix, No. XI.

‡ "A Castilla y a Leon
Nuevo Mundo diò Colon,"

was the inscription on the costly monument that was raised over the remains of Columbus in the Carthusian Monastery of La Cuevas at Seville. "The like of which," says his son Ferdinand, with as much truth as simplicity, "was never recorded of any man in ancient or modern times."—*Hist. del Almirante*, cap. cviii.

His ashes were finally removed to Cuba, where they now repose in the Cathedral church of its capital.—Navarrete, *Coleccion de Viages*, tom. ii.

"E dandogli il titol di Don volsero che egli aggiungesse presso all'armè di casa sua quattro altre, cioè quelle del Regno de Castiglio di Leon, e il Mar Oceano con tutte l'isole e quattro anchore per dimostrare l'ufficio d'Almirante, con un motto d'intorno che dicea, 'Per Castiglia e per Leon, Nuovo Mundo trovo Colon.'"—Ramusio, *Discorso*, tom. iii.

The heir of Columbus was always to bear the arms of the admiral, to seal with them, and in his signature never to use any other title than simply "the Admiral."

§ See Appendix, No. XII.—In the Middle Ages the prevalent opinion was that the sea covered but one seventh of the surface of the globe; an opinion which Cardinal d'Ailly (Imago Mundi, cap. viii.) founded on the apocryphal fourth book of Ezra. Columbus, who always derived much of his cosmological knowledge from the cardinal's work,

ventures, his numerous voyages, his industry, acquirements, and speculations, and how at length the great idea arose in his mind, and matured itself into a conviction; then how conviction led to action, checked and interrupted, but not weakened, by the doubts of pedantic ignorance,* and the treachery,† coolness, or contempt of courts. On Friday,‡

was much interested in upholding this idea of the smallness of the sea, to which the misunderstood expression of "the ocean-stream" contributed not a little. He was also accustomed to cite Aristotle, and Seneca, and St. Augustine, in confirmation of this opinion.—Humboldt's *Examen Critique de l'Hist. de la Géographie*, tom. i., p. 186.

* See, especially, the details of the conference held at Salamanca (the great seat of learning in Spain), given in the fourth chapter of Washington Irving's "Columbus." One of the objections advanced was, that, admitting the earth to be spherical, and should a ship succeed in reaching in this way the extremity of India, she could never get back again; for the rotundity of the globe would present a kind of mountain, up which it would be impossible for her to sail with the most favorable wind.—*Hist. del Almirante*, cap. ii.; *Hist. de Chiapa por Remesel*, lib. ii., cap. 27.

† Columbus was required by King John II., of Portugal, to furnish a detailed plan of his proposed voyages, with the charts and other documents according to which he proposed to shape his course, for the alleged purpose of having them examined by the royal counselors. He readily complied; but while he remained in anxious suspense as to the decision of the council, a caravel was secretly dispatched with instructions to pursue the route designated in the papers of Columbus. This voyage had the ostensible pretext of carrying provisions to the Cape de Verde Islands; the private instructions given were carried into effect when the caravel departed thence. It stood westward for several days; but then the weather grew stormy, and the pilots having no zeal to stimulate them, and seeing nothing but an immeasurable waste of wild, trembling waves still extending before them, lost all courage to proceed. They put back to the Cape de Verde Islands, and thence to Lisbon, excusing their own want of resolution by ridiculing the project of Columbus. On discovering this act of treachery, Columbus instantly quitted Portugal.—*Hist. del Almirante*, cap. viii.; Herrera, Dec. I., lib. i., cap. vii.; Munoz, *Hist. del Nuevo Mundo*, lib. ii.—Quoted by Prescott.

‡ "Le Vendredi n' étant pas regardé dans la Chrétienté comme un jour de bon augure pour le commencement d'une entreprise, les historiens du 17me siècle, qui gémissaient dejà sur les maux dont, selon eux, l'Europe a été accablé par la découverte de l'Amérique, on fait remarque que Colomb est parti pour la première expédition *vendredi*, 3 août 1492, et que la première terre d'Amérique a été découverte *vendredi* 12 Octobre de la même année. La réformation du calendrier

the 3d of August, 1492, a squadron of three small, crazy ships, bearing ninety men, sailed from the port of Palos, in Andalusia. Columbus, the commander and pilot, was deeply impressed with sentiments of religion; and, as the spread of Christianity was one great object of the expedition, he and his followers before their departure had implored the blessing of Heaven* upon the voyage, from which they might never return.

They steered at first for the Canaries, over a well-known course; but on the 6th of September they sailed from Gomera, the most distant of those islands, and, leaving the usual track of navigation, stretched westward into the unknown sea. And still ever westward for six-and-thirty days they bent their course through the dreary desert of waters; terrified by the changeless wind that wafted them hour after hour further into the awful solitude, and seemed to forbid the prospect of return; bewildered by the altered hours of day and night, and more than all by the mysterious variation of their only guide, for the magnetic needle no longer pointed to the pole.† Then strange appearances in the sea aroused new

appliquée au journal de Colomb, qui indique toujours à la fois, les jours de la semaine et la date du mois, feroit disparoître le pronostic du jour fatal."—Humboldt's *Géog. du Nouveau Continent*, vol. iii., p. 160.

* His first landing in the New World partook of the same character as his departure from the Old.

"Christoforo Colombo—primo con una bandiera nella quale era figurato il nostro Signore Jesu Christo in croce, saltô in terra, e quella piantò, e poi tutti gli alti smontarono, e inginocchiati baciarono la terra, tre volti piangendo di allegrezza. Di poi Colombo alzate le mani al cielo lagrimando disse, Signor Dio Eterno, Signore omnipotente, tu creasti il cielo, e la terra, e il mare con la tua santa parola, sia benedetto e glorificato il nome tuo, sia ringraziata la tua Maestà, la quale si è degnata per mano d' uno umil suo servo far ch' él suo santo nome sia conosciuto e divulgato in questa altra parte del mondo."—Pietro Martire, *Dell' Indie Occidentali*, in Ramusio, tom. iii., p. 2; Oviedo, *Hist. Gen. dell' India.*

† Columbus not only has, incontestably, the merit of first discovering the line where there is no declination of the needle, but also of first inducing a study of terrestrial magnetism in Europe, by his observations concerning the increasing declination as he sailed in a westerly direction from that line. It had been already easily recognized in the Mediterranean, and in all places where, in the twelfth century, the declination was as much as eight or ten degrees, even though their

fears: vast quantities of weeds covered the surface, retarding the motion of the vessels; the sailors imagined that they had reached the utmost boundary of the navigable ocean, and that they were rushing blindly into the rocks and quicksands of some submerged continent.

The master mind turned all these strange novelties into omens of success. The changeless wind was the favoring breath of the Omnipotent; the day lengthened as they followed the sun's course; an ingenious fiction explained the inconstancy of the needle; the vast fields of sea-weed bespoke a neighboring shore; and the flight of unknown birds* was hailed with happy promise. But as time passed on, and brought no fulfillment of their hopes, the spirits of the timid began to fail; the flattering appearances of land had repeat-

instruments were so imperfect that the ends of a magnetic needle did not point exactly to the geographical north or south. It is improbable that the Arabs or Crusaders drew attention to the fact of the compass pointing to the northeast and northwest in different parts of the world, as to a phenomenon which had long been known. The merit which belongs to Columbus is, not for the first observance of the existence of the declination, which is given, for example, upon the map of Andrew Bianca, in 1436, but for the remark which he made on the 13th of September, 1492, that about two degrees and a half to the east of the Island of Corvo the magnetic variation changed, and that it passed over from northeast to northwest. This discovery of a magnetic line without any variation indicates a remarkable epoch in nautical astronomy. It was celebrated with just praise by Oviedo, Casas, and Herrera. If with Livio Sanuto we ascribe it to the renowned mariner Sebastian Cabot, we forget that his first voyage, which was undertaken at the expense of some merchants of Bristol, and which was crowned with success by his touching the main-land of America, falls five years later than the first expedition of Columbus.—Humboldt's *Cosmos*, vol. ii., p. 318; Las Casas, *Hist. Ind.*, lib. i., cap. 6.

* "In sailing toward the West India Islands birds are often seen at the distance of two hundred leagues from the nearest coast."—Sloane's *Nat. Hist. of Jamaica*, vol. i., p. 30.

Captain Cook says, "No one yet knows to what distance any of the Oceanic birds go to sea; for my own part, I do not believe that there is any one of the whole tribe that can be relied on in pointing out the vicinity of land."—*Voyage toward the South Pole*, vol. i., p. 275.

The Portuguese, however, only keeping along the African coast and watching the flight of birds with attention, concluded that they did not venture to fly far from land. Columbus adopted this erroneous opinion from his early instructors in navigation.

edly deceived them; they were now very far beyond the limit of any former voyage. From the timid and ignorant these doubts spread upward, and by degrees the contagion extended from ship to ship: secret murmurs rose to conspiracies, complaints, and mutiny. They affirmed that they had already performed their duty in so long pursuing an unknown and hopeless course, and that they would no more follow a desperate adventurer to destruction. Some even proposed to cast their leader into the sea.

The menaces and persuasions that had so often enabled Columbus to overcome the turbulence and fears of his followers now ceased to be of any avail. He gave way to an irresistible necessity, and promised that he would return to Spain, if unsuccessful in their search for three days more. To this brief delay the mutineers consented. The signs of land now brought almost certainty to the mind of the great leader. The sounding-line brought up such soil as is only found near the shore: birds were seen of a kind supposed never to venture on a long flight. A piece of newly-cut cane floated past, and a branch of a tree bearing fresh berries was taken up by the sailors. The clouds around the setting sun wore a new aspect, and the breeze became warm and variable. On the evening of the 11th of October every sail was furled, and strict watch kept, lest the ships might drift ashore during the night.

On board the admiral's vessel all hands were invariably assembled for the evening hymn; on this occasion a public prayer for success was added, and with those holy sounds Columbus hailed the appearance of that small, shifting light,* which crowned with certainty his long-cherished hope,† turned

* "Puesto que el amirante a los diez de la noche viò lumbre. . . . y era como una candelilla de cera que se alzaba y levantaba, lo cual a pocos pareciera ser indicio de tierra. Pero el amirante tuvò por cierto estar junto a la tierra. Por lo qual quando dijeron la 'Salve' que acostumbran decir y cantar a su manera todos los marineros, y de hallan todos, vogo y amonestòlos el amirante que hiciesen buena guarda al castillo de proa, y mirasen bien por la tierra."—*Diar. de Colon. Prem. Viag.* 11 *de Oct.*

† "Let those who are disposed to faint under difficulties, in the prosecution of any great and worthy undertaking, remember that eight-

his faith into realization,* and stamped his name forever upon the memory of man.†

It was by accident only that England had been deprived of the glory of these great discoveries. Columbus, when repulsed by the courts of Portugal and Spain, sent his brother Bartholomew to London,‡ to lay his projects before Henry VII., and seek assistance for their execution. The king, although the most penurious of European princes, saw the vast advantage of the offer, and at once invited the great Genoese to his court. Bartholomew was, however, captured by pirates on his return voyage, and detained till too late, for in the mean while Isabella of Castile had adopted the project of Columbus, and supplied the means for the expedition.

Henry VII. was not discouraged by this disappointment: two years after the discoveries of Columbus became known in England, the king entered into an arrangement with John Cabot, an adventurous Venetian merchant, resident at Bristol, and, on the 5th of March, 1495, granted him letters patent for conquest and discovery. Henry stipulated that one-fifth of the gains in this enterprise was to be retained for the crown, and that the vessels engaged in it should re-

een years elapsed after the time that Columbus conceived his enterprise before he was enabled to carry it into effect; that most of that time was passed in almost hopeless solicitation, amid poverty, neglect, and taunting ridicule; that the prime of his life had wasted away in the struggle, and that, when his perseverance was finally crowned with success, he was about in his fifty-sixth year. This example should encourage the enterprising never to despair."—Washington Irving's *Life of Columbus*, vol. i., p. 174.

* "While Columbus lay on a sick-bed by the River Belem, he was addressed in a dream by an unknown voice, distinctly uttering these words: 'Maravillósamente Dios hizo sonar tu nombre en la tierra; de los atamientos de la Mar Oceana, que estaban cerradas con cadenas tan fuertes, te dió las llaves.' (Letter to the Catholic monarch, July 7th, 1503.)"—Humboldt's *Cosmos*. † See Appendix, No. XIII.

‡ "The application to King Henry VII. was not made until 1488, as would appear from the inscription on a map which Bartholomew presented to the king. Las Casas intimates, from letters and writings of Bartholomew Columbus, in his possession, that the latter accompanied Bartholomew Diaz in his voyage from Lisbon, in 1486, along the coast of Africa, in the course of which he discovered the Cape of Good Hope."—Las Casas, *Hist. Ind.*, lib. i., cap. vii.

turn to the port of Bristol. On the 24th of June, 1497, Cabot discovered the coast of Labrador, and gave it the name of *Primavista*. This was, without doubt, the first visit of Europeans to the Continent of North America,* since the time of the Scandinavian voyages. A large island lay opposite to this shore: from the vast quantity of fish frequenting the neighboring waters, the sailors called it *Bacallaos*.† Cabot gave this country the name of St. John's, having landed there on St. John's day. Newfoundland has long since superseded both appellations. John Cabot returned to

* "The American Continent was first discovered under the auspices of the English, and the coast of the United States by a native of England (Sebastian Cabot told me that he was born in Bristowe)."—*History of the Travayles in the East and West Indies*, by R. Eden and R. Willes, 1577, fol. 267. Posterity hardly remembered that they[1] (the Cabots) had reached the American Continent nearly four months before Columbus, on his third voyage, came in sight of the main-land. —Bancroft's *Hist. of the United States*, vol. i., p. 11. Charlevoix's "Histoire de la Nouvelle France," and the "Fastes Chronologiques," endeavor to discredit the discoveries of John and Sebastian Cabot, but the testimonies of cotemporary authors are decisive. Unfortunately, no journal or relation remains of the voyages of the Cabots to North America, but several authors have handed down accounts of them, which they received from the lips of Sebastian Cabot himself. See Hakluyt, iii., 27; Galearius Butrigarius, in Ramusio, tom. ii.; Ramusio, Preface to tom. iii.; Peter Martyr ab Angleria, Dec. III., cap. vi.; Gomara, *Gen. Hist. of the West Indies*, b. ii., c. vi. In Fabian's Chronicle, the writer asserts that he saw, in the sixteenth year of Henry VII., two out of three men who had been brought from "New-found Island" two years before). The grant made by Edward VI. to Sebastian Cabot of a pension equal to £1000 per annum of our money, attests that "the good and acceptable service" for which it was conferred was of a very important nature. The words of the grant are handed down to us by Hakluyt, vol. iii., p. 31.—See *Life of Henry VII.*, by Lord Bacon; Bacon's *Works*, vol. iii., p. 356, 357.

† Baccalaos was the name given by the natives to the codfish with which these waters abounded. Pietro Martire, who calls Sebastian Cabot his "dear and familiar friend," speaks of Newfoundland as Baccalaos; also, Lopez de Gomara and Ramusio.

[1] "The only immediate fruit of Cabot's first enterprise is said to have been the importation from America of the first turkeys ever seen in Europe. Why this bird received the name it enjoys in England has never been satisfactorily explained. By the French it was called 'Coq d'Inde,' on account of its American original, America being then generally termed Western India."—Graham's *Hist. of the United States*, vol. i., p. 7.

England in August of the same year, and was knighted and otherwise rewarded by the king; he survived but a very short time in the enjoyment of his fame, and his son Sebastian Cabot, although only twenty-three years of age, succeeded him in the command of an expedition destined to seek a northwest passage to the South Seas.

Sebastian Cabot sailed in the summer of 1498: he soon reached Newfoundland, and thence proceeded north as far as the fifty-eighth degree. Having failed in discovering the hoped-for passage, he returned toward the south, examining the coast as far as the southern boundary of Maryland, and perhaps Virginia. After a long interval, the enterprising mariner again, in 1517, sailed for America, and entered the bay* which, a century afterward, received the name of Hudson. If prior discovery confer a right of possession, there is no doubt that the whole eastern coast of the North American Continent may be justly claimed by the English race.†

Gaspar Cortereal was the next voyager in the succession of discoverers: he had been brought up in the household of the King of Portugal, but nourished an ardent spirit of enterprise and thirst for glory, despite the enervating influences of a court. He sailed early in the year 1500, and pursued the track of John Cabot as far as the northern point of Newfoundland; to him is due the discovery of the Gulf of St. Lawrence,‡ and he also pushed on northward, by the coast

* Mr. Bancroft pronounces this "fact to be indisputable," though he acknowledges that "the testimony respecting this expedition is confused and difficult of explanation." Sebastian Cabot wrote "A Discourse of Navigation," in which the entrance of the strait leading into Hudson's Bay was laid down with great precision "on a card, drawn by his own hand."—Ortelius, *Map of America in Theatrum Orbis Terrarum;* Eden and Willis, p. 223; Sir H. Gilbert, in Hakluyt, vol. iii., p. 49, 50; Bancroft, vol. i., p. 12.

† The learned and ingenious author of the "Memoirs of Sebastian Cabot" has brought forward strong arguments against the discovery of the Continent of America by Jean Vas Cortereal in 1494.—Humboldt's *Géog. du Nouveau Continent*, vol. i., p. 279; vol. ii., p. 25.

"The discoverer of the territory of our country was one of the most extraordinary men of his age. There is deep cause for regret that time has spared so few memorials of his career. He gave England a continent, and no one knows his burial-place."—Bancroft, vol. i., p. 14.

‡ Ramusio, vol. iii., p. 417. This discovery is also attributed to

of Labrador,* almost to the entrance of Hudson's Bay. The adventurer returned to Lisbon in October of the same year. This expedition was undertaken more for mercantile advantage than for the advancement of knowledge; timber and slaves seem to have been the objects; no less than fifty-seven of the natives were brought back to Portugal, and doomed to bondage. These unhappy savages proved so robust and useful, that great benefits were anticipated from trading on their servitude;† the dreary and distant land of their birth, covered with snow for half the year, was despised by the Portuguese, whose thoughts and hopes were ever turned to the fertile plains, the sunny skies, and the inexhaustible treasures of the East.‡

But disaster and destruction soon fell upon these bold and merciless adventurers. In a second voyage, the ensuing year, Cortereal and all his followers were lost at sea: when some time had elapsed without tidings of their fate, his broth-

Jacques Cartier, who entered the gulf on the 10th of August, 1535, and gave it the name of the saint whose festival was celebrated on that day.—Charlevoix.

* In an old map published in 1508, the Labrador coast is called Terra Corterealis.

† It has been conjectured that the name Terra de Laborador was given to this coast by the Portuguese slave merchants, on account of the admirable qualities of the natives as laborers.—*Picture of Quebec.*

‡ It was an idea entertained by Columbus, that, as he extended his discoveries to climates more and more under the torrid influence of the sun, he should find the productions of nature sublimated by its rays to more perfect and precious qualities. He was strengthened in this belief by a letter written to him, at the command of the queen, by one Jayme Ferrer, an eminent and learned lapidary, who, in the course of his trading for precious stones and metals, had been in the Levant and in various parts of the East; had conversed with the merchants of the remote parts of Asia and Africa, and the natives of India, Arabia, and Ethiopia, and was considered deeply versed in geography generally, but especially in the nature of those countries from whence the valuable merchandise in which he dealt was procured. In this letter Ferrer assured Columbus that, according to his experience, the rarest objects of commerce, such as gold, precious stones, drugs, and spices, were chiefly to be found in the regions about the equinoctial line, where the inhabitants were black, or darkly colored, and that until the admiral should arrive among people of such complexions, he did not think he would find those articles in great abundance.—Navarrete, *Coleccion*, tom. ii., Document 68

er sailed to seek them; but he too, probably, perished in the stormy waters of the North Atlantic, for none of them were ever heard of more. The King of Portugal, feeling a deep interest in these brothers, fitted out three armed vessels and sent them to the northwest. Inquiries were made along the wild shores which Cortereal had first explored, without trace or tidings being found of the bold mariner, and the ocean was searched for many months, but the deep still keeps it secret.

Florida was discovered in 1512 by Ponce de Leon, one of the most eminent among the followers of Columbus. The Indians had told him wonderful tales of a fountain called Birnini, in an island of these seas; the fountain possessed the power, they said, of restoring instantly youth and vigor to those who bathed in its waters. He sailed for months in search of this miraculous spring, landing at every point, entering each port, however shallow or dangerous, still ever hoping; but in the weak and presumptuous effort to grasp at a new life, he wasted away his strength and energy, and prematurely brought on those ills of age he had vainly hoped to shun. Nevertheless, this wild adventure bore its wholesome fruits, for Ponce de Leon then first brought to the notice of Europe that beautiful land which, from its wonderful fertility and the splendor of its flowers, obtained the name of Florida.*

The first attempt made by the French to share in the advantages of these discoveries was in the year 1504. Some Basque and Breton fishermen at that time began to ply their calling on the Great Bank of Newfoundland, and along the adjacent shores. From them the Island of Cape Breton received its name. In 1506, Jean Denys, a man of Harfleur, drew a map of the Gulf of St. Lawrence. Two years afterward, a pilot of Dieppe, named Thomas Aubert, excited great curiosity in France by bringing over some of the savage natives from the New World: there is no record whence they were taken, but it is supposed from Cape Breton. The

* Ramusio, vol. iii., p. 347; Charlevoix, vol. i., p. 36; see Osorio, History of the Portuguese, b. i.; Barrow's Voyages, p. 37–48; Herrera, Dec. I., lib. vii., cap. ix.; Ensayo Chronologico para la Historia general de la Florida. En Madrid, 1723.—Quoted by Murray.

reports borne back to France by these hardy fishermen and adventurers were not such as to raise sanguine hopes of riches from the bleak northern regions they had visited: no teeming fertility or genial climate tempted the settler, no mines of gold or silver excited the avarice of the soldier;* and for many years the French altogether neglected to profit by their discoveries.

In the mean time, Pope Alexander VI. issued a bull bestowing the whole of the New World upon the kings of Spain and Portugal.† Neither England nor France allowed the right of conferring this magnificent and undefined gift; it did not throw the slightest obstacle in the path of British enterprise and discovery, and the high-spirited Francis I. of France refused to acknowledge the papal decree.‡

In the year 1523, Francis I. fitted out a squadron of four ships to pursue discovery§ in the west; the command was intrusted to Giovanni Verazzano, of Florence, a navigator of great skill and experience, then residing in France: he

* "Les demandes ordinaires qu'on nous fait sont, 'Y a-t-il des tresors? Y a-t-il de l'or et de l'argent?' Et personne ne demande, 'Ces peuples là sont il disposés à entendre la doctrine Chrétienne?' Et quant aux mines, il y en a vraiment, mais il les faut fouiller avec industrie, labeur et patience. La plus belle mine que je sache, c'est du bled et du vin, avec la nourriture du bestial; qui a de ceci, il a de l'argent, et des mines, nous n'en vivons point."—Marc l'Escarbot.

† This bold stretch of papal authority, so often ridiculed as chimerical and absurd, was in a measure justified by the event, since it did, in fact, determine the principle on which the vast extent of unappropriated empire in the eastern and western hemispheres was ultimately divided between two petty states of Europe. Alexander had not even the excuse that he thought he was disposing of uncultivated and uninhabited regions, since he specifies in his donation both towns and castles: "Civitates et castra in perpetuum tenore præsentium donamus."

‡ "What," said Francis I., "shall the kings of Spain and Portugal divide all America between them, without suffering me to take a share as their brother? I would fain see the article in Adam's will that bequeaths that vast inheritance to them."—*Encyclopedia*, vol. iv., p. 695.

§ "In the latter years of his life, Francis, by a strict economy of the public money, repaired the evils of his early extravagance, while, at the same time, he was enabled to spare sufficient for carrying on the magnificent public institutions he had undertaken, and for forwarding the progress of discovery, of the fine arts, and of literature."—Bacon's *Life and Times of Francis I.*, p. 399–401.

was about thirty-eight years of age, nobly born, and liberally educated; the causes that induced him to leave his own country and take service in France are not known. It has often been remarked as strange that three Italians should have directed the discoveries of Spain, England, and France, and thus become the instruments of dividing the dominions of the New World among alien powers, while their own classic land reaped neither glory nor advantage from the genius and courage of her sons. Of this first voyage the only record remaining is a letter from Verazzano to Francis I., dated 8th of July, 1524, merely stating that he had returned in safety to Dieppe.

At the beginning of the following year Verazzano fitted out and armed a vessel called the Dauphine, manned with a crew of thirty hands, and provisioned for eight months. He first directed his course to Madeira; having reached that island in safety, he left it on the 17th of January and steered for the west. After a narrow escape from the violence of a tempest, and having proceeded for about nine hundred leagues, a long, low line of coast rose to view, never before seen by ancient or modern navigators. This country appeared thickly peopled by a vigorous race, of tall stature and athletic form; fearing to risk a landing at first with his weak force, the adventurer contented himself with admiring at a distance the grandeur and beauty of the scenery, and enjoying the delightful mildness of the climate. From this place he followed the coast for about fifty leagues to the south, without discovering any harbor or inlet where he might shelter his vessel; he then retraced his course and steered to the north. After some time Verazzano ventured to send a small boat on shore to examine the country more closely: numbers of savages came to the water's edge to meet the strangers, and gazed on them with mingled feelings of surprise, admiration, joy, and fear. He again resumed his northward course, till, driven by want of water, he armed the small boat and sent it once more toward the land to seek a supply; the waves and surf, however, were so great that it could not reach the shore. The natives assembled on the beach, by their signs and gestures, eagerly invited the French to approach: one young sailor, a bold swimmer, threw himself into the water, bearing some presents for the savages, but his heart failed him on a nearer approach, and he turned to regain the boat; his strength was exhausted, however, and a heavy sea washed him, almost insensible, up upon the beach. The Indians treated him with great kindness, and, when he had sufficiently recovered, sent him back in safety to the ship.*

Verazzano pursued his examination of the coast with untiring zeal, narrowly searching every inlet for a passage through to the westward, until he reached the great island known to the Breton fishermen—Newfoundland. In this important voyage he surveyed more than two thousand miles of coast, nearly all that of the present United States, and a great portion of British North America.

A short time after Verazzano's return to Europe, he fitted out another expedition, with the sanction of Francis I., for the establishment of a colony in the newly-discovered countries. Nothing certain is known of the fate of this enterprise, but the bold navigator returned to France no more; the dread inspired by his supposed fate† deterred the French king and people from any further adventure across the Atlantic during many succeeding years. In later times it has come to light that Verazzano was alive thirteen years after

* See Appendix, No. XIV.

† "Navigò anche lungo la detta terra l'anno 1524 un gran capitano del Re Christianissimo Francesco, detto Giovanni da Verazzano, Fiorentino, e scorse tutta la costa fino alla Florida, come per una sua lettera scritta al detto Re, particolarmente si vedià la qual sola abbiamo potuto avere perciocchè l'altre si sono smarrite nelli travagli della povera città di Fiorenza e nell' ultimo viaggio che esso fece, avendo voluto smontar in terra con alcuni compagni, furono tutti morti da quei popoli, e in presentia di colóro che erano rimasi nelle navi, furono arrostiti e mangeati." (Ramusio, tom. iii., p. 416.) The Baron La Houtan and La Potherie give the same account of Verazzano's end; they are not, however, very trustworthy authorities. Le Beau repeats the same story; but Charlevoix's words are, "Je ne trouve aucun fondement à ce que quelques uns ont publié, qu'ayant mis pied à terre dans un endroit où il voulait bâtir un fort, les sauvages se jetèrent sur lui, le massacrèrent avec tous ses gens et le mangèrent." A Spanish historian has asserted, contrary to all probability, that Verazzano was taken by the Spaniards, and hung as a pirate.—D. Andrès Gonzalez de Barcia, *Ensayo Chronologico para la Historia della Florida.*

this period :* those best informed on the subject are of opinion that the enterprise fell to the ground in consequence of Francis I. having been captured by the Emperor Charles V., and that the adventurer withdrew himself from the service of France, having lost his patron's support.

The year after the failure of Verazzano's last enterprise, 1525, Stefano Gomez sailed from Spain for Cuba and Florida ; thence he steered northward in search of the long-hoped-for passage to India, till he reached Cape Race, on the south-eastern extremity of Newfoundland. The further details of his voyage remain unknown, but there is reason to suppose that he entered the Gulf of St. Lawrence and traded upon its shores. An ancient Castilian tradition existed that the Spaniards visited these coasts before the French, and having perceived no appearance of mines or riches, they exclaimed frequently, "Aca nada ;"† the natives caught up the sound, and when other Europeans arrived, repeated it to them. The strangers concluded that these words were a designation, and from that time this magnificent country bore the name of CANADA.‡

* Tiraboschi, *Storia della Literatura Italiana*, vol. vii., p. 261, 262. —Quoted in the *Picture of Quebec*, to which valuable work J. C. Fisher, Esq., president of the Literary and Historical Society of Quebec, largely contributed.

† Signifying "here is nothing." The insatiable thirst of the Spanish discoverers for gold is justified by the greatest of all discoverers, the disinterested Columbus himself, on high religious principles. When acquainting their Castilian majesties with the abundance of gold[1] to be procured in the newly-found countries, he thus speaks, "El oro es excelentisimo, del oro se hace tesoro; y con el quien lo tiene hace quanto quiere en el mundo, y elega a que echa las animas al paraiso." (Navarrete, *Coleccion de los Viages*, vol. i., p. 309.) A passage which the modern editor of his papers affirms to be in conformity with many texts of Scripture.

‡ Father Hennepin asserts that the Spaniards were the first dis-

[1] The historian Herrera, writing in the light of experience, makes use of the strong expression, that "mines were a lure devised by the evil spirit to draw the Spaniards on to destruction." "L'Espagne," says Montesquieu, "a fait comme ce roi insensé, qui demanda que tout ce qu'il toucheroit se convertît en or, et qui fut obligé de revenir aux Dieux, pour les prier de finir sa misère."—*Esprit des Loix*, lib. xxi., cap. 22.

"Les mines du Pérou et du Mexique ne valoient pas même pour l'Espagne ce qu'elle auroit tiré de son propre fonds en los cultivant. Avec tant de trésors Philippe II. fit banqueroute."—Millot. "Pâturage et labourage," said the wise Sully, "valent mieux que tout l'or du Pérou."

coverers of Canada, and that, finding nothing there to gratify their extensive desires for gold, they bestowed upon it the appellation of El Capo di Nada, "Cape Nothing," whence, by corruption, its present name.—*Nouvelle Description d'un trés grand pays situé dans l'Amérique entre le Nouveau Mexique et la Mer Glaciale, depuis l'an* 1667 *jusqu' en* 1670. *Par le Père Louis Hennepin, Missionaire Recollet à Utrecht*, 1697.

La Potherie gives the same derivation. *Histoire de l'Amérique Septentrionale par M. de Bacqueville de la Potherie, à Paris*, 1722. The opinion expressed in a note of Charlevoix (Histoire de la Nouvelle France, vol. i., p. 13), is that deserving most credit. "D'autres dérivent ce nom du mot Iroquois 'Kannata,' qui se prononce Cannada, et signifie un amas de cabanes." This derivation would reconcile the different assertions of the early discoverers, some of whom give the name of Canada to the whole valley of the St. Lawrence; others, equally worthy of credit, confine it to a small district in the neighborhood of Stadacona (now Quebec). *Seconda Relatione di Jacques Cartier*, in Ramusio, tom. iii., p. 442, 447. "Questo popolo (di Hochelaga) non partendo mai del loro paese, ne essendo vagabondi, come quelli di Canada e di Saguenay benchè dette di Canada sieno lor suggetti con otte o nove altri villaggi posti sopra detto fiume." Father du Creux, who arrived in Canada about the year 1625, in his "Historia Canadensis," gives the name of Canada to the whole valley of the St. Lawrence, confessing, however, his ignorance of the etymology: "Porro de Etymologiâ vocis Canada nihil satis certè potui comperire; priscam quidem esse, constat ex eo, quod illam ante annos prope sexaginta passim usurpari audiebam puer."

Duponçeau, in the Transactions of the Philosophical Society of Philadelphia, founds his conjecture of the Indian origin of the name of Canada upon the fact that, in the translation of the Gospel of St. Matthew into the Mohawk tongue, made by Brandt, the Indian chief, the word Canada is always used to signify a village. The mistake of the early discoverers, in taking the name of a part for that of the whole, is very pardonable in persons ignorant of the Indian language. It is highly improbable that at the period of its discovery the name of Canada was extended over this immense country. The migratory habits of the aborigines are alone conclusive against it. They distinguished themselves by their different tribes, not by the country over which they hunted and rode at will. They more probably gave names to localities than adopted their own from any fixed place of residence. The Iroquois and the Ottawas conferred their appellations on the rivers that ran through their hunting grounds, and the Huron tribe gave theirs to the vast lake now bearing their name. It has, however, never been pretended that any Indian tribe bore the name of Canada, and the natural conclusion therefore is, that the word "Canada" was a mere local appellation, without reference to the country; that each tribe had their own "Canada," or collection of huts, which shifted its position according to their migrations.

Dr. Douglas, in his "American History," pretends that Canada derives its name from Monsieur Kane or Cane, whom he advances to have been the first adventurer in the River St. Lawrence.—Knox's *Historical Journal*, vol. i., p. 303.

CHAPTER II.

In the year 1534, Philip Chabot, admiral of France, urged the king to establish a colony in the New World,* by representing to him in glowing colors the great riches and power derived by the Spaniards from their transatlantic possessions. Francis I., alive to the importance of the design, soon agreed to carry it out. Jacques Cartier, an experienced navigator of St. Malo, was recommended by the admiral to be intrusted with the expedition, and was approved of by the king. On the 20th of April, 1534, Cartier sailed from St. Malo with two ships of only sixty tons burden each, and one hundred and twenty men for their crews:† he directed his course westward, inclining rather to the north; the winds proved so favorable, that on the twentieth day of the voyage he made Cape Bonavista, in Newfoundland. But the harbors of that dreary country were still locked up in the winter's ice, forbidding the approach of shipping: he then bent to the southeast, and at length found anchorage at St. Catharine, six degrees lower in latitude. Having remained here ten days, he again turned to the north, and on the 21st of May reached Bird Island, fourteen leagues from the coast.

Jacques Cartier examined all the northern shores of Newfoundland, without having ascertained that it was an island, and then passed southward through the Straits of Belleisle. The country appeared every where the same bleak and inhospitable wilderness;‡ but the harbors were numerous, con-

* Hist. de la Nouvelle France, par le Père Charlevoix, de la Compagnie de Jésus, vol. i., p. 11; Fastes Chronologiques, 1534.

† Prima Relatione de Jacques Cartier della Terra Nouva, detta la Nouva Francia, in Ramusio, tom. iii., p. 435.

‡ "Se la terra fosse cosi buono, come vi sono buoni porti, sarebbe

venient, and abounding in fish. He describes the natives as well-proportioned men, wearing their hair tied up over their heads like bundles of hay, quaintly interlaced with birds' feathers.* Changing his course still more to the south, he then traversed the Gulf of St. Lawrence, approached the main-land, and on the 9th of July entered a deep bay; from the intense heat experienced there, he named it the "Baye de Chaleurs." The beauty of the country, and the kindness and hospitality of his reception, alike charmed him; he carried on a little trade with the friendly savages, exchanging European goods for their furs and provisions.

Leaving this bay, Jacques Cartier visited a considerable extent of the gulf coast; on the 24th of July he erected a cross thirty feet high, with a shield bearing the fleurs-de-lys of France, on the shore of Gaspé Bay.† Having thus taken possession‡ of the country for his king in the usual manner

un gran bene, ma ella non si debba chiamar Terra Nouva, anzi sassi e grebani salvatichi, e proprij luoghi da fiere, per ciò che in tutto l'isola di Tramontana—[translated by Hakluyt "the northern part of the island"]—io non vidi tanta terra che se ne potesse coricar un carro, e vi smontai in parecchi luoghi, e all' isola di Bianco Sabbione non v'è altro che musco, e piccioli spini dispersi, secchi, e morti, e in somma io penso che questa sia la terra che Iddio dette a Caino."—J. Cartier, in Ramusio, tom. iii., p. 436.

The journal of the first two voyages of Cartier is preserved almost entire in the "Histoire de la Nouvelle France," by L'Escarbot; there is an Italian translation in the third volume of Ramusio. They are written in the third person, and it does not appear that he was himself the author.

* "Sono uomini d'assai bella vita e grandezza ma indomiti e salvatichi: portano i capelli in cuna legati e stretti a guisa d'un pugno di fieno rivolto, mettendone in mezzo un legnetto, o altra cosa in vece di chiodo, e vi legano insieme certe penne d'uccelli."—J. Cartier, in Ramusio, tom. iii., p. 436.

† De Laët., vol. i., p. 58.

‡ This was ingeniously represented to the natives as a religious ceremony, and, as such, excited nothing but the "grandissima ammirazione" of the natives present; it was, however, differently understood by their chief. "Ma essendo noi ritornati alle nostra navi, venne il Capitano lor vestito d'im pella vecchia d'orso negro in una barca con tre suoi figliuoli, e ci fece un lungo sermone mostrandaci detta croce e facendo il segno della croce con due dita poi ci mostrava la terra tutta intorno di noi come s'avesse voluto dice che tutta era sua, e che noi non dovevamo piantar detta croce senza sua licenza."—J. Cartier, in Ramusio, tom. iii., p. 439.

of those days, he sailed, the 25th of July, on his homeward voyage: at this place two of the natives were seized by stratagem, carried on board the ships, and borne away to France. Cartier coasted along the northern shores of the Gulf till the 15th of August, and even entered the mouth of the River St. Lawrence, but the weather becoming stormy, he determined to delay his departure no longer: he passed again through the Straits of Belleisle, and arrived at St. Malo on the 5th of September, 1534, contented with his success, and full of hope for the future.

Jacques Cartier was received with the consideration due to the importance of his report. The court at once perceived the advantage of an establishment in this part of America, and resolved to take steps for its foundation. Charles de Moncy, Sieur de la Mailleraye, vice-admiral of France, was the most active patron of the undertaking; through his influence Cartier obtained a more effective force, and a new commission, with ampler powers than before. When the preparations for the voyage were completed, the adventurers all assembled in the Cathedral of St. Malo, on Whitsunday, 1535, by the command of their pious leader; the bishop then gave them a solemn benediction, with all the imposing ceremonials of the Romish Church.

On the 19th of May Jacques Cartier embarked, and started on his voyage with fair wind and weather. The fleet consisted of three small ships, the largest being only one hundred and twenty tons burden. Many adventurers and young men of good family accompanied the expedition as volunteers. On the morrow the wind became adverse, and rose to a storm; the heavens lowered over the tempestuous sea; for more than a month the utmost skill of the mariners could only enable them to keep their ships afloat, while tossed about at the mercy of the waves. The little fleet was dispersed on the 25th of June: each vessel then made for the coast of Newfoundland as it best might. The general's vessel, as that of Cartier was called, was the first to gain the land, on the 7th of July, and there awaited her consorts; but they did not arrive till the 26th of the month. Having taken in supplies of fuel and water, they sailed in company to explore the Gulf of St. Lawrence. A violent storm arose on the 1st of August, forcing them to seek shelter. They happily found a port on the north shore, at the entrance of the Great River, where, though difficult of access, there was a safe anchorage. Jacques Cartier called it St. Nicolas, and it is now almost the only place still bearing the name he gave. They left their harbor on the 7th, coasting westward along the north shore, and on the 10th came to a gulf filled with numerous and beautiful islands.* Cartier gave this gulf the name of St. Lawrence, having discovered it on that saint's festival day.†

On the 15th of August they reached a long, rocky island toward the south, which Cartier named L'Isle de l'Assumption, now called Anticosti.‡ Thence they continued their course, examining carefully both shores of the Great River,§

* "Trovavamo un molto bello e gran golfo pieno d'isole e buone entrate e passaggi, verso qual vento si possa fare."—J. Cartier, in Ramusio, tom. iii., p. 441.

† "Carthier donna au golphe le nom de St. Laurent, ou plutôt il le donna à une baye qui est entre l'isle d'Anticoste et la côte septentrionale, d'où ce nom s'est étendu à tout le golphe dont cette baye fait partie."—*Hist. de la Nouvelle France*, tom. i., p. 15.

‡ "Des sauvages l'appelloient Natiscotec, le nom d'Anticosti paraît lui avoir été donné par les Anglais."—Charlevoix, tom. i., p. 16. This island is one hundred and twenty-five miles long, and in its widest part thirty miles, dividing the River St. Lawrence into two channels. Throughout its whole extent it has neither bay nor harbor sufficiently safe to shelter ships. It is uncultivated, being generally of an unprofitable soil, upon which any attempted improvements have met with very unpromising results. Since the year 1809, establishments have been formed on the island for the relief of shipwrecked persons; two men reside there, at two different stations, all the year round, furnished with provisions for the use of those who may have the misfortune to need them. Boards are placed in different parts describing the distance and direction to these friendly spots; instances of the most flagrant inattention have, however, occurred, which were attended with the most distressing and fatal consequences."—Bonchetti, vol. i., p. 169.

"At present the whole island might be purchased for a few hundred pounds. It belongs to some gentlemen in Quebec; and you might, for a very small sum, become one of the greatest land-owners in the world, and a Canadian *seigneur* into the bargain."—Grey's *Canada*.

§ This is the first discovery of the River St. Lawrence, called by

and occasionally holding communication with the inhabitants, till, on the 1st of September, they entered the mouth of the deep and gloomy Saguenay. The entrance of this great tributary was all they had leisure to survey; but the huge rocks, dense forests, and vast body of water, forming a scene of somber magnificence such as had never before met their view, inspired them with an exalted idea of the country they had discovered. Still passing to the southwest up the St. Lawrence, on the 6th they reached an island abounding in delicious filberts, and on that account named by the voyagers Isle aux Coudres. Cartier, being now so far advanced into an unknown country, looked out anxiously for a port where his vessels might winter in safety. He pursued his voyage till he came upon another island, of great extent, fertility, and beauty, covered with woods and thick, clustering vines. This he named Isle de Bacchus:* it is now

the natives the River Hochelaga, or the River of Canada. Jacques Cartier accurately determined the breadth of its mouth ninety miles across. Cape Rosier, a small distance to the north of the point of Gaspé, is properly the place which marks the opening of the gigantic river. "V'è tra le terre d'ostro e quelle di tramontana la distantia di trenta léghe in circa, e più di dugento braccia di fondo. Ci dissero anche i detti salvatichi e certificarono quivi essere il cammino e principio del gran fiume di Hochelaga e strada di Canada."—J. Cartier, in Ramusio, tom. iii., p. 442.

J. Cartier always afterward speaks of the St. Lawrence as the River of Hochelaga, or Canada. Charlevoix says, "Parceque le fleuve qu'on appelloit auparavant la Rivière de Canada se décharge dans le Golphe de St. Laurent, il a insensiblement pris le nom de Fleuve de St. Laurent, qu'il porte aujourd'hui (1720)."

* "Lorsque Jacques Carthier découvrit cette île, il la trouva toute remplie de vignes, et la nomma l'Ile de Bacchus. Ce navigateur était Bréton, après lui sont venus des Normands qui ont arraché les vignes et à Bacchus ont substitué Pomone et Cérès. En effet elle produit de bon froment et d'excellent fruits."—*Journal Historique*, lettre ii., p. 102.

Charlevoix also mentions that, when he visited the islands in 1720, the inhabitants were famed for their skill in sorcery, and were supposed to hold intercourse with the devil!

The Isle of Orleans was, in 1676, created an earldom, by the title of St. Laurent, which, however, has long been extinct. The first Comte de St. Laurent was of the name of Berthelot.—Charlevoix, vol. v., p. 99.

called Orleans. On the 7th of September, Donnacona, the chief of the country,* came with twelve canoes filled by his train, to hold converse with the strangers, whose ships lay at anchor between the island and the north shore of the Great River. The Indian chief approached the smallest of the ships with only two canoes, fearful of causing alarm, and began an oration, accompanied with strange and uncouth gestures. After a time he conversed with the Indians who had been seized on the former voyage, and now acted as interpreters. He heard from them of their wonderful visit to the great nation over the salt lake, of the wisdom and power of the white men, and of the kind treatment they had received among the strangers. Donnacona appeared moved with deep respect and admiration ; he took Jacques Cartier's arm and placed it gently over his own bended neck, in token of confidence and regard. The admiral cordially returned these friendly demonstrations. He entered the Indian's canoe, and presented bread and wine, which they ate and drank together. They then parted in all amity.

After this happy interview, Jacques Cartier, with his boats, pushed up the north shore against the stream, till he reached a spot where a little river flowed into a "goodly and pleasant sound," forming a convenient haven.† He moored

* "Il signor de Canada (chiamato Donnacona per nome, ma per signore il chiamano Agouhanna)."—J. Cartier, in Ramusio, tom. iii., p. 442. Agouhanna signified chief or lord.

Here, says Jacques Cartier, begins the country of Canada. "Il settimo giorno di detto mese la vigilia della Madonna, dopo udita la messa ci partimmo dall' isola de' nocellari per andar all'insu di detta fiume, e arrivamo a quattordici isole distanti dall' isola de Nocellari intorno setto in otto leghe, e quivi è il principio della provincia, e terra di Canada."—J. Cartier, in Ramusio, tom. iii., p. 442.

† The writer of these pages adds the testimony of an eye-witness to the opinion of the ingenious author of the "Picture of Quebec," as to the localities here described. The old writers, even Charlevoix himself, have asserted that the "Port St. Croix was at the entrance of the river now called Jacques Cartier, which flows into the St. Lawrence about fifteen miles above Quebec." Charlevoix, indeed, mentions that "Champlain prétend que cette rivière est celle de St. Charles, mais," he adds, "il se trompe," &c. However, the localities are still unchanged; though three centuries have since elapsed, the description of Jacques Cartier is easily recognized at the present day, and marks

his vessels here for the winter on the 16th of September, and gave the name of St. Croix to the stream, in honor of the day

out the mouth of the little River St. Charles[1] as the first winter station of the Europeans in Canada. The following are J. Cartier's words: "Per cercar luogo e porto sicuro da metter le navé, e andammo al contrario per detto fiume intorno di dieci leghe costezziando detta isola (di Bacchus) e in capo di quella trovammo un gorgo d'acqua bello e ameno ("the beautiful basin of Quebec," as it is called in the "Picture of Quebec")—nel quel luogo e un picciol fiume e porto, dove per il flusso è alta l'acqua intorno a tre braccia, ne parve questo luogo comodo per metter le nostre navi, per il che quivi le mettemmo in sicuro, e lo chiamammo Santa Croce, percio che nel detto giorno v' eramo giunti. . . Alla riva e lito di quell' isola (di Bacchus verso ponente v'è un goejo d'acque molto bello e dilettevole, e convenientemente da mettere navilij, dove è uno stretto del detto fiume molto corrente e profondo ma non e lungo più d'un terzo di lega intorno, per traverso del quale vi è una terra tutta di colline di buona altezza . . . quive è la stanza e la terra di Donnacona, e chiamasi il luogo Stadacona . . . . sotto la qual alta terra verso tramontana è il fiume e porto di Santa Croce, nel qual luogo e porto siamo stati dalli 15 di Settembre fino alli 16 di Maggio 1536, nel qual luogo le navi rimasero in secco." The "one place" in the River St. Lawrence, "deep and swift running," means, of course, that part directly opposite the Lower Town, and no doubt it appeared, by comparison, "very narrow" to those who had hitherto seen the noble river only in its grandest forms. The town of Stadacona stood on that part of Quebec which is now covered by the suburbs of St. Roch, with part of those of St. John, looking toward the St. Charles. The area, or ground adjoining, is thus described by Cartier, as it appeared three centuries ago: "terra Tanta buona, quanto sia possibile di vedere, e è molto fertile, piena di bellissimi arbori della sorte di quelli di Francia, come sarebbeno quercie, olmi, frassinè, najare, nassi, cedri, vigne, specie bianchi, i quali producono il frutto cosi grosso come susinè damaschini, e di molte altre specie d'arbori, sotto de quali vi nasce e cresce cosi bel canapo come quel di Francia, e nondimeno vi nasce senza semenza, e senza opera umana o lavoro alcuno.—Jacques Cartier, in Ramusio, tom. iii., p. 443, 449, 450.

The exact spot in the River St. Charles where the French passed the winter is supposed, on good authority, to have been the site of the old bridge, called Dorchester Bridge, where there is a ford at low water, close to the Marine Hospital. That it was on the east bank, not far from the residence of Charles Smith, Esq., is evident from the river having been frequently crossed by the natives coming from Stadacona to visit the French.—*Picture of Quebec*, p. 43–46; 1834.

1 It received this name, according to La Potherie, in compliment to Charles des Boûes, grand vicar of Pontoise, founder of the first mission of Recollets in New France. The River St. Charles was called Coubal Coubat by the natives, from its windings and meanderings.—Smith's *Canada*, vol. i., p. 104.

on which he first entered its waters; Donnacona, accompanied by a train of five hundred Indians, came to welcome his arrival with generous friendship. In the angle formed by the tributary stream and the Great River, stood the town of Stadacona, the dwelling-place of the chief; thence an irregular slope ascended to a lofty height of table-land: from this eminence a bold headland frowned over the St. Lawrence, forming a rocky wall three hundred feet in height. The waters of the Great River—here narrowed to less than a mile in breath—rolled deeply and rapidly past into the broad basin beyond. When the white men first stood on the summit of this bold headland, above their port of shelter, most of the country was fresh from the hand of the Creator; save the three small barks lying at the mouth of the stream, and the Indian village, no sign of human habitation met their view. Far as the eye could reach, the dark forest spread; over hill and valley, mountain and plain; up to the craggy peaks, down to the blue water's edge; along the gentle slopes of the rich Isle of Bacchus, and even from projecting rocks, and in fissures of the lofty precipice, the deep green mantle of the summer foliage hung its graceful folds. In the dim distance, north, south, east, and west, where mountain rose above mountain in tumultuous variety of outline, it was still the same; one vast leafy vail concealed the virgin face of Nature from the stranger's sight. On the eminence commanding this scene of wild but magnificent beauty, a prosperous city now stands; the patient industry of man has felled that dense forest, tree by tree, for miles and miles around, and where it stood, rich fields rejoice the eye; the once silent waters of the Great River below now surge against hundreds of stately ships; commerce has enriched this spot, art adorned it; a memory of glory endears it to every British heart. But the name QUEBEC* still remains unchang-

* "Quebec en langue Algonquine signifie *retrécissement*. Les Abenaquis dont la langue est une dialecte Algonquine, le nomment Quelibec, qui veut dire *ce qui est fermé*, parceque de l'entrée de la petite rivière de la Chaudière par où ces sauvages venaient à Quebec, le port de Quebec ne paroît qu'une grande barge."—Charlevoix, vol. i., p. 50.

"Trouvant un lieu le plus étroit de la rivière que les habitans du

ed ; as the savage first pronounced it to the white stranger, it stands to-day among the proudest records of our country's story.

The chief Donnacona and the French continued in friendly intercourse, day by day exchanging good offices and tokens of regard. But Jacques Cartier was eager for further discoveries ; the two Indian interpreters told him that a city of much larger size than Stadacona lay further up the river, the capital of a great country ; it was called in the native tongue Hochelaga ; thither he resolved to find his way. The Indians endeavored vainly to dissuade their dangerous guests from this expedition ; they represented the distance, the lateness of the season, the danger of the great lakes and rapid currents ; at length they had recourse to a kind of masquerade or pantomime, to represent the perils of the voyage, and the ferocity of the tribes inhabiting that distant land. The interpreters earnestly strove to dissuade Jacques Cartier from proceeding on his enterprise, and one of them refused to accompany him. The brave Frenchman would not heark-

pays nomment Québec ;" "la pointe de Québec, ainsi appellée des sauvages."—Champlain, vol. i., p. 115, 124.

Others give a Norman derivation for the word : it is said that Quebec was so called after Caudebec, on the Seine.

La Potherie's words are : "On tient que les Normands qui étoient avec J. Cartier à sa première découverte, apercevant en bout de l'isle d'Orléans, un cap fort élevé, s'écrièrent 'Quel bec !' et qu' à la suite du tems la nom de Quebec lui est resté. Je ne suis point garant de cette étymologie." Mr. Hawkins terms this "a derivation entirely illusory and improbable," and asserts that the word is of Norman origin. He gives an engraving of a seal belonging to William de la Pole, earl of Suffolk, dated in the 7th of Henry V., or A.D. 1420. The legend or motto is, "Sigillum Willielmi de la Pole, Comitis Suffolckiæ, Domine de Hamburg et de Quebec." Suffolk was impeached by the Commons of England in 1450, and one of the charges brought against him was, his unbounded influence in Normandy, where he lived and ruled like an independent prince ; it is not, therefore, improbable that he enjoyed the French title of Quebec in addition to his English honors.

The Indian name Stadacona had perished before the time of Champlain, owing, probably, to the migration of the principal tribe and the succession of others. The inhabitants of Hochelaga, we are told by Jacques Cartier, were the only people in the surrounding neighborhood who were not migratory.

en to such dissuasions, and treated with equal contempt the verbal and pantomimic warnings of the alleged difficulties. As a precautionary measure to impress the savages with an exalted idea of his power as a friend or foe, he caused twelve cannon loaded with bullets to be fired in their presence against a wood ; amazed and terrified at the noise, and the effects of this discharge, they fled, howling and shrieking, away.

Jacques Cartier sailed for Hochelaga on the 19th of September ; he took with him the Hermerillon, one of his smallest ships, the pinnace, and two long-boats, bearing thirty-five armed men, with their provisions and ammunition. The two larger vessels and their crews were left in the harbor of St. Croix, protected by poles and stakes driven into the water so as to form a barricade. The voyage presented few of the threatened difficulties ; the country on both sides of the Great River was rich and varied, covered with stately timber, and abounding in vines. The natives were every where friendly and hospitable ; all that they possessed was freely offered to the strangers. At a place called Hochelai, the chief of the district visited the French, and showed much friendship and confidence, presenting Jacques Cartier with a girl seven years of age, one of his own children.

On the 29th, the expedition was stopped in Lake St. Pierre by the shallows, not having hit upon the right channel. Jacques Cartier took the resolution of leaving his larger vessels behind and proceeding with his two boats ; he met with no further interruption, and at length reached Hochelaga on the 2d of October, accompanied by De Pontbriand, De la Pommeraye, and De Gozelle, three of his volunteers. The natives welcomed him with every demonstration of joy and hospitality ; above a thousand people, of all ages and sexes, came forth to meet the strangers, greeting them with affectionate kindness. Jacques Cartier, in return for their generous reception, bestowed presents of tin, beads, and other bawbles upon all the women, and gave some knives to the men. He returned to pass the night in the boats, while the savages made great fires on the shore, and danced merrily all night long. The place where the French first landed was probably about eleven miles from the city of Hochelaga, below the rapid of St. Mary.

On the day after his arrival Jacques Cartier proceeded to the town; his volunteers and some others of his followers accompanied him, arrayed in full dress; three of the natives undertook to guide them on their way. The road was well beaten, and bore evidence of having been much frequented: the country through which it passed was exceedingly rich and fertile. Hochelaga stood in the midst of great fields of Indian corn; it was of a circular form, containing about fifty large huts, each fifty paces long and from fourteen to fifteen wide, all built in the shape of tunnels, formed of wood, and covered with birch bark; the dwellings were divided into several rooms, surrounding an open court in the center, where the fires burned. Three rows of palisades encircled the town, with only one entrance; above the gate, and over the whole length of the outer ring of defense, there was a gallery, approached by flights of steps, and plentifully provided with stones and other missiles to resist attack. This was a place of considerable importance, even in those remote days, as the capital of a great extent of country, and as having eight or ten villages subject to its sway.

The inhabitants spoke the language of the great Huron nation, and were more advanced in civilization than any of their neighbors: unlike other tribes, they cultivated the ground and remained stationary. The French were well received by the people of Hochelaga; they made presents, the Indians gave fêtes; their fire-arms, trumpets, and other warlike equipments filled the minds of their simple hosts with wonder and admiration, and their beards and clothing excited a curiosity which the difficulties of an unknown language prevented from being satisfied. So great was the veneration for the white men, that the chief of the town; and many of the maimed, sick, and infirm, came to Jacques Cartier, entreating him, by expressive signs, to cure their ills. The pious Frenchman disclaimed any supernatural power, but he read aloud part of the Gospel of St. John, made the sign of the cross over the sufferers, and presented them with chaplets and other holy symbols; he then prayed earnestly that the poor savages might be freed from the night of ignorance and infidelity. The Indians regarded these acts and words with deep gratitude and respectful admiration.

Three miles from Hochelaga, there was a lofty hill, well tilled and very fertile;* thither Jacques Cartier bent his way, after having examined the town. From the summit he saw the river and the country for thirty leagues around, a scene of singular beauty. To this hill he gave the name of Mont Royal; since extended to the large and fertile island on which it stands, and to the city below. Time has now swept away every trace of Hochelaga; on its site the modern capital of Canada has arisen; fifty thousand people of European race, and stately buildings of carved stone, replace the simple Indians and the huts of the ancient town.

Jacques Cartier, having made his observations, returned to the boats, attended by a great concourse; when any of his men appeared fatigued with their journey, the kind Indians carried them on their shoulders. This short stay of the French seemed to sadden and displease these hospitable people, and on the departure of the boats they followed their course for some distance along the banks of the river. On the 4th of October Jacques Cartier reached the shallows, where the pinnace had been left; he resumed his course the following day, and arrived at St. Croix on the 11th of the same month.

* "In mezzo di quelle campagne, è posta la terra d'Hochelaga appresso e congiunta con una montagna coltivata tutta attorno e molto fertile, sopra la qual si vede molto lontano. Noi la chiamammo il Monto Regal. . . . . . Parecchi uomini e donne ci vennero a condur e menar sopra la montagna, qui dinanzi detta, la qual chiamammo Monte Regal, distante da detto luogo poco manco d'un miglio, sopra la quale essendo noi, vedemmo e avemmo notitia di più di trenta leghe attorno di quella, e verso la parte di tramontana si vede una continuazione di montagne, li quali corrono avante e ponente, e altra tante verso il mezzo giorno, fra le quali montagna è la terra, più bella che sia possibile a veder."—J. Cartier, in Ramusio, tom. iii., p. 447, 448.

"Cartier donna le nom de Mont Royal à la montagne au pied de laquelle étoit la bourgade de Hochelaga. Il découvrit de là une grande étendue de pays dont la vue le charma, et avec raison, car il en est peu au monde de plus beau et de meilleur."—Charlevoix, tom. i., p. 20.

The men who had remained at St. Croix had busied themselves during their leader's absence in strengthening their position, so as to secure it against surprise, a wise precaution under any circumstances among a savage people, but especially in the neighborhood of a populous town, the residence of a chief whose friendship they could not but distrust, in spite of his apparent hospitality.

The day after Jacques Cartier's arrival, Donnacona came to bid him welcome, and entreated him to visit Stadacona. He accepted the invitation, and proceeded with his volunteers and fifty sailors to the village, about three miles from where the ships lay. As they journeyed on, they observed that the houses were well provided and stored for the coming winter, and the country tilled in a manner showing that the inhabitants were not ignorant of agriculture ; thus they formed, on the whole, a favorable impression of the docility and intelligence of the Indians during this expedition.

When the awful and unexpected severity of the winter set in, the French were unprovided with necessary clothing and proper provisions ; the scurvy attacked them, and by the month of March twenty-five were dead, and nearly all were infected ; the remainder would probably have also perished ; but when Jacques Cartier was himself attacked with the dreadful disease, the Indians revealed to him the secret of its cure : this was the decoction of the leaf and bark of a certain tree, which proved so excellent a remedy that in a few days all were restored to health.*

Jacques Cartier, on the 21st of April, was first led to suspect the friendship of the natives from seeing a number of strong and active young men make their appearance in the neighboring town ; these were probably the warriors of the tribe, who had just then returned from the hunting grounds, where they had passed the winter, but there is now no reason to suppose that their presence indicated any hostility. However, Jacques Cartier, fearing treachery, determined to

* "This tree is supposed to have been the spruce fir, *Pinus Canadensis.* It is called 'Ameda' by the natives. Spruce-beer is known to be a powerful anti-scorbutic."—Champlain, part i., p. 124.

Charlevoix calls the tree *Epinette Blanche.*

anticipate it. He had already arranged to depart for France. On the 3d of May he seized the chief, the interpreters, and two other Indians, to present them to Francis I. : as some amends for this cruel and flagrant violation of hospitality, he treated his prisoners with great kindness ; they soon became satisfied with their fate. On the 6th of May he made sail for Europe, and, after having encountered some difficulties and delays, arrived safely at St. Malo the 8th of July, 1536.

The result of Jacques Cartier's expedition was not encouraging to the spirit of enterprise in France ; no mines had been discovered,* no rare and valuable productions found.†

* Any information given by the natives as to the existence of mines was vague and unsatisfactory. "Poscia ci mostrarono con segni, che passate dette tre cadute si poteva navigar per detto fiume il spazio di tre lune : noi pensammo che quello sia il fiume che passa per il passe di Saguenay, e senza che li facessimo dimanda presero la catena del subiotto del capitano che era d'argento, e il manico del pugnale di uno de nostre compagni marinari, qual era d'ottone giallo quanto l'oro, e ci mostrarono che quello veniva di sopra di detto fiume. . . Il capitan mostro loro del rame rosso, qual chiamano *Caignetadze* dimostrandoli con segni voltandosi verso detto paese li dimandava se veniva da quelle parti, e eglino cominciarono a crollar il capo, volendo dir no, ma ben ne significarono che veniva da *Saguenay*.

"Più ci hanno detto e fatto intendere, che in quel paese di *Saguenay* sono genti vestite di drappi come noi, . . . e che hanno gran quantità d'oro e rame rosso . . . e che gli uomini e donne di quella terra sono vestite di pelli come loro, noi li dimandammo se ci è oro e rame rosso, ci risposero di si. Io penso che questo luogo sia verso la Florida per quanto ho potuto intendere dalli loro segni e indicij."—J. Cartier, in Ramusio, tom. iii., p. 448–450.

† The only valuable the natives seemed to have in their possession was a substance called *esurgny*, white as snow, of which they made beads and wore them about their necks. This they looked upon as the most precious gift they could bestow on the white men. The mode in which it was prepared is said by Cartier to be the following : When any one was adjudged to death for a crime, or when their enemies are taken in war, having first slain the person, they make long gashes over the whole of the body, and sink it to the bottom of the river in a certain place, where the esurgny abounds. After remaining ten or twelve hours, the body is drawn up and the esurgny or *cornibotz* is found in the gashes. These necklaces of beads the French found had the power to stop bleeding at the nose. It is supposed that in the above account the French misunderstood the natives or were imposed upon by them ; and there is no doubt that the "valuable substance" described by Cartier was the Indian wampum.

The miserable state to which the adventurers had been reduced by the rigorous climate and loathsome diseases, the privations they had endured, the poverty of their condition, were sufficient to cool the ardor of those who might otherwise have wished to follow up their discoveries. But, happily for the cause of civilization, some of those powerful in France judged more favorably of Jacques Cartier's reports, and were not to be disheartened by the unsuccessful issue of one undertaking; the dominion over such a vast extent of country, with fertile soil and healthy climate, inhabited by a docile and hospitable people, was too great an object to be lightly abandoned. The presence of Donnacona, the Indian chief, tended to keep alive an interest in the land whence he had come; as soon as he could render himself intelligible in the French language, he confirmed all that had been said of the salubrity, beauty, and richness of his native country. The pious Jacques Cartier most of all strove to impress upon the king the glory and merit of extending the blessed knowledge of a Savior to the dark and hopeless heathens of the West; a deed well worthy of the prince who bore the title of Most Christian King and Eldest Son of the Church.

Jean François de la Roque, lord of Roberval, a gentleman of Picardy, was the most earnest and energetic of those who desired to colonize the lands discovered by Jacques Cartier; he bore a high reputation in his own province, and was favored by the friendship of the king. With these advantages he found little difficulty in obtaining a commission to command an expedition to North America; the title and authority of lieutenant general and viceroy was conferred upon him; his rule to extend over Canada, Hochelaga, Saguenay, Newfoundland, Belle Isle, Carpon, Labrador, La Grand Baye, and Baccalaos, with the delegated rights and powers of the crown. This patent was dated the 15th of January, 1540. Jacques Cartier was named second in command. The orders to the leaders of the expedition enjoined them to discover more than had been hitherto accomplished, and, if possible, to reach the country of Saguenay, where, from some reports of the Indians, they still hoped to find mines of gold and silver. The port of St. Malo was again chosen for the fitting out of the expedition: the king furnished a sum of money to defray the expenses.*

Jacques Cartier exerted himself vigorously in preparing the little fleet for the voyage, and awaited the arrival of his chief with the necessary arms, stores, and ammunition; Roberval was meanwhile engaged at Honfleur in fitting out two other vessels at his own cost, and being urged to hasten by the king, he gave his lieutenant orders to start at once, with full authority to act as if he himself were present. He also promised to follow from Honfleur with all the required supplies. Jacques Cartier sailed on the 23d of May, 1541, having provisioned his fleet for two years. Storms and adverse winds dispersed the ships for some time, but in about a month they all met again on the coast of Newfoundland, where they hoped Roberval would join them. They awaited his coming for some weeks, but at length proceeded without him to the St. Lawrence; on the 23d of August they reached their old station near the magnificent headland of Quebec.

Donnacona's successor as chief of the Indians at Stadacona came in state to welcome the French on their return, and to inquire after his absent countrymen. They told him of the chief's death, but concealed the fate of the other Indians, stating that they were enjoying great honor and happiness in France, and would not return to their own country. The savages displayed no symptoms of anger, surprise, or distrust at this news; their countenances exhibited the same impassive calm, their manners the same quiet dignity as ever; but from that hour their hearts were changed; hatred and hostility took the place of admiration and respect, and a sad foreboding of their approaching destruction darkened their simple minds. Henceforth the French were hindered and molested by the inhabitants of Stadacona to such an extent that it was deemed advisable to seek another settlement for the winter. Jacques Cartier chose his new position at the mouth of a small river three leagues higher on the St. Lawrence;†

* See Appendix, No. XIV.

† The precise spot on which the upper fort of Jacques Cartier was built, afterward enlarged by Roberval, has been fixed by an ingenious

here he laid up some of his vessels under the protection of two forts, one on a level with the water, the other on the summit of an overhanging cliff; these strong-holds communicated with each other by steps cut in the solid rock; he gave the name of Charlesbourg Royal to this new station. The two remaining vessels of the fleet he sent back to France with letters to the king, stating that Roberval had not yet arrived.

Under the impression that the country of the Saguenay, the land of fabled wealth, could be reached by pursuing the line of the St. Lawrence, Jacques Cartier set forth to explore the rapids above Hochelaga on the 7th of September, 1541. The season being so far advanced, he only undertook this expedition with a view to being better acquainted with the route, and to being provided with all necessary preparations for a more extensive exploration in the spring. In passing up the Great River he renewed acquaintance with the friendly and hospitable chief of Hochelai, and there left two boys under charge of the Indians to learn the language. On the 11th he reached the sault or rapids above Hochelaga, where the progress of the boats was arrested by the force of the stream; he then landed and made his way to the second rapid. The natives gave him to understand that above the next sault there lay a great lake; Cartier, having obtained this information, returned to where he had left the boats; about four hundred Indians had assembled and met him with demonstrations of friendship; he received their good offices and made them presents in return, but still regarded them with distrust on account of their unusual numbers. Having gain-

gentleman at Quebec at the top of Cape Rouge Height, a short distance from the handsome villa of Mr. Atkinson. A few months ago, Mr. Atkinson's workmen, in leveling the lawn in front of the house, and close to the point of Cape Rouge Height, found beneath the surface some loose stones which had apparently been the foundation of some building or fortification. Among these stones were found several iron balls of different sizes, adapted to the caliber of the ship guns used at the period of Jacques Cartier's and Roberval's visit. Upon the whole, the evidence of the presence of the French at Cape Rouge may be considered as conclusive. Nor is there any good reason to doubt that Roberval took up his quarters in the part which Jacques Cartier had left.—*Picture of Quebec*, p. 62–469.

ed as much information as he could, he set out on his return to Charlesbourg Royal, his winter-quarters. The chief was absent when Jacques Cartier stopped at Hochelai on descending the river; he had gone to Stadacona to hold counsel with the natives of that district for the destruction of the white men. On arriving at Charlesbourg Royal, Jacques Cartier found confirmation of his suspicions against the Indians; they now avoided the French, and never approached the ships with their usual offerings of fish and other provisions; a great number of men had also assembled at Stadacona. He accordingly made every possible preparation for defense in the forts, and took due precautions against a surprise. There are no records extant of the events of this winter in Canada, but it is probable that no serious encounter took place with the natives; the French, however, must have suffered severely from the confinement rendered necessary by their perilous position, as well as from want of the provisions and supplies which the bitter climate made requisite.

Roberval, though high-minded and enterprising, failed in his engagements with Jacques Cartier: he did not follow his adventurous lieutenant with the necessary and promised supplies till the spring of the succeeding year. On the 16th of April, 1542, he at length sailed from Rochelle with three large vessels, equipped principally at the royal cost. Two hundred persons accompanied him, some of them being gentlemen of condition, others men and women purposing to become settlers in the New World. Jean Alphonse, an experienced navigator of Saintonge, by birth a Portuguese, was pilot of the expedition. After a very tedious voyage, they entered the Road of St. John's, Newfoundland, on the 8th of June, where they found no fewer than seventeen vessels engaged in the inexhaustible fisheries of those waters.

While Roberval indulged in a brief repose at this place, the unwelcome appearance of Jacques Cartier filled him with disappointment and surprise. The lieutenant gave the hostility of the savages and the weakness of his force as reasons for having abandoned the settlement where he had passed the winter. He still, however, spoke favorably of the richness and fertility of the country, and gladdened the eyes of the adventurers by the sight of a substance that resembled gold ore, and crystals that they fancied were diamonds, found on the bold headland of Quebec. But, despite these flattering reports and promising specimens, Jacques Cartier and his followers could not be induced, by entreaties or persuasions, to return. The hardships and dangers of the last terrible winter were too fresh in memory, and too keenly felt, to be again braved. They deemed their portion of the contract already complete, and the love of their native land overcame the spirit of adventure, which had been weakened, if not quenched, by recent disappointment and suffering. To avoid the chance of an open rupture with Roberval, the lieutenant silently weighed anchor during the night, and made all sail for France. This inglorious withdrawal from the enterprise paralyzed Roberval's power, and deferred the permanent settlement of Canada for generations then unborn. Jacques Cartier died soon after his return to Europe.* Having sacrificed his fortune in the pursuit of discovery, his heirs were granted an exclusive privilege of trade to Canada for twelve years, in consideration of his sacrifices for the public good; but this gift was revoked four months after it was bestowed.

Roberval determined to proceed on his expedition, although deprived of the powerful assistance and valuable experience of his lieutenant. He sailed from Newfoundland for Canada, and reached Cap Rouge, the place where Jacques Cartier had wintered, before the end of June, 1542. He immediately fortified himself there, as the situation best adapted for defense against hostility, and for commanding the navigation of the Great River. Very little is known of Roberval's proceedings during the remainder of that year and the following winter. The natives do not appear to have molested the new settlers; but no progress whatever was made to-

* Jacques Cartier was born at St. Malo about 1500. The day of his birth can not be discovered, nor the time and place of his death. Most probably he finished his useful life at St. Malo; for we find, under the date of the 29th of November, 1549, that the celebrated navigator with his wife, Catharine des Granges, founded an obit in the Cathedral of St. Malo, assigning the sum of four francs for that purpose. The mortuary registers of St. Malo make no mention of his death, nor is there any tradition on the subject.

ward a permanent establishment. During the intense cold, the scurvy caused fearful mischief among the French; no fewer than fifty perished from that dreadful malady during the winter. Demoralized by misery and idleness, the little colony became turbulent and lawless, and Roberval was obliged to resort to extreme severity of punishment before quiet and discipline were re-established.

Toward the close of April the ice broke up, and released the French from their weary and painful captivity. On the 5th of June, 1543, Roberval set forth from Cap Rouge to explore the province of Saguenay, leaving thirty men and an officer to protect their winter-quarters: this expedition produced no results, and was attended with the loss of one of the boats and eight men. In the mean time the pilot, Jean Alphonse, was dispatched to examine the coasts north of Newfoundland, in hopes of discovering a passage to the East Indies; he reached the fifty-second degree of latitude, and then abandoned the enterprise; on returning to Europe, he published a narrative of Roberval's expedition and his own voyage, with a tolerably accurate description of the River St. Lawrence, and its navigation upward from the Gulf. Roberval reached France in 1543; the war between Francis I. and the Emperor Charles V. for some years occupied his ardent spirit, and supplied him with new occasions for distinction, till the death of the king, his patron and friend, in 1547. In the year 1549 he collected some adventurous men, and, accompanied by his brave brother, Achille, sailed once again for Canada; but none of this gallant band were ever heard of more. Thus, for many a year, were swallowed up in the stormy Atlantic all the bright hopes of founding a new nation in America:* since these daring men had failed, none others might expect to be successful.

* The name of America was first given to the New World in 1507. "L'opinion anciennement émise et encore très répandue que Vespuce, dans l'exercice de son emploi de Piloto mayor, et chargé de corriger les cartes hydrographiques de 1508 à 1512, ait profité de sa position pour appeler de son nom le Nouveau Monde, n'a aucun fondement. La dénomination d'Amérique a été proposée loin de Seville, en Lorraine, en 1507, une année avant la création de l'office d'un Piloto mayor de Indias. Les Mappe Mondes qui portent le nom d'Amérique

In the reign of Henry II., attention was directed toward Brazil; splendid accounts of its wealth and fertility were brought home by some French navigators who had visited that distant land. The Admiral Gaspard de Coligni was the first to press upon the king the importance of obtaining a footing in South America, and dividing the magnificent prize with the Portuguese monarch. This celebrated man was convinced that an extensive system of colonization was necessary for the glory and tranquillity of France. He purposed that the settlement in the New World should be founded exclusively by persons holding that Reformed faith to which he was so deeply attached, and thus would be provided a refuge for those driven from France by religious proscription and persecution. It is believed that Coligni's magnificent scheme comprehended the possession of the St. Lawrence and the Mississippi, gradually colonizing the banks of these great rivers into the depths of the Continent, till the whole of North America, from the Gulf of St. Lawrence to the Gulf of Mexico, should be hemmed in by this gigantic line of French outposts. However, the first proposition was to establish a colony on the coast of Brazil; the king approved the project, and Durand de Villegagnon, vice-admiral of Brittany, was selected to command in 1555; the expedition, however, entirely failed, owing to religious differences.

Under the reigns of Francis II. and Charles IX., while France was convulsed with civil war, America seemed altogether forgotten. But Coligni availed himself of a brief interval of calm to turn attention once more to the Western

n'ont paru que 8 our 10 ans après la mort de Vespuce, et dans des pays sur lequels ni lui ni ses parents n'exerçaient aucune influence. Il est probable que Vespuce n'a jamais su quelle dangereuse gloire on lui préparoit à Saint Dié, dans un petit endroit, situé au pied des Vosges, et dont vraisembablement le nom même lui étoit inconnu. Jusqu' à l'époque de sa mort, le mot Amérique, employé comme dénomination d'un continent ne s'est trouvé imprimé que dans deux seuls ouvrages, dans la Cosmographiæ Introductio de Martin Waldseemüller, et dans le Globus Mundi (Argentor, 1509). On n'a jusqu'ici aucun rapport direct de Waldseemüller imprimateur de Saint Dié, avec le navigateur Florentin."—Humboldt's *Géogr. du Nouveau Continent*, vol. v., p. 206.

World. He this time bethought himself of that country to which Ponce de Leon had given the name of Florida, from the exuberant productions of the soil and the beauty of the scenery and climate. The River Mississippi* had been discovered by Ferdinand de Soto,† about the time of Jacques Cartier's last voyage, 1543 ; consequently, the Spaniards had this additional claim upon the territory, which, they affirmed, they had visited in 1512, twelve years before the date of Verazzano's voyage in 1524. However, the claims and rights of the different European nations upon the American Continent were not then of sufficient strength to prevent each state from pursuing its own views of occupation. Coligni obtained permission from Charles IX. to attempt the establishment of a colony in Florida,‡ about the year 1562. The king was the more readily induced to approve of this enterprise, as he hoped that it would occupy the turbulent spirits of the Huguenots, many of them his bitter enemies, and elements of discord in his dominions. On the 18th of February, 1562, Jean de Ribaut, a zealous Protestant, sailed from Dieppe with two vessels and a picked crew ; many volunteers, including some gentlemen of condition, followed his fortunes. He landed on the coast of Florida, near St. Mary's River, where he established a settlement and built a fort. Two years afterward Coligni sent out a re-enforcement, under the command of René de Laudonnière ; this was the

* Nomœsi-Sipu, *Fish River*, Mœsisip by corruption. This river is called Cucagna by Garcilasso.

† For the romantic details of Ferdinand de Soto's perilous enterprise, see Vega Garcilasso de Florida del Ynca, b. i., ch. iii., iv. ; Herrera, Dec. VI., b. vii., ch. ix. ; Purchas, 4, 1532; "Purchas, his Pilgrimage," otherwise called "Hackluytus Posthumus ;" a voluminous compilation by a chaplain of Archbishop Abbot's, designed to comprise whatever had been related concerning the religion of all nations, from the earliest times.—Miss Aikin's *Charles I.*, vol. i., p. 39.

‡ "La colonie Française établie sous Charles IX. comprenoit la partie méridionnale de la Caroline Angloise, la Nouvelle Georgie, d'aujourd'hui (1740) San Matteo, appellé par Laudonnière Caroline en l'honneur du roi Charles, St. Augustin, et tout ce que les Espagnols ont sur cette côte jusqu'au Cap François, n'a jamais été appellée autrement que la Floride Française, ou la Nouvelle France, ou la France Occidentale."—Charlevoix, tom. vi., p. 383.

only portion of the admiral's great scheme ever carried into effect: when he fell, in the awful massacre of Saint Bartholomew, his magnificent project was abandoned. [1568.] After six years of fierce struggle with the Spaniards, the survivors of this little colony returned to France.*

CHAPTER III.

LITTLE or no effort was made to colonize any part of Canada for nearly fifty years after the loss of Roberval; but the Huguenots of France did not forget that hope of a refuge from religious persecution which their great leader, Coligni, had excited in their breasts. Several of the leaders of subsequent expeditions of trade and discovery to Canada and Acadia were Calvinists, until 1627, when Champlain, zealous for the Romish faith, procured a decree forbidding the free exercise of the Reformed religion in French America.

Although the French seemed to have renounced all plan of settlement in America by the evacuation of Florida, the fishermen of Normandy and Brittany still plied their calling on the Great Bank and along the stormy shores of Newfoundland, and up the Gulf and River of St. Lawrence. By degrees they began to trade with the natives, and soon the greater gains and easier life of this new pursuit transformed many of these hardy sailors into merchants.

When, after fifty years of civil strife, the strong and wise sway of Henry IV. restored rest to troubled France, the spirit of discovery again arose. The Marquis de la Roche, a Breton gentleman, obtained from the king, in 1598, a patent granting the same powers that Roberval had possessed. He speedily armed a vessel, and sailed for Nova Scotia in the same year, accompanied by a skillful Norman pilot named Chedotel. He first reached Sable Island, where he left forty miserable wretches, convicts drawn from the prisons of

* See Appendix, Nos. XV., XVI.

France, till he might discover some favorable situation for the intended settlement, and make a survey of the neighboring coasts. When La Roche ever reached the Continent of America remains unknown; but he certainly returned to France, leaving the unhappy prisoners upon Sable Island to a fate more dreadful than even the dungeons or galleys of France could threaten. After seven years of dire suffering, twelve of these unfortunates were found alive, an expedition having been tardily sent to seek them by the king. When they arrived in France, they became objects of great curiosity; in consideration of such unheard-of suffering, their former crimes were pardoned, a sum of money was given to each, and the valuable furs collected during their dreary imprisonment, but fraudulently seized by the captain of the ship in which they were brought home, were allowed to their use. In the mean time, the Marquis de la Roche, who had so cruelly abandoned these men to their fate, harassed by lawsuits, overwhelmed with vexations, and ruined in fortune by the failure of his expedition, died miserably of a broken heart.

The misfortunes and ruin of the Marquis de la Roche did not stifle the spirit of commercial enterprise which the success of the fur trade had excited. Private adventurers, unprotected by any especial privilege, began to barter for the rich peltries of the Canadian hunters. [1600.] A wealthy merchant of St. Malo, named Pontgravé, was the boldest and most successful of these traders; he made several voyages to Tadoussac, at the mouth of the Saguenay, bringing back each time a rich cargo of rare and valuable furs. He saw that this commerce would open to him a field of vast wealth, could he succeed in obtaining an exclusive privilege to enjoy its advantages, and managed to induce Chauvin, a captain in the navy, to apply to the king for powers such as De la Roche had possessed: the application was successful, a patent was granted to Chauvin, and Pontgravé admitted to partnership. [1602.] It was, however, in vain that they attempted to establish a trading post at Tadoussac:* after

* "Parceque les relations et les voyageurs parloient beaucoup de Tadoussac, les Géographes ont supposé que e'était une ville, mais il n'y a jamais eu qu'une maison Française, et quelques cabannes de

having made two voyages thither without realizing their sanguine expectations of gain, Chauvin died while once more preparing to try his fortune.

At this time the great object of colonization was completely forgotten in the eager pursuit of the fur trade, till De Chatte, the governor of Dieppe, who succeeded to the privileges of Chauvin, founded a company of merchants at Rouen, for the further development of the resources of Canada. [1603.] An armament was fitted out under the command of the experienced Pontgravé; he was commissioned by the king to make further discoveries in the St. Lawrence, and to establish a settlement upon some suitable position on the coast. Samuel de Champlain, a captain in the navy, accepted a command in this expedition at the request of De

sauvages, qui y venoient au tems de la traité, et qui emportoient ensuite leurs cabannes; comme on fait les loges d'une foire. Il est vrai que ce port a été lontems l'abord de toutes les nations sauvages du nord et de l'est; que les François s'y rendoient dès que la navigation étoit libre; soit de France, soit du Canada; que les missionnaires profitoient de l'occasion, et y venoient négocier pour le ciel. . . . Au reste Tadoussac est un bon port, et on m'a assuré que vingt cinq vaisseaux de guerre y pouvoient être à l'abri de tous les vents, que l'ancrage y est sûr, et que l'entrée en est facile."—Charlevoix, tom. v., p. 96, 1721.

"Tadoussac, one hundred and forty miles below Quebec, is a post belonging to the Hudson Bay Company, and is the residence of one of its partners and an agent. They alone are allowed to trade with the Indians in the interior. At Tadoussac is a Roman Catholic chapel, a store and warehouse, and some eight or ten dwellings. Here is erected a flag-staff, surrounded by several pieces of cannon, on an eminence elevated about fifty feet, and overlooking the inner warehouse, where is a sufficient depth of water to float the largest vessels. This place was early settled by the French, who are said to have here erected the first dwelling built of stone and mortar in Canada, and the remains of it are still to be seen. The view is exceedingly picturesque from this point. The southern shore of the St. Lawrence may be traced, even with the naked eye, for many a league; the undulating line of snow-white cottages stretching far away to the east and west; while the scene is rendered gay and animated by the frequent passage of the merchant vessel plowing its way toward the port of Quebec, or hurrying upon the descending tide to the Gulf; while, from the summit of the hill upon which Tadoussac stands, the sublime and impressive scenery of the Saguenay rises to view."—*Picturesque Tourist*, p. 267 (New York, 1844).

Chatte; he was a native of Saintonge, and had lately returned to France from the West Indies, where he had gained a high name for boldness and skill. Under the direction of this wise and energetic man the first successful efforts were made to found a permanent settlement in the magnificent province of Canada, and the stain of the errors and disasters of more than seventy years was at length wiped away.

Pontgravé and Champlain sailed for the St. Lawrence in 1603. They remained a short time at Tadoussac, where they left their ships; then, trusting themselves to a small, open boat, with only five sailors, they boldly pushed up the Great River to the sault St. Louis, where Jacques Cartier had reached many years before. By this time Hochelaga, the ancient Indian city, had, from some unknown cause, sunk into such insignificance that the adventurers did not even notice it, nor deem it worthy of a visit; but they anchored for a time under the shade of the magnificent headland of Quebec. On the return of the expedition to France, Champlain found, to his deep regret, that De Chatte, the worthy and powerful patron of the undertaking, had died during his absence. Pierre du Guast, sieur de Monts, had succeeded to the powers and privileges of the deceased, with even a more extensive commission.

De Monts was a Calvinist, and had obtained from the king the freedom of religious faith for himself and his followers in America, but under the engagement that the Roman Catholic worship should be established among the natives. Even his opponents admitted the honesty and patriotism of his character,* and bore witness to his courage and ability; he was, nevertheless, unsuccessful; many of those under his command failed in their duty, and the jealousy excited by his exclusive privileges and obnoxious doctrines† involved him in ruinous embarrassments.

* "The colony that was sent to Canada this year was among the number of those things that had not my approbation; there was no kind of riches to be expected from all those countries of the New World which are beyond the fortieth degree of latitude. His majesty gave the conduct of this expedition to the Sieur de Monts."—*Memoirs of Sully*, b. xvi., p. 241, English translation.

† The pious Romanist, Champlain, thus details the inconveniences

The trading company established by De Chatte was continued and increased by his successor. With this additional aid De Monts was enabled to fit out a more complete armament than had ever hitherto been engaged in Canadian commerce. He sailed from Havre on the 7th of March, 1604, with four vessels. Of these, two under his immediate command were destined for Acadia. Champlain, Poutrincourt, and many other volunteers, embarked their fortunes with him, purposing to cast their future lot in the New World. A third vessel was dispatched under Pontgravé to the Strait of Canso, to protect the exclusive trading privileges of the company. The fourth steered for Tadoussac, to barter for the rich furs brought by the Indian hunters from the dreary wilds of the Saguenay.

On the 6th of May De Monts reached a harbor on the coast of Acadia, where he seized and confiscated an English vessel, in vindication of his exclusive privileges. Thence he sailed to the Island of St. Croix, where he landed his people, and established himself for the winter. In the spring of 1605 he hastened to leave this settlement, where the want of wood and fresh water, and the terrible ravages of the scurvy, had disheartened and diminished the number of his followers. In the mean time Champlain had discovered and named Port Royal, now Annapolis, a situation which presented many natural advantages. De Monts removed the establishment thither, and erected a fort, appointing

caused by the different creeds of the Frenchmen composing the expedition of De Monts: "Il se trouva quelque chose à redire en cette entreprise, qui est en ce que deux religions contraires ne font jamais un grand fruit pour la gloire de Dieu parmi les infidèles que l'on veut convertir. J'ai vu le ministre et notre curé s'entre battre à coups de poing, sur le différend de la religion. Je ne sçais pas qui étoit le plus vaillant et qui donnoit le meilleur coup, mas je sçais trés bien que le ministre se plaignoit quelquefois au Sieur de Monts d'avoir été battue, et vuidoit en cette façon les points de controversie. Je vous laisse à penser si cela étoit beau à voir; les sauvages étoient tantôt d'une partie, tantôt d'une autre, et les François mêlés selon leurs diverses croyances, disoit pis que pendre de l'une et de l'autre religion, quoique le Sieur de Monts y apportât la paix le plus qu'il pouvoit."—*Voyages de la Nouvelle France Occidentale, dite Canada, faits par le Sieur de Champlain à Paris*, 1632.

Pontgravé to its command. Soon afterward he bestowed Port Royal and a large extent of the neighboring country upon De Poutrincourt, and the grant was ultimately confirmed by letters patent from the king. This was the first concession of land made in North America since its discovery.

When De Monts returned to France in 1605, he found that enemies had been busily and successfully at work in destroying his influence at court. Complaints of the injustice of his exclusive privileges poured in from all the ports in the kingdom. It was urged that he had interfered with and thwarted the fisheries, under the pretense of securing the sole right of trading with the Indian hunters. These statements were hearkened to by the king, and all the Sieur's privileges were revoked. De Monts bore up bravely against this disaster. He entered into a new engagement with De Poutrincourt, who had followed him to France, and dispatched a vessel from Rochelle on the 13th of May to succor the colony in Acadia. The voyage was unusually protracted, and the settlers at Port Royal, at length reduced to great extremities, feared that they had been abandoned to their fate. The wise and energetic Pontgravé did all that man could do to reassure them; but, finally, their supplies being completely exhausted, he was constrained to yield to the general wish, and embark his people for France. He had scarcely sailed, however, when he heard of the arrival of Poutrincourt and the long-desired supplies. He then immediately returned to Port Royal, where he found his chief already landed. Under able and judicious management,* the colony

* De Poutrincourt had been accompanied, in his last voyage from France, by Marc Lescarbot, well known as one of the best historians of the early French colonists. His memoirs and himself are thus described by Charlevoix: "Un avocat de Paris, nommé Marc L'Escarbot, homme d'esprit et fort attaché à M. de Poutrincourt, avoit eu la curiosité de voir le Nouveau Monde. Il animoit les uns, il picquoit les autres d'honneur, il se faisoit aimer de tous, et ne s'épargnoit lui-même en rien. Il inventoit tous les jours quelque chose de nouveau pour l'utilité publique, et jamais on ne comprit mieux de quelle ressource peut être dans un nouvel établissement, un esprit cultivé par l'étude. . . . C'est à cet avocat, que nous sommes redevable des meilleurs mémoires que nous ayons de ce qui s'est passé sous ses yeux. On y voit un auteur exact, judicieux, et un homme, qui eût été aussi

increased and prospered until 1614, when it was attacked and broken up by Sir Samuel Argall with a Virginian force.*

The enemies of De Monts did not relax in their efforts till he was deprived of his high commission. A very insufficient indemnity was granted for the great expenses he had incurred. Still he was not disheartened: in the following year, 1607, he obtained a renewal of his privileges for one year, on condition that he should plant a colony upon the banks of the St. Lawrence. The trading company did not lose confidence in their principal, although his courtly influence had been destroyed; but their object was confined to the prosecution of the lucrative commerce in furs, for which reason they ceased to interest themselves in Acadia, and turned their thoughts to the Great River of Canada, where they hoped to find a better field for their undertaking. They equipped two ships at Honfleur, under the command of Champlain and Pontgravé, to establish the fur trade at Tadoussac. De Monts remained in France, vainly endeavoring to obtain an extension of his patent. Despite his disappointments, he fitted out some vessels in the spring of 1608, with the as-

capable d'établir une colonie que d'en écrire une histoire." (Charlevoix, vol. i., p. 185.) The title of L'Escarbot's work is "Histoire de la Nouvelle France, par Marc L'Escarbot, Avocat en Parlement, témoin oculaire d'une partie des choses y récitées: à Paris, 1609."

* "Argall se fondait sur une concession de Jacques I., qui avait permis à ses sujets de s'établir jusqu'au quarante cinq degrés, et il crut pouvoir profiter de la foiblesse des Français pour les traitre en usurpateurs. . . . Si Poutrincourt avoit été dans son fort avec trente hommes bien armés, Argall n'auroit pas même eu l'assurance de l'attaquer . . . en deux heures de tems le feu consuma tout ce que les Français possedoient dans une colonie où l'on avait déja depensé plus de cent mille écus. . . . Celui qui y perdit davantage, fut M. de Poutrincourt qui, depuis ce tems là ne songea plus à l'Amérique. Il rentra dans le service, où il s'était déja par plusieurs belles actions et mourut au lit d'honneur."—Jean de Laët.

In 1621, James I. conferred Acadia upon Sir William Alexander, who gave it the name of Nova Scotia. At the treaty of St. Germain-en-Laye, in 1632, it was restored to the French; again taken by the English, it was again restored to France by the treaty of Breda, in 1667. In 1710, when Acadia was taken by General Nicholson, the English perceived its importance for their commerce. They obtained its formal and final cession at the treaty of Utrecht, 1713.

sistance of the company, and dispatched them to the River St. Lawrence on the 13th of April, under the same command as before.

Champlain reached Tadoussac on the 3d of June; his views were far more extended than those of a mere merchant; even honest fame for himself, and increase of glory and power for his country, were, in his eyes, objects subordinate to the extension of the Catholic faith. After a brief stay, he ascended the Great River, examining the shore with minute care, to seek the most fitting place where the first foundation of French empire might be laid. On the 3d of July he reached QUEBEC, where, nearly three quarters of a century before, Jacques Cartier had passed the winter. This magnificent position was at once chosen by Champlain as the site of the future capital of Canada: centuries of experience have proved the wisdom of the selection; admirably situated for purposes of war or commerce, and completely commanding the navigation of the Great River, it stands the center of a scene of beauty that can nowhere be surpassed.

On the bold headland overlooking the waters of the basin, he commenced his work by felling the trees, and rooting up the wild vines and tangled underwood from the virgin soil. Some rude huts were speedily erected for shelter; spots around them were cultivated to test the fertility of the land: this labor was repaid by abundant production. The first permanent work undertaken in the new settlement was the erection of a solid building as a magazine for their provisions. A temporary barrack on the highest point of the position, for the officers and men, was subsequently constructed. These preparations occupied the remainder of the summer. The first snow fell on the 18th of November, but only remained on the ground for two days: in December it again returned, and the face of nature was covered till the end of April, 1609. From the time of Jacques Cartier to the establishment of Champlain, and even to the present day, there has been no very decided amelioration of the severity of the climate; indeed, some of the earliest records notice seasons milder than many of modern days.

The town of Stadacona, like its prouder neighbor of Hochelaga, seems to have dwindled into insignificance since the time when it had been an object of such interest and suspicion to Jacques Cartier. Some Indians still lived in huts around Quebec, but in a state of poverty and destitution, very different from the condition of their ancestors. During the winter of 1608, they suffered dire extremities of famine; several came over from the southern shores of the river, miserably reduced by starvation, and scarcely able to drag along their feeble limbs, to seek aid from the strangers. Champlain relieved their necessities and treated them with politic kindness. The French suffered severely from the scurvy during the first winter of their residence.

On the 18th of April, 1609, Champlain, accompanied by two Frenchmen, ascended the Great River with a war party of Canadian Indians. After a time, turning southward up a tributary stream, he came to the shores of a large and beautiful lake, abounding with fish; the shores and neighboring forests sheltered, in their undisturbed solitude, countless deer and other animals of the chase. To this splendid sheet of water he gave his own name, which it still bears. To the south and west rose huge snow-capped mountains, and in the fertile valleys below dwelt numbers of the fierce and hostile Iroquois. Champlain and his savage allies pushed on to the furthest extremity of the lake, descended a rapid, and entered another smaller sheet of water, afterward named St. Sacrement. On the shore they encountered two hundred of the Iroquois warriors; a battle ensued; the skill and the astonishing weapons of the white men soon gave their Canadian allies a complete victory. Many prisoners were taken, and, in spite of Champlain's remonstrances, put to death with horrible and protracted tortures. The brave Frenchman returned to Quebec, and sailed for Europe in September, leaving Captain Pierre Chauvin, an experienced officer, in charge of the infant settlement. Henry IV. received Champlain with favor, and called him to an interview at Fontainebleau:* the king listened attentively to the re-

* "It was at this time that the name of New France was first given to Canada."—Charlevoix, tom. i., p. 232.

port of the new colony, expressing great satisfaction at its successful foundation and favorable promise. But the energetic De Monts, to whom so much of this success was due, could find no courtly aid : the renewal of his privilege was refused, and its duration had already expired. By the assistance of the Merchant Company, he fitted out two vessels in the spring of 1610, under the tried command of Champlain and Pontgravé : the first was destined for Quebec, with some artisans, settlers, and necessary supplies for the colony; the second was commissioned to carry on the fur trade at Tadoussac. Champlain sailed from Honfleur on the 8th of April, and reached the mouth of the Saguenay in eighteen days, a passage which even all the modern improvements in navigation have rarely enabled any one to surpass in rapidity. He soon hastened on to Quebec, where, to his great joy, he found the colonists contented and prosperous; the virgin soil had abundantly repaid the labors of cultivation, and the natives had in no wise molested their dangerous visitors. He joined the neighboring tribes of Algonquin and Montagnez Indians, during the summer, in an expedition against the Iroquois. Having penetrated the woody country beyond Sorel for some distance, they came upon a place where their enemies were intrenched; this they took, after a bloody resistance. Champlain and another Frenchman were slightly wounded in the encounter.

In 1612 Champlain found it necessary to revisit France; some powerful patron was wanted to forward the interests of the colony, and to provide the supplies and resources required for its extension. The Count de Soissons readily entered into his views, and delegated to him the authority of viceroy, which had been conferred upon the count.* Soissons died soon after, and the Prince of Condé became his successor. Champlain was wisely continued in the command he had so long and ably held, but was delayed in France for some time by difficulties on the subject of commerce with the merchants of St. Malo.

Champlain sailed again from St. Malo on the 6th of March, 1613, in a vessel commanded by Pontgravé, and

* Champlain, part i., p. 231; Charlevoix, vol. i., p. 236.

anchored before Quebec on the 7th of May. He found the state of affairs at the settlement so satisfactory that his continued presence was unnecessary; he therefore proceeded at once to Montreal, and, after a short stay at that island, explored for some distance the course of the Ottawa, which there pours its vast flood into the main stream of the St. Lawrence. The white men were filled with wonder and admiration at the magnitude of this great tributary, the richness and beauty of its shores, the broad lakes and deep rapids, and the eternal forests, clothing mountain, plain, and valley for countless leagues around. As they proceeded they found no diminution in the volume of water; and when they inquired of the wandering Indian for its source, he pointed to the northwest, and indicated that it lay in the unknown solitudes of ice and snow, to which his people had never reached. After this expedition Champlain returned with his companion Pontgravé to St. Malo, where they arrived in the end of August.

Having engaged some wealthy merchants of St. Malo, Rouen, and Rochelle in an association for the support of the colony, through the assistance of the Prince of Condé, viceroy of New France, he obtained letters patent of incorporation for the company [1614]. The temporal welfare of the settlement being thus placed upon a secure basis, Champlain, who was a zealous Catholic, next devoted himself to obtain spiritual aid. By his entreaties four Recollets were prevailed upon to undertake the mission. These were the first* ministers of religion settled in Canada. They

* Seven or eight years before the arrival of the PP. Recollets at Quebec, Roman Catholic missionaries had found their way to Nova Scotia. They were Jesuits. It was remarkable that Henry IV., whose life had been twice attempted by the Jesuits,[1] should have earnestly urged their establishment in America. When Port Royal was ceded to Poutrincourt by De Monts, the king intimated to him that it was time to think of the conversion of the savages, and that it was *his desire* that the Jesuits should be employed in this work. Charlevoix acknowledges that De Poutrincourt was "un fort honnête homme, et

1 By Barrière in 1593; by Jean Châtel in 1594. He finally perished by the hand of Ravaillac, in 1610. See Sully's Memoirs, b. vi., vii.; Cayet, Chron. Noven., b. v.; Père de Chalons, tom. iii., p. 245, quoted by Sully.

reached Quebec in the beginning of April, 1615, accompanied by Champlain, who, however, at once proceeded to Montreal.

On arriving at this island, he found the Huron and other allied tribes again preparing for an expedition against the Iroquois. With a view of gaining the friendship of the savages, and of acquiring a knowledge of the country, he injudiciously offered himself to join a quarrel in which he was in no wise concerned. The father Joseph Le Caron accompanied him, in the view of preparing the way for religious instruction, by making himself acquainted with the habits and language of the Indians. Champlain was appointed chief by the allies, but his savage followers rendered slight obedience to this authority. The expedition proved very disastrous: the Iroquois were strongly intrenched, and protected by a quantity of felled trees; their resistance proved successful; Champlain was wounded, and the allies were forced to retreat with shame and with heavy loss.

The respect of the Indians for the French was much diminished by this untoward failure; they refused to furnish

sincèrement attaché à la religion Catholique" — nevertheless, his prejudices against Jesuits were so strong, that "il étoit bien résolu de ne les point mene au Port Royal." On various pretexts he evaded obeying the royal commands, and when, the year after, the Jesuits were sent out to him, at the expense of Madame de Gruercheville, and by the orders of the queen's mother, he rendered their stay at Port Royal as uncomfortable as was consistent with his noble and generous character, vigilantly guarding against their acquiring any dangerous influence. His former prejudices could not have been lessened by the assassination of Henry IV.[1] The two Jesuits selected by P. Cotton, Henry IV.'s confessor, for missionary labors in Acadia, were P. Pierre Biast and P. Enemond Masse. They were taken prisoners at the time of Argall's descent on Acadia, 1614, and conveyed to England. —Charlevoix, tom. i., p. 189, 216.

[1] Henri s' etait montré bienveillant pour les Jésuites, encore que les parlemens et tous ceux qui tenoient, á la magistrature ressentoient plus de prévention contre ces religieux que les Hugonots eux-mêmes. . . . . . . Henri IV. fit abattre la pyramide qui avait été élevée en mémoire de l' attentat de Jean Châtel contre lui, parce que l' inscription qu' elle portait inculpait les Jésuites d' avoir excité à cet assassinat.— Sismondi: *Histoire des Français*. See De Thou, tom ix., p. 696, 704; tom. x., p. 26 à 30.

Champlain with a promised guide to conduct him to Quebec, and he was obliged to pass the winter among them as an unwilling guest. He, however, made the best use of his time; he visited many of the principal Huron and Algonquin towns, even those as distant as Lake Nipissing, and succeeded in reconciling several neighboring nations. At the opening of the navigation, he gained over some of the Indians to his cause, and, finding that another expedition against the Iroquois was in preparation, embarked secretly and arrived at Quebec on the 11th of July, 1616, when he found that he and the father Joseph were supposed to have been dead long since. They both sailed for France soon after their return from among the Hurons.

In the following year, a signal service was rendered to the colony by a worthy priest named Duplessys: he had been engaged for some time at Three Rivers in the instruction of the savages, and had happily so far gained their esteem, that some of his pupils informed him of a conspiracy among all the neighboring Indian tribes for the utter destruction of the French; eight hundred chiefs and warriors had assembled to arrange the plan of action. Duplessys contrived, with consummate ability, to gain over some of the principal Indians to make advances toward a reconciliation with the white men, and, by degrees, succeeded in arranging a treaty, and in causing two chiefs to be given up as hostages for its observance.

For several years Champlain was constantly obliged to visit France for the purpose of urging on the tardily provided aids for the colony. The court would not interest itself in the affairs of New France since a company had undertaken their conduct, and the merchants, always limited in their views to mere commercial objects, cared but little for the fate of the settlers so long as their warehouses were stored with the valuable furs brought by the Indian hunters. These difficulties would doubtless have smothered the infant nation in its cradle, had it not been for the untiring zeal and constancy of its great founder. At every step he met with new trials from the indifference, caprice, or contradiction of his associates, but, with his eye steadily fixed upon the future, he devoted his fortune and the energies of his life to the cause, and rose superior to every obstacle.

In 1620, the Prince of Condé sold the vice-royalty of New France to his brother-in-law, the Marshal de Montmorenci, for eleven thousand crowns. The marshal wisely continued Champlain as lieutenant governor, and intrusted the management of colonial affairs in France to M. Dolu, a gentleman of known zeal and probity. Champlain being hopeful that these changes would favorably affect Canada, resolved now to establish his family permanently in that country. Thaking them with him, he sailed from France in the above-named year, and arrived at Quebec in the end of May. In passing by Tadoussac, he found that some adventurers of Rochelle had opened a trade with the savages, in violation of the company's privileges, and had given the fatal example of furnishing the hunters with fire-arms in exchange for their peltries.

A great danger menaced the colony in the year 1621. The Iroquois sent three large parties of warriors to attack the French settlements. This savage tribe feared that if the white men obtained a footing in the country, their alliance with the Hurons and Algonquins, of which the effects had already been felt, might render them too powerful. The first division marched upon Sault St. Louis, where a few Frenchmen were established. Happily, there was warning of their approach; the defenders, aided by some Indian allies, repulsed them with much loss, and took several prisoners. The Iroquois had, however, seized Father Guillaume Poulain, one of the Recollets, in their retreat; they tied him to a stake, and were about to burn him alive, when they were persuaded to exchange the good priest for one of their own chiefs, who had fallen into the hands of the French. Another party of these fierce marauders dropped down the river to Quebec in a fleet of thirty canoes, and suddenly invested the Convent of the Recollets, where a small fort had been erected; they did not venture to attack this little stronghold, but fell upon some Huron villages near at hand, and massacred the helpless inhabitants with frightful cruelty; they then retreated as suddenly as they had come. Alarmed by this ferocious attack, which weakness and the want of sufficient supplies prevented him from avenging, Champlain sent Father Georges le Brebeuf as an agent, to represent to the king the deplorable condition of the colony, from the criminal neglect of the company. The appeal was successful; the company was suppressed, and the exclusive privilege transferred to Guillaume and Emeric de Caen, uncle and nephew.

The king himself wrote to his worthy subject Champlain, expressing high approval of his eminent services, and exhorting him to continue in the same career. This high commendation served much to strengthen his hands in the exercise of his difficult authority. He was embarrassed by constant disputes between the servants of the suppressed company, and those who acted for the De Caens; religious differences also served to embitter these dissensions, as the new authorities were zealous Huguenots.

This year Champlain discovered that his ancient allies, the Hurons, purposed to detach themselves from his friendship, and unite with the Iroquois for his destruction. To avert this danger, he sent among them Father Joseph la Caron and two other priests, who appear to have succeeded in their mission of reconciliation. The year after, he erected a stone fort* at Quebec for the defense of the settlement, which then only numbered fifty souls of all ages and sexes. As soon as the defenses were finished, Champlain departed for France with his family, to press for aid from the government for the distressed colony.

On his arrival, he found that Henri de Levi, duke de Ventadour, had purchased the vice-royalty of New France from the Marshal de Montmorenci, his uncle, with the view of promoting the spiritual welfare of Canada, and the general conversion of the heathen Indians to the Christian faith. He had himself long retired from the strife and troubles of

* When Champlain first laid the foundations of the fort in 1623, to which he gave the name of St. Louis, it is evident that he was actuated by views, not of a political, but a commercial character. When Montmagny rebuilt the fort in 1635, it covered about four acres of ground, and formed nearly a parallelogram. Of these works only a few vestiges remain, except the eastern wall, which is kept in solid repair.—Bonchette.

the world, and entered into holy orders. Being altogether under the influence of the Jesuits, he considered them as the means given by heaven for the accomplishment of his views. The pious and exemplary Father Lallemant, with four other priests and laymen of the Order of Jesus, undertook the mission, and sailed for Canada in 1625. They were received without jealousy by their predecessors of the Recollets, and admitted under their roof on their first arrival.* The following year three other Jesuit fathers reached Quebec in a little vessel provided by themselves; many artisans accompanied them. By the aid of this re-enforcement, the new settlement soon assumed the appearance of a town.

The Huguenot De Caens used their powerful influence to foment the religious disputes now raging in the infant settlement; † they were also far more interested in the profitable pursuit of the fur trade than in promoting the progress of colonization; for these reasons, the Cardinal de Richelieu judged that their rule was injurious to the prosperity of the country; he revoked their privileges, and caused the formation of a numerous company of wealthy and upright men; to this he transferred the charge of the colony. This body was chartered under the name of "The Company of One Hundred Associates:" ‡ their capital was 100,000 crowns; their privileges as follows: To be proprietors of Canada; to

* Charlevoix, tom. i., p. 247.

† "Ce fut Guillaume de Caën qui les conduisit (les Jésuites) à Quebec. Il avoit donné sa parole au Duc de Ventadour qu'il ne laisseroit les Jésuites manquer de rien; cependant, dès qu'ils furent débarqués, il leur déclara que, si les PP. Recollets ne vouloient pas les recevoir et les loger chez eux, ils n'avoient point d'autre parti à prendre que retourner en France. Ils s'aperçurent même bientôt qu'on avoit travaillé a prévénir contre eux les habitans de Quebec, en leur mettant entre les mains les écrits les plus injurieux, que les Calvinistes de France avoient publiés contre leur compagnie. Mais leur présence eut bientôt effacé tous ces préjugés."—Charlevoix, tom. i., p. 248.

‡ Charlevoix highly extols this brilliant conception of the Cardinal de Richelieu, "et ne craint point d'avancer que la Nouvelle France seroit aujourd'hui la plus puissante colonie de l'Amerique, si l'execution avoit répondue à la beauté du projet, et si les membres de ce grand corps eussent profité des dispositions favorables du souverain et de son ministre à leur égard." — Charlevoix, tom. i., p. 250; *Memoires des Commissaires*, vol. i., p. 346.

govern in peace and war; to enjoy the whole trade for fifteen years (except the cod and whale fishery), and the fur trade in perpetuity; untaxed imports and exports. The king gave them two ships of 300 tons burden each, and raised twelve of the principal members to the rank of nobility. The company, on their part, undertook to introduce 200 or 300 settlers during the year 1628, and 16,000 more before 1643, providing them with all necessaries for three years, and settling them afterward on a sufficient extent of cleared land for their future support. The articles of this agreement were signed by the Cardinal de Richelieu on the 19th of April, 1627, and subsequently approved by the king.

At this time the Indians were a constant terror to the settlers in Canada: several Frenchmen had been assassinated by the ruthless savages, and their countrymen were too feeble in numbers to demand the punishment of the murderers. Conscious of their strength, the natives became daily more insolent; no white man could venture beyond the settlement without incurring great danger. Building languished, and much of the cleared land remained uncultivated. Such was the disastrous state of the colony.

The commencement of the company's government was marked by heavy misfortune. The first vessels sent by them to America fell into the hands of the English, at the sudden breaking out of hostilities. In 1628, Sir David Kertk, a French Calvinist refugee in the British service, reached Tadoussac with a squadron, burned the fur houses of the free traders, and did other damage; thence he sent to Quebec, summoning Champlain to surrender. The brave governor consulted with Pontgravé and the inhabitants; they came to the resolution of attempting a defense, although reduced to great extremities, and sent Kertk such a spirited answer that he, ignorant of their weakness, did not advance upon the town. He, however, captured a convoy under the charge of De Roquemont, with several families on board, and a large supply of provisions for the settlement. This expedition against Canada was said to have been planned and instigated by De Caen, from a spirit of vengeance against those who had succeeded to his lost privileges.

In July, 1629, Lewis and Thomas, brothers of Sir David Kertk, appeared with an armament before Quebec. As soon as the fleet had anchored, a white flag with a summons to capitulate was sent ashore. This time the assailants were well informed of the defenders' distress, but offered generous terms if Champlain would at once surrender the fort. He, having no means of resistance, was fain to submit. The English took possession the following day, and treated the inhabitants with such good faith and humanity, that none of them left the country. Lewis Kertk remained in command at Quebec; Champlain proceeded with Thomas to Tadoussac, where they met the admiral, Sir David, with the remainder of the fleet. In September they sailed for England, and Champlain was sent on to France, according to treaty.*

When the French received the news of the loss of Canada, opinion was much divided as to the wisdom of seeking to regain the captured settlement.† Some thought its possession of little value in proportion to the expense it caused, while others deemed that the fur trade and fisheries were of great importance to the commerce of France, as well as a useful nursery for experienced seamen. Champlain strongly urged the government not to give up a country where they had already overcome the principal difficulties of settlement, and where, through their means, the light of religion was dawning upon the darkness of heathen ignorance. His solicitations were successful, and Canada was restored to France at the same time with Acadia and Cape Breton, by the treaty of St. Germain-en-Laye‡ [1632]. At this period the fort of Quebec, surrounded by a score of hastily-built dwellings and barracks, some poor huts on the island of Montreal, the like at Three Rivers and Tadoussac, and a

* Champlain's proposals of capitulation (Smith's Canada, vol. i., p. 22) sufficiently prove that, down to 1629, France had scarcely any permanent footing in the country. By stipulating for the removal of "all the French" in Quebec, Champlain seems to consider that the whole province was virtually lost to France, and "the single vessel," which was to furnish the means of removal, reduces "all the French" in Quebec to a very small number.

† Charlevoix.

‡ Charlevoix, tom. i., p. 273.

few fishermen's log-houses elsewhere on the banks of the St. Lawrence, were the only fruits of the discoveries of Verazzano, Jacques Cartier, Roberval, and Champlain, the great outlay of La Roche and De Monts, and the toils and sufferings of their followers, for nearly a century.*

By the treaty of St. Germain-en-Laye the company were restored to all their rights and privileges, and obtained compensation for the losses they had sustained, but it was some time before the English could be effectually excluded from the trade which they had established with the Indians during their brief possession of the country. In 1633 Champlain was reappointed governor of New France, and on his departure for the colony took with him many respectable settlers: several Protestants were anxious to join him; this, however, was not permitted. Two Jesuits, Fathers de Brebeuf and Enemond Masse, accompanied the governor: they purposed to devote themselves to the conversion of the Indians to Christianity, and to the education of the youth of the colony. The Recollets had made but little progress in proselytism; as yet, very few of the natives had been baptized, nor were the Jesuits at first † much more successful: these persevering men were, however, not to be disheartened by difficulties, and they were supported by the hope that when they became better acquainted with the language and manners of their pupils, their instructions would yield a richer harvest.‡

* "L'île au Cap Breton (c'étoit bien peu de choses que l'établissement que nous avions alors dans cette île) le fort de Quebec environné de quelques méchantes maisons et de quelques baraques, deux ou trois cabanes dans l'Ile de Montreal, autant peutêtre à Tadoussac, et en quelques autres endroits sur le fleuve St. Laurent, pour la commodité de la pêché et de la Traité, un commencement d'habitation aux Trois Rivières et les rivières de Port Royal, voilà en quoi consistoit la Nouvelle France et tout le fruit des découvertes de Verazzani, de Jaques Cartier, de M. de Roberval, de Champlain, des grandes dépenses de Marquis de la Roche, et de M. de Monts et de l'industrie d'un grand nombre de Français qui auroient pu y faire un grand établissement, s'ils eussent été bien conduits."—Charlevoix, tom. i., p. 274.

† See Appendix, No. XVI.

‡ The Jesuits always retained the superior position they held from the first among the Roman Catholic missionaries of Canada. There

As New France advanced in population and prosperity, the sentiments of religion became strengthened among the settlers. On the first arrival of the Jesuits, Rénè Rohault, the eldest son of the Marquis de Gamache, and himself one of the order, adopted the idea of founding a college at Quebec for the education of youth and the conversion of the Indians, and offered 6000 crowns of gold as a donation to forward the object. The capture of the settlement by the English had, for a time, interrupted the execution of this plan; but Rohault at length succeeded in laying the foundation of the building in December, 1635, to the great joy of the French colonists.

In the same month, to the deep regret of all good men, death deprived his country of the brave, high-minded, and wise Champlain. He was buried in the city of which he was the founder, where, to this day, he is fondly and gratefully remembered among the just and good. Gifted with high ability, upright, active, and chivalrous, he was, at the same time, eminent for his Christian zeal and humble piety. "The salvation of one soul," he often said, "is of more value than the conquest of an empire." To him belongs the glory of planting Christianity and civilization among the snows of those northern forests; during his life, indeed, a feeble germ, but, sheltered by his vigorous arm—nursed by his tender care—the root struck deep. Little more than two centuries have passed since the faithful servant went to rest upon the field of his noble toils. And now a million and a half of Christian people dwell in peace and plenty upon that magnificent territory, which his zeal and wisdom first redeemed from the desolation of the wilderness.

is a well-known Canadian proverb, "Pour faire un Recollet il faut une hachette, pour un Prêtre un ciseau, mais pour un Jésuite il faut un pinceau." See Appendix, No. XVII., for Professor Kalm's account of these three classes.

CHAPTER IV.

Having followed the course of discovery and settlement in New France up to the death of the man who stamped the first permanent impression upon that country, it is now time to review its character and condition at the period when it became the abode of a civilized people. Champlain's deputed commission of governor gave him authority over all that France possessed or claimed on the continent and islands of North America; Newfoundland, Isle Royale, and Acadia, were each portions of this vast but vague territory; and those unknown, boundless solitudes of ice and snow, lying toward the frozen north, whose very existence was a speculation, were also, by the shadowy right of a European king, added to his wide dominion. Of that portion, however, called Canada, it is more especially the present subject to treat.

Canada is a vast plain, irregular in elevation and feature, forming a valley between two ranges of high land; one of these ranges divides it, to the north, from the dreary territories of Hudson's Bay; the other, to the south, from the republic of the United States and the British province of New Brunswick. None of the hills rise to any great height; with one exception, Man's Hill, in the State of Maine, 2000 feet is their greatest altitude above the sea. The elevated districts are, however, of very great extent, broken, rugged, and rocky, clothed with dense forests, intersected with rapid torrents, and varied with innumerable lakes. The great plain of Canada narrows to a mere strip of low land by the side of the St. Lawrence, as it approaches the eastern extremity. From Quebec to the gulf on the north side, and toward Gaspé on the south, the grim range of mountains reaches almost to the water's edge; westward of that city the plain expands, gradually widening into a district of great beauty and fertility; again, westward of Montreal, the level country becomes far wider and very rich, including the broad and valuable flats that lie along the lower waters of the Ottawa. The rocky, elevated shores of Lake Huron bound this vast valley to the west; the same mountain range extends along the northern shore of Lake Superior; beyond lie great tracts of fertile soil, where man's industrious hand has not yet been applied.

Canada may be described as lying between the meridians of 57° 50′ and 90° west; from the mouth of the Esquimaux River on the confines of Labrador, to the entrance of the stream connecting the waters of Lake Superior and the Rainy Lake, bordering on Prince Rupert's Land. The parallels of 42° and 52° inclose this country to the south and north. The greatest length is about 1300 miles, the breadth 700. A space of 348,000 square miles is inclosed within these limits.

The great lakes in Canada give a character to that country distinct from any other in the Old World or the New. They are very numerous; some far exceed all inland waters elsewhere in depth and extent; they feed, without apparent diminution, the great river St. Lawrence; the tempest plows their surface into billows that rival those of the Atlantic,* and they contain more than half of all the fresh water upon the surface of the globe.†

* "The sea (if it may be so termed) on Lake Ontario is so high during a sharp gale, that it was at first thought the smaller class steamboats could not live on it; and on Lake Superior, the waves almost rival those of the far-famed Cape of Storms, while the ground-swell, owing to the comparative shallowness, or little specific gravity of the fresh water, is such as to make the oldest sailor sick. Whether the water in the lowest depths of Lakes Superior and Ontario be salt or fresh, we can not ascertain; for the greater density of the former may keep it always below, or there may be a communication with the fathomless abysses of the ocean."—Montgomery Martin, p. 181.

† "Beyond Lake Superior, stretching into the vast interior of North America, we find first a long chain of little lakes connected by narrow channels, and which, combined, form what in the early narratives and even treaties is called Long Lake. Next occur, still connected by the same channel, the larger expanses of Lake La Pluie and Lake of the Woods. Another channel of about 100 miles connects this last with the Winnipeg Lake, whose length from north to south is almost equal to the Superior; but in a few parts only it attains the breadth

Superior* is the largest and most elevated of these lakes: it is crescent-shaped, convex to the north; to the southeast and southwest its extremities are narrow points: the length through the curve is 360 geographical miles, the breadth in the widest part 140, the circumference 1500. The surface of this vast sheet of fresh water is 627 feet above the level of the Atlantic; from various indications upon the shores, there is good reason to conclude that at some remote period it was forty or fifty feet higher. The depth of Lake Superior varies much in different parts, but is generally very great; at the deepest it is probably 1200 feet. The waters are miraculously pure and transparent; many fathoms down, the eye can distinctly trace the rock and shingle of the bottom, and follow the quick movements of the numerous and beautiful fish inhabiting these crystal depths. No tides vary the stillness of this inland sea, but when a strong prevailing wind sweeps over the surface, the waves are lashed to fury, and the waters, driven by its force, crowd up against the leeward shore. When in the spring the warm sun melts the mountain snows, and each little tributary becomes an impetuous

of 50 miles. The whole of this wonderful series of lakes, separated by such small intervals, may almost be considered as forming one inland sea. There is nothing parallel to this in the rest of the globe. The Tzad, the great interior sea of Africa, does not equal the Ontario. The Caspian, indeed, is considerably greater than any of these lakes, almost equal to the whole united; but the Caspian forms the final receptacle of many great rivers, among which the Volga is of the first magnitude. But the northern waters, after forming this magnificent chain of lakes, are not yet exhausted, but issue forth from the last of them, to form one of the noblest river channels either in the old or new continent."—*History of Discoveries and Travels in North America*, by H. Murray, Esq., vol. ii., p. 458.

* "Lake Superior is called, also, Keetcheegahmi and Missisawgaiegon. It is remarkable, that while every other large lake is fed by rivers of the first order, this, the most capacious on the surface of the globe, does not receive a third or even fourth rate stream; the St. Louis, the most considerable, not having a course of more than 150 miles. But, whatever deficiency there may be in point of magnitude, it is compensated by the vast number which pour in their copious floods from the surrounding heights. The dense covering of wood and the long continuance of frost must also, in this region, greatly diminish the quantity drawn off by evaporation."—Bouchette, vol. i., p. 127, 128. Darby's *View of the United States* (1828), p. 200.

torrent pouring into this great basin, the level of the surface rises many feet. Although no river of any magnitude helps to supply Lake Superior, a vast number of small streams fall in from among clefts and glens along the rugged shores;* there are also many large islands; one, Isle Royale, is more than forty miles in length. In some places lofty hills† rise abruptly from the water's edge; in others there are intervals of lower lands for sixty or seventy miles, but every where stands the primeval forest, clothing height and hollow alike. At the southeastern extremity of this lake, St. Mary's Channel carries the superabundant waters for nearly forty miles, till they fall into Lake Huron; about midway between, they rush tumultuously down a steep descent, with a tremendous roar, through shattered masses of rock, filling the pure air above with clouds of snowy foam.

Lake Huron is the next in succession and the second in magnitude of these inland seas. The outline is very irreg-

* "The *Pictured* Rocks (so called from their appearance) are situated on the south side of the lake, toward the east end, and are really quite a natural curiosity; they form a perpendicular wall 300 feet high, extending about twelve miles, with numerous projections and indentations in every variety of form, and vast caverns, in which the entering waves make a tremendous sound. The Pictured Rocks of Lake Superior have been described as 'surprising groups of overhanging precipices, towering walls, caverns, waterfalls, and prostrate ruins, which are mingled in the most wonderful disorder, and burst upon the view in ever-varying and pleasing succession.' Among the more remarkable objects are the Cascade La Portaille and the Doric Arch. The Cascade consists of a considerble stream precipitated from a height of 70 feet by a single leap into the lake, and projected to such a distance that a boat may pass beneath the fall and the rock perfectly dry. The Doric Arch has all the appearance of a work of art, and consists of an isolated mass of sandstone, with four pillars supporting an entablature of stone, covered with soil, and a beautiful grove of pine and spruce trees, some of which are 60 feet in height." —Montgomery Martin's *History of Canada*, vol. i., p. 211.

† "The Thunder Mountain is one of the most appalling objects of the kind that I have ever seen, being a bleak rock, about twelve hundred feet above the level of the lake, with a perpendicular face of its full height toward the west; the Indians have a superstition, which one can hardly repeat without becoming giddy, that any person who may scale the eminence, and turn round on the brink of its fearful wall, will live forever."—Simpson, vol. i., p. 33.

ular, to the north and east formed by the Canadian territory, to the southwest by that of the United States. From where the Channel of St. Mary enters this lake to the furthest extremity is 240 miles, the greatest breadth is 220, the circumference about 1000; the surface is only 32 feet lower than that of Superior; in depth and in pure transparency the waters of this lake are not surpassed by its great neighbor. Parallel to the north shore runs a long, narrow peninsula called Cabot Head, which, together with a chain of islands, shuts in the upper waters so as almost to form a separate and distinct lake. The Great Manitoulin Island, the largest of this chain, is seventy-five miles in length. In the Indian tongue the name denotes it the abode of the Great Spirit,* and the simple savages regard these woody shores with reverential awe.

To the north and west of Lake Huron the shores are generally rugged and precipitous; abrupt heights of from 30 to 100 feet rise from the water's edge, formed of clay, huge stones, steep rocks, and wooded acclivities; further inland, the peaks of the Cloche Mountains ascend to a considerable height. To the east, nature presents a milder aspect; a plain of great extent and richness stretches away toward the St. Lawrence. Many streams pour their flood into this lake; the principal are the Maitland, Severn, Moon, and French Rivers; they are broad and deep, but their sources lie at no great distance. By far the largest supply of water comes from the vast basin of Lake Superior, through the Channel of St. Mary. Near the northwestern extremity of Huron, a narrow strait† connects it with Lake Michi-

* "The Indian appellation of 'Sacred Isles' first occurs at Lake Huron, and thence westward is met with in Superior, Michigan, and the vast and numerous lakes of the interior. Those who have been in Asia, and have turned their attention to the subject, will recognize the resemblance in sound between the North American Indian and the Tartar names."—Montgomery Martin's *History of Canada*, vol. i., p. 117.

† "The remarkable post of Michillimackinack is a beautiful island or great rock, planted in the strait of the same name, which forms the connection between Lakes Huron and Michigan. The meaning of the Indian word Michillimackinack is *Great Turtle*. The island is crowned with a cap 300 feet above the surrounding waters, on the

gan in the United States; there is a slight difference of level between these two great sheets of water, and a current constantly sets into the southern basin: this lake is also remarkable for its depth and transparency.*

At the southern extremity of Lake Huron, its overflow pours through a river about thirty miles in length into a small lake; both lake and river bear the name of St. Clair.† Thence the waters flow on, through the broad but shallow stream of the Detroit, until they fall into Lake Erie thirty miles below; on either side, the banks and neighboring districts are rich in beauty and abundantly fertile.

Lake Erie is shallow and dangerous, the anchorage is bad, the harbors few and inconvenient. Long, low promontories project for a considerable distance from the main land, and embarrass the navigation; but the coasts, both on the Canadian and American side, are very fertile.‡ Lake Erie

top of which is a fortification. If Quebec is the Gibraltar of North America, Mackinaw (the vulgar appellation for this fort) is only second in its physical character, and in its susceptibilities of improvement as a military post. It is also a most important position for the facilities it affords in the fur trade between New York and the North-west."—Mr. Colton's *American Lakes*, vol. i., p. 92.

The value of canals and steam navigation may be judged of from the fact that, in 1812, the news of the declaration of war against Great Britain by the United States did not reach the post of Michillimackinack (1107 miles from Quebec) in a shorter time than two months; the same place is now within the distance of ten days' journey from the Atlantic.

* "So clear are the waters of these lakes, that a white napkin, tied to a lead, and sunk thirty fathoms beneath a smooth surface, may be seen as distinctly as when immersed three feet."—Colton, vol. i., p. 93.

† "The St. Clair (according to Dr. Bigsby) is the only river of discharge for Lakes Superior, Michigan, and Huron, which cover a surface of thirty-eight and a half million of acres, and are fed by numerous large rivers. Other able observers are of opinion that the Missouri and the Mississippi receive some of the waters of Superior and Michigan. Many persons think that a subterraneous communication exists between all the great lakes, as is surmised to be the case between the Mediterranean and the Euxine."—Montgomery Martin.

‡ "The Lake Erie is justly dignified by the illustrious name of Conti, for assuredly it is the finest lake upon earth. Its circumference extends to 230 leagues; but it affords every where such a charming prospect, that its banks are decked with oak-trees, elms, chesnut-trees, walnut-trees, apple-trees, plum-trees, and vines, which bear

is about 265 miles long, and 63 wide at its greatest breadth; the circumference is calculated at 658 miles; its surface lies 30 feet below the level of Lake Huron.* The length of the lake stretches northeast, almost the same direction as the line of the River St. Lawrence.

The Niagara River flows from the northeastern extremity

their fine clusters up to the very top of the trees, upon a sort of ground that lies as smooth as one's hand. Such ornaments as these are sufficient to give rise to the most agreeable idea of a landscape in the world."—La Hontan, in Pinkerton, vol. xiii., p. 343 (1683).

"Le nom que le Lac Erié porte est celui d'une nation de la langue Huronne, qui était établie sur ses bords et que les Iroquois ont entièrement détruite. Erié veut dire Chat, et les Eriés sont nommés dans quelques relations la nation du Chat. Ce nom vient apparemment de la quantité de ces animaux qu'on trouve dans le pays. Quelques cartes modernes ont donné au Lac Erié le nom de Conti, mais ce nom n'a pas fait fortune, non plus que ceux de Condé, de Tracy, et d'Orleans, donnés au Lac Huron, au Lac Supérieur, et au Lac Michigan."—Charlevoix, tom. v., p. 374 (1721).

* "In extreme depth Lake Erie varies from forty to forty-five fathoms, with a rocky bottom. Lakes Superior and Huron have a stiff, clayey bottom, mixed with shells. Lake Erie is reported to be the only one of the series in which any current is perceptible. The fact, if it is one, is usually ascribed to its shallowness; but the vast volume of its outlet—the Niagara River—with its strong current, is a much more probable cause than the small depth of its water, which may be far more appropriately adduced as the reason why the navigation is obstructed by ice much more than either of the other great lakes. As connected with trade and navigation, this lake is the most important of all the great chain, not only because it is bordered by older settlements than any of them except Ontario, but still more because from its position it concentrates the trade of the vast West. The Kingston Herald notices a most extraordinary occurrence on Lake Erie during a late storm (1836). A channel was made by the violence of the tempest through Long Point, N. Foreland, 300 yards wide, and from 11 to 15 feet deep. It had been in contemplation to cut a canal at this very spot, the expenses of which were estimated at £12,000. The York Courier confirms this extraordinary intelligence, stating that the storm made a breach through the point near the main land, converted the peninsula into an island, and actually made a canal 400 yards wide, and eight or ten feet deep, almost at the very point where the proposed canal was to be cut, and rendered nothing else now necessary in order to secure a safe channel for the vessels, and a good harbor on both sides, than the construction of a pier on the west side, to prevent the channel being filled up with sand."—Montgomery Martin.

of Lake Erie to Lake Ontario in a course of 33 miles, with a fall of not less than 334 feet. About twenty miles below Lake Erie is the grandest sight that nature has laid before the human eye—the Falls of Niagara. A stream three quarters of a mile wide, deep and rapid, plunges over a rocky ledge 150 feet in height; about two thirds of the distance across from the Canadian side stands Goat Island, covered with stately timber: four times as great a body of water precipitates itself over the northern or Horse-shoe Fall as that which flows over the American portion. Above the cataract the river becomes very rapid and tumultuous in several places, particularly at the Ferry of Black Rock, where it rushes past at the rate of seven miles an hour; within the last mile there is a tremendous indraught to the Falls. The shores on both sides of the Niagara River are of unsurpassed natural fertility, but there is little scenic beauty around to divert attention from the one object. The simplicity of this wonder adds to the force of its impression: no other sight over the wide world so fills the mind with awe and admiration. Description may convey an idea of the height and breadth*—the vast body of water†—the

* "The Horse-shoe Cataract on the British side is the largest of the Falls. The curvatures have been geometrically computed at 700 yards, and its altitude, taken with a plumb-line from the surface of the Table Rock, 149 feet; the American fall, narrowed by Goat Island, does not exceed 375 yards in curvilinear length (the whole irregular semicircle is nearly three quarters of a mile), its perpendicular height being 162 feet, or 13 feet higher than the top of the Great Fall, adding 57 feet for the fall. The rapids thus give only a total of 219 feet, which is less than many other falls; but their magnificence consists in the volume of the water precipitated over them, which has been computed at 2400 millions of tons per day, 102 millions per hour! A calculation made at Queenston, below the Falls, is as follows: The river is here half a mile broad; it averages 25 feet deep; current three miles an hour; in one hour it will discharge a current of water three miles long, half a mile wide, and twenty-five feet deep, containing 1,111,400,000 cubic feet, being 18,524,000 cubic feet, or 113,510,000 gallons of water each minute."—Montgomery Martin's *History of Canada*.

† "The total area of the four great lakes which pour forth their waters to the ocean over the Falls of Niagara is estimated at 100,000 square miles."—Montgomery Martin.

profound abyss—the dark whirlpools—the sheets of foam* —the plumy column of spray† rising up against the sky—the dull, deep sound that throbs through the earth, and fills the air for miles and miles with its unchanging voice‡—but of the magnitude of this idea, and the impression stamped upon the senses by the reality, it is vain to speak to those who have not stood beside Niagara.

The descent of the land from the shores of Lake Erie to those of Ontario is general and gradual,§ and there is no

* Colonel Bouchette observes, that, according to the altitude of the sun, and the situation of the spectator, a distinct and bright iris is seen amid the revolving columns of mist that soar from the foaming chasm, and shroud the broad front of the gigantic flood. Both arches of the bow are seldom entirely elicited, but the interior segment is perfect, and its prismatic hues are extremely glowing and vivid. The fragments of a plurality of rainbows are sometimes to be seen in various parts of the misty curtain.

† Symptons of the Falls are discerned from a vast distance. From Buffalo, twenty miles off, two small fleecy specks are distinctly seen, appearing and disappearing at intervals. These are the clouds of spray arising from the Falls; it is even asserted that they have been seen from Lake Erie, a distance of fifty-four miles.—Weld, p. 374.

‡ The sound of the Falls appears to have been heard at the distance of twenty or even forty miles; but these effects depend much on the direction of the wind, and the tranquil or disturbed state of the atmosphere. Mr. Weld mentions having approached the Falls within half a mile without hearing any sound, while the spray was but just discernible.—Weld, p. 374.

§ "The shores of Lake Erie, though flat, are elevated about 400 feet above those of Lake Ontario. The descent takes place in the short interval between the two lakes traversed by the Niagara Channel. This descent is partly gradual, producing only a succession of rapids. It is at Queenston, about seven miles below the present site of the Falls, that a range of hills marks the descent to the Ontario level. Volney conceives it certain that this must have been the place down which the river originally fell, and that the continued and violent action of its waves must have gradually worn away the rocks beneath them, and in the course of ages carried the Fall back to its present position, from which it continues gradually receding. Mr. Howison confirms the statement, that, in the memory of persons now living in Upper Canada, a considerable change has been observed. The whole course of the river downward to Queenston is through a deep dell, bordered by broken and perpendicular steeps, rudely overhung by trees and shrubs, and the opposite strata of which correspond, affording thus the strongest presumption that it is a channel hewn out by

feature in the neighborhood of the Falls to mark its locality. From the Erie boundary the river flows smoothly through a level but elevated plain, branching round one large and some smaller islands. Although the deep, tremulous sound of Niagara tells of its vicinity, there is no unusual appearance till within about a mile, when the waters begin to ripple and hasten on; a little further it dashes down a magnificent rapid, then again becomes tranquil and glassy, but glides past with astonishing swiftness. There are numberless points whence the fall of this great river may be well seen: the best is Table Rock, at the top of the cataract; the most wonderful is the recess between the falling flood and the cliff over which it leaps.

For some length below Niagara the waters are violently agitated; however, at the distance of half a mile, a ferry plies across in safety. The high banks on both sides of the river extend to Queenston and Lewiston, eight miles lower, confining the waters to a channel of no more than a quarter of a mile in breadth, between steep and lofty cliffs; midway is the whirlpool,* where the current rushes furious-

the river itself."—H. Murray's *Historical Description of America*, vol. ii., p. 466.

"It is now considered that there is clear geological proof that the Fall once existed at Queenston. The 710,000 tons of water which each minute pour over the precipice of the Niagara, are estimated to carry away a foot of the cliff every year; therefore we must suppose a period of 20,000 years occupied in the recession of the cataract to its present site."—Lyell's *Geology*.

* "The mouth of the whirlpool is more than 1000 feet wide, and in length about 2000. Mr. Howison, in his sketches of Upper Canada, says that the current of the river has formed a circular excavation in the high and perpendicular banks, resembling a bay. The current, which is extremely rapid, whenever it reaches the upper point of this bay, forsakes the direct channel, and sweeps wildly round the sides of it; when, having made this extraordinary circuit, it regains its proper course, and rushes with perturbed velocity between two perpendicular precipices, which are not more than 400 feet asunder. The surface of the whirlpool is in a state of continual agitation. The water boils, mantles up, and wreaths in a manner that proves its fearful depth, and the confinement it suffers; the trees that come within the sphere of the current are swept along with a quivering, zigzag motion, which it is difficult to describe. This singular body of water must be several hundred feet deep, and has not hitherto been frozen over, although in

ly round within encircling heights. Below Queenston the river again rolls along a smooth stream, between level and cultivated banks, till it pours its waters into Lake Ontario.

Ontario is the last* and the most easterly of the chain of

spring the broken ice that descends from Lake Erie descends in such quantities upon its surface, and becomes so closely wedged together, that it resists the current, and remains till warm weather breaks it up. The whirlpool is one of the greatest natural curiosities in the Upper Province, and its formation can not be rationally accounted for."—Martin's *History of Canada*, p. 139.

* "This inland sea, though the smallest of the great chain with which it is connected, is of such extent, that vessels in crossing it lose sight of land, and must steer their way by the compass; and the swell is often equal to that of the ocean. During the winter, the northeast part of Ontario, from the Bay of Quinté to Sacket's Harbor, is frozen across; but the wider part of the lake is frozen only to a short distance from the shore. Lake Erie is frozen still less; the northern parts of Huron and Michigan more; and Superior is said to be frozen to a distance of seventy miles from its coasts. The navigation of Ontario closes in October; ice-boats are sometimes used when the ice is *glare* (smooth). One, mentioned by Lieutenant de Roos, was twenty-three feet in length, resting on three skates of iron, one attached to each end of a strong cross-bar, fixed under the fore-feet, the remaining one to the stern, from the bottom of the rudder; the mast and sail those of a common boat: when brought into play on the ice, she could sail (if it may be so termed) with fearful rapidity, nearly twenty-three miles an hour. One has been known to cross from Toronto to Fort George or Niagara, a distance of forty miles, in little more than three quarters of an hour; but, in addition to her speed before the wind, she is also capable of beating well up to windward, requiring, however, an experienced hand to manage her, in consequence of her extreme sensibility of the rudder during her quick motion."—Martin's *History of Canada*.

"The great earthquake that destroyed Lisbon happened on the 1st of November, 1755, and on Lake Ontario strong agitations of the water were observed from the month of October, 1755."—*Lettera Rarissima data nelle Indie nella Isola di Jamaica a 7 Julio del* 1503 (Bassano, 1810, p. 29).

"From some submarine center in the Atlantic, this earthquake spread one enormous convulsion over an area of 700,000 square miles, agitating, by a single impulse, the lakes of Scotland and Sweden, and the islands of the West Indian Sea. Not, however, by a simultaneous shock, for the element of time comes in with the distance of undulation; and, together with this, another complexity of action in the transmission of earthquake movements through the sea, arising from the different rate of progression at different depths. In the fact that the wave of the Lisbon earthquake reached Plymouth at the rate of

lakes.* The greatest length is 172 miles; at the widest it measures 59 miles across; the circumference is 467 miles, and the surface is 334 feet below the level of Lake Erie. The depth of Ontario varies very much along the coast, being seldom more than from three to 50 fathoms; and in the center, a plummet, with 300 fathoms of line, has been tried in vain for soundings. A sort of gravel, small pieces of limestone, worn round and smooth by the action of water, covers the shores, lying in long ridges sometimes miles in extent. The waters, like those of the other great lakes, are very pure and beautiful, except where the shallows along the margin are stirred up by violent winds: for a few days in June a yellow, unwholesome scum covers the surface at the edge every year. There is a strange phenomenon connected with Ontario, unaccounted for by scientific speculation; each seventh year, from some inscrutable cause, the waters reach to an unusual height, and again subside, mysteriously as they arose. The beautiful illusion of the mirâge spreads its dreamy enchantment over the surface of Ontario in the summer calms, mixing islands, clouds, and waters in strange confusion.†

2·1 miles per minute, and Barbadoes at 7·3 miles per minute, there is illustration of the law that the velocity of a wave is proportional to the square root of its depth, and becomes a substitute for the sounding line in fixing the mean proportional depth of different parts of this great ocean."—Humboldt.

* "There are two lakes in Lower Canada, Matapediac and Memphremagog. The former is about 16 miles long, and three broad in its greatest breadth, about 21 miles distant from the St. Lawrence River, in the county of Rimouski; amid the islands that separate the waters running into the St. Lawrence from those that run to the Bay of Chaleurs, it is navigable for rafts of all kinds of timber, with which the banks of the noble River Matapediac are thickly covered. Memphremagog Lake, in the county of Stanstead, stretching its south extremity into the State of Vermont, is of a semicircular shape, 30 miles long, and very narrow. It empties itself into the fine river St. Francis, by means of the River Magog, which runs through Lake Scaswaninepus. The Memphremagog Lake is said to be navigable for ships of 500 tons burden."—Martin's *History of Canada*, p. 102.

† "It is worthy of remark, that the great lakes of Upper Canada are liable to the formation of the Prester or water-spout, and that

The outline of the shores is much diversified: to the northeast lie low lands and swampy marshes; to the north and northeast extends a bold range of elevated grounds; southward the coast becomes again flat for some distance inland, till it rises into the ridge of heights that marks the position of Niagara. The country bordering the lake is generally rich and productive, and was originally covered with forest. A ridge of lofty land runs from the beautiful Bay of Quinté, on the northwest of the lake, westward along the shore, at a distance of nine or more miles: from these heights innumerable streams flow into Ontario on one side, and into the lakes and rivers of the back country on the other. At Toronto the ridge recedes to the distance of twenty-four miles northeast from the lake, separating the tributary waters of Lakes Huron and Ontario; thence merging in the Burlington Heights, it continues along the southwest side from four to eight miles distant from the shore to the high grounds about Niagara.

Besides the great stream of Niagara, many rivers flow into Ontario both on the Canadian and American sides. The bays and harbors are also very numerous, affording great facilities for navigation and commerce: in this respect the northern shore is the most favored—the Bays of Quinté and Burlington are especially remarkable for their extent and security.*

several instances are recorded of the occurrence of that truly extraordinary phenomenon, the theory of which, however, is well known. Whether electricity be a cause or a consequence of this formidable meteor, appears, nevertheless, to be a question of some doubt among natural philosophers; Gassendi being disposed to favor the former opinion, while Cavallo espouses the latter."—Bouchette's *Topographical and Statistical Description of Upper and Lower Canada*, vol. i., p. 346.

* "The most considerable harbors on the English side are Toronto (York, the former name, has recently been changed to the Indian name of the place, Toronto) and Kingston. Toronto is situated near the head of Lake Ontario, on the north side of an excellent harbor or elliptical basin, of an area of eight or nine miles, formed by a long, low, sandy peninsula or island, stretching from the land east of the town to Gibraltar Point, abreast of a good fort. The town of Toronto, at that period York, was twice captured by the Americans, in April and August, 1813, owing to its defenseless state, and a large ship of war on the

The northeast end of Lake Ontario, where its waters pour into the St. Lawrence, is a scene of striking beauty;* numerous wooded islands, in endless variety of form and extent, divide the entrance of the Great River† into a lab-

stocks burned. The Americans would not now find its capture such an easy task. Little more than forty years ago, the site whereon Toronto now stands, and the whole country to the north and west of it, was a perfect wilderness; the land is now fast clearing—thickly settled by a robust and industrious European-descended population, blessed with health and competence, and on all sides indicating the rapid progress of civilization. The other British town of importance on this shore is Kingston, formerly Cataraqui or Frontenac, distant from Toronto 184 miles, and from Montreal 180 miles. It is, next to Quebec and Halifax, the strongest British post in America, and, next to Quebec and Montreal, the first in commercial importance. It is advantageously situate on the north bank of Lake Ontario, at the head of the River St. Lawrence, and is separated from Points Frederic and Henry by a bay, which extends a considerable distance to the northwest beyond the town, where it receives the water of a river flowing from the interior. Point Frederic is a long, narrow peninsula, extending about half a mile into the lake, distant from Kingston about three quarters of a mile on the opposite side of its bay. This peninsula forms the west side of a narrow and deep inlet called Navy Bay, from its being our chief naval dépôt on Lake Ontario."—Martin's *History of Canada.*

* "The channel of the St. Lawrence is here so spacious that it is called the Lake of the Thousand Islands. The vast number implied in this name was considered a vague exaggeration, till the commissioners employed in fixing the boundary with the United States actually counted them, and found that they amounted to 1692. They are of every imaginable size, shape, and appearance; some barely visible, others covering fifteen acres; but, in general, their broken outline presents the most picturesque combinations of wood and rock. The navigator, in steering through them, sees an ever-changing scene: sometimes he is inclosed in a narrow channel; then he discovers before him twelve openings, like so many noble rivers; and, soon after, a spacious lake seems to surround him on every side."—Bouchette, vol. i., p. 156; Howison's *Sketches of Canada*, p. 46.

† "The St. Lawrence traverses the whole extent of Lower Canada, as the lakes every where border and inclose Upper Canada. There is a difficulty in tracing its origin, or, at least, which of the tributaries of Lake Superior is to be called the St. Lawrence. The strongest claim seems to be made by the series of channels which connect all the great upper lakes, though, strictly speaking, till after the Ontario, there is nothing which can very properly be called a river. There are only a number of short canals connecting the different lakes, or, rather, separating one immense lake into a number of great branches. It seems

yrinth of tortuous channels, for twelve miles in breadth from shore to shore: this width gradually decreases as the stream flows on to Prescot, fifty miles below; a short distance beyond that town the rapids commence,* and thence to Montreal the navigation is interrupted for vessels of burden; boats, rafts, and small steamers, however, constantly descend these tumultuous waters, and not unfrequently are lost in the dangerous attempt. The most beautiful and formidable of these rapids is called the Cedars, from the rich groves of that fragrant tree covering numerous and intricate islands, which distort the rushing stream into narrow and perilous channels: the water is not more than ten feet deep in some places, and flows at the rate of twelve miles an hour. The river there

an interesting question how this northern center of the continent, at the precise latitude of about 50°, should pour forth so immense and overwhelming a mass of waters; for through a great part of its extent it is quite a dead flat, though the Winnepeg, indeed, draws some tributaries from the Rocky Mountains. The thick forests with which the surface is covered, the slender evaporation which takes place during the long continuance of cold, and, at the same time, the thorough melting of the snows by the strong summer heat, seem to be the chief sources of this profuse and superabundant moisture."—H. Murray's *Historical Account of Discoveries and Travels in North America*, vol. ii., p. 459, 1829.

* "The statements laid before Parliament thus enumerate and describe the five rapids of the St. Lawrence, which are impassable by steam, and occur between Montreal and Kingston, a distance, by the St. Lawrence River, of 171 miles, and by the Rideau Canal, 267 miles. The rapids vary in rapidity, intricacy, depth and width of channel, and in extent, from half a mile to nine miles. The Cedar Rapid, twenty-four miles from La Chine, is nine miles long, very intricate, running from nine to twelve miles an hour, and in some places only from nine to ten feet water in the channel. The Coteau du Lac Rapid, six miles above the former, is two miles long, equally intricate in channel, and in some places only sixteen feet wide. Long Sault, forty-five miles above the preceding, is nine or ten miles long, with generally the same depth of water throughout. It is intersected by several islands, through whose channels the water rushes with great velocity, so that boats are carried through it, or on it, at the rate of twenty-seven miles an hour; at the foot of the rapid the water takes a sudden leap over a slight precipice, whence its name. From the Long Sault to Prescot is forty-one miles shoal water, running from six to eight miles an hour, and impassable by steamboats. Then the Rapid du Plas, half a mile long, and Rapid Galoose, one and half a mile long, intervene."

widens into Lake St. Francis, and again into Lake St. Louis, which drains a large branch of the Ottawa at its south-western extremity. The water of this great tributary is remarkably clear and of a bright emerald color; that of the St. Lawrence at this junction is muddy, from having passed over deep beds of marl for several miles above its entrance to Lake St. Louis: for some distance down the lake the different streams can be plainly distinguished from each other. From the confluence of the first branches above Montreal these two great rivers seem bewildered among the numerous and beautiful islands, and, hurrying past in strong rapids, only find rest again in the broad, deep waters many miles below.

The furthest sources of the Ottawa River are unknown.* It rises to importance at the outlet from Lake Temiscaming,

* "According to Mr. M'Gregor (*Brit. Amer.*, vol. ii., p. 525), the Ottawa, or Grand River, is said to have its source near the Rocky Mountains, and to traverse in its windings a distance of 2500 miles. The more sober statement of Bouchette attributes to the Ottawa a course of about 450 miles before joining the St. Lawrence."—Bouchette, vol. i., p. 187.

"A tremendous scene is presented at the eastern part of Lake St. Louis, where the St. Lawrence and its grand tributary, the Ottawa, rush down at once and meet in dreadful conflict. The swell is then equal to that produced by a high gale in the British Channel, and the breakers so numerous, that all the skill of the boatmen is required to steer their way. The Canadian boatmen, however, are among the most active and hardy races in the world, and they have boats expressly constructed for the navigation of these perilous channels. The largest of these, called, it is not known why, the Durham boat, is used both here and in the rapids of the Mohawk. It is long, shallow, and nearly flat-bottomed. The chief instrument of steerage is a pole ten feet long, shod with iron, and crossed at short intervals with small bars of wood like the feet of a ladder. The men place themselves at the bow, two on each side, thrust their poles into the channel, and grasping successively the wooden bars, work their way toward the stern, thus pushing on the vessel in that direction. At other times, by the brisk and vigorous use of the oar, they catch and dash through the most favorable lines of current. In this exhausting struggle, however, it is needful to have frequent pauses for rest, and in the most difficult passages there are certain positions fixed for this purpose, which the Canadians call *pipes*."—H. Murray's *Hist. Descr. of America*, vol. ii., p. 473.

350 miles west of its junction with the St. Lawrence.* Beyond the Falls and Portage des Allumettes, 110 miles above Hull, this stream has been little explored. There it is divided into two channels by a large island fifteen miles long: the southernmost of these expands into the width of four or five miles, and communicates by a branch of the river with the Mud and Musk Rat Lakes. Twelve miles further south the river again forms two branches, including an extensive and beautiful island twenty miles in length; numerous rapids and cascades diversify this wild but lovely scene; thence to the foot of the Chenaux, wooded islands in picturesque variety deck the bosom of the stream, and the bright blue waters here wind their way for three miles through a channel of pure white marble. Nature has bestowed abundant fertility as well as beauty upon this favored district. The Gatineau River joins the Ottawa near Hull, after a course of great length. This stream is navigated by canoes for more than 300 miles, traversing an immense valley of rich soil and picturesque scenery.

At the foot of the Chenaux the magnificent Lake des

* "From the sea to Montreal, this superb river is called the St. Lawrence; from thence to Kingston, in Upper Canada, the Cataraqui or Iroquois; between Lakes Ontario and Erie, the Niagara; between Lakes Erie and St. Clair, the Détroit; between Lakes St. Clair and Huron, the St. Clair; and between Lakes Huron and Superior, the distance is called the Narrows, or Falls of St. Mary. The St. Lawrence discharges to the ocean annually about 4,277,880 millions of tons of fresh water, of which 2,112,120 millions of tons may be reckoned melted snow; the quantity discharged before the thaw comes on, being 4512 millions of tons per day for 240 days, and the quantity after the thaw begins, being 25,560 millions per day for 125 days, the depths and velocity when in and out of flood being duly considered: hence a ton of water being nearly equal to 55 cubic yards of pure snow, the St. Lawrence frees a country of more than 2000 miles square, covered to the depth of three feet. The embouchure of this first-class stream is that part of the Gulf of St. Lawrence where the island of Anticosti divides the mouth of the river into two branches. According to Mr. M'Taggart, a shrewd and humorous writer, the solid contents in cubic feet of the St. Lawrence, embracing Lakes Superior, Huron, Michigan, Erie, and Ontario, is estimated at 1,547,792,360,000 cubic feet, and the superficial area being 72,930 square miles, the water therein would form a cubic column of nearly 22 miles on each side!"—Montgomery Martin's *History of Canada*.

Chats opens to view, in length about fifteen miles; the shores are strangely indented, and numbers of wooded islands stud the surface of the clear waters. At the foot of the lake there are falls and rapids;* thence to Lake Chaudière, a distance of six miles, the channel narrows, but expands again to form that beautiful and extensive basin. Rapids again succeed, and continue to the Chaudière Falls. The boiling pool into which these waters descend is of great depth: the sounding-line does not reach the bottom at the length of 300 feet. It is supposed that the main body of the river flows by a subterraneous passage, and rises again half a mile lower down. Below the Chaudière Falls the navigation is uninterrupted to Grenville, sixty miles distant. The current is scarcely perceptible; the banks are low, and generally overflowed in the spring; but the varying breadth of the river, the numerous islands, the magnificent forests, and the crystal purity of the waters, lend a charm to the somewhat monotonous beauty of the scene. At Grenville commences the Long Sault, a swift and dangerous rapid, which continues with intervals till it falls into the still Lake of the Two Mountains. Below the heights from whence this sheet of water derives its name, the well-known Rapids of St. Anne's discharge the main stream into the waters of the St. Lawrence.†

Below the island of Montreal the St. Lawrence continues, in varying breadth and considerable depth, to Sorel, where it is joined by the Richelieu River from the south; thence opens the expanse of Lake St. Peter, shallow and uninteresting; after twenty-five miles the Great River contracts again, receives in its course the waters of the St. Maurice, and other large streams; and 180 miles below Montreal the

* "Kinnel Lodge, the residence of the celebrated Highland chieftain M'Nab, is romantically situated on the south bank of the lake, about five miles above the head of the Chats Rapids, which are three miles long, and pass amid a labyrinth of varied islands, until the waters of the Ottawa are suddenly precipitated over the Falls of the Chats, which, to the number of fifteen or sixteen, form a curved line across the river, regularly divided by woody islands, the falls being in depth from sixteen to twenty feet."—M. Martin's *History of Canada*.

† See Appendix, No. XIX.

vast flood pours through the narrow channel that lies under the shadow of Quebec.* Below this strait lies a deep basin, nearly four miles wide, formed by the head of the Island of Orleans: the main channel continues by the south shore. It would be wearisome to tell of all the numerous and beautiful islands that deck the bosom of the St. Lawrence from Quebec to the Gulf. The river gradually expands till it reaches a considerable breadth at the mouth of the Saguenay. There is a dark shade for many miles below where this great tributary pours its gloomy flood into the pure waters of the St. Lawrence: 120 miles westward it flows from a large, circular sheet of water, called Lake St. John; but the furthest sources lie in the unknown regions of the west and north. For about half its course, from the lake to Tadoussac at the mouth, the banks are rich and fertile; but thence cliffs rise abruptly out of the water to a lofty height—sometimes 2000 feet—and two or three miles apart. The depth of the Saguenay is very great, and the surrounding scenery is of a magnificent but desolate character.

Below the entrance of the Saguenay the St. Lawrence increases to twenty miles across, at the Bay of Seven Islands to seventy, at the head of the large and unexplored island of Anticosti to ninety, and at the point where it may be said to enter the Gulf between Gaspé and the Labrador coast, reaches the enormous breadth of 120 miles. In mid-channel both coasts can be seen; the mountains on the north shore rise to a great height in a continuous range, their peaks capped with eternal snows.

Having traced this vast chain of water communication from its remotest links, it is now time to speak of the mag-

* "At Quebec, the River St. Lawrence narrows to 1314 yards; yet the navigation is completely unobstructed, while there is formed near the city a capacious harbor. About twenty-one miles lower, its waters, beginning to mingle with those of the sea, acquire a saline taste, which increases till, at Kamauraska, seventy-five miles nearer its mouth, they become completely salt. Yet custom, with somewhat doubtful propriety, considers the river as continued down to the island of Anticosti, and bounded by Cape Rosier on the southern, and Mingau settlement on the northern shore."—Bouchette's *Top. and Stat. Descr. of Canada*, vol. i., p. 164–169.

nificent territory which it opens to the commerce and enterprise of civilized man.

Upper or Western Canada* is marked off from the eastern province by the natural boundary of the Ottawa or Grand River. It consists almost throughout of one uniform plain. In all those districts hitherto settled or explored, there is scarcely a single eminence that can be called a hill, although traversed by two wide ridges, rising above the usual level of the country. The greater of these elevations passes through nearly the whole extent of the province from southeast to northwest, separating the waters falling into the St. Lawrence and the great lakes from those tributary to the Ottawa: the highest point is forty miles north of Kingston, being also the most elevated level on that magnificent modern work, the Rideau Canal; † it is 290 feet above the Ottawa at Bytown, and 160 feet higher than the surface of Lake Ontario. Toward these waters the plain descends at the gradient of about four feet in the mile; this declivity is imperceptible to the eye, and is varied by gently undulating slopes and inequalities. Beyond the broad, rich valley lying to the north of this elevation there is a rocky and mountainous country; still farther north are seen snow-covered peaks of a great but unknown height; thence to the pole extends the dreary region of the Hudson Bay territory.

The lesser elevation begins near the eastern extremity of Ontario, and runs almost parallel with the shores of the lake to a point about twenty-four miles northwest from Toronto, where it separates the streams flowing into Lakes Huron and Ontario: it then passes southeast between Lakes Erie and Ontario, and terminates on the Genesee in the United States. This has a more perceptible elevation than the southern ridge, and in some places rises into bold heights.

* See Appendix, No. XX.

† "The Falls of the Rideau are about fifty feet in height and 300 in breadth, being, at the time we saw them, more magnificent than usual, by reason of the high state of the waters. It is from their resemblance to a curtain that they are distinguished by the name of Rideau, and they also give this name to the river that feeds them, which again lends the same appellation to the canal that connects the Ottawa with Lake Ontario."—Simpson, vol. i., p. 16.

The only portion of the vast plain of Western Canada surveyed or effectually explored is included by a line drawn from the eastern coast of Lake Huron to the Ottawa River, and the northern shores of the great chain of lake and river; this is, however, nearly as large as the whole of England.

The natural features of Lower or Eastern Canada are unsurpassed by those of any other country in grace and variety: rivers, lakes, mountains, forests, prairies, and cataracts are grouped together in endless combinations of beauty and magnificence. The eastern districts, beginning with the bold sea-coast and broad waters of the St. Lawrence, are high, mountainous, and clothed with dark forests on both sides, down to the very margin of the river. To the north, a lofty and rugged range of heights runs parallel with the shore as far westward as Quebec; thence it bends west and southwest to the banks of the Ottawa. To the south, the elevated ridge, where it reaches within sixty miles of Quebec, turns from the parallel of the St. Lawrence southwest and south into the United States; this ridge, known by the name of the Alleganies, rises abruptly out of the Gulf of St. Lawrence at Percé, between the Baye de Chaleur and Gaspé Cape, and is more distant from the Great River than that upon the northern shore. Where the Alleganies enter the United States they divide the plains of the Atlantic coast from the basin of the Ohio; their greatest height is about 4000 feet above the level of the sea.

The Valley of the St. Lawrence, lying between these two ranges of heights, is marked by great diversities of hill, plain, and valley. Both from the north and south numerous rivers pour their tributary flood into the great waters of Canada; of those eastward of the Saguenay little is known beyond their entrance; they flow through cliffs of light-colored sand, rocky, wooded knolls, or, in some places, deep, swampy moss-beds nearly three feet in depth. From the Saguenay to Quebec the mountain ridge along the shore of the St. Lawrence is unbroken, save where streams find their way to the Great River, but beyond this coast-border the country is in some places level, in others undulating, with hills of moderate height, and well-watered valleys. From Quebec westward to the St. Maurice, which joins the St. Lawrence at Three Rivers, the land rises in a gentle ascent from the banks of the Great River, and presents a rich tract of fertile plains and slopes: in the distance, a lofty chain of mountains protects this favored district from the bitter northern blast. Along the north bank of the St. Lawrence, from the St. Maurice, the country toward the Ottawa is slightly elevated into table ridges, with occasional abrupt declivities and some extensive plains. In this portion of Canada are included the islands of Montreal, Jesus, and Perrot, formed by the various branches of the Great River and the Ottawa, where their waters unite. Montreal is the largest and most fertile of these islands; its length is thirty-two miles and breadth ten; the general shape is triangular. Isle Jesus is twenty-one miles by six in extent, and also very rich; there are, besides, several other smaller islands of considerable fertility. Isle Perrot is poor and sandy. The remote country to the north of the Ottawa is but little known.

On the south shore of the St. Lawrence, the peninsula of Gaspé is the most eastern district; this large tract of country has been very little explored: so far as it has been examined, it is uneven, mountainous, and intersected with deep ravines; but the forests, rivers, and lakes are very fine, and the valleys fertile. The sea-beach is low and hard,* answering the purposes of a road; at the Cape of Gaspé, however, there are some bold and lofty cliffs. Behind the beach the land rises into high, round hills, well wooded; sheltered from the Gaspé district to the Chaudière River, the country is not so stern as on the northern side of the St. Lawrence; though somewhat hilly, it abounds in large and fertile valleys. The immediate shores of the river are flat; thence irregular ridges arise, till they reach an elevated table-land fifteen or

* Modern alluvial accumulations are rapidly increasing on some points of this coast, owing to the enormous mass of fresh water, charged with earthy matter, that here mingles with the sea. The surface of the water at the mouth of the St. Lawrence, where the depth is 100 fathoms, is stated by Bayfield to be turbid from this cause; yet that this discoloration is superficial is evident, for in the wake of a ship moving through the turbid surface, the clear blue waters of the sea are seen below.

twenty miles from the beach. From the Chaudière River westward extends that rich and valuable country now known by the name of the Eastern Townships. At the mouth of the Chaudière the banks of the St. Lawrence are bold and lofty, but they gradually lower to the westward till they sink into the flats of Baye du Febre, and form the marshy shores of Lake St. Peter, whence a rich plain extends to a great distance. This district contains several high, isolated mountains, and is abundantly watered by lakes and rivers To the south lies the territory of the United States.

CHAPTER V.

Upon the surface of Canada are found manifest indications of that tremendous deluge, the effects of which are so plainly visible in the Old World. Huge bowlder stones* abound in almost every part of the province; sometimes they are seen rounded, piled in high heaps on extensive horizontal beds of limestone, swept together by the force of some vast flood. Masses of various kinds of shells lie in great quantities in hollows and valleys, some of them hundreds of feet above the level of Lake Ontario. Near to great rivers, and often where now no waters are at hand, undulations of rocks are seen like those found in the beds of rapids where the chan-

* "The neighborhood of Quebec, as well as Canada in general, is much characterized by bowlders, and the size and position of some of them is very striking. There are two crowning the height which overlooks the domain farm at Beauport, whose collective weight is little short, by computation, of forty tons. The Heights of Abraham also are, or rather were, crowded with them; and it should never be forgotten that it was upon one of these hoary symbols, the debâcles of the deluge, as they are supposed to be, that the immortal and mortal parts of two heroes separated from each other. It has often occurred to us, that one of the most suitable monuments to the memory of Wolfe and Montcalm might have been erected with these masses, in the form of a pyramid or pile of shot, instead of burying them, as in many instances has been done, in order to clear the ground."—*Picture of Quebec*, p. 456.

nels are waved. These have evidently, at some remote period, been the courses of floods now no longer existing. On the shores of the Gulf of St. Lawrence detached bowlder stones appear, some of enormous size, many tons in weight; they must have come from a great distance, for nowhere in that region is there any rock of similar material. In the upper strata of the country are abundant fossil remains of distinct animal existences now unknown; they are blended with the limestone in which they lie.

It seems certain that the whole of Canada has been violently convulsed by some effort of nature since the floods of the deluge passed away; the mountains are abrupt and irregular in outline, and in some places cleft with immense chasms; the rivers also show singular contortions. North of Quebec and in St. Paul's Bay are many traces of volcanic eruptions, and vast masses of alluvial rocks, bearing marks of vitrification, frequently appear on the surface of the earth. There is, besides, strong evidence that the American Continent has lain for unknown ages beneath the great deep, or that it is of later formation than Europe or Asia.

As far as it has been explored, the general geological structure of Canada exhibits a granite country, with some calcareous rocks of a soft texture in horizontal strata. The lower islands in the St. Lawrence are merely inequalities of the vast granite strata which occasionally stand above the level of the waters; the whole neighboring country appears as if the Great River had at one time covered it. The banks of the St. Lawrence are in many places formed of a schistus substance in a decaying state, but still granite is every where found in strata, inclined, but never parallel to the horizon. In the Gaspé District, many beautiful quartz, and a great variety of cornelians, agates, copals, and jaspers have been found, and traces of coal have also been observed.*

* Gray says, in 1809, that "no coal has ever yet been found in Canada, probably because it has never been thought worth searching after. It is supposed that coal exists in the neighborhood of Quebec; at any rate, there can be no doubt that it exists in great abundance in the island of Cape Breton, which may one day become the Newcastle of Canada."—P. 287.

"No idea can be formed of the importance of the American coal-

The north shore of the St. Lawrence, from thirty miles below Quebec eastward, and along the coast of Labrador, is generally of the primitive formations. Except in the marshes and swamps, rocks obtrude upon the surface in all quarters; in many places, deep fissures of from six inches to two feet wide are seen bearing witness to volcanic violence; the Indians describe some of these rents as several miles long, and forty or fifty deep; when covered with the thick underwood, they are, at times, very dangerous to the traveler. These chasms are probably owing to some great subterranean action; there is a manuscript in the Jesuits' College at Quebec which records the occurrence of an earthquake on the 5th of February, 1663, at about half past 5 P.M., felt through the whole extent of Canada: trees in the forests were torn up and dashed against each other with inconceivable violence; mountains were raised from their foundations and thrown into valleys, leaving awful chasms behind; from the openings issued dense clouds of smoke, dust, and sand; many rivers disappeared, others were diverted from their course, and the great St. Lawrence became suddenly white as far down as the mouth of the Saguenay. The first shock lasted for more than half an hour, but the greatest violence was only for fifteen minutes. At Tadoussac, a shower of volcanic ashes descended upon the rivers, agitating the waters like a tempest. This tremendous earthquake extended simultane-

seams until we reflect on the prodigious area over which they are continuous. The elliptical area occupied by the Pittsburg seam is 225 miles in its largest diameter, while its maximum breadth is about 100 miles, its superficial extent being about 14,000 square miles.

"The Apalachian coal-field extends for a distance of 720 miles from northeast to southwest, its greatest width being about 180 miles.

"The Illinois coal-field is not much inferior in dimensions to the whole of England."—Lyell's *America*, vol. ii., p. 31.

"It was the first time I had seen the true coal in America, and I was much struck with its surprising analogy in mineral and fossil characters to that of Europe; . . . . the whole series resting on a coarse grit and conglomerate, containing quartz pebbles, very like our millstone grit, and often called by the Americans, as well as the English miners, the 'Farewell Rock,' because, when they have reached it in their borings, they take leave of all valuable fuel."—*Ibid.*, vol. i., p. 61.

ously over 180,000 square miles of country, and lasted for nearly six months almost without intermission.*

In the neighborhood of Quebec, a dark clay slate generally appears, and forms the bed of the St. Lawrence as far as Lake Ontario, and even at Niagara; bowlders and other large masses of rock, however, of various kinds, occur in detached portions at many different places. The great elevated ridge of broken country running toward the Ottawa River, at the distance of from fifty to one hundred miles from the north shore of Lake Ontario, and the course of the St. Lawrence, is rich in silver, lead, copper, and iron. On the north shore of the Saguenay, the rugged mountains abound in iron to such an extent as to influence the mariner's compass. The iron mines of St. Maurice† have been long

* See Appendix, No. XXI.

† Professor Kalm visited the iron-works of St. Maurice in 1748, eleven or twelve years after their first establishment. "The iron-work, which is the only one in the country, lies three miles to the west of Trois Rivières. Here are two great forges, besides two lesser ones to each of the great ones, and under the same roof with them. The bellows were made of wood, and every thing else as in the Swedish forges. The ore is got two and a half miles from the iron-works, and is carried thither on sledges. It is a kind of moor-ore (Tophus Tubalcaini: *Linn. Syst. Nat.*, lib. iii., p. 187, note 5), which lies in veins within six inches or a foot from the surface of the ground. Each vein is from six to eighteen inches deep, and below it is a white sand. The veins are surrounded with this sand on both sides, and covered at the top with a thin mold. The ore is pretty rich, and lies in loose lumps in the veins of the size of two fists, though there are a few which are near eighteen inches thick. These lumps are full of holes which are filled with ocher. The ore is so soft that it may be crushed between the fingers. They make use of a gray limestone, which is broke in the neighborhood, for promoting the fusibility of the ore; to that purpose they likewise employ a clay marl, which is found near this place. Charcoals are to be had in great abundance here, because the country round this place is covered with wood which has never been stirred. The charcoals from evergreen trees, that is, from the fir kind, are best for the forge, but those of deciduous trees are best for the smelting-oven. The iron which is here made was to me described as soft, pliable, and tough, and is said to have the quality of not being attacked by rust so easily as other iron. This iron-work was first founded in 1737 by private persons, who afterward ceded it to the king; they cast cannon and mortars here of different sizes, iron stoves, which are in use all over Canada, kettles, &c. They have likewise tried to make

known, and found abundantly productive of an admirable metal, inferior to none in the world; it is remarkably pliant and malleable, and little subject to oxydation. In 1667, Colbert sent M. de la Potardière, an experienced mineralogist, to examine these mines; he reported the iron very abundant, and of excellent quality, but it was not till 1737 that the forges were established by the French: they failed to pay the expenses of the speculation; the superintendent and fourteen clerks, however, gained fortunes by the losses of their employers.

There is no doubt that immense mineral resources remain undiscovered among the rocky solitudes of Lower Canada. Marble of excellent quality, and endless variety of color, is

steel here, but can not bring it to any great perfection, because they are unacquainted with the best method of preparing it. Here are many officers and overseers, who have very good houses built on purpose for them. It is agreed on all hands that the resources of the iron-work do not pay the expenses which the king must every year be at in maintaining it. They lay the fault on the bad state of population, and say that the few inhabitants in the country have enough to do with agriculture, and that it therefore costs great trouble and large sums to get a sufficient number of workmen. But, however plausible this may appear, yet it is surprising that the king should be a loser in carrying on this work, for the ore is easily broken, being near the iron-work, and very fusible. The iron is good; and this is, moreover, the only iron-work in the country, from which every body must supply himself with tools, and what other iron he wants. But the officers and servants belonging to the iron-work appear to be in very affluent circumstances. A river runs down from the iron-work into the River St. Lawrence, by which all the iron can be sent in boats throughout the country at a low rate."—Kalm in Pinkerton, vol. xiii., p. 631.

"M. Dantic, after a number of experiments to class the different kinds of iron, discovered that the iron of Styria was the best, and that the iron of North America, of Danemara in Sweden, of Spain, Bayonne, Roussillon, Foix, Berri, Thierache in Sweden, the communes of France, and Siberia, was the next class."—Abbé Raynal, vol. iii., p. 268.

Weld and Heriot mention that the bank of iron ore at the forges of St. Maurice was nearly exhausted in their time; new veins, however, have been since discovered.

Charlevoix says, in 1720: "Il est certain que ces mines de fer, que l'œil perçant de M. Colbert et la vigilance de M. Talon avoit fait découvrir, après avoir presqú entièrement disparu pendant plus de soixante dix ans, viennent d'être retrouvées par les soins de ceux qui occupent aujourd'hui leur place."—Charlevoix, tom. ii., p. 166.

found in different parts of the country, and limestone is almost universal. Labrador produces a beautiful and well-known spar of rich and brilliant tints, ultra-marine, greenish yellow, red, and some of a fine pearly gray.

In Upper Canada, the country north of Lake Ontario is generally characterized by a limestone subsoil resting on granite. The rocks about Kingston are usually a very compact limestone, of a bluish-gray color, having a slight silicious admixture, increasing as the depth increases, with occasional intrusions of quartz or hornstone. The limestone strata are horizontal, with the greatest dip when nearest to the elder rock on which it rests; their thickness, like the depths of the soil, varies from a few feet to a few inches: in these formations many minerals are observed; genuine granite is seldom or never found.

West of Lake Ontario, the chasm at the Falls of Niagara shows the strata of the country to be limestone, next slate, and lowest sandstone. Limestone and sandstone compose the secondary formations of a large portion of Canada, and of nearly all that vast extent of country in the United States drained by the Mississippi. At Niagara the interposing structure of slate is nearly forty feet thick, and fragile, like shale crumbling away from under the limestone, thus strengthening the opinion that there has been for many ages a continual retrocession of the Great Falls. Around Lake St. Clair, masses of granite, mica slate, and quartz are found in abundance. The level shores of Lake Huron offer little geological variety; secondary limestone, filled with the usual reliquiæ, is the general structure of the coast, but detached blocks of granite and other primitive rocks are occasionally found: this district appears poor in minerals. The waters of Lakes Huron, Michigan, and Superior have evidently, at some remote period, formed one vast sheet, which probably burst its bounds by a sudden action of nature, and subsided into the present divisions, all lower than the former general level: the separating ridges of these waters are but slightly elevated; great masses of rock and huge bowlders of granite are found rolled at least 100 miles from their original situations, and immense alluvial beds of fresh-water shells, apparently formed since the deluge, but when the waters were still of a vast depth and extent, are found in the east of Lake Huron.

Little or nothing is known of the dreary solitudes beyond Lake Superior; enormous muddy ponds and marshes are succeeded by open, dry, sandy plains; then forests of hemlock and spruce arise, again swamp, bog, windfalls, and stagnant water succeed; in the course of many miles there may not be one dry spot found for a resting-place. The cold is intense in this desolate region; in winter spirits freeze into a consistency like honey; and even in the height of summer the thermometer only shows thirty-six degrees at sunrise. Part of the north and east shore of this greatest of the lakes present old formations—sienite, stratified greenstone, more or less chloritic, and alternating five times with vast beds of granite—the general direction east, with a north or perpendicular dip. Great quantities of the older shell limestone are found strewn in rolled masses on the beach. Amygdaloid occupies also a very large tract to the north, mingled with porphyries, conglomerates, and various other substances. From Thunder Mountain westward, trappose greenstone is the prevailing rock: it gives rise to some strange pilastered precipices near Fort William. Copper* abounds in this

* Henry and others speak of a rock of pure copper, from which the former cut off 100 lbs. weight. W. Schoolcraft examined the remainder of the mass in 1820, and found it of irregular shape; in its greatest length three feet eight inches, greatest breadth three feet four inches, making about eleven cubic feet, and containing, of metallic matter, about 2200 lbs.; but there were many marks of chisels and axes upon it, as if a great deal had been carried off. The surface of the block, unlike most metals which have suffered a long exposure to the atmosphere, presents a metallic brilliancy.—Martin's *History of Canada*, p. 175.

Weld mentions having seen in the possession of a gentleman at Niagara a lump of copper, of several ounces weight, apparently as pure as if it had passed through the fire, which had been struck off with a chisel from a piece equally pure, growing on one of the islands in Lake Superior. Rich veins of copper are visible in almost all the rocks on these islands near the shore; and copper ore, resembling copperas, is likewise found in deep beds near the water.—Weld, p. 346.

In Charlevoix's time (1720), "on trouvoit sur les bords du Lac Supérieur et autour de certains isles, de grosses pièces de cuivre qui sont l'objet de cette superstition des sauvages; ils les regardent avec

region to an extent, perhaps, unsurpassed any where in the world. At the Coppermine River, three hundred miles from

vénération comme un présent des Dieux qui habitent sous les eaux; ils en ramassent les plus petits fragmens et les conservent avec soin, mais ils n'en font aucune usage. J'ai connu un de nos frères lequel étoit orfévre de son métier, et qui, pendant qu'il étoit dans la mission du Sault Sainte Marie, en étoit allé chercher là, et en avoit fait des chandeliers, des croix, et des encensoirs, car ce cuivre est souvent presque tout pur."—Tom. v., p. 415.

Kalm says that the copper found is so pure that it does not require melting over again, but is fit for working immediately.—Kalm in Pinkerton, vol. xiii., p. 691 (1748).

"Before saying good-by to Lake Superior, let me add, that since the date of my visit, the barren rocks which we passed have become an object of intense interest, promising to rival, in point of mineral wealth, the Altai chain and the Uralian Mountains. Iron had long been known to abound on the northern shore, two mines having been at one time worked and abandoned, chiefly on account of temporary obstacles, which the gradual advance of agriculture and civilization was sure to remove; and, more recently, the southern shore, though of a much less favorable character in that respect, was found to possess rich veins of copper and silver. Under these circumstances, various enterprising persons in Canada have prosecuted investigations which appear to have satisfactorily proved that, in addition to their iron, the forbidding wastes of the northern shore contain inexhaustible treasures, both of the precious and of the useful metals, of gold and of silver, of copper and tin, and already have associations been formed to reap the teeming harvest."—Sir G. Simpson's *Journey round the World*, vol. i., p. 35 (1841).

The following extract is from a Quebec newspaper, bearing date 25th June, 1848:

"THE COPPER REGION: SINGULAR DISCOVERY.—A correspondent of the Buffalo Express, writing under date June 14, from Ontonagon, Lake Superior, says:

"'Mr. Knapp, of the Vulcan Mining Company, has lately made some very singular discoveries here in working one of the veins which he lately found. He worked into an old cave which has been excavated centuries ago. This led them to look for other works of the same sort, and they have found a number of sinks in the earth which they have traced a long distance. By digging into those sinks they find them to have been made by the hand of man. It appears that the ancient miners went on a different principle from what they do at the present time. The greatest depth yet found in these holes is thirty feet: after getting down to a certain depth, they drifted along the vein, making an open cut. These cuts have been filled nearly to a level by the accumulation of soil; and we find trees of the largest growth standing in this gutter, and also find that trees of a very large growth

the Sault de St. Marie, this metal, in a pure state, nearly covers the face of a serpentine rock, and is also found within the stone in solid masses. Iron is abundant in many parts of Upper Canada; at Charlotteville, eight miles from Lake Erie, the metal produced is of a very fine quality. The Marmora Iron Works, about thirty-two miles north of the Bay of Quinté, on the River Trent, are situated on an extensive white rocky flat, apparently the bed of some dried-up river; the ore is found on the surface, and is very rich, yielding ninety-two per cent.: the necessary assistants, lime and fuel, abound close at hand. Various other minerals have also been found there; among the rest, small specimens of a metal like silver.

There are many strong mineral springs in different parts

have grown up and died, and decayed many years since; in the same places there are now standing trees of over three hundred years' growth. Last week they dug down into a new place, and about twelve feet below the surface found a mass of copper that will weigh from eight to ten tons. This mass was buried in ashes, and it appears they could not handle it, and had no means of cutting it, and probably built fire to melt or separate the rock from it, which might be done by heating, and then dashing on cold water. This piece of copper is as pure and clean as a new cent; the upper surface has been pounded clear and smooth. It appears that this mass of copper was taken from the bottom of a shaft, at the depth of about thirty feet. In sinking this shaft from where the mass now lies, they followed the course of the vein, which pitches considerably: this enabled them to raise it as far as the hole came up with a slant. At the bottom of a shaft they found skids of black oak, from eight to twelve inches in diameter: these sticks were charred through, as if burned: they found large wooden wedges in the same situation. In this shaft they found a miner's gad and a narrow chisel made of copper. I do not know whether these copper tools are tempered or not, but their make displays good workmanship. They have taken out more than a ton of cobble-stones, which have been used as mallets. These stones were nearly round, with a score cut around the tenter, and look as if this score was cut for the purpose of putting a withe round for a handle. The Chippewa Indians all say that this work was never done by Indians. This discovery will lead to a new method of finding veins in this country, and may be of great benefit to some. I suppose they will keep finding new wonders for some time yet, as it is but a short time since they first found the old mine. There is copper here in abundance, and I think people will begin to dig it in a few years. Mr. Knapp has found considerable silver during the past winter.' "

of Canada; the most remarkable of these is the Burning Spring above Niagara; its waters are black, hot and bubbling, and emit, during the summer, a gas that burns with a pure bright flame; this sulphureted hydrogen is used to light a neighboring mill. Salt springs are also numerous; gypsum is obtained in large quantities, with pipe and potter's clay; yellow ocher sometimes occurs; and there are many kinds of valuable building stones. It is gathered from the Indians that there are incipient volcanoes in several parts of these regions, particularly toward the Chippewa hunting grounds.

The soil of Lower Canada is generally fertile; about Quebec it is light and sandy in some parts, in others it is a mixture of loam and clay. Above the Richelieu Rapids, where the great valley of the St. Lawrence begins to widen, the low lands consist of a light and loose dark earth, with ten or twelve inches of depth, lying on a stratum of cold clay, all apparently of alluvial formation. Along the banks of the Ottawa there is a great extent of rich alluvial soil; each year develops large districts of fertile land, before unknown. The soils of Upper Canada are various; brown clay and loam, intermixed with marl, predominates, particularly in the rich district between the St. Lawrence and the Ottawa: north of Ontario it is more clayey and extremely fertile. A rich black mold prevails in the district between Lakes Ontario and Erie. There is in this upper country an almost total absence of stone or gravel for building and other common purposes. So great is the fertility of the soil in Canada, that fifty bushels of wheat an acre are frequently produced, even where the stumps of trees still occupy a considerable portion of the ground: near Toronto one hundred bushels of wheat have been grown upon a single acre, and in some districts the land has yielded rich crops of that grain for twenty successive years, without being manured.

The quality of the soil in wild lands may be known by the timber growing upon it. Hard-wood trees, those that shed their leaves during winter, show the best indication, such as maple, bass-wood, elm, black walnut, hickory, butternut, iron-wood, hemlock, and a giant species of nettle. A mixture of beech is good, but where it stands alone the soil is generally light. Oak is uncertain as an indication, being found on various bottoms. Soft or evergreen wood, such as pine, fir, larch, and others of the species, are considered decisive of a very light soil. The larch or tamarack on wide, flat plains, indicates sand upon a substratum of marly clay, which the French Canadians hold in high estimation. It is, however, right to add, that some very respectable authorities dispute that the nature of the timber can be fully relied on as a guide to the value of the land. The variety of trees found in the Canadian forest is astonishing, and it is supposed that many kinds still remain unknown. Of all these, none is more beautiful and useful than the maple; its brilliant foliage, changing with each season of the year, is the richest ornament of the forest. The timber is valuable for many purposes, and from the sap might be produced an immense quantity of excellent sugar. A great deal is at present made, but, like all the other resources of this magnificent country, it is very partially turned to the use of man: the sap of the maple is valuable also for distillation.

There is a considerable variety of climate in Canada, from the northeast, chilled by the winds of the Atlantic,*

* Acosta is the first philosopher who endeavored to account for the different degrees of heat in the Old and New Continents by the agency of the winds which blow in each. (*Hist. Moral.*, lib. ii. and iii.) M. de Buffon adopted the same theory, and illustrated it with many new observations. "The prevailing winds, both in Upper and Lower Canada, are the northeast, northwest, and southwest, which all have a considerable influence on the temperature of the atmosphere and the state of the weather. The southwest wind is the most prevalent, but it is generally moderate, and accompanied by clear skies; and the northeast and easterly winds usually bring with them continued rain in summer, and snow in winter; the northwest is remarkable for its dryness and elasticity, and, from its gathering an intense degree of frigor as it sweeps over the frozen plains and ice-bound hills in that quarter of the continent, invariably brings with it a perceptible degree of cold. Winds from due north, south, or west are not frequent. At Quebec, the direction of the wind often changes with the tide, which is felt for nearly sixty miles higher up the stream of the St. Lawrence."—Bonchette, vol. i., p. 343.

"The northwest wind is uncommonly dry, and brings with it fresh animation and vigor to every living thing. Although this wind is so

to the southwest, five degrees lower, and approaching the center of the continent; the neighborhood of ranges of bare and rugged mountains,* has also a marked effect upon the temperature of different localities. However, in all parts the winters are very severe, while the heat of summer is little inferior to that of the tropics. But, on the whole, the clear blue sky, unobscured by fog or mist, and the pure elastic air, bespeak the salubrity of these provinces in all seasons.

In Lower Canada the extreme severity of the winter is, in a measure, caused by the vicinity of the range of lofty and rugged mountains, as well as by its more northern

very piercing in winter, yet the people never complain so much of cold as when the northeast wind blows. The northeast wind is also cold, but it renders the air raw and damp. That from the southeast is damp, but warm. Rain or snow usually falls when the wind comes from any point toward the east. The northwest wind, from coming over such an immense tract of land, must necessarily be dry; and, coming from regions eternally covered with mounds of snow and ice, it must also be cold. The northeast wind, from traversing the frozen seas, must be cold likewise; but, from passing over such a large portion of the watery main afterward, it brings damp and moisture with it. All those from the northeast are damp, and loaded with vapors from the same cause. Southerly winds, from crossing the warm regions between the tropics, are attended with heats; and the southwest wind, from passing, like the northwest, over a great extent of land, is dry at the same time."—Weld's *Travels in America*, 4th ed., p. 184.

Kalm says, p. 748, that he was assured that "the northeast wind, when it is very violent in winter, pierces through walls of a moderate thickness, so that the whole wall on the inside of the house is covered with snow, or a thick hoar frost. The wind damages severely the houses that are built of stone, so that the owners are frequently obliged to repair them on the northeast side. In summer the north wind is generally attended with rain."—Kalm in Pinkerton, vol. xiii., p. 651.

* "Many of these mountains are very high. During my stay in Canada, I asked many people who have traveled much in North America whether they ever met with mountains so high that the snow never melts on them in summer, to which they always answered in the negative. They say that the snow sometimes stays on the highest, viz., on some of those between Canada and the English colonies during a part of the summer, but that it melts as soon as the great heat begins."—Kalm, p. 671.

position. The fall of snow commences in November, but seldom remains long on the ground till December; in that month constantly successive falls of snow rapidly cover the whole surface of the country. Toward the end of December the heavy clouds disperse, and the rude storm is followed by a perfect calm; the air becomes pure and frosty, and the skies of a clear and beautiful azure. The River St. Lawrence* is frozen over every winter from Montreal to the Richelieu Rapids, but from thence to Quebec only once in about five years; at other times, however, enormous fields and masses of ice drift up and down with the changing tides, increasing or diminishing with the severity or mildness of the weather; where the Island of Orleans divides the Great River into two branches, the northern channel is narrow and less acted upon by tides; here these huge frozen masses are forced together by the winds and waters, and form an enormous bridge from shore to shore. The greatest degree of cold prevails toward the end of January, for a few days occasionally so intense that the human frame can scarcely endure exposure to it for any length of time. When winter has set in nearly every bird disappears, and few wild animals are any longer to be seen; some, like the bear, remain torpid, others change their color to a snowy white, and are rarely observed. Rocks of the softer kinds are often rent asunder, as if with the explosion of gunpowder, by the irresistible expansive power of the frost.† Dogs be-

* "It is worthy of remark, and not a little surprising, that so large a river as the St. Lawrence, in latitude 47°, should be shut up with ice as soon, and continue as long shut up, as the comparatively small river, the Neva, in latitude 60°."—Gray's *Canada*, p. 320.

† "The following curious experiments were made some years ago at Quebec, by Major Williams, of the Artillery. Iron shells of different sizes, from the thirteen-inch shell to the cohorn of four inches diameter, were nearly filled with water, and an iron plug was driven in at the fuse-hole by a sledge-hammer. It was found, however, that the plug could never be driven so firmly into the fuse-hole as to resist the expanding ice, which pushed it out with great force and velocity, and a bolt or cylinder of ice immediately shot up from the hole; but when a plug was used that had springs which would expand and lay hold of the inside of the cavity, so that it could not possibly be pushed out, the force of expansion split the shell. The

come mad from the severity of the cold, and polished iron or other metal, when exposed in the air for a little time, *burns* the hand at the touch as if it were red hot.* During the still nights of intense frost the woods send forth a creaking sound, like the noise of chopping with thousands of hatchets. Sometimes a brief thaw occurs in the middle of winter, when a very extraordinary effect, called by the Canadians *ver glas*, is occasionally produced upon the bare trees: they are covered with an incrustation of pure ice from the stem to the extremities of the smallest branches; the slight frost of the night freezes the moisture that covered the bark during the day; the branches become at last unable to bear their icy burden, and when a strong wind arises, the destruction among trees of all kinds is immense. When the sun shines upon the forest covered with this brilliant incrustation, the effect is indescribably beautiful.

The months of March and April are usually very hot, and the power of the sun's rays is heightened by the reflection of the ice and snows. Toward the end of April or the beginning of May, the dreary winter covering has altogether disappeared; birds of various kinds return from their wintery exile; the ice accumulated in the great lakes and streams that are tributary to the St. Lawrence breaks up with a tremendous noise, and rushes down in vast quantities toward the ocean, till again the tides of the Gulf drive them back. Sometimes the Great River is blocked up from shore to shore with these frozen masses; the contending currents force them together with terrible violence, and pile them over each other in various fantastic forms. The navigation of the river is not fairly practicable till all these have disappeared, which is generally about the 10th of May.

amazing force of expansion is also shown from the distance to which these iron plugs are thrown out of the fuse-hole. A plug of two pounds and a half weight was thrown no less than 415 feet from the shell; the fuse axis was at an angle of 45°; the thermometer showed 51° below the freezing point. Here you see ice and gunpowder performing the same operations. That similar effects should proceed from such dissimilar causes is very extraordinary."—Gray's *Canada*, p. 309.

* See Appendix, No. XXII.

When the young summer fairly sets in, nothing can be more charming than the climate—during the day bright and genial, with the air still pure and clear; the transition from bare brown fields and woods to verdure and rich green foliage is so rapid, that its progress is almost perceptible. Spring has scarcely begun before summer usurps its place, and the earth, awakened from nature's long, wintery sleep, gives forth her increase with astonishing bounty. This delightful season is usually ushered in by moderate rains, and a considerable rise in the meridian heat; but the nights are still cool and refreshing. In June, July, and August, the heat becomes great, and for some days intense; the roads and rocks at noon are so hot as to be painful to the touch, and the direct rays of the sun possess almost tropical power; but the night brings reinvigorating coolness, and the breezes of the morning are fresh and tempered as in our own favored land. September is usually a delightful month, although at times oppressively sultry. The autumn or fall rivals the spring in healthy and moderate warmth, and is the most agreeable of the seasons. The night-frosts destroy the innumerable venomous flies that have infested the air through the hot season, and, by their action on the various foliage of the forest, bestow an inconceivable richness of coloring to the landscape.

During the summer there is a great quantity of electric fluid in the atmosphere, but storms of thunder and lightning are not of very frequent occurrence. When they do take place, their violence is sometimes tremendous, and serious damage often occurs. These outbursts, however, usually produce a favorable effect upon the weather and temperature.

The most remarkable meteoric phenomenon that has occurred in Canada since the country became inhabited by civilized man, was first seen in October, 1785, and again in July, 1814. At noonday a pitchy darkness, of a dismal and sinister character, completely obscured the light of the sun, continuing for about ten minutes at a time, and being frequently repeated during the afternoon. In the interval between each mysterious eclipse dense masses of black clouds, streaked with yellow, drove athwart the darkened sky, with fitful gusts of wind; thunder, lightning, black rain, and showers of ashes added to the terrors of the scene; and, when the sun appeared, its color was a bright red. The Indians ascribe this wonderful phenomenon to a vast volcano in the unknown regions of Labrador. The testimony of M. Gagnon gives corroboration to this idea. In December, 1791, when at St. Paul's Bay, in the Saguenay country, he saw the flames of an immense volcano, mingled with black smoke, rising to a great height in the air. Several violent shocks, as of an earthquake, accompanied this strange appearance.

The prevailing winds of Lower Canada are the northeast, northwest, and southwest, and these exercise considerable influence on the temperature of the atmosphere and the state of the weather. The southwest wind, the most prevalent, is generally moderate, accompanied by clear, bright skies; the northeast and east wind bring rain in summer, and snow in winter, from the dreary regions of Labrador; and the northwest blast is keen and dry, from its passage over the vast frozen solitudes that lie between the Rocky Mountains* and Hudson's Bay. Winds from the north, south, or west are seldom felt: the currents of the neighboring air are often affected by the direction of the tidal streams, which act as far as 400 miles from the mouth of the Great River.

The effect of a long continuance of snow upon the earth is favorable to vegetation; were the surface exposed to the intense severity of wintery frosts, unprotected by this ample covering, the ground could not regain a proper degree of heat, even under a Canadian sun, before the autumn frosts had again chilled the energies of nature. The natural heat of the earth is about 42°; the surface waters freeze at 32°, and thus present a non-conducting incrustation to the keen atmosphere; then the snow becomes a warm garment till the April sun softens the air above; the latent heat of the earth begins to be developed; the snow melts, and penetrates the ground through every pore, rendering friable the stiffest soil. For a month or more before the visible termination

* "These mountains were known to the French missionaries by the name of Montagnes des Pierres Brillantes."—Chateaubriand.

of the Canadian winter, vegetation is in active progress on the surface of the earth, even under snow several feet thick.

In Upper Canada the climate does not present such extremes of heat and cold as in the Lower Province. In the Newcastle District, between latitude 44° and 45°, the winter is little more severe than in England, and the warmth of summer is tempered by a cool and refreshing southwest breeze, which blows throughout the day from over the waters of the great lakes. In spring and autumn the southwest wind brings with it frequent rains; the northwest wind prevails in winter, and is dry, cold, and elastic; the southeastern breezes are generally accompanied by thaw and rain: from the west, south, or north, the wind rarely blows. The most sudden changes of weather consequent upon varying winds are observed from the northwest, when the air becomes pure and cool; thunder storms generally clear away with this wind: the heaviest falls of snow, and the most continued rains, come with the eastern breezes.

The great lakes are never frozen in their centers, but a strong border of thick ice extends for some distance from the shore: in severe weather, a beautiful evaporation in various fantastic shapes ascends from the vast surfaces of these inland seas, forming cloudy columns and pyramids to a great height in the air: this is caused by the water being of a higher temperature than the atmosphere above. The chain of shallow lakes from Lake Simco toward the midland district are rarely frozen over more than an inch in thickness till about Christmas, and are free from ice again by the end of March. The earth in Upper Canada is seldom froze more than twelve or eighteen inches deep, and the general covering of the snow is about a foot and a half in thickness.

In Canada the Indian summer is perhaps the most delightful period of the year. During most of November the weather is mild and serene; a soft, dry haze pervades the air, thickening toward the horizon; in the evenings the sun sets in a rich crimson flush, and the temperature is mild and genial: the birds avail themselves of the Indian summer for their migration. A phenomenon called the "tertian intervals" has excited much interest, and is still unexplained: at the end of the third day the greatest intensity of frost is always remittent, and succeeded by several days of mild weather. The climate is so dry that metals rarely are rusted by exposure to the air. This absence of humidity prevents the extremes of heat and cold from being so powerful here in their effect upon the sensations of the human frame as in other countries.

The Aurora Borealis, or northern lights,* appear with great brilliancy in the clear Canadian sky, especially during the winter nights. Starting from behind the distant horizon, they race up through the vault of heaven, spreading over all space one moment, shrinking to a quivering streak the next, shooting out again where least expected, then vanishing into darkness deeper than before; now they seem like vast floating banners of variegated flame, then as crescents, again as majestic columns of light, ever changing in form and color. It is said that a rustling sound like that of silk accompanies this beautiful appearance.

The climate of Canada has undergone a slight change since the discovery of the country; especially from the year 1818, an amelioration has been perceptible, partly owing to the motion of the magnetic poles, and partly to the gradual cultivation and clearing of the country. The winters are somewhat shorter and milder, and less snow falls than of old; the summers are also hotter.† The felling of the forests, the draining of the morasses, partial though it may still be, together with the increasing population, have naturally some effect. The thick foliage, which before interposed its shade between the sun and the earth, intercepting the genial warmth from the lower atmosphere, has now been removed in many extensive tracts of country: the cultivated soil imbibes the heat, and returns it to the surrounding air in warm and humid vapors. The exhalations arising from a much increased amount of animal life, together with the burning of so many combustibles, are not altogether without their influence in softening the severity of the climate.‡

Canada abounds in an immense and beautiful variety of

* See Appendix, No. XXIII. † See Appendix, No. XXIV.
‡ See Appendix, No. XXV.

trees* and shrubs. Among the timber trees, the oak, pine, fir, elm, ash, birch, walnut, beech, maple, chestnut, cedar, and aspen, are the principal. Of fruit-trees and shrubs there are walnut, chestnut, apple, pear, cherry, plum, elder, vines,† hazel, hickory, sumach, juniper, hornbeam, thorn, laurel, whortleberry, cranberry, gooseberry, raspberry, blackberry, blueberry, sloe, and others; strawberries of an excellent flavor are luxuriantly scattered over every part of the country. Innumerable varieties of useful and beautiful herbs and grasses enrich the forests, whose virtues and peculiarities are as yet but little known to Europeans.‡ In many places, pine-

* "In Europe, in Asia, in Africa, and even in South America, the primeval trees, however much their magnitude may arrest admiration, do not grow in the promiscuous style that prevails in the general character of the North American woods. Many varieties of the pine, intermingled with birch, maple, beech, oak, and numerous other tribes, branch luxuriantly over the banks of lakes and rivers, extend in stately grandeur along the plains, and stretch proudly up to the very summits of the mountains. It is impossible to exaggerate the autumnal beauty of these forests; nothing under heaven can be compared to its effulgent grandeur. Two or three frosty nights in the decline of autumn transform the boundless verdure of a whole empire into every possible tint of brilliant scarlet, rich violet, every shade of blue and brown, vivid crimson, and glittering yellow. The stern, inexorable fir tribes alone maintain their eternal somber green. All others, in mountains or in villages, burst into the most glorious vegetable beauty, and exhibit the most splendid and most enchanting panorama on earth."—M'Gregor, p. 79, 80.

Mr. Weld says, "The varied hues of the trees at this season of the year (autumn) can hardly be imagined by those who never have had an opportunity of observing them; and, indeed, as others have often remarked before, were a painter to attempt to color a picture from them, it would be condemned in Europe as totally different from any thing that ever existed in nature."—Weld, p. 510.

"I can only compare the brightness of the faded leaves, scarlet, purple, and yellow, to that of tulips."—Lyell's *America*, vol. i., p. 107.

† See Appendix, No. XXVI.

‡ "One of the most striking features in the vegetation of Canada is the number of species belonging to the *genera* Solidago, Aster, Quercus, and Pinus. It is also distinguished for the many plants contained in the Orders, or natural families—Grossulaceæ, Onograceæ, Hypericaceæ, Aceraceæ, Betulaceæ, Juglandaceæ, and Vacciniaceæ; and for the presence of the peculiar families—Podophyllæ, Sarraceniaceæ, and Hydrophyllaceæ. There is, on the contrary, the climate being considered, a remarkable paucity of Cruciferæ and Umbelliferæ, and,

trees grow to the height of 120 feet and upward, and are

what is most extraordinary, a total absence of the genus Erica (heath),[1] which covers so many thousands of acres in corresponding latitudes in Europe. Mrs. Butler mentions, in her Journal, 'that some poor Scotch peasants, about to emigrate to Canada, took away with them some roots of the "bonny blooming heather," in hopes of making this beloved adorner of their native mountains the cheerer of their exile. The heather, however, refused to grow in the Canadian soil. The person who told me this said that the circumstance had been related to him by Sir Walter Scott, whose sympathy with the disappointment of these poor children of the romantic heather-land betrayed itself even in tears.'

"Canada is not rich in roses; only three species occur throughout the two provinces. Among the Ribes and the Ericaceæ, however, are found many of the most beautiful ornaments of the English garden: Andromedas, Rhododendrons, Azaleas, and Kalmias belong to the latter order. The Azalea was thus described by one of the earlier European botanical travelers, Professor Kalm[2] (in 1748): 'the May-flowers, as the Swedes call them, were plentiful in the woods wherever I went to-day, especially on a dry soil, or one that is somewhat moist. The Swedes have given them this name because they are in full blossom in May. Some of the Swedes and the Dutch call them "Pinxter Bloem" (Whitsunday flowers), as they are in blossom about Whitsuntide. The English call them wild honeysuckles, and at a distance they really have a resemblance to the honeysuckle or lonicera. Dr. Linnæus and other botanists call it an Azalea (Azalea Nudiflora, *Linn. Spec. Plant.*, p. 214.) Its flowers were now open, and added a new ornament to the woods, being little inferior to the flowers of the honey-

[1] Seven hours' journey above the sources of the Bow River, Sir George Simpson mentions meeting with "an unexpected reminiscence of my own native hills, in the shape of a plant which appeared to me to be the very heather of the mountains of Scotland; and I might well regard the reminiscence as unexpected, inasmuch as in all my wanderings, of more than twenty years, I had never found any thing of the kind in North America. As I took a considerable degree of interest in the question of the supposed identity, I carried away two specimens, which, however, proved, on a minute comparison, to differ from the genuine staple of the brown heaths of the 'Land o' Cakes.'"—Vol. i., p. 120.

"We missed, also, the small 'crimson-tipped daisy' on the green lawns, and were told that they have been often cultivated with care, but are found to wither when exposed to the dry air and bright sun of this climate. When weeds so common with us can not be reared here, we cease to wonder at the dissimilarity of the native Flora of the New World. Yet, wherever the aboriginal forests are cleared, we see orchards, gardens, and arable lands filled with the same fruit-trees, the same grain and vegetables, as in Europe, so bountifully has Nature provided that the plants most useful to man should be capable, like himself, of becoming cosmopolites."—Lyell's *Travels in North America*, vol. i., p. 5.

[2] The Kalmias were so named by Linnæus in honor of Professor Kalm, a favorite pupil of the great botanist.

from nine to ten feet in circumference.* Of this and of the fir species there are many varieties, some of them valuable from their production of pitch, tar, and turpentine. The American oak † is quicker in its growth and less durable than that of England; one species, however, called the live oak, grown in the warmer parts of the continent, is said to be equal, if

suckle and hedysarum. They sit in a circle round the stem's extremity, and have either a dark red or lively red color; but by standing some time, the sun bleaches them, and at last they get a whitish hue. The height of the bush is not always alike. Some were as tall as a full-grown man, and taller; others were but low, and some were not above a palm from the ground; yet they were all full of flowers. They have some smell, but I can not say it is very pleasant. However, the beauty of the color entitles them to a place in every flower garden.' "—*Travels in North America*, by Professor Kalm, in Pinkerton, vol. xiii., p. 557.

* See Appendix, No. XXVII.

† The oak from the dense forests of Canada, into which the sun's rays never penetrate, is more porous, more abundant in sap, and more prone to the dry rot than the oak grown in any other country. Canadian timber has increased in value since the causes of its former rapid decay have been more fully understood. Mr. Nathaniel Gould asserts that the wane of the moon is now universally considered the best season for felling timber, both in the United States and in Canada. The Americans contract for their ship timber to be felled or girdled between the 20th of October and the 12th of February. Dry rot being probably caused by the natural moisture or sap being left in the wood, the less there is in the tree when cut, the longer it will keep sound. As regards the Canadian oak, it is stated by Mr. M'Taggart (the engineer, who so ably distinguished himself while in the colony), that it is not so durable as that of the British, the fiber not being so compact and strong; it grows in extensive groves near the banks of large lakes and rivers, sometimes found growing to 50 feet in length by 2 feet 6 inches; its specific gravity is greater than water, and therefore, when floated down in rafts, it is rendered buoyant with cross bars of pine. It is easily squared with the hatchet, and answers well for ship-building and heavy work; will endure the seasons for about fifteen years,[1] and does not decay in England so soon as in Canada.—Montgomery Martin's *Canada*, p. 257; Gray's *Canada*, p. 207.

[1] Kalm says, in 1748, "They were now building several ships below Quebec for the king's account. However, before my departure, an order arrived from France prohibiting the further building of ships of war, because they had found that the ships built of American oak do not last so long as those of European oak. Near Quebec is found very little oak, and what grows there is not fit for use, being very small; therefore they are obliged to fetch their oak timber from those parts of Canada which border upon New England. But all the North American oaks have the quality of lasting longer, and withstanding putrefaction better, the further north they grow."—Kalm, p. 663.

not superior, to any in Europe for ship-building. The white oak is the best found in the Canadian settlements, and is in high repute. Another description is called the scrubby oak —it resembles the British gnarled oak, and is remarkably hard and durable. The birch* tribe is very numerous: the bark is much used by the Indians in making canoes,† baskets, and roofings; the wood is of a useful quality, and the sap, when extracted in the spring, produces by fermentation a pleasant but weak wine. The maple‡ is one of the most variable and beautiful of all the forest trees, and is adopted as the emblem of Canadian nationality.

Two plants, formerly of great importance in these counties, are now almost extirpated, or little noticed as articles of commerce—ginseng§ and capillaire. The first was found in

* The most useful American plants in the small order Betulaceæ are the birches, of which Canada contains six species. The most celebrated is Betula Papyracea, the canoe birch, so called from the use made of the bark in the construction of the Indian boats. It ex tends from the shore of the Hudson in New York to a considerable range of country northward of Canada. The bark is obtained with facility in large pieces, and is sewed together with the tough and slender roots of the pine-tree. La Hontan relates a characteristic story respecting the birch bark: "I remember I have seen, in a certain library in France, a manuscript of the Gospel of St. Matthew, written in Greek upon this sort of bark; and which is yet more surprising, I was there told that it had been written above a thousand years; and, at the same time, I dare swear that it was the genuine birch bark of New France, which, in all appearance, was not then discovered."—La Hontan, in Pinkerton, vol. xiii., p. 361.

Mr. Weld says that "the bark resembles in some degree that of the cork-tree, but it is of a closer grain, and also much more pliable, for it admits of being rolled up the same as a piece of cloth. The Indians of this part of the country always carry large rolls of it in their canoes when they go on a hunting party, for the purpose of making temporary huts. The bark is spread on small poles over their heads, and fastened with strips of elm bark, which is remarkably tough, to stakes, so as to form walls on the sides."—Weld, p. 311.

† See Appendix, No. XXVIII.

‡ See Appendix, No. XXIX.

§ The ginseng belongs to the small order Araliaceæ. The botanical name is Panax quinquefolium: it was called Aureliana Canadensis by Lafitau, who was the first to bring it from Canada to France.—(Charlevoix, tom. iv., p. 309, fig. 13.) It was discovered in the forests of Canada in 1718. It is herbaceous, scarcely a foot and a

great abundance by the French in their earlier settlement of the colony, and large quantities were exported to Europe,

half in height, and toward the upper part of the stem arise three quinate-digitate leaves, from the center of which springs the flower stalk. The root is fusiform and fleshy, and is the part most valued. We are informed that among the Chinese many volumes have been written upon its virtues; and that, besides the name already mentioned, it is known by several others, expressive of the high estimation in which it is universally held throughout the Celestial Empire; two of these appellations are, 'the pure spirit of the earth,' and 'the plant that gives immortality.' An ounce of ginseng bears the surprising price of seven or eight ounces of silver at Pekin. When the French botanists in Canada first saw a figure of it, they remembered to have seen a similar plant in this country. They were confirmed in their conjecture by considering that several settlements in Canada lie under the same latitude with those parts of Chinese Tartary and China where the true ginseng grows wild. They succeeded in their attempt, and found the same ginseng wild and abundant in several parts of North America, both in French and English plantations, in plain parts of the woods. It is fond of shade, and of a deep, rich mold, and of land which is neither wet nor high. It is not every where very common, for sometimes one may search the woods for the space of several miles without finding a single plant of it; but in those spots where it grows it is always found in great abundance. It flowers in May and June, and its berries are ripe at the end of August. The trade which is carried on with it here is very brisk, for they gather great quantities of it, and send them to France, from whence they are brought to China, and sold there to great advantage. The Indians in the neighborhood of Montreal were so taken up with the business of collecting ginseng, that the French farmers were not able during that time to hire a single Indian, as they commonly do, to help them in the harvest. The ginseng formerly grew in abundance round Montreal, but at present there is not a single plant of it to be found, so effectually have they been rooted out. This obliged the Indians this summer to go far within the English boundaries to collect these roots. After the Indians have sold the fresh roots to the merchants, the latter must take a great deal of pains with them. They are spread on the floor to dry, which commonly requires two months and upward, according as the season is wet or dry. During that time they must be turned once or twice every day, lest they should putrefy or molder. The roots prepared by the Chinese are almost transparent, and look like horn in the inside; and the roots which are fit for use are heavy and compact in the inside. No one has ever discovered the Chinese method of preparing it. It is thought, among other preparations, they dip the roots in a decoction of the leaves of ginseng." Kalm wrote thus of the ginseng in 1749 (Kalm, in Pinkerton, vol. xiii., p. 639). Mr. Heriot mentions that "one article of commerce the Canadians had, by their own imprudence, rendered altogether

from whence it was forwarded to China. The high value it then possessed in that distant market induced the Canadians to collect the roots prematurely; and the Indians also gathered them wherever they could be found; consequently, this useful production was soon exhausted, and is now rarely seen. The capillaire * is now either become rare or neglected

unprofitable. From the time that Canada ginseng had been imported to Canton, and its quality pronounced equal to that of Corea or Tartary, a pound of this plant, which before sold in Quebec for twenty pence, became, when its value was once ascertained, worth one pound and tenpence sterling. The export of this article amounted in 1752 to £20,000 sterling. But the Canadians, eager suddenly to enrich themselves, reaped this plant in May when it should not have been gathered until September, and dried it in ovens when its moisture should have been gradually evaporated in the shade. This fatal mistake, arising from cupidity, and in some measure from ignorance, ruined the sale of their ginseng among the only people on earth who are partial to its use, and at an early period cut off from the colony a new branch of trade, which, under proper regulations, might have been essentially productive."—Heriot's *Travels through the Canadas*, p. 99, 1807.

"Mountainous woods in Tartary are mentioned as the place where the ginseng is produced in the greatest abundance. In 1709, the emperor ordered an army of ten thousand men to collect all the ginseng they could find, and each person was to give him two ounces of the best, while for the remainder payment was to be made in silver, weight for weight. It was in the same year that Father Jartoux, a Jesuit missionary in China, prepared a figure and accurate description of the plant, in which he bears testimony to the beneficial effects of the root. He tried it in many instances himself, and always with the same result, especially when exhausted with fatigue. His pulse was increased, his appetite improved, and his whole frame invigorated. Judging from the accounts before us, we should say that the Chinese were extravagant in their ideas of the virtues of this herb; but that it is undoubtedly a cordial stimulant, to be compared, perhaps, in some degree, with the aromatic root of Meum athamanticum, so much esteemed by the Scottish Highlanders. It has nevertheless disappeared from our Materia Medica."—Murray's *Canada*, vol. iii., p. 308. Charlevoix, tom. vi., p. 24.

"Ginseng a véritablement la vertu de soutenir, de fortifier, et de rappeller les forces épuisées."—Lafitau, tom. ii., p. 142.

* In La Hontan's time (1683), he speaks of "maiden-hair" being as common in the forests of Canada as fern in those of France, and is esteemed beyond that of other countries, insomuch that the inhabitants of Quebec prepare great quantities of its syrup, which they send to Paris, Nantes, Rouen, and several other cities of France. Charlevoix

for other objects; a small quantity is, however, still exported. In the woods there is a vast variety of wild plants and flowers, many of them very beautiful. The sweet garlic especially deserves notice: two large pale-green leaves arise from the root; between them stands the delicate stem, about a foot in height, bearing a cluster of graceful flowers, resembling blue-bells in shape and color. The wild turnip is also very beautiful. There are, besides, many valuable herbs and roots, which the Indians use for various purposes. The reindeer moss* often serves for support and refreshment to

gives a figure of the maiden-hair (tom. iv., p. 301), under the name of Adiantum Americanum.—"Cette plante a la racine fort petite, et enveloppée de fibres noires, fort déliées; sa tige est d'un pourpre foncé, et s'élève en quelques endroits à trois ou quatre pieds de haut; il en sort des branches, qui se courbent en tous sens. Les feuilles sont plus larges que celles de notre Capillaire de France, d'un beau verd d'un côté, et de l'autre, semées de petits points obscurs; nulle part ailleurs cette plante n'est si haute ni si vive, qu'en Canada. Elle n'a aucune odeur tandis qu'elle est sur pied, mais quand elle a été renfermée, elle répand une odeur de violette, qui embaume. Sa qualité est aussi beaucoup audessus de tous les autres capillaires."

The Herba capillaris is the Adiantum pedatum of Linnæus (Sp. Pl., p. 1557). Cornutus, in his *Canadens. Plant. Historia*, p. 7, calls it Adiantum Americanum, and gives a figure of it, p. 6. Kalm says that "it grows in all the British colonies of America, and likewise in the southern parts of Canada, but I never found it near Quebec. It grows in the woods in shady places, and in a good soil. Several people in Albany and Canada assured me that its leaves were very much used instead of tea in consumptions, coughs, and all kinds of pectoral diseases. This they have learned from the Indians, who have made use of it for these purposes from time immemorial. This American maiden-hair is reckoned preferable in surgery to that which we have in Europe, and therefore they send a great quantity of it to France every year. Commonly the price at Quebec is between five and fifteen sols a pound. The Indians went into the woods about this time (August), and traveled far above Montreal in quest of this plant."—Kalm, in Pinkerton, vol. xiii., p. 641.

* "This moss is called by the Canadian voyageurs, *Tripe de Roche*; it belongs to the order Gyrophara. They who have perused the affecting narrative of the sufferings of Captain Franklin and his gallant party, on their return from their first journey to the Arctic Sea, will remember that it was on *Tripe de Roche* that they depended, under God, for their very existence. 'We looked,' says Captain Franklin, 'with humble confidence to the Great Author and giver of all good, for a continuance of the support which had been hitherto

the exhausted hunter; when boiled down into a liquid, it is very nourishing; and an herb called Indian tea produces a pleasant and wholesome draught, with a rich aromatic flavor. Wild oats and rice* are found in some of the marshy lands. The soil and climate are also favorable to the production of hops and a mild tobacco, much esteemed for the manufacture of snuff. Hemp† and flax are both indigenous in America. Father Hennepin, in the seventeenth century, found the former growing wild in the country of the Illinois; and Sir Alexander Mackenzie, in his travels to the western coast, met with flax in the interior, where no European was ever known to have been before. The Indian hemp‡ is seen in abundance upon the Canadian soil, particularly in light and sandy places; the bark is so strong that the natives use it for bow-strings; the pod bears a substance that rivals down in softness and elasticity; the culture is easy; the root, penetrating deep into the earth, survives the frosts of winter, and shoots out fresh stalks every spring. When five or six

always supplied to us at our greatest need,' and he was not disappointed."—Murray's *Canada*, vol. iii., p. 330. "Parmi les sauvages errans, et qui ne cultivent point du tout la terre, lorsque la chasse et la pêche leur manquent, leur unique ressource est une espèce de mousse, qui croît sur certains rochers, et que nos Français ont nommée Tripe de Roche; rien n'est plus insipide que ce mets, lequel n'a pas même beaucoup de substance, c'est bien là être réduit au pur nécessaire pour ne pas mourir de faim."—Charlevoix, tom. vi., p. 24.

* See Appendix, No. XXX. † See Appendix, No. XXXI.

‡ "The Swedes gave the name of Indian hemp to Apocynum cannabinum, because the Indians apply it to the same purposes as the Europeans do hemp; for the stalk may be divided into filaments, and is easily prepared. This plant grows in abundance in old corn grounds, in woods, on hills, and on high glades. The Indians make ropes of this Apocynum, which the Swedes buy, and employ them as bridles, and for nets. These ropes are stronger, and kept longer in water than such as were made of common hemp. The Swedes commonly got fourteen yards of these ropes for one piece of bread. On my journey through the country of the Iroquois, I saw the women employed in manufacturing this hemp. The plant is perennial, which renders the annual planting of it altogether unnecessary. Out of the root and stalk of this plant, when it is fresh, comes a white, milky juice, which is somewhat poisonous. Sometimes the fishing tackle of the Indian consists entirely of this hemp."—Kalm, in Pinkerton, vol xiii., p. 544

years old it attains the greatest perfection. It may be added that in these favored provinces all European plants, fruits, vegetables, grain,* legumes, and every other production of the earth required for the subsistence or luxury of man, yield their increase even more abundantly than in the old continents.

The animals originally belonging to America appear to be of an inferior race—neither so robust, fierce, or numerous as those of the other continents: some are peculiar to the New World; but there is reason to suppose that several species have become utterly extinct, and the spread of cultivation and increase of the human race rapidly extirpate many of those that still remain. America gives birth to no creature of equal bulk to the elephant and rhinoceros, or of equal strength and ferocity to the lion and tiger. The particular qualities in the climate, stinting the growth and enfeebling the spirit of the native animals, have also proved injurious to such as have been transported to the Canadas by their present European inhabitants. The soil, as well as temperature, of the country seems to be rather unfavorable to the development of strength and perfection in the animal creation.† The general quality of the natural grasses covering those boundless pastures is not good or sufficiently nutritious.‡

The native animals of Canada are the buffalo, bison, and musk bull, belonging to the ox kind. The buffalo is still

* See Appendix, No. XXXII.

† Buffon, Hist. Nat., tom. ix., p. 13, 203; Acosta, Hist., lib. iv., cap. xxxiv.; Pisonis Hist., p. 6; Herrera, Dec. IV., lib. iv., cap. i.; lib. x., cap. xiii.

‡ Canada has not the fine natural pastures of Ireland, England, Holland, and other countries enjoying a cool, moist, and equable climate. Artificial grasses, now a most valuable branch of British husbandry, are peculiarly important in Canada, where so large a quantity of hay should be stored for winter use. They are also most useful in preparing the soil for grain crops, but have the disadvantage of requiring to stand the severe winter, so trying to all except annual plants. Clover, which is supposed to yield three times the produce of natural grass, grows luxuriantly; but in the second year its roots are often found to have been destroyed by frost. For this reason, it is necessary to have recourse to the species named Timothy, which is extremely hardy, and will set at defiance even a Canadian winter.—Talbot, vol. i., p. 301; Gould, p. 67.

found in herds of immense numbers upon the prairies of the remote western country, where they have wandered from the hated neighborhood of civilized man: the skin* is invaluable to the Canadians as a protection from the keen wintery air, and is abundantly supplied to them by the hunters of the Hudson's Bay Company.† This animal is about the size of an ox, with the head disproportionably large; he is of a lighter color, less ferocious aspect, and inferior strength to those of the Old World. Both the bison and musk ox are varieties of the domestic cow, with a covering of shaggy hair; they possess considerable strength and activity. There are different descriptions of deer: the black and gray moose or elk, the cariboo or reindeer,‡ the stag§

* "In the western parts of Lower Canada, and throughout Upper Canada, where it is customary for travelers to carry their own bedding with them, these skins are very generally made use of for the purpose of sleeping upon. For upward of two months we scarcely ever had any other bed than one of the skins spread on the floor and a blanket to each person. The skins are dressed by the Indians with the hair on, and they are rendered by a peculiar process as pliable as cloth. When the buffalo is killed in the beginning of the winter, at which time he is fenced against the cold, the hair resembles very much that of a black bear; it is then long, straight, and of a blackish color; but when the animal is killed in the summer, the hair is short and curly, and of a light brown color, owing to its being scorched by the rays of the sun."—Weld, p. 313.

† Charlevoix says, "que la peau, quoique très forte, devient souple et moëlleuse comme le meilleur chamois. Les sauvages en font des boucliers, qui sont très légers, et que les bals de fusil ne perçent pas aisément."—Tom. v., p. 193.

‡ The height of the domesticated reindeer is about three feet; of the wild ones, four. It lives to the age of sixteen years. The reindeer is a native of the northern regions only. In America it does not extend further south than Canada. The Indians often kill numbers for the sake of their tongue only; at other times they separate the flesh from the bones, and preserve it by drying it in the smoke. The fat they sell to the English, who use it for frying instead of butter. The skins, also, are an article of extensive commerce with the English.—Rees's *Cyclopædia*, art. Cervus Tarandus.

Charlevoix says that the Cnnadian *caribou* differs in nothing from the *Renne* of Buffon except in the color of its skin, which is brown or reddish.—Tom. v., p. 191. La Hontan calls the *caribou* a species of wild ass; and Charlevoix says that its form resembles that of the ass, but that it at least equals the stag in agility.

§ Pennant is persuaded that the stag is not a native of America,

and fallow deer.* The moose deer† is the largest wild animal of the continent; it is often seen upward of ten feet high, and weighing twelve hundred weight; though savage in aspect, the creature is generally timid and inoffensive even when attacked by the hunter, and, like the sheep, may be easily domesticated: the flesh and skin are both of some value.

The black and brown bear‡ is found in various parts of America, but chiefly in the northwest: some few are seen in the forests to the north of Quebec. This animal chooses for his lurking-place the hollow trunk of an old tree, which he prepares with sticks and branches, and a coating of warm moss; on the approach of the cold season he retires to his lair, and sleeps through the long winter till the return of spring enables him again to seek his prey. The bear is rather shy than fierce, but very powerful and dangerous when driven to extremities; he displays a strong degree of instinct, and is very dexterous and cunning in procuring food: the flesh is considered a delicacy, and the skin highly prized for beauty and warmth. Foxes§ are numerous; they are of various colors and very cunning. Hares‖ are abundant, and turn white in winter like those of Norway. The wolverine or carcajou is called by the hunters beaver-eater, and somewhat resembles a badger; the skin is soft and handsome. A species of porcupine or urchin is found to the

and considers the deer known in that country by the name of stag as a distinct species. The American stag is the Cervus Canadensis of Erxleben. The Americans hunt and shoot those animals not so much for the sake of the flesh as of the fat, which serves as tallow in making candles, and the skins, which they dispose of to the Hudson's Bay Company. They are caught principally in the inland parts, near the vicinity of the lakes.—Rees's *Cyclopædia*, art. Cervus Elaphus.

Charlevoix says that "le Cerf en Canada est absolument le même qu'en France, peut être communément un peu plus grand."—Tom. v., p. 189.

* The fallow deer in America have been introduced there from Europe; for the animal called the American fallow is of a very different kind, and is peculiar to the New Continent. This, the *Cervus* Virginianus, inhabits all the provinces south of Canada.—Rees's *Cyclopædia*, art. Cervus Virginianus.

† See Appendix, No. XXXIII. ‡ See Appendix, No. XXXIV.

§ See Appendix, No. XXXV. ‖ See Appendix, No. XXXVI.

northward, and supplies the Indians with quills about four inches long, which, when dyed, are worked into showy ornaments. Squirrels * and various other small quadrupeds with fine furs are abundant in the forests. The animals of the cat kind are the cougar or American lion, the loup-cervier, the catamount, and the manguay or lynx.

Beavers † are numerous in North America; these amphibious animals are about two feet nine inches in length, with very short fore feet and divided toes, while the hinder are membranous, and adapted for swimming; the body is covered with a soft, glossy, and valuable fur; the tail is oval, scaly, destitute of hair, and about a foot long. These industrious creatures dam up considerable streams, and construct dwellings of many compartments, to protect them from the rigor of the climate, as well as from their numerous enemies; their winter food, consisting of poplar logs, pieces of willows, alder, and fragments of other trees, is collected in autumn, and sunk in the water near the habitation. The beaver exhibits an extraordinary degree of instinct, and may be easily tamed; when caught or surprised by the approach of an enemy, it gives warning to its companions by striking the water with the flat of its tail. The musk rat and otter resemble the beaver in some of their habits, but are inferior in ingenuity, and of less value to the hunter.

The walrus has now disappeared from the frequented waters of the Gulf of St. Lawrence, but is still found on the northern coasts of Labrador; in shape he somewhat resembles the seal, but is of much greater size, sometimes weighing 4000 pounds; when protecting their young, or when wounded, they are dangerous from their immense tusks; when out of the water, however, they are very helpless.

Nearly all these wild animals are pursued by the Indians, and the hunters of the Hudson's Bay Company, ‡ for their skins; they are consequently growing rarer, and their haunts become more remote each succeeding year: probably, at no distant time, they will be altogether extinct.

* See Appendix, No. XXXVII. † See Appendix, No. XXXVIII.
‡ See Appendix, No. XXXIX.

The birds of Canada differ little from those of the same names in Europe, but the severe climate is generally uncongenial to them. There are eagles, vultures, hawks, falcons, kites, owls, ravens, crows, rooks, jays, magpies, daws, cuckoos, woodpeckers, hoopers, creepers, humming-birds, thrushes, blackbirds, linnets, finches, sparrows, fly-catchers, pigeons, turkeys, ducks, geese, swans, grouse, ptarmigans, snipes, quails, and many others. The plumage of the American birds is very brilliant; but the sweet voices that fill the European woods with melody are never heard. Many of the birds of Lower Canada are migratory; the water-fowl seek the cooler north during the heat of summer, and other species fly to the south to shun the wintery frosts. In the milder latitudes of Upper Canada, birds are more numerous. They are known by the same names as those of corresponding species in England, but differ from them to some extent in plumage and character.

In Lower Canada the reptiles are few and innocuous, and even these are not met with in the cultivated parts of the country. In the Upper Province, however, they are more numerous; some species are very dangerous, others harmless and exquisitely beautiful. Two kinds of rattlesnakes* are found here: one of a deep brown and yellow color, and seldom more than thirty inches in length; it frequents marshes and low meadows, and is very dangerous to cattle, often fastening its fangs upon their lips while grazing. The other is a bright greenish yellow clouded with brown, and twice the size of the former. These reptiles are thicker in proportion to their length than any others; the rattle is at the end of the tail, and consists of a number of dry, horny shells inclosed within each other. When wounded or enraged, the skin of the rattlesnake assumes a variety of beautiful colors; the flesh is white as that of the most delicate fish, and is esteemed a great luxury by the Indians. Cold weather weakens or destroys their poisonous qualities. In the spring, when they issue from their place of winter concealment, they are harmless till they have got to water, and at that time emit a sickening smell so as to injure those

* See Appendix, No. XL.

who hunt them. In some of the remoter districts they are still numerous, but in the long-settled parts of the country they are now rarely or never seen.

Several varieties of lizards and frogs abound; the latter make an astonishing noise in marshy places during the summer evening by their harsh croaking. The land crab is found on the northern shore of Lake Erie. A small tortoise, called a terrapin,* is taken in some rivers, creeks, and swampy grounds, and is used as an article of food. Seals have been occasionally seen on the islands in Lake Ontario.

Insects† are very numerous and various, some of them both troublesome and mischievous: locusts or grasshoppers

* "While we were roaming along the shore of Lake Ontario we caught a species of tortoise (testudo picta), which was a gayly-colored shell, and I carried it a day's journey in the carriage, and then turned it out, to see whether, as I was told, it would know its way back to Lake Ontario. I am bound to admit that its instinct on this occasion did not fail, for it made directly for a ravine, in the bottom of which was a stream that would lead it in time to the Genesee River, and this would carry it to its native lake if it escaped destruction at the Falls below Rochester, where the celebrated diver, Sam Patch, perished, after he had succeeded in throwing himself with impunity down several other great waterfalls. There is a fresh-water tortoise in Europe (Terrapena Europea) found in Hungary, Prussia, and Silesia, as far north as latitude 50° to 52°. It also occurs near Bordeaux, and in the north of Italy, 44° and 45° north latitude, which precisely corresponds with the latitude of Lake Ontario."—Lyell's *Travels in North America*, vol. i., p. 25.

† "To the Malacodermous division belongs the remarkable genus Lampyris, which contains the insects commonly called glow-worms. The substance from which the luminous property results has been the subject of frequent experiment and observation. It is obviously under the control of the animal, which, when approached, may frequently be observed to diminish or put out its light. The only species with which we are acquainted in British America is Lampyris corusca. It occurs in Canada, and has been taken at least as far north as latitude 54°. It was originally described by Simmons as a native of Finland and Russia, on the authority of Uddman, but has not since been found there."—Murray, vol. iii., p. 277.

"We saw numerous yellow butterflies, very like a British species. Sometimes forty of them clustering on a small spot resembled a plot of primroses, and as they rose altogether, and flew off slowly on every side, it was like the play of a beautiful fountain."—Lyell's *America*, vol. i., p. 25.

have been known to cause great destruction to the vegetable world. Musquitoes and sand-flies infest the woods, and the neighborhood of water, in incredible numbers, during the hot weather. There are many moths and butterflies resembling those seen in England. The beautiful fire-fly is very common in Canada, their phosphorescent light shining with wonderful brightness through the shady forests in the summer nights.

The lakes and rivers of Upper Canada abound in splendid fish of almost every variety known in England, and others peculiar to the country: sturgeon of 100 lbs. weight are frequently taken, and a giant species of pike, called the maskenongi, of more than 60 lbs. The trout of the upper lakes almost rivals the sturgeon in size, but not in flavor. The delicious white-fish, somewhat resembling a shad, is very plentiful, as is also the black bass, which is highly prized. A fresh-water herring abounds in great shoals, but is inferior in delicacy to the corresponding species of the salt seas. Salmon are numerous in Lake Ontario, but above the Falls of Niagara they are never seen.

CHAPTER VI.

PERHAPS the saddest chapter in the history of the sons of Adam is furnished by the Red Man of America. His origin is unknown; no records tell the tale of his ancient deeds. A foundling in the human family, discovered by his stronger brethren wandering wild through the forests and over the prairies of the western desert, no fraternal welcome greeted this lost child of nature; no soothing voice of affection fell upon his ear; no gentle kindness wooed him from his savage isolation. The hand of irresistible power was stretched out, not to raise him from his low estate and lead him into the brotherhood of civilized man, but to thrust him away with cruel and unjust disdain.

Little more than three centuries and a half have elapsed

since the Indian first gazed with terror and admiration upon the white strangers, and already three fourths of his inheritance are rent away, and three fourths of his race have vanished from the earth; while the sad remnant, few and feeble, faint and weary, "are fast traveling to the shades of their fathers, toward the setting sun."* Year by year they wither away; to them the close breath of civilized man is more destructive than the deadliest blight.† The arts and appliances which the accumulated ingenuity of ages has provided to aid the labor and enhance the enjoyments of others, have been but a curse to these children of the wilderness. That blessed light which shines to the miserable of this world through the vista of the "shadowy valley," cheering the fainting spirit with the earnest of a glorious future, sheds but a few dim and distorted rays upon the outskirts of the Red Man's forest land.

All the relations of Europeans to the Indian have been alike fatal to him, whether of peace or war; as tyrants or suppliants; as conquerors armed with unknown weapons of destruction; as the insidious purchasers of his hunting-grounds, betraying him into an accursed thirst for the deadly fire-water; as the greedy gold-seekers, crushing his feeble frame under the hated labors of the mine; as shipwrecked and hungry wanderers, while receiving his simple alms, marking the fertility and defenselessness of his lands; as

* "Driven by the European populations toward the northwest of North America,[1] the savage tribes are returning, by a singular destiny, to expire on the same shore where they landed, in unknown ages, to take possession of America. In the Iroquois language, the Indians gave themselves the appellation of *Men of Always* (Ongoueonoue); these *men of always* have passed away, and the stranger will soon have left to the lawful heirs of a whole world nothing but the mold of their graves."—Chateaubriand's *Travels in America* (Eng. trans.), vol. ii., p. 93.

† See Appendix, No. XLI.

[1] De Tocqueville calculated that along the borders of the United States, from Lake Superior to the Gulf of Mexico, extending a distance of more than 1200 miles, as the bird flies, the whites advance every year at a mean rate of seventeen miles; and he truly observes that there is a grandeur and solemnity in this gradual and continuous march of the European race toward the Rocky Mountains. He compares it to "a deluge of men rising, unabatedly, and daily driven onward by the hand of God."—*Democracy in America*, vol. ii., cap. x., § 4; Lyell, vol. ii., p. 77.

sick men enjoying his hospitality, and, at the same time, imparting that terrible disease* which has swept off whole nations; as woodmen in his forest, and intrusive tillers of his ground, scaring away to the far West those animals of the chase given by the Great Spirit for his food: there is to him a terrible monotony of result. In the delicious islands of the Caribbean Sea, and in the stern and magnificent regions of the northeast, scarcely now remains a mound, or stone, or trace even of tradition, to point out the place where any among the departed millions sleep.

The discovery of the American Indians brought to light not only a new race, but also a totally new condition of men. The rudest form of human society known in the Old World was far advanced beyond that of the mysterious children of the West, in arts, knowledge, and government. Even among the simplest European and Asiatic nations the principle of individual possession was established; the beasts of the field were domesticated to supply the food and aid the labors of man, and large bodies of people were united under the sway of hereditary chiefs. But the Red Man roamed over the vast forests and prairies of his undiscovered continent, accompanied by few of his fellows, unassisted by beasts of burden,† and trusting alone to his skill and fortune in the chase for a support. The first European visitors to the New World were filled with such astonishment at the appearance and complexion of the Red Man, that they hastily concluded he belonged to a different species from themselves. As the native nations became better known, their warriors, statesmen, and orators commanded the admiration of the strangers. Especially in the northern people, every savage virtue was

* See Appendix, No. XLII.

† "Generally speaking, the American races of mankind were characterized by a want of domestic animals, and this had considerable influence on their domestic life." (*Cosmos*, note, vol. ii., p. 481.) Contrasting the Bedouin with the Red Indian, Volney observes, "the American savage is, on the contrary, a hunter and a butcher, who has had daily occasion to kill and slay, and in every animal has beheld nothing but a fugitive prey, which he must be quick to seize. He has thus acquired a roaming, wasteful, and ferocious disposition; has become an animal of the same kind with the wolf and tiger; has united in bands or troops, but not into organized societies."

conspicuous; they were gentle in peace, but terrible in war; of a proud and noble bearing, honest, faithful, and hospitable, loving order though without laws, and animated by the strongest and most devoted loyalty to their tribe. At the same time, while willingly recording their high and admirable qualities, pity for the devoted race must not blind us to their ferocious and degrading vices.

It was not until the end of the seventeenth century that the manners and characteristics of this strange race attracted to any considerable degree the attention of philosophers and theorists; a chasm in human history then seemed about to be filled. Eager to throw light upon the subject, but too impatient to inquire into the facts necessary for the formation of opinions, the conclusions formed were often unjust to the native dignity of the Red Indian,* and have been proved erroneous by subsequent and more perfect information. On the other hand, one of the most gifted but dangerous of modern philosophers would exalt these untutored children of nature to a higher degree of honor and excellence than civilization and knowledge can confer. He deemed that the elevation and independence of mind, resulting from the rude simplicity of savage life, is sought in vain among the members of refined and organized societies.†

Every thing tended to render inquiry into the state of

* "On ne prit pas d'abord les Américains pour des hommes, mais pour des orang-otangs, pour des grands singes, qu'on pouvoit détruire sans remords et sans reproche. Un pape fit une Bulle originale dans laquelle il déclara qu' ayant envie de fonder des Evêchés dans les plus riches contrées de l'Amérique, il plaisoit à lui et au Saint Esprit de reconnoitre les Américains pour des hommes véritables; de sorte que, sans cette décision d'une Italien, les habitans du Nouveau Monde seroient encore maintenant, aux yeux des fidèles, une race d'animaux équivoques. . . . . Qui auroit cru que malgré cette sentence de Rome, on eût agité violemment au conseil de Lima, 1583, si les Américains avoient assez d'esprit pour être admis aux sacrements de l'Eglise. Plusieurs évêques persistèrent à les leur refuser pendant que les Jésuites faisoient communier tous les jours leurs Indiens esclaves au Paraquai, afin de les accoutumer, disoient-ils, à la discipline, et pour les détourner de l'horrible coutûme de se nourrir de chair humain."—*Récherches Philosophiques sur les Américains*, De Pauw, tom. i., p. 35.

† Rousseau, opposed by Buffon, Volney, &c.

the rude tribes of America difficult and obscure. In the generality of cases they presented characteristics of a native simplicity, elsewhere unknown; and even in the more favored districts, where a degree of civilization appeared, it had assumed a form and direction totally different from that of the Old World.*

The origin of this mysterious people has been the subject of an immense variety of speculations, and has involved the question, whether all men are the sons of Adam, or whether the distinctions of the human race were owing to the several sources from whence its members sprung? The skeptic supposition that each portion of the globe gave its own original type of man to the human family at once solves the difficulty of American population; but as both Christianity and philosophy alike forbid acceptance of this view, †

* "Notwithstanding the striking analogies existing between the nations of the New Continent and the Tartar tribes who have adopted the religion of Bouddah, I think I discover in the mythology of the Americans, in the style of their paintings, in their languages, and especially in their external conformation, the descendants of a race of men, which, early separated from the rest of mankind, has followed for a lengthened series of years a peculiar road in the unfolding of its intellectual faculties, and in its tendency toward civilization."—Humboldt's *Ancient Inhabitants of America*, vol. i., p. 200.

"It can not be doubted that the greater part of the nations of America belong to a race of men who, isolated ever since the infancy of the world from the rest of mankind, exhibit in the nature and diversity of language, in their features, and the conformation of their skull, incontestable proofs of an early and complete civilization."—*Ibid.*, vol. i., p. 250.

On the American races in general, Humboldt refers to the beautiful work of Samuel George Morton, *Craniæ Americanæ*, 1839, p. 62–86; and an account of the skulls brought by Pentland from the Highlands of Titicaca, in the '*Dublin Journal of Medical and Chemical Science*,' vol. v., p. 475, 1834; also, Alcide d'Orbigny, *L'Homme Américain considéré sous ses Rapports Physiol. et Mor.*, p. 221, 1839; and, further, the work, so full of delicate ethnographical observations, of Prinz Maximilian of Wied, *Reise in das Innere von Nordamerika*, 1839.

† "With regard to their origin, I have no doubt, independent of theological considerations, but that it is the same with ours. The resemblance of the North American savages to the Oriental Tartars renders it probable that they originally sprang from the same stock."—Buffon, Eng. trans., vol. iii., p. 193.

it becomes necessary to consider the relative probabilities in favor of the other different theories which enthusiasm, ingenuity, and research have contributed to lay before the world.

Without referring to the most sacred and ancient of authorities, we may find existing natural evidence abundantly sufficient to establish the belief of the common descent of our race. There are not in the human form differences such as distinguish separate species of the brute creation. All races of men are nearly of like stature and size, varying only by the accidents of climate and food favorable or adverse to their full development. The number, shape, and uses of limbs and extremities are alike, and internal construction is invariably the same. These are circumstances the least acted upon by situation and temperature, and therefore the surest tests of a particular species. Color is the most obvious and the principal indication of difference in the human families, and is evidently influenced to a great extent by the action of the sun,* as the swarthy cheek of the harvest

* "The Ethiopians," sings the old tragedian, Theodectes of Phaselis, "are dyed by the near sun-god in his course with a dark and sooty luster; the sun's heat crisps and dries up their hair." The expeditions of Alexander, which were so influential in exciting ideas of the physical cosmography, first fanned the dispute on the uncertain influence of climate upon races of men. Humboldt's *Cosmos*, vol. i., p. 386. Volney, p. 506, and Oldmixon, vol. i., p. 286, assert that the savages are born white, and in their infancy continue so. An intelligent Indian said to Volney, "Why should there be any difference of color between us and them? (some Spaniards who had been bronzed in America). In them, as in us, it is the work of *the father of colors*, the sun, that burns us. You whites yourselves compare the skin of your faces with that of your bodies." This brought to my remembrance that, on my return from Turkey, when I quitted the turban, half my forehead above the eyebrows was almost like bronze, while the other half next the hair was as white as paper. If, as natural philosophy demonstrates, there be no color but what originates from light, it is evident that the different complexions of people are owing entirely to the various modifications of this fluid with other elements that act on our skin, and even compose its substance. Sooner or later it will be provod that the blackness of the African has no other source. —P. 408.

"Vespuce décrit les indigènes du Nouveau Continent dans sa première lettre comme des hommes à face large et à physionomie

laborer will witness. Under the equator we find the jet black of the negro; then the olive-colored Moors of the southern shores of the Mediterranean; again, the bronzed face of the Spaniard and Italian; next, the Frenchman, darker than those who dwell under the temperate skies of England; and, last, the bleached and pallid visages of the north. Along the arctic circle, indeed, a dusky tint again appears: that, however, may be fairly attributed to the scorching power of the sun, constantly over the horizon, through the brief and fiery summer. The natives remain generally in the open air during this time, fishing, or in the chase; and the effect of exposure stamps them with a complexion which even the long-continued snows can not remove. In the rigorous winter season, the people of those dreary countries pass most of their time in wretched huts or subterranean dwellings, where they heap up large fires to warm their shivering limbs. The smoke has no proper vent in these ill-constructed abodes; it fills the confined air, and tends to darken the complexions of those constantly exposed to its influence.

The difference of color in the human race is doubtless influenced by many causes, modifying the effect of position with regard to the tropics. The great elevation of a particular district, its proximity to the sea, the shades of a vast forest, the exhalations from extensive marshes, all tend to diminish materially the power of a southern sun.* On the other hand, intensity of heat is aggravated by the neighborhood of arid and sandy deserts, or rocky tracts. The action

tartare, dont la couleur rougeâtre n'étoit due qu'à l'habitude de ne pas être vêtus. Il revient à cette même opinion en examinant les Brésiliens." (Canovai, p. 87, 90.) "Leur teint, dit il, est rougeâtre, ce qui vient de leur nudité absolue et de l'ardeur du soleil auquel ils sont constamment exposés. Cette erreur a été partagée par un des voyageurs modernes les plus spirituels, mais des plus systématiques, par Volney." (*Essai Politique sur la Mexique.*) Humboldt's *Géog. du Nouv. Continent*, vol. v., p. 25.

* On the influence of humidity much stress has been laid by M. D'Orbigny and Sir R. Schomburgh, each of whom has made the remark as the result of personal and independent observation on the inhabitants of the New World, that people who live under the damp shade of dense and lofty forests are comparatively fair.

of long-continued heat creates a more permanent effect than the mere darkening of the outer skin: it alters the character of those subtile juices that display their color through the almost transparent covering.* We see that, from a constitutional peculiarity in individuals, the painful variety of the albino is sometimes produced in the hottest countries. Certain internal diseases, and different medicines, change the beautiful bloom of the young and healthy into repulsive and unnatural tints. A peculiar secretion of the carbon abounding in the human frame produces the jet black of the negro's skin, and enables him to bear without inconvenience the terrible sultriness of his native land.† The dark races, inferior in animal and intellectual powers to the white man, are yet nearly free from the deformities he so often exhibits, perhaps on account of a less susceptible and delicate structure. The Caucasian or European races, born and matured under a temperate climate, manifestly enjoy the highest gifts of man. Wherever they come in contact with their colored brother, he ultimately yields to the irresistible superiority, and becomes, according to the caprice of their haughty will, the victim, the dependent, or the slave.‡

There are other characteristics different from, but generally combined with color, which are influenced by constitutional varieties. The hair usually harmonizes with the complexion, and, like it, shows the influence of climate. In cold countries, the natural covering of every animal becomes rich and soft; the plentiful locks and manly beard of the European show a marked contrast to the coarse and scanty hair of the inhábitants of tropical countries. The development of mental power and refined habits of life have also a strong but slow effect upon the outward form.§ Certain African

* See Appendix, No. XLI.

† Mr. Jarrold asserts that the negro becomes the most perfect specimen of the human species, in consequence of his possessing the coarsest and most impassive integument.—*Anthropologia.*

‡ See Appendix, No. XLII.

§ "It is intellectual culture which contributes most to diversify the features. Barbarous nations have rather a physiognomy of tribe or horde than one peculiar to such or such an individual. The savage and civilized man are like those animals of the same species, several

nations of a higher intelligence and civilization than their rude neighbors, show much less of the peculiarities of the negro features. The refined Hindoo displays a delicate form and expression under his dark complexion. The black color and the negro features are accidentally not necessarily connected, and it seems to require both climate and inferiority of intellect to unite them in the same race.

When circumstances of climate or situation have effected peculiar appearances in a nation or tribe, the results will long survive the causes when people are removed to widely-different latitudes: a dark color is not easily effaced, even under the influence of moderate temperature and heightened civilization. For these reasons, there appear many cases where the complexion of the inhabitants and the climate of the country do not correspond, but the original characteristics will be found undergoing the process of gradual change, ultimately adapting themselves to their new country and situation.* The marked and peculiar countenances of the once

of which rove in the forest, while others connected with us share in the benefits and evils that accompany civilization. The varieties of form and color are frequent only in domestic animals. How great is the difference with respect to mobility of feature and variety of physiognomy between dogs again become savage in the New World, and those whose slightest caprices are indulged in the houses of the opulent. Both in men and animals the emotions of the soul are reflected in the features; and the features acquire the habit of mobility in proportion as the emotions of the mind are more frequent, more varied, and more durable. In every condition of man, it is not the energy or the transient burst of the passions which give expression to the features; it is rather that sensibility of the soul which brings us continually into contact with the external world, multiplies our sufferings and our pleasures, and reacts at once on the physiognomy, the manners, and the language. If the variety and mobility of the features embellish the domain of animated nature, we must admit also that both increase by civilization without being produced by it alone. In the great family of nations, no other race unites these advantages to a higher degree than that of Caucasus or the European. It must be admitted that this insensibility of the features is not peculiar to every race of men of a very dark complexion: it is much less apparent in the African than in the natives of America."—Humboldt's *Personal Narrative*, vol. iii., p. 230.

* Tacitus, in his speculations on the peopling of Britain, distinguishes very beautifully between what may belong to the ultimate in-

"chosen people" vary, in color at least, wherever they are seen over the world, although uninfluenced by any admixture of alien blood. In England the children of Israel and the descendant of the Saxon are alike of a fair complexion, and on the banks of the Nile the Jew and the Egyptian show the same swarthy hue.*

At first sight this American race would appear to offer evidence against the supposed influence of climate upon color, as one general form and complexion prevail in all latitudes of the New World, from the tropics to the frozen regions of the north. Great varieties, however, exist in the shade of the red or copper† color of the Indians. There are two extremes of complexion among mankind—those of the northern European and the African negro; between these there is a series of shades, that of the American Indian being about midway. The structure of the New World, and the circumstances of its inhabitants, may account for the generally equal color of their skin. The western Indian never becomes black, even when dwelling directly under the equator. He lives among stupendous mountain ranges, where cool breezes from

fluences of the country, and what may pertain to an old, unalterable type in the immigrated race. "Britanniam qui mortales initio coluerunt, indigenæ an advecti, ut inter barbaros, parum compertum. Habitus corporis varii, atque ex eo argumenta; namque rutilæ Caledoniam habitantium comæ, magni artus Germanicam originem adseverant. Silurum colorati vultus et torti plerumque crines, et posita contra Hispania, Iberos veteres trajecisse, easque sedes occupâsse fidem faciunt: proximi Gallis et similes sunt, seu durante originis vi; seu, procurrentibus in divisa terris, positio cœli corporibus habitum dedit." —*Agricola*, cap. ii.

"No ancient author has so clearly stated the two forms of reasoning by which we still explain in our days the differences of color and figure among neighboring nations as Tacitus. He makes a just distinction between the influence of climate and hereditary dispositions, and, like a philosopher persuaded of our profound ignorance of the origin of things, leaves the question undecided."—Humboldt's *Personal Narrative.*

* See Smith on *The Variety of Complexion of the Human Species.*

† Mr. Lawrence's precise definition is "an obscure orange or rusty-iron color, not unlike the bark of the cinnamon-tree." Among the early discoverers, Vespucius applies to them the epithet "rougeâtre." Verazzano says, "sono di color berrettini e non molto dalli Saracini differenti."

the snowy heights sweep through the valleys and over the plains below. The vast rivers springing from under those lofty peaks inundate a great extent of country, and turn it into swamps, whence perpetual exhalations arise and lower the temperature. There are no fiery deserts to heat the passing wind and reflect the rays of the sun; a continual forest, with luxuriant foliage, and a dense underwood, spreads a pleasant shade over the surface of the earth. America, under the same latitudes, especially on the eastern coast, is every where colder than the Old World. The nearest approach to a black complexion is seen in the people of Brazil, a country comparatively low, and immediately under the equator. The inhabitants of the lofty Mexican table-land are also very dark, and on those arid plains the sun pours down its scorching rays upon a surface almost devoid of sheltering vegetation.

The habits of savage life, and the constant exposure to the elements, seem sufficient to cause a dark tint upon the human skin even in the temperate regions of America, where the cold is far greater than in the same latitude in Europe. The inhabitants of those immense countries are badly clothed, imperfectly defended against the weather, miserably housed; wandering in war or in the chase, exposed for weeks at a time to the mercy of the elements, they soon darken into the indelible red or copper color of their race. On the northwest coasts, about latitude 50°, in Nootka Sound, and a number of other smaller bays, dwell a people more numerous and better provided with food and shelter than their eastern neighbors. They are free from a great part of the toils and hardships of the hunter, and from the vicissitudes of the season. When cleansed from their filthy and fantastic painting, it appears that their complexion and features resemble those of the European.*

* Cook's Narrative calls their color an *effete* white, like that of the southern nations of Europe. Meares expressly says that some of the females, when cleaned, were found to have the fair complexions of Europe.

Somewhat further north, at Cloak Bay, in lat. 54° 10′, Humboldt remarks, that "in the midst of copper-colored Indians, with small, long eyes, there is a tribe with large eyes, European features, and

Modern discoveries have to a great extent dispelled the mystery of the Indian origin, and proved the fallacy of the numerous and ingenious theories formerly advanced with so much pertinacity and zeal. Since the northwest coasts of America and the northeast of Asia have been explored, little difficulty remains on this subject. The two continents approach so nearly in that direction that they are almost within sight of each other, and small boats can safely pass the narrow strait. Ten degrees further south, the Aleutian and Fox Islands* form a continuous chain between Kamtschatka and the peninsula of Alaska, in such a manner as to leave the passage across a matter of no difficulty. The rude and hardy Tschutchi, inhabiting the northeast of Asia, frequently sail from one continent to the other.† From the remotest antiquity, this ignorant people possessed the wonderful secret of the existence of a world hidden from the wisest and most adventurous of civilized nations. They were unconscious of the value of their vast discovery; they passed over a stormy strait from one frozen shore to another, as stern and desolate as that they had left behind, and knew not that they had crossed one of the great boundaries of earth. When they first entered upon the wilderness of America, probably the most adventurous pushed down toward the genial regions of the south, and so through the long ages of the past the stream of population flowed slowly on, wave by wave, to the remotest limits of the east and south. The Indians resemble the people of northeastern Asia in form and feature more than any other of the human race. Their population is most dense along the districts nearest to Asia; and among the Mexicans, whose records of the past deserve credence, there is a constant tradition that their Aztec and Toultec chiefs came from the northwest. Every where but to the north, America is surrounded with a vast ocean unbroken by any chain of islands that could connect it with the Old World.

a skin less dark than that of our peasantry."—*New Spain*, vol. i., p. 145.

Humboldt considers this as the strongest argument of an original diversity of race which has remained unaffected by climate.

* See Appendix, No. XLV. † Cochrane's *Pedestrian Journey*.

Most probably no living man ever crossed this immense barrier before the time of Columbus. It is certain that in no part of America have any authentic traces been found of European civilization; the civilization of America, such as it was, arose, as it flourished, in the fertile plains of Mexico* and in the delightful valleys of Peru;† there, where the bounty of nature supplied an abundance of the necessaries of life, the population rapidly multiplied, and the arts became objects of cultivation.

There is something almost mysterious in the total differ-

* Prescott remarks, that the progress made by the Mexicans in astronomy, and especially the fact of their having a general board for education and the fine arts, proves more in favor of their advancement than the noble architectural monuments which they and their kindred tribes erected. "Architecture," he observes, "is a sensual gratification, and addresses itself to the eye: it is the form in which the resources of a semi-civilized people are most likely to be lavished."—*Conquest of Mexico*, vol. i., p. 155; Lyell's *America*, vol. i., p. 115.

† "Dans les régions anciennement agricoles de l'Amérique méridionale les conquérans Européens n'ont fait que suivre les traces d'une culture indigène. Les Indiens sont restés attachés au sol qu'ils ont défriché depuis des siécles. Le Mexique seul compte un million sept cent mille indigènes de race pure, dont le nombre augmente avec la même rapidité que celui des autres castes. Au Mexique, à Guatémala, à Quito, au Perou, à Bolivia, la physionomie du pays, à l'exception de quelques grandes villes, est essentiellement Indienne; dans les campagnes la varieté des langues s'est conservée avec les mœurs, le costume et les habitudes de la vie domestique. Il n'y a de plus que des troupeaux de vaches et de brebis, quelques céreales nouvelles et les cérémonies d'une culte qui se mêle à d'antiques superstitions locales. Il faut avoir vécu dans les hautes plaines de l'Amérique Espagnole ou dans la conféderation Anglo-Américain pour sentir vivement combien ce contraste entre des peuples chasseurs et des peuples agricoles, entre des pays longtemps barbares ou des pays offrant d'anciennes institutions politiques et une législation indigène très developpée, a facilité ou entravé la conquête, influé sur les formes des premiers établissement européens, conservé même de nos jours aux differentes parties de l'Amérique indépendante, un caractère ineffaçable. Déjà le père Joseph Acosta qui a étudié sur les lieux mêmes les suites du grand drame sanguinaire de la conquête a bien saisi ces différences frappantes de civilisation progressive et d'absence entière d'ordre social qu'offrait le nouveau-monde à l'époque de Christopher Colomb, ou peu de tems après la colonisation par les Espagnols.—*Hist. Nat. y Moral.* lib. vi., cap. ii.; Humboldt's *Géographie du Nouveau Continent*, tom. i., p. 130.

ence between the languages of the Old and New World.* All the tongues of civilized nations spring from a few original roots, somewhat analogous to each other; but it would seem that, among wandering tribes, dispersed over a vast extent of country, carrying on but little intercourse, and having no written record or traditionary recital to preserve any fixed standard, language undergoes a complete change in the course of ages. The great varieties of tongues in America, and their dissimilarity to each other, tend to confirm this supposition.

In various parts of America, remains are found which place beyond a doubt the ancient existence of a people more numerous, powerful, and civilized than the present race of Indians; but the indications of this departed people are not such as to bespeak their having been of very remote antiquity: the ruined cities of Central America, concealed by the forest growth of centuries, and the huge mounds of earth† in the Valley of the Mississippi and upon the tablelands of Mexico, their dwellings and mausoleums, although long swept over by the storm of savage conquest, afford no proofs of their having existed very far back into those dark ages when the New World was unknown to Europe. The history of these past races of men will probably forever remain a sealed book, but there is no doubt that a great population once covered those rich countries which the first English visitors found the wild hunting-grounds for a few savage tribes.‡ Probably the existing race of Red Men

* See Appendix, No. XLVI.

† "In both Americas it is a matter of inquiry what was the intention of the natives when they raised so many artificial hills, several of which appear to have served neither as mounds, nor watch-towers, nor the base of a temple. A custom established in Eastern Asia may throw some light on this important question. Two thousand three hundred years before our era, sacrifices were offered in China to the Supreme Being, Chan-Ty, on four great mountains called the Four Yo. The sovereigns, finding it inconvenient to go thither in person, caused eminences representing these mountains to be erected by the hands of men near their habitations."—*Voyage of Lord Macartney*, vol. i., p. 58; Hager, *Monument of Yu*, p. 10, 1802.

‡ Mr. Flint asserts, "that the greatest population clearly has been in those positions where the most dense future population will be."—P. 166.

were the conquerors and exterminators of the feeble but civilized aboriginal nations, and as soon as they possessed the land they split into separate and hostile communities, waging perpetual war with each other so as constantly to diminish their numbers.

Far up the Mississippi and the Missouri the exploration of the country brings to light incontestable proofs of the existence of the mysterious aboriginal race: wells artificially walled, and various other structures for convenience or defense, are frequently seen; ornaments of silver, copper, and even brass are found, together with various articles of pottery and sculptured stone; sepulchers filled with vast numbers of human bones have often been discovered, and human bodies in a state of preservation are sometimes exhumed. On one of these the hair was yellow or sandy, and it is well known that an unvarying characteristic of the present red race is the lank black hair. A splendid robe of a kind of linen, made apparently from nettle fibers, and interwoven with the beautiful feathers of the wild turkey, encircled this long-buried mummy. The number and the magnitude of the mounds bear evidence that the concurrent labors of a vast assembly of men were employed in their construction.*

* "The bones of animals and snakes have sometimes been found mixed with human bones in these tumuli, and out of one near Cincinnati were dug two large marine shells, one of which was the *Cassis cornutus* of the Asiatic islands, the other the *Fulgur perversus* of the coast of Georgia and East Florida; and this is an additional argument used in favor of the alleged intercourse existing anciently between the Indians of this part of North America and the inhabitants of Asia, and between them and those of the Atlantic. Many circumstances still existing give probability to the popular belief that the American Indians had their origin in Asia. In their persons, color, and reserved disposition, they have a strong resemblance to the Malays of the Oriental Archipelago—that is to say, to some of the Tartar tribes of Upper Asia; and it is a remarkable circumstance, that, like these, they shave the head, leaving only a single lock of hair. The picture language of the Mexicans, as corresponding with the ancient picture language of China, and the quipos of Peru with the knotted and party-colored cords which the Chinese history informs us were in use in the early period of the empire, may also be adduced as corroborative evidence. The high cheek bones and the elongated eye of the two people, besides

In the progress of early discovery and settlement, striking views were presented of savage life among the Red Men inhabiting the Atlantic coast; but later researches along the banks of the Mississippi and its tributaries, and by the great Canadian lakes, exhibited this people under a still more remarkable aspect. The most prominent among the natives of the interior for power, policy, and courage, were the Iroquois or Five Nations.* Their territory extended west-

other personal resemblances, suggest the probability of a common origin."—*Quarterly Review*, No. LVII., p. 13.

"The Iroquois and Hurons made hieroglyphic paintings on wood, which bear a striking resemblance to those of the Mexicans."—Lafitau, vol. ii., p. 43, 225; La Houtan, p. 193.

"A long struggle between two religious sects, the Brahmans and the Buddhists, terminated by the emigration of the Chamans to Thibet, Mongolia, China, and Japan. If tribes of the Tartar race have passed over to the northwest coast of America, and thence to the south and the east, toward the banks of Gila, and those of the Missouri, as etymological researches serve to indicate, we should be less surprised at finding among the semi-barbarous nations of the New Continent idols and monuments of architecture, a hieroglyphical writing, and exact knowledge of the duration of the year, and traditions respecting the first state of the world, recalling to our minds the arts, the sciences, and religious opinions of the Asiatic nations."—Humboldt's *Researches*.

In his description of a Mexican painting, Humboldt observes, "The slave on the left is like the figure of those saints which we see frequently in Hindoo paintings, and which the navigator Roblet found on the northwest coast of America, among the hieroglyphical paintings of the natives of Cox's Channel."—Marchant's *Voyage*, vol. i., p. 312.

"It is probably by philosophical and antiquarian researches in Tartary that the history of those civilized nations of North America, of whose great works only the wreck remains, will alone be elucidated." —See Bancroft's *History of the United States*, vol. iii., chap. xxii.; and Stephens's *Central America*, vol. i., p. 96; vol. ii., chap. xxvi., p. 186, 357, 413, 433. See Appendix, No. XLVII.

* "The five nations were the Mohawks, the Oneidas, the Cayugas, the Onondagas, and the Senecas. The Dutch called them Maquas, the French Iroquois; their appellation at home was the Mingoes, and sometimes the Aganuschion, or United People."—Governor Clinton's *Discourse before New York Historical Society*, 1811.

The Iroquois have often, among Europeans, been termed the Romans of the West. "Le nom d'Iroquois est purement françois, et a été formé du terme *Hiro*, qui signifie, *J'ai dit*, par lequel ces sauvages finissent tout leur discours, comme les Latins faisaient autrefois par

ward from Lake Champlain, to the farthest extremity of Ontario, along the southern banks of the St. Lawrence, and of the Great Lake. Although formed by the alliance of five independent tribes, they always presented a united front to their foes, whether in defense or aggression. Their enemies, the Algonquins, held an extensive domain on the northern bank of the St. Lawrence; these last were at one time the masters of all that portion of America, and were the most polished and mildest in manners of the northern tribes. They depended altogether for subsistence on the produce of the chase, and disdained those among their neighbors who attempted the cultivation of the soil. The Hurons* were a numerous nation, generally allied with the Algon-

leur *Dixi;* et *de Koué*, qui est un cri, tantôt de tristesse, lorsqu' on le prononce en traînant, et tantôt de joie, lorsqu' on le prononce plus court. Leur nom propre est Agonnonsionni, qui veut dire, *Faiseurs de Cabannes;* parcequ'ils les bâtissent beaucoup plus solides, que la plupart des autres sauvages."—Charlevoix, tom. i., p. 421.

Lafitau gives the Iroquois the same name of Agonnonsionni; they used to say of themselves that the five nations of which they were composed formed but one "Cabane."

* "Le Père Brebeuf comptoit environ trente mille âmes de vrais Hurons, distribués en vingt villages de la nation. Il y avoit outre cela, douze nations sédentaires et nombreuses, qui parloient leur langue. La plupart de ces nations ne subsistent plus, les Iroquois ces ont detruites. Les vrais Hurons sont réduits aujourd'hui à la petite mission de Lorette, qui est près de Quebec, où l'on voit le Christianisme fleurir avec l'édification de tous les Français, à la nation des Tionnontatès qui sont établis au Détroit, et à une autre nation qui s'est refugiée à la Carolina."—Charlevoix, 1721.

"The Tionnontatès mentioned above now bear the name of Wyandots, and are a striking exception to the degeneracy which usually attends the intercourse of Indians with Europeans. The Wyandots have all the energy of the savage warrior, with the intelligence and docility of civilized troops. They are Christians, and remarkable for orderly and inoffensive conduct; but as enemies, they are among the most dreadful of their race. They were all mounted (in the war of 1812–13), fearless, active, enterprising; to contend with them in the forest was hopeless, and to avoid their pursuit, impossible.

"It is worthy of remark, that the Wyandots are the only part of the Huron nation who ever joined in alliance with the English. The mass of the Hurons were always the faithful friends of the French during the times of the early settlement of Canada."—*Quarterly Review.*

quins, inhabiting the immense and fertile territory extending westward to the Great Lake, from which they take their name: they occupied themselves with a rude husbandry, which the fertile soil of the west repaid, by affording them an abundant subsistence; but they were more effeminate and luxurious than their neighbors, and inferior in savage virtue and independence. The above-named nations were those principally connected with the events of Canadian history.

Man is less affected by climate in his bodily development than any other animal; his frame is at the same time so hardy and flexible, that he thrives and increases in every variety of temperature and situation, from the tropic to the pole; nevertheless, in extremes such as these, his complexion, size, and vigor usually undergo considerable modifications.* Among the Red Men of America, however, there is a re-

* The extremes of heat and cold are as unfavorable to intellectual as to physical superiority,[1] a fact which may be easily traced throughout the vast and varied extent of the two Americas. "As far as the parallel of 53°, the temperature of the northwest coast of America is milder than that of the eastern coasts: we are led to expect, therefore, that civilization had anciently made some progress in this climate, and even in higher latitudes. Even in our own times, we perceive that in the 59th degree of latitude, in Cox's Channel and Norfolk Sound, the natives have a decided taste for hieroglyphical paintings on wood."—Humboldt *on the Ancient Inhabitants of America.*

It has been ascertained that this western coast is populous, and the race somewhat superior to the other Indians in arts and civilization.—Ramusio, tom. iii., p. 297–303; Venegas's *California*, Part ii., § ii.

"From the happy coincidence of various circumstances, man raises himself to a certain degree of cultivation, even in climates the least favorable to the development of organized beings. Near the polar circle, in Iceland, in the twelfth century, we know the Scandinavians cultivated literature and the arts with more success than the inhabitants of Denmark and Prussia."—Humboldt.

[1] The most temperate climate lies between the 40th and 50th degree of latitude, and it produces the most handsome and beautiful people. It is from this climate that the ideas of the genuine color of mankind and of the various degrees of beauty ought to be derived. The two extremes are equally remote from truth and from beauty. The civilized countries situated under this zone are Georgia, Circassia, the Ukraine, Turkey in Europe, Hungary, the south of Germany, Italy, Switzerland, France, and the northern parts of Spain. The natives of these territories are the most handsome and most beautiful people in the world.—Buffon, English trans., vol. iii., p. 205.

markable similarity of countenance, form, manners, and habits, in every part of the continent. No other race can show people speaking different languages, inhabiting widely different climates, and subsisting on different food, who are so wonderfully alike.* There are, indeed, varieties of stature, strength, intellect, and self-respect to be found among them; but the savage of the frozen north, and the Indian of the tropics, have the same stamp of person, and the same instincts.† There is a language of signs common to all, conveying similar ideas, and providing a means of mutual intelligence to every Red Man from north to south.

The North American Indians are generally of a fair

* Mr. Flint says, "I have inspected the northern, middle, and southern Indians for a length of ten years; my opportunities of observation have, therefore, been considerable, and I do not undertake to form a judgment of their character without, at least, having seen much of it. I have been forcibly struck by a general resemblance in their countenance, make, conformation, manners, and habits. I believe that no race of men can show people who speak different languages, inhabit different climes, and subsist on different food, and who are yet so wonderfully alike."—(1831.)

Don Antonio Ulloa, who had extensive opportunities of forming an opinion on the natives of both the continents of America, asserts that "If we have seen one American, we may be said to have seen all, their color and make are so nearly the same."—*Notic. Americanas*, p. 308. See, likewise, Garcia, *Origin de los Indios*, p. 55–242; Torquemada, *Monarch. Indiana*, vol. ii., p. 571.

"If we except the northern regions, where we find men similar to the Laplanders, all the rest of America is peopled with inhabitants among whom there is little or no diversity. This great uniformity among the natives of America seems to proceed from their living all in the same manner. All the Americans were, or still are, savages; the Mexicans and Peruvians were so recently polished that they ought not to be regarded as an exception. Whatever, therefore, was the origin of these savages, it seems to have been common to the whole. All the Americans have sprung from the same source, and have preserved, with little variation, the characters of their race; for they have all continued in a savage state, and have followed nearly the same mode of life. Their climates are not so unequal with regard to heat and cold as those of the ancient continent, and their establishment in America has been too recent to allow those causes which produce varieties sufficient time to operate so as to render their effects conspicuous."—Buffon, Eng. trans., vol. iii., p. 188.

† See Appendix, No. XLVIII.

height and proportion. Deformities or personal defects* are rare among them; and they are never seen to fall into corpulency. Their features, naturally pleasing and regular, are often distorted by absurd attempts to improve their beauty, or render their appearance more terrible. They have high cheek bones, sharp and rather aquiline noses, and good teeth. Their skin is generally described as red or copper-colored, approaching to the tint of cinnamon bark, a complexion peculiar to the inhabitants of the New World. The hair of the Americans, like that of their Mongolian ancestors, is coarse, black, thin, but strong, and growing to a great length. Many tribes of both these races remove it from every part of the head except the crown, where a small tuft is left, and cherished with care. It is a universal habit among the tribes of the New World to eradicate every symptom of beard: hence the early travelers were led to conclude that the smoothness of their faces resulted from a natural deficiency. One reason for the adoption of this strange custom was to enable them to paint themselves with greater ease. Among old men, who have become indifferent to their appearance, the beard is again seen to a small extent.†

* See Appendix, No. XLIX.

† There would never have been any difference of opinion between physiologists, as to the existence of the beard among the Americans, if they had paid attention to what the first historians of the conquest of their country have said on this subject; for example, Pigafetta, in 1519, in his Journal preserved in the Ambrosian library at Milan, and published (in 1800) by Amoretti, p. 18.—Benzoni, *Hist. del Mundo Nuovo*, p. 35, 1572; Bembo, *Hist. Venet.*, p. 86, 1557; Humboldt's *Personal Narrative*, vol. iii., p. 235.

"The Indians have no beard, because they use certain receipts to extirpate it, which they will not communicate."—Oldmixon, vol. i., p. 286.

"Experience has made known that these receipts were little shells which they used as tweezers; since they have become acquainted with metals, they have invented an instrument consisting of a piece of brass wire rolled round a piece of wood the size of the finger, so as to form a special spring; this grasps the hairs within its turns, and pulls out several at once. No wonder if this practice, continued for several generations, should enfeeble the roots of the beard. Did the practice of eradicating the beard, originate from the design of depriv-

On the continent, especially toward the north, the natives were of robust and vigorous constitution. Their sole employment was the chase of the numerous wild animals of the forest and prairies: from their continual activity, their frame acquired firmness and strength;* but in the islands, where game was rare, and the earth supplied spontaneously an abundant subsistence, the Indians were comparatively feeble, being neither inured to the exertions of the chase nor the labors of cultivation. Generally, the Americans were more remarkable for agility than strength, and are said to have been more like beasts of prey than animals formed for labor. Toil was hateful, and even destructive to them; they broke down and perished under tasks that would not have wearied a European. Experience proves that the physical strength of civilized man exceeds that of the savage.† Hand to hand in war, in wrestling, leaping, and even in running for a short distance, this superiority usually appears. In a long journey, however, the endurance of the Indian has no parallel among Europeans. A Red Man has been known to travel nearly eighty miles between sunrise and sunset, without apparent fatigue. He performs a long journey, bearing a heavy burden, and indulging in no refreshment or repose; an enemy can not escape his persevering pursuit, even when mounted on a strong horse.

It has been already observed that the Americans are rarely or never deformed, or defective in their senses, while in their wild state, but in those districts where the restraints of law are felt, an extraordinary number of blind, deaf, dwarfs, and cripples, are observed. The terrible custom

ing the enemy of such a dangerous hold on the face? This seems to me probable."—Volney, p. 412.

* When the statue of Apollo Belvedere was shown to Benjamin West on his first arrival at Rome, he exclaimed, "It is a model from a young North American Indian."—*Ancient America.*

† "It is a notorious fact, that every European who has embraced the savage life has become stronger and better inured to every excess than the savages themselves. The superiority of the people of Virginia and Kentucky over them has been confirmed, not only in troop opposed to troop, but man to man, in all their wars."—Volney, p. 417.

among the savage tribes of destroying those children who do not promise a vigorous growth, accounts for this apparent anomaly. Infancy is so long and helpless that it weighs as a heavy burden upon a wandering people; food is scanty and uncertain of supply, hunters and their families must range over extensive countries, and often remove from place to place. Judging that children of feeble or defective formation are not likely to survive the hardships of this errant life, they destroy all such unpromising offspring,* or desert them to a slower and more dreadful fate. The lot of all is so hard that few born with any great constitutional defect could long survive, and arrive at maturity.

In the simplicity of savage life, where labor does not oppress, nor luxury enervate the human frame, and where harassing cares are unknown, we are led to expect that disease and suffering should be comparatively rare, and that the functions of nature should not reach the close of their gradual decay till an extreme old age. The decrepit and shriveled forms of many American Indians would seem to indicate that they had long passed the ordinary time of life. But it is difficult or impossible to ascertain their exact age, as the art of counting is generally unknown among them, and they are strangely forgetful and indifferent to the past. Their longevity, however, varies considerably, according to differences of climate and habits of life. These children of nature are naturally free from many of the diseases afflicting civilized nations; they have not even names in their language to distinguish such ills, the offspring of a luxury to them unknown. The diseases of the savage, however, though few,

* Yet infanticide is condemned among the Red Indians both by their theology and their feelings. Dr. Richardson relates that those tribes who hold the idea that "the souls of the departed have to scramble up a great mountain, at whose top they receive the reward of their good or bad deeds, declare that women who have been guilty of infanticide never reach the top of this mountain at all. They are compelled instead to travel around the scenes of their crimes with branches of trees tied to their legs. The melancholy sounds which are heard in the still summer evenings, and which the ignorance of the white people looks upon as the screams of the goat-suckers, are really, according to my informant, the moanings of these unhappy beings"—Franklin's *Journey to the Polar Seas*, p. 77, 78.

are violent and fatal; the severe hardships of his mode of life produce maladies of a dangerous description. From improvidence they are often reduced for a considerable time to a state bordering on starvation. When successful in the chase, or in the seasons when earth supplies her bounty, they indulge in enormous excesses. These extremes of want and abundance prove equally pernicious, for, although habit and necessity enable them at the time to tolerate such sudden transitions, the constitution is ultimately injured: disorders arising from these causes strike down numbers in the prime and vigor of youth, and are so common that they appear the necessary consequences of their mode of life. The Indian is likewise peculiarly subject to consumption, pleurisy, asthma, and paralysis, engendered by the fatigues and hardships of the chase and war, and constant exposure to extremes of heat and cold. Experience supports the conclusion that the average life is greater among people in an advanced condition of society than among those in a state of nature; among savages, all are affected by circumstances of over-exertion, privation, and excess, but in civilized societies the diseases of luxury only affect the few.

CHAPTER VII.

The Indian is endowed with a far greater acuteness of sense than the European. Despite the dazzling brightness of the long-continued snows, and the injurious action of the smoke of burning wood to which he is constantly exposed, he possesses extraordinary quickness of sight. He can also hear and distinguish the faintest sounds, alike through the gentle rustling of the forest leaves and in the roar of the storm; his power of smell is so delicate that he scents fire long before it becomes visible. By some peculiar instinct the Indian steers through the trackless forests, over the vast prairies, and even across wide sheets of water with unerring certainty. Under the gloomiest and most obscure sky, he can follow the course of the sun* as if directed by a compass. These powers would seem innate in this mysterious race; they can scarcely be the fruit of observation or practice, for children who have never left their native village can direct their course through pathless solitudes as accurately as the experienced hunter.

In the early stages of social progress, when the life of man is rude and simple, the reason is little exercised, and his wants and wishes are limited within narrow bounds; consequently, his intellect is feebly developed, and his emotions are few but concentrated. These conditions were generally observable among the rudest tribes of the American Indians.

There are, however, some very striking peculiarities in the intellectual character of the Red Men. Without any aid from letters or education, some of the lower mental faculties are developed in a remarkable degree. As orators, strategists, and politicians, they have frequently exhibited very great power.† They are constantly engaged in dangerous and difficult enterprises, where ingenuity and presence of mind are essential for their preservation. They are vigorous in the thought which is allied to action, but altogether incapable of speculation, deduction, or research. The ideas and attention of a savage are confined to the objects relating to his sub-

* "At night the savages direct their course by the polar star; they call it the *motionless star*. It is a curious coincidence that the constellation of the Bear should be called by the savages the Bear. This is certainly a very ancient name among them, and given long before any Europeans visited the country. They turn into ridicule the large imaginary tail which astronomers have given to an animal that has scarcely any such appendage, and they call the three stars that compose the tail of the Bear, three hunters who are in pursuit of it. The second of these stars has a very small one very close to it. This, they say, is the kettle of the second hunter, who is the bearer of the baggage and the provision belonging to all three.[1] The savages also call the Pleiades 'the Dancers,' and Hygin tells us that they were thus called by the ancients, because they seem, from the arrangement of their stars, to be engaged in a circular dance."—Lafitau, vol. ii., p. 236. Hygin., lib. ii., art. Taurus.

† See Appendix, No. L.

[1] "Even at the present time" (1720), Lafitau writes, "these three stars are called in Italy, *i tre cavalli*"—the three knights—on the celestial globe of Caronelli.

sistence, safety, or indulgence: every thing else escapes his observation or excites little interest in his mind. Many tribes appear to make no arrangement for the future; neither care nor forethought prevents them from blindly following a present impulse, regardless of its consequences.

The natives of North America were divided into a number of small communities; in the relation of these to each other, war or negotiation was constantly carried on; revolutions, conquests, and alliances frequently occurred among them. To raise the power of his tribe, and to weaken or destroy that of his enemy, was the great aim of every Indian. For these objects schemes were profoundly laid, and deeds of daring valor achieved: the refinements of diplomacy were employed, and plans arranged with the most accurate calculation. These peculiar circumstances also developed the power of oratory to an extraordinary degree.* Upon all occasions of importance, speeches were delivered with eloquence, and heard with deep attention. When danger threatened, or opportunity of aggrandizement or revenge offered itself, a council of the tribe was called, where those most venerable from age and illustrious for wisdom deliberated for the public good. The composition of the Indian orator is studied and elaborate; the language is vigorous, and, at the same time, highly imaginative; all ideas are expressed by figures addressed to the senses; the sun and stars, mountains and rivers, lakes and forests, hatchets of war and pipes of peace, fire and water, are employed as illustrations of his subject with almost Oriental art and

* Charlevoix says that the eloquence of the savages was such as the Greeks admired in the barbarians, "strong, stern, sententious, pointed, perfectly undisguised."

Decanesora's oratory was greatly admired by the most cultivated among the English: his bust was said to resemble that of Cicero. The celebrated address of Logan is too well known to be cited here. Mr. Jefferson says of it, "I may challenge the whole orations of Demosthenes and Cicero, and of any other more eminent orator, if Europe has furnished more eminent, to produce a single passage superior to the speech of Logan." An American statesman and scholar, scarcely less illustrious than the former, has expressed his readiness to subscribe to this eulogium. — Clinton's *Historical Discourse*, 1811.

richness. His eloquence is unassisted by action or varied intonation, but his earnestness excites the sympathy of the audience, and his persuasion sinks into their hearts.*

The want of any written or hieroglyphic records of the past among the Northern Indians was, to some extent, supplied by the accurate memories of their old men; they were able to repeat speeches of four or five hours' duration, and delivered many years before, without error or even hesitation, and to hand them down from generation to generation with equal accuracy, their recollection being only assisted by small pieces of wood corresponding to the different subjects of discourse. On great and solemn occasions, belts of wampum were used as aid to recollection whenever a conference was held with a neighboring tribe, or a treaty or compact is negotiated. One of these belts, differing in some respects from any other hitherto used, was made for the occasion; each person who speaks holds this in his hand by turns, and all he says is recorded in the "living books" of the by-standers' memory in connection with the belt. When the conference ends, this memorial is deposited in the hands of the principal chief. As soon as any important treaty is ratified, a broad wampum belt of unusual splendor is given by each contracting party to the other, and these tokens are deposited among the other belts, that form, as it were, the archives of the nation. At stated intervals they are reproduced before the people, and the events which they commemorate are circumstantially recalled. Certain of the Indian women are intrusted with the care of these belts: it is their duty to relate to the children of the tribe the circumstances of each treaty or conference, and thus is kept alive the remembrance of every important event.

* Catlin gives the following account of a native preacher, known by the name of the Shawnee Prophet: "I soon learned that he was a very devoted Christian, regularly holding meetings in his tribe on the Sabbath, preaching to them, and exhorting them to a belief in the Christian religion, and to an abandonment of the fatal habit of whisky-drinking. I went on the Sabbath to hear this eloquent man preach, when he had his people assembled in the woods; and although I could not understand his language, I was surprised and pleased with the natural ease, and emphasis, and gesticulation which carried their own

On the matters falling within his limited comprehension, the Indian often displays a correct and solid judgment; he pursues his object without hesitation or diversion. He is quickly perceptive of simple facts or ideas, but any artificial combination or mechanical contrivance he is slow to comprehend, especially as he considers every thing beneath his notice which is not necessary to his advantage or enjoyment. It is very difficult to engage him in any labor of a purely mental character, but he often displays vivacity and ardor in matters that interest him, and is frequently quick and happy in repartee.*

evidence of the eloquence of his sermon. I was singularly struck with the noble efforts of this champion of the mere remnant of a poisoned race, so strenuously laboring to rescue the remainder of his people from the deadly bane that has been brought among them by enlightened Christians. It is quite certain that his exemplary endeavors have completely abolished the practice of drinking whisky in his tribe."—Catlin, vol. ii., p. 98.

* "Whatever may be the estimate of the Indian character in other respects, it is with me an undoubting conviction, that they are by nature a shrewd and intelligent race of men, in no wise, as regards combination of thought or quickness of apprehension, inferior to uneducated white men. This inference I deduce from having instructed Indian children.[1] I draw it from having seen the men and women in all situations calculated to try and call forth their capacities. When they examine any of our inventions, steamboats, steam-mills, and cotton factories, for instance; when they contemplate any of our institutions in operation, by some quick analysis or process of reasoning, they seem immediately to comprehend the principle or the object. No spectacle affords them more delight than a large and orderly school. They seem instinctively to comprehend, at least they explained to me that they felt, the advantages which this order of things gave our children over theirs."—Flint's *Ten Years in the Valley of the Mississippi*, 1831.

Mr. Flint, an experienced and intelligent observer, takes so dark a view of the moral character of the Red Indian that his favorable opinion of their mental faculties may be looked upon as probably accurate, though differing strongly from that more generally held. On the other side of the question, among the early writers may be cited M. Bouguer, *Voyage au Pérou*, p. 102; *Voyage d' Ulloa*, tom. i., p. 335–337. "They

[1] All those who have expressed an opinion on the subject seem to agree that *children* of most native races are fully, or more than a match, for those of Europeans, in aptitude for intellectual acquirement. Indeed, it appears to be a singular law of Nature, that there is less precocity in the European race than almost any other. In those races in which we seem to have reason for believing that the intellectual organization is lower, perception is quicker, and maturity earlier.—Merivale *On Colonization*, vol. ii., p. 197.

The Red Man is usually characterized by a certain savage elevation of soul and calm self-possession, that all the aid of religion and philosophy can not enable his civilized brethren to surpass. Master of his emotions, the expression of his countenance rarely alters for a moment even under the most severe and sudden trials. The prisoner, uncertain as to the fate that may befall him, preparing for his dreadful death, or racked by agonizing tortures, still raises his unfaltering voice in the death song, and turns a fearless front toward his tormentors.*

seem to live in a perpetual infancy," is the striking expression of De la Condamine, *Voyage de la Riv. Amazon*, p. 52, 53. Chauvelon, *Voyage à la Martinique*, p. 44, 50. P. Venegas, *Hist. de la Californie.*

* "Thus, on the whole, it may be said that the virtues of the savages are reducible to intrepid courage in danger, unshaken firmness amid tortures, contempt of pain and death, and patience under all the anxieties and distresses of life. No doubt these are useful qualities, but they are all confined to the individual, all selfish, and without any benefit to the society. Farther, they are proofs of a life truly wretched, and a social state so depraved or null, that a man, neither finding nor hoping any succor or assistance from it, is obliged to wrap himself up in despair, and endeavor to harden himself against the strokes of fate. Still it may be urged that these men, in their leisure hours, laugh, sing, play, and live without care for the past as well as for the future. Will you then deny that they are happier than we? Man is such a pitiable and variable creature, and habits have such a potent sway over him, that in the most disastrous situations he always finds some posture that gives him ease, something that consoles him, and, by comparison with past suffering, appears to him well-being and happiness; but if to laugh, sing, or play constitute bliss, it must likewise be granted that soldiers are perfectly happy beings, since there are no men more careless or more gay in dangers or on the eve of battle. It must be granted, too, that during the Revolution, in the most fatal of our jails, the Conciergerie, the prisoners were very happy, since they were, in general, more careless and gay than their keepers, or than those who only feared the same fate. The anxieties of those who were at large were as numerous as the enjoyments they wished to preserve; they who were in the other prisons felt but one, that of preserving their lives. In the Conciergerie, where a man was condemned in expectation or in reality, he had no longer any care; on the contrary, every moment of life was an acquisition, the gain of a good that was considered as lost. Such is nearly the situation of a soldier in war, and such is really that of the savage throughout the whole course of his life. If this be happiness, wretched indeed must be the country where it is an object of envy. In pursuing my investigation, I do not find

The art of numbering was unknown in some American tribes, and even among the most advanced it was very imperfect; the savage had no property to estimate, no coins to count, no variety of ideas to enumerate. Many nations could not reckon above three, and had no words in their language to distinguish a greater number; some proceeded as far as ten, others to twenty; when they desired to convey an idea of a larger amount, they pointed to the hair of the head, or declared that it could not be counted. Computation is a mystery to all rude nations; when, however, they acquire the knowledge of a number of objects, and find the necessity of combining or dividing them, their acquaintance with arithmetic increases; the state of this art is therefore, to a considerable extent, a criterion of their degree of progress. The wise and politic Iroquois had advanced the farthest, but even

that I am led to more advantageous ideas of the liberty of the savage; on the contrary, I see in him only the slave of his wants, and of the freaks of a sterile and parsimonious nature. Food he has not at hand; rest is not at his command; he must run, weary himself, endure hunger and thirst, heat and cold, and all the inclemency of the elements and seasons; and as the ignorance in which he was born and bred gives him or leaves him a multitude of false and irrational ideas and superstitious prejudices, he is likewise the slave of a number of errors and passions, from which civilized man is exempted by the science and knowledge of every kind that an improved state of society has produced." —Volney's *Travels in the United States*, p. 467.

"Their impassible fortitude and endurance of suffering are, after all, in my mind, the result of a greater degree of physical insensibility. It has been told me, and I believe it, that in amputation and other surgical operations, their nerves do not shrink, do not show the same tendency to spasm with those of the whites. When the savage, to explain his insensibility to cold, called upon the white man to recollect how little his own face was affected by it, in consequence of its constant exposure, he added, 'My body is all face.'[1] This increasing insensibility, transmitted from generation to generation, finally becomes inwrought with the whole web of animal nature, and the body of the savage seems to have little more sensibility than the hoofs of horses." —Flint's *Ten Years in the Valley of the Mississippi*. See, also, Ulloa's *Notic. Amer.*, p. 313.

Charlevoix quotes a passage from Cicero to the effect that "l'habitude au travail donne de la facilité à supporter la douleur."—2 *Tusc.*, 25.

[1] Delicacy of skin is observed to be in proportion to civilization among nations, in proportion to degrees of refinement among individuals.—Sharon Turner.

they had not got beyond one thousand; the smaller tribes seldom reached above ten.

The first ideas are suggested to the mind of man by the senses: the Indian acquires no other. The objects around him are all important; if they be available for his present purposes, they attract his attention, otherwise they excite no curiosity: he neither combines nor arranges them, nor does he examine the operations of his own mind upon them; he has no abstract or universal ideas, and his reasoning powers are generally employed upon matters merely obvious to the senses. In the languages of the ruder tribes there were no words to express any thing that is not material, such as faith, time, imagination, and the like. When the mind of the savage is not occupied with matters relating to his animal existence, it is altogether inactive. In the islands, and upon the exuberant plains of the south, where little exertion of ingenuity was required to obtain the necessaries of life, the rational faculties were freqently dormant, and the countenance remained vacant and inexpressive. Even the superior races of the north loiter away their time in thoughtless indolence, when not engaged in war or the chase, deeming other objects unworthy of their consideration. Where reason is so limited in a field for exertion, the mind can hardly acquire any considerable degree of vigor or enlargement. In civilized life men are urged to activity and perseverance by a desire to gratify numerous artificial wants; but the necessities of the Indian are few, and provided for by nature almost spontaneously. He detests labor, and will sometimes sit for whole days together without uttering a word or changing his posture. Neither the hope of reward nor the prospect of future want can overcome this inveterate indolence.

Among the northern tribes, however, dwelling under a rigorous climate, some efforts are employed, and some precautions taken, to procure subsistence; but the necessary industry is even there looked upon as a degradation: the greater part of the labor is performed by women, and man will only stoop to those portions of the work which he considers least ignominious. This industry, so oppressive to one half of the community, is very partial, and directed by a limited foresight. During one part of the year they depend upon fishing for a subsistence, during another upon the chase, and the produce of the ground is their resource for the third. Regardless of the warnings of experience, they neglect to apportion provision for their wants, or can so little restrain their appetites, that, from imprudence or extravagance, they often are exposed to the miseries of famine like their ruder neighbors. Their sufferings are soon forgotten, and the horrors of one year seem to teach no lesson of providence for the next.

The Indians, for the most part, are very well acquainted with the geography of their own country. When questioned as to the situation of any particular place, they will trace out on the ground with a stick, if opportunity offer, a tolerably accurate map of the locality indicated. They will show the course of the rivers, and, by pointing toward the sun, explain the bearings of their rude sketch. There have been recorded some most remarkable instances of the accuracy with which they can travel toward a strange place, even when its description had only been received through the traditions of several generations, and they could have possessed no personal knowledge whatever of the surrounding country.

The religion of the natives of America can not but be regarded with an interest far deeper than the gratification of mere curiosity. The forms of faith, the rites, the ideas of immortality; the belief in future reward, in future punishment; the recognition of an invisible Power, infinitely surpassing that of the warrior or the chief; the dim traditions of a first parent, and a general deluge—all these, among a race so long isolated from the rest of the human family, distinct in language, habits, form, and mind, and displaying, when societies began to exist, a civilization utterly dissimilar from any before known, afford subject for earnest thought and anxious inquiry. Those who in the earlier times of American discovery supplied information on these points, were generally little qualified for the task. Priests and missionaries alone had leisure or inclination to pursue the subject; and their minds were often so preoccupied with their own peculiar doctrines, that they accommodated to them all that fell under their observation, and explained it by analogies which had no existence but in their own zealous imaginations. They seldom attempted to consider what they saw or heard in relation to the rude notions of the savages themselves. From a faint or fancied similarity of peculiar Indian superstitions to certain articles of Christian faith, some missionaries imagined they had discovered traces of an acquaintance with the divine mysteries of salvation: they concluded that the savage possessed a knowledge of the doctrine of the Trinity,* of the Incarnation, of the sacrifice of a Saviour, and of sacraments, from their own interpretation of certain expressions and ceremonies.† But little

* Conical stones, wrapped up in 100 goat skins, were the idols preserved in the temple of the Natchez. Many authors assert that the Amazons and many Eastern people had nothing in their temples but these pyramidal stones, which represented to them the Divinity. . . . . . "Peut-être aussi vouloient ils (les fondateurs des Pyramides) figurer en même tems la Divinité, et ce qui leur restoit d'ideés du mystère de la Sainte Trinité, dans les trois faces de ces pyramides. Du moins est ce ainsi qu'aux Indes un Brame paroissoit concevoir les choses et s'expliquer d'après les anciennes. 'Il faut,' disoit il, 'se réprésenter Dieu et ses trois noms différents qui répondent à ces trois principaux attributs, à peu près sous l'idée de ces Pyramides triangulaires qu'on voit élevées devant la poste de quelques temples."—*Lettre du Père Bouchet à M. Huet, Evêque d'Avranches.* Three logs are always employed to keep up the fire in the Natchez temple.—Lafitau, vol. i., p. 167.

Extract from a dialogue between John Wesley and the Chickasaw Indians:

"*Wesley.* Do you believe there is One above who is over all things?

"*Answer.* We believe there are four beloved things above—the clouds, the sun, the clear sky, and He that lives in the clear sky.

"*Wesley.* Do you believe there is but One who lives in the clear sky?

"*Answer.* We believe there are two with Him, three in all."—Wesley's *Journal*, No. 1., p. 39.

† See Stephens's "Incidents of Travel in Central America," vol. ii., p. 346.

"Les croix qui ont tant excité la curiosité des conquistadores à Coqumel, à Yucatan, et dans d'autres contrées de l'Amerique ne sont pas 'des contes de moines,' et méritent, comme tout ce qui a rapport

confidence can be placed in any evidence derived from such sources.

The earlier travelers in the interior of the New World received the impression that the Indians had no religious belief; they saw neither priests, temples, idols, nor sacrifices among any of the various and numerous tribes. A further knowledge of this strange people disproved the hastily-formed opinion, and showed that their whole life and all their actions were influenced by a belief in the spiritual world.* It is now known that the American Indians were pre-eminent among savage nations for the superior purity of their religious faith,† and, indeed, over even the boasted elegance of poetical

au culte des peuples indigènes du Nouveau Continent, un examen plus sérieux. Je me sers du mot culte, car un relief conservé dans les ruines de Palenque, de Guatemala, et dont je possède une copie, ne me paraît laisser aucun doute qu'une figure symbolique en forme de croix étoit un objet d'adoration. Il faut faire observer cependant qu'à cette croix manque le prolongement supérieur, et qu'elle forme plutôt la lettre *tau*. Des idées qui n'ont aucun rapport avec le Christianisme ont pu être symboliquement attachées à cet emblême Egyptien d'Hermès, si célébre parmi les Chrétiens depuis la destruction du temple de Sérapis à Alexandrie sous Théodose le Grand. (Rufinus, *Hist. Eccles.*, lib. ii., cap. xxix., p. 294; Zozomenes, *Eccl. Hist.*, lib. iii., cap. xv.) Un bâton terminé par une croix se voit dans la main d'Astarté sur les monnaies de Sidon au 3me siècle avant notre ère. En Scandinavie, un signe de l'alphabet *runique* figurait le *marteau de Thor*, très semblable à la croix du relief de Palenque. On marquoit de cette *rune*, dans les tems payens, les objets qu'on vouloit sanctifier." (Voyez l'excellent Traité de M. Guillaume Grimm, *Ueber Deutsche Runen*, p. 242.)—Humboldt, *Géographie de Nouveau Continent*, vol. ii., p. 356.

"Laët avoue qu' Herrera parle d'une espèce de baptême, et de confession usitée dans Yucatan et dans les isles voisines, mais il ajoute qu'il est bien plus naturel d'attribuer toutes ces marques équivoques de Christianisme qu'on a cru apercevoir en plusieurs provinces du Nouveau Monde au démon qui a toujours affecté de contrefaire le culte du vrai Dieu." Charlevoix adds, "Cette remarque est de tous les bons auteurs qui ont parlé de la religion des peuples nouvellement découverts, et fondée sur l'autorité des pères de l'Eglise."—Charlevoix, tom. v., p. 28.

* See Appendix, No. LI.

† "The most sensual, degraded, and least intellectual tribes of Northern Asia and America have purer notions of a Spiritual Deity than were possessed of old by the worshipers of Jupiter and Juno under Pericles."—*Progression by Antagonism.*

mythology. From the reports of all those worthy of credence, who have lived intimately among these children of the forest, it is certain that they firmly believe in the power and unity of the Most High God, and in an immortality of happiness or misery. They worship the Great Spirit, the Giver of life, and attribute to him the creation of the world, and the government of all things with infinite love, wisdom, and power. Of the origin of their religion they are altogether ignorant. In general they believe that, after the world was created and supplied with animal life by the Great Spirit, he formed the first red man and woman, who were very large of stature, and lived to an extreme old age; that he often held council with his creatures, gave them laws and instructed them, but that the red children became rebels against their Great Father, and he then withdrew himself in sorrowful anger from among them, and left them to the vexations of the Bad Spirit. But still this merciful Father, from afar off, where he may be seen no more, showers down upon them all the blessings they enjoy. The Indians are truly filial and sincere in their devotions; they pray for what they need, and return hearty thanks for such mercies as they have enjoyed.* They supplicate him to

This, according to Lord Lindsay's theory, is to be accounted for by the absence of imagination, these nations being only governed by Sense and Spirit, to the exclusion of intellect in either of its manifestations, Imagination, or Reason.—P. 21, 26.

* "At the breaking up of the winter," says Hunter, "after having supplied ourselves with such things as were necessary and the situation afforded, all our party visited the spring from which we had procured our supplies of water, and there offered up our orisons to the Great Spirit for having preserved us in health and safety, and for having supplied all our wants. This is the constant practice of the Osages, Kansas, and many other nations of Indians on breaking up their encampments, and is by no means an unimportant ceremony." The habitual piety of the Indian mind is remarked by Heckewelder, and strongly insisted upon by Hunter, and it is satisfactorily proved by the whole tenor of his descriptions, where he throws himself back, as it were, into the feelings peculiar to Indian life. And, indeed, after hearing at a council the broken fragments of an Indian harangue, however imperfectly rendered by an ignorant interpreter, or reading the few specimens of Indian oratory which have been preserved by translation, no one can fail to remark a perpetual and earnest reference

bestow courage and skill upon them in the battle; the endurance which enables them to mock the cruel tortures of their enemies is attributed to his aid; their preparation for war is a long-continued religious ceremony; their march is supposed to be under omnipotent guidance, and their expeditions in the chase are held to be not unworthy of divine superintendence. They reject all idea of chance on the fortune of war, and believe firmly that every result is the decision of a Superior Power.* Although this elevated conception of the One God† is deeply impressed upon the Indian's mind, it is tainted with some of the alloy which ever must characterize the uninspired faith. Those who have inquired into the religious opinions of the uneducated and laborious classes of men, even in the most enlightened and civilized communities, find that their system of belief is derived from instruction, and not from instinct or the results of their own

to the power and goodness of the Deity. "Brothers! we all belong to one family; we are all children of the Great Spirit," was the commencement of Tecumthé's harangue to the Osages; and he afterward tells them: "When the white men first set foot on our grounds, they were hungry; they had no places on which to spread their blankets or to kindle their fires. They were feeble; they could do nothing for themselves. Our fathers commiserated their distress, and shared freely with them whatever the Great Spirit has given to his red children."—*Quarterly Review.*

* On the remarkable occasion on which our forces were compelled, in 1813, to evacuate the Michigan territory, Tecumthé, in the name of his nation, refused to consent to retreat; he closed his denial with these words: "Our lives are in the hand of the Great Spirit: He gave the lands which we possess to our fathers; if it be his will, our bones shall whiten upon them, but we will never quit them." An old Oneida chief, who was blind from years, observed to Heckewelder, "I am an aged hemlock; the winds of one hundred years have whistled through my branches; I am dead at the top. Why I yet live, the great, good Spirit only knows." This venerable father of the forest lived long enough to be converted to Christianity.—*Quarterly Review.*

† A Huron woman under the instruction of a missionary, who detailed to her the perfections of God, exclaimed, in a species of ecstasy, "I understand, I understand; and I always felt convinced that our Areskoui was exactly such a one as the God you have described to me."—Lafitau, tom. i., p. 127. The Great Spirit was named Areskoui among the Hurons, Agriskoué among the Iroquois, Manitou among the Algonquins.

examination: in savage life it is vain to expect that men should reason accurately, from cause to effect, and form a just idea of the Creator from the creation. The Indian combines the idea of the Great Spirit with others of a less perfect nature. The word used by him to indicate this Sovereign Being does not convey the notion of an immaterial nature; it signifies with him some one possessed of lofty and mysterious powers, and in this sense may be applied to men and even to animals.

To the first inquirers into the religious faith of the native Americans, the subject of their mythology presented very great difficulties and complications; those Indians who attempted to explain it to Europeans had themselves no distinct or fixed opinions. Each man put forward peculiar notions, and was constantly changing them, without attempting to reconcile his self-contradictions.

Some of the southern tribes, who were more settled in their religious faith, exhibited a remarkable degree of bigotry and spiritual pride. They called the Europeans "men of the accursed speech," while they styled themselves "the beloved of the Great Spirit." The Canadian and other northern nations, however, were less intolerant, and at any time easily induced to profess the recantation of their heathen errors for some small advantage. Among these latter, the hare was deemed to possess some mystic superiority over the rest of the animal creation; it was even raised to be an object of worship, and the Great Hare was confounded in their minds with the Great Spirit. The Algonquins believed in a Water God, who opposes himself to the benevolent designs of the Great Spirit; it is strange that the name of the Great Tiger should be given to this Deity, as the country does not produce such an animal, and from this it appears probable that the tradition of his existence had come from elsewhere. They have also a third Deity, who presides over their winter season. The gods of the Indians have bodies like the sons of men, and subsist in like manner with them, but are free from the pains and cares of mortality; the term "spirit" among them only signifies a being of a superior and more excellent nature than man. However, they believe in the omnipresence of their deities, and invoke their aid in all times and places.

Besides the Great Spirit and the lesser deities above mentioned, every Indian has his own Manitou, Okki, or guardian power; this divinity's presence is represented by some portable object, often of the most insignificant nature, such as the head, beak, or claw of a bird, the hoof of a deer or cow. No youth can be received among the brotherhood of warriors till he has placed himself, in due form, under the care of this familiar. The ceremony is deemed of great importance: several days of strict fasting are always observed in preparation for the important event, and the youth's dreams are carefully noted during this period. While under these circumstances, some object usually makes a deep impression upon his mind; this is then chosen for his Manitou or guardian spirit, and a specimen of it is procured. He is next placed for some time in a large vapor bath, and having undergone the process of being steamed, is laid on the ground, and the figure of the Manitou is pricked on his breast with needles of fish-bone dipped in vermilion; the intervals between the scars are then rubbed with gunpowder, so as to produce a mixture of red and blue. When this operation is performed, he cries aloud to the Great Spirit, invoking aid, and praying to be received as a warrior.

The Indian submits with resignation to the chastening will of the Great Spirit. When overtaken by any disaster, he diligently examines himself to discover what omission of observance or duty has called down the punishment, and endeavors to atone for past neglect by increased devotion. But if the Manitou be deemed to have shown want of ability or inclination to defend him, he upbraids the guardian power with bitterness and contempt, and threatens to seek a more effectual protector. If the Manitou continue useless, this threat is fulfilled. Fasting and dreaming are again resorted to in the same manner as before, and the vision of another Manitou is obtained. The former representation is then, as much as possible, effaced, and the figure of the newly-adopted amulet painted in its place. All the veneration and confidence forfeited by the first Manitou is now transferred to the successor.*

It is also part of the Indian's religious belief that there are inferior spirits to rule over the elements, under the control of the Supreme Power, he being so great that he must, like their chiefs, have attendants to execute his behests. These inferior spirits see what passes on earth, and report it to their Great Ruler: the Indian, trusting to their good offices, invokes these spirits of the air in times of peril, and endeavors to propitiate them by throwing tobacco or other simple offerings to the winds or upon the waters. But, amid all these corrupt and ignorant superstitions, the One Spirit, the Creator and Ruler of the World, is the great object of the Red Man's adoration. On him they rest their hopes; to him they address their daily prayers, and render their solemn sacrifice.

The worship of the Indians, although frequently in private, is generally little regulated either by ceremonies or stated periodical devotions. But there are, at times, great occasions, when the whole tribe assembles for the purpose,† such as in declaring war or proclaiming peace, or when visited by storms or earthquakes. Their great feasts all partake of a religious character; every thing provided must be consumed by the assembly, as being consecrated to the Great Spirit. The Ottawas seem to have had a more complicated mythology than any other tribe: they held a regular festival in honor of the sun; and, while rendering thanks for past benefit, prayed that it might be continued to the future. They have also been observed to erect an idol in their village, and offer it sacrifice: this ceremony was, however, very rare. Many Western tribes visit the

* See Appendix, No. LII.

† Every spring the Arkansas go in a body to some retired place, and there turn up a large space of land, which they do with the drums beating all the while. After this they call it the *Desart*, or the Field of the Spirit, and thither they go when they are in their enthusiastic fits, and there wait for inspiration from their pretended deity. In the mean while, as they do this every year, it proves of no small advantage to them, for by this means they turn up all their land by degrees, and it becomes abundantly more fruitful.—Tonti.

spring whence they have been supplied with water during the winter, at the breaking up of the ice, and there offer up their grateful worship to the Great Spirit for having preserved them in health and safety, and having supplied their wants. This pious homage is performed with much ceremony and devotion.

Among this rude people, who were at one time supposed to have been without any religion, habitual piety may be considered the most remarkable characteristic: every action of their lives is connected with some acknowledgment of a Superior Power. Many have imagined that the severe fasts sometimes endured by the Indians were only for the purpose of accustoming themselves to support hunger; but all the circumstances connected with these voluntary privations leave no doubt that they were solemn religious exercises. Dreams and visions during these fasts were looked upon as oracular, and respected as the revelations of Heaven. The Indian frequently propitiates the favor of the inferior spirits by vows; when for some time unsuccessful in the chase, or suffering from want in long journeys, he promises the genius of the spot to bestow upon one of his chiefs, in its honor, a portion of the first fruits of his success;* if the chief be too distant to receive the gift, it is burned in sacrifice.

The belief of the Indian in a future state, although deeply cherished and sincere, can scarcely be regarded as a defined idea of the immortality of the soul.† There is little spiritual or exalted in his conception. When he attempts to form a distinct notion of the spirit, he is blinded by his senses; he

* Lafitau asserts that the first beast killed by a young hunter was always offered in sacrifice.—Vol. i., p. 515. See Catlin's description of the sacrifices and ceremonies practiced when the first fruits of corn are ripe.—Catlin, vol. i., p. 189.

† Peter Martyr speaks of the general opinion among the early discoverers that the Indians believed in a species of immortality. "They confess the soul to be immortal; having put off the bodily clothing, they imagine it goeth forth to the woods and the mountains, and that it liveth there perpetually in caves; nor do they exempt it from eating or drinking, but that it should be fed there. The answering voices heard from caves and hollows, which the Latines call echoes, they suppose to be the souls of the departed wandering through those places."—Peter Martyr, Decad. VIII., cap. ix., M. Lock's translation, 1612.

calls it the shadow or image of his body, but its acts and enjoyments are all the same as those of its earthly existence. He only pictures to himself a continuation of present pleasures. His Heaven is a delightful country, far away beyond the unknown Western seas, where the skies are ever bright and serene, the air genial, the spring eternal, and the forests abounding in game; no war, disease, or torture are known in that happy land; the sufferings of life are endured no more, and its sweetest pleasures are perpetuated and increased; his wife is tender and obedient, his children dutiful and affectionate. In this country of eternal happiness, the Indian hopes to be again received into the favor of the Great Spirit, and to rejoice in his glorious presence.* But in his simple mind there is a deep and enduring conviction that admission to this delightful country of souls can only be attained by good and noble actions in this mortal life. For the bad men there is a fate terribly different—endless afflictions, want, and misery; a land of hideous desolation; barren, parched, and dreary hunting-grounds, the abode of evil and malignant spirits, whose office is to torture, whose pleasure is to enhance the misery of the condemned. It is also almost universally believed that the Great Spirit manifests his wrath or his favor to the evil and the good in their journey to the land of souls. After death the Indian believes that he is supplied with a canoe; and if he has been a virtuous warrior, or otherwise worthy, he is guided across the vast deep to a haven

* "Une jeune sauvagesse voyant sa sœur mourante, par la quantité de ciguë qui elle avoit pris dans un dépit, et determiné à ne faire aucun remède pour se garantir de la mort, pleuroit à chaudes larmes, et s'efforçoit de la toucher par les liens du sang, et de l'amitié qui les unissoit ensemble. Elle lui disoit sans cesse, 'C'en est donc fait; tu veux que nous ne nous retrouvions jamais plus, et que nous ne nous revoyions jamais?' Le missionnaire, frappé de ces paroles, lui en demanda la raison. 'Il me semble,' dit-il, 'que vous avez un pays des âmes, où vous devez tous vous reünir à vos ancêtres; pourquoi donc est ce que tu parles ainsi à la sœur?' 'Il est vrai,' reprit-elle, 'que nous allons tous au pays des âmes; mais les mechants, et ceux en particulier, qui se sont dêtruits eux-mêmes par un mort violente, y portent la peine de leur crime; ils y sont séparés des autres, et n'ont point de communication avec eux: c'est là le sujet de mes peines.'"—Lafitau, tom. i., p. 404. See Appendix, LII.

of eternal happiness and peace by the hand of the Great Spirit; but if his life be stained with cowardice, vice, or negligence of duty, he is abandoned to the malignity of evil genii, driven about by storms and darkness over that unknown sea, and at length cast ashore on the barren land, where everlasting torments are his portion.*

The Indians generally believe in the existence of a Spirit of Evil, and occasionally pray to him in deprecation of his wrath. They do not doubt his inferiority to the Great Spirit, but they believe that he has the power to inflict torments and punishments upon the human race, and that he has a malignant delight in its exercise.

The souls of the lower animals are also held by the Red Man to be immortal: he recognizes a certain portion of understanding in them, and each creature is supposed to possess a guardian spirit peculiar to itself. He only claims a superiority in degree of intelligence and power over the beasts of the field. Man is but the king of animals. In the world of souls are to be found the shades of every thing

* Hunter gives the following view of the Indian mythology, while describing his own and his companions' first sight of the Pacific Ocean: "Here the surprise and astonishment of our whole party was indescribably great. The unbounded view of waters, the incessant and tremendous dashing of the waves along the shore, accompanied with a noise resembling the roar of loud and distant thunder, filled our minds with the most sublime and awful sensation, and fixed on them as immutable truths the tradition we had received from our old men, that the great waters divide the residence of the Great Spirit from the temporary abodes of his red children. We have contemplated in silent dread the immense difficulties over which we should be obliged to triumph after death before we could arrive at those delightful hunting-grounds, which are unalterably destined for such only as do good, and love the Great Spirit. We looked in vain for the stranded and shattered canoes of those who had done wickedly; we could see none, and were led to hope they were few in number. We offered up our devotions, or, I might say, our minds were serious, and our devotions continued all the time we were in this country, for we had ever been taught to believe that the Great Spirit resided on the western side of the Rocky Mountains; and this idea continued throughout the journey, notwithstanding the more specific boundary assigned to Him by our traditionary dogmas."—*Memoirs of a Captivity among the North American Indians from Childhood to the Age of Nineteen.* By John D. Hunter, p. 69. 1824.—See Appendix, No. LIII.

that breathes the breath of life. However, he takes little pains to arrange or develop these strange ideas. The enlightened heathen philosophers of antiquity were not more successful.

To penetrate the mysteries of the future has always been a favorite object of superstition,* and has been attempted by a countless variety of means. The Indian trusts to his dreams for this revelation, and invariably holds them sacred. Before he engages in any important undertaking, particularly in war, diplomacy, or the chase, the dreams of his principal chiefs are carefully watched and examined; by their interpretation his conduct is guided. In this manner the fate of a whole nation has often been decided by the chance visions of a single man. The Indian considers that dreams are the mode by which the Great Spirit condescends to hold converse with man; thence arises his deep veneration for the omens and warnings they may shadow forth.†

Many other superstitions, besides those of prognostics from dreams, are cherished among the Indians. Each remarkable natural feature, such as a great cataract, a lake, or a difficult and dangerous pass, possesses a spirit of the spot, whose favor they are fain to propitiate by votive offerings: skins, bones, pieces of metal, and dead dogs are hung up in the neighborhood, and dedicated to its honor. Supposed visions of ghosts are sometimes, but rarely, spoken of: it is, however, generally believed that the souls of the dead continue for some time to hover round the earthly remains: dreading, therefore, that the spirits of those they have tortured watch near them to seek opportunity of vengeance, they beat the air violently with rods, and raise frightful cries to scare the shadowy enemy away.

Among some of the Indian tribes, an old man performed the duty of a priest at their religious festivals; he broke the bread and cast it in the fire, dedicated the different offerings, and officiated in the sacrifice. It was also his calling to declare the omens from dreams and other signs, as the warnings of Heaven. These religious duties of the priest were totally distinct from the office of the juggler, or "medicine-

* See Appendix, No. LIV. † See Appendix, No. LV.

man," although some observers have confounded them together. There were also vestals in many nations of the continent who were supposed to supply by their touch a precious medicinal efficacy to certain roots and simples.

The "medicine-men," or jugglers, undertook the cure of diseases, the interpretation of omens, the exorcising of evil spirits, and magic in all its branches. They were men of great consideration in the tribe, and were called in and regularly paid as physicians; but this position could only be attained by undergoing certain ordeals, which were looked upon as a compact with the spirits of the air. The process of the vapor bath was first endured; severe fasting followed, accompanied by constant shouting, singing, beating a sort of drum, and smoking. After these preliminaries the jugglers were installed by extravagant ceremonies, performed with furious excitement and agitation. They possessed, doubtless, some real knowledge of the healing art; and in external wounds or injuries, the causes of which are obvious, they applied powerful simples, chiefly vegetable, with considerable skill. With decoctions from ginseng, sassafras, hedisaron, and a tall shrub called bellis, they have been known to perform remarkable cures in cases of wounds and ulcers. They scarified the seat of inflammation or rheumatic pain skillfully with sharp-pointed bones, and accomplished the cupping process by the use of gourd shells as substitutes for glasses. For all internal complaints, their favorite specific was the vapor bath, which they formed with much ingenuity from their rude materials. This was doubtless a very efficient remedy, but they attached to it a supernatural influence, and employed it in the ceremonies of solemn preparation for great councils.

All cases of disease, when the cause could not be discovered, were attributed to the influence of malignant spirits. To meet these, the medicine-man, or juggler, invested himself with his mysterious character, and endeavored to exorcise the demon by a great variety of ceremonies, a mixture of delusion and imposture. For this purpose, he arrayed himself in a strange and fanciful dress, and on his first arrival began to sing and dance round the sufferer, invoking the spirits with loud cries. When exhausted with these exertions, he attributed the hidden cause of the malady to the first unusual idea that suggested itself to his mind, and in the confidence of his supposed inspiration, proclaimed the necessary cure. The juggler usually contrived to avoid the responsibility of failure by ordering a remedy impossible of attainment when the patient was not likely to recover. The Iroquois believed that every ailment was a desire of the soul, and, when death followed, it was from the desire not having been accomplished.

Among many of the Indian tribes, the barbarous custom of putting to death those who were thought past recovery, existed, and still exists. Others abandoned these unfortunates to perish of hunger and thirst, or under the jaws of the wild beasts of the forest. Some nations put to death all infants who had lost their mother, or buried them alive in her grave, under the impression that no other woman could rear them, and that they must perish by hunger. But the dreadful custom of deserting the aged and emaciated among the wandering tribes is universal.* When these miserable creatures become incapable of walking or riding, and there is no means of carrying them, they themselves uniformly insist upon being abandoned to their fate, saying that they are old and of no further use—they left their fathers in the same manner—they wish to die, and their children must not mourn for them. A small fire and a few pieces of wood, a scanty supply of meat, and perhaps a buffalo skin, are left as the old man's sole resources. When in a few months the wandering tribe may revisit the spot where he was deserted, a skull and a few scattered bones will be all that the wolves and vultures have left as tokens of his dreadful fate.

The Indian father and mother display great tenderness for their children,† even to the weakness of unlimited indul-

* See Appendix, No. LVI.

† "While I remained among the Indians, a couple, whose tent was adjacent to mine, lost a son of four years of age. The parents were so much affected at the death of their child, that they observed the usual testimonies of grief with such extreme rigor as through the

gence; this affection, however, appears to be merely instinctive, for they use no exertion whatever to lead their offspring to the paths of virtue. Children, on their part, show very little filial affection, and frequently treat their parents, especially their father, with indignity and violence. This vicious characteristic is strongly exemplified in the horrible custom above described.

When the Indian believes that his death is at hand, his conduct is usually stoical and dignified. If he still retain the power of speech, he harangues those who surround him in a funeral oration, advising and encouraging his children, and bidding them and all his friends farewell. During this time, the relations of the dying man slay all the dogs they can catch, trusting that the souls of these animals will give notice of the approaching departure of the warrior for the world of spirits; they then take leave of him, wish him a happy voyage, and cheer him with the hope that his children will prove worthy of his name. When the last moment arrives, all the kindred break into loud lamentations, till some one high in consideration desires them to cease. For weeks afterward, however, these cries of grief are daily renewed at sunrise and sunset. In three days after death the funeral takes place, and the neighbors are invited to a feast of all the provisions that can be procured, which must be all consumed. The relations of the deceased do not join in the banquet; they cut off their hair, cover their heads, blacken

weight of sorrow and loss of blood to occasion the loss of the father. The woman, who had hitherto been inconsolable, no sooner saw her husband expire than she dried up her tears, and appeared cheerful and resigned. I took an opportunity of asking her the reason of so extraordinary a transition, when she informed me that her child was so young it would have been unable to support itself in the world of spirits, and both she and her husband were apprehensive that its situation would be far from happy. No sooner, however, did she behold her husband depart for the same place, who not only loved the child with the tenderest affection, but was a good hunter, and would be able to provide plentifully for its support, than she ceased to mourn. She said she had now no reason to continue her tears, as the child on whom she doted was under the care and protection of a fond father, and she had now only one wish remaining ungratified, that of herself being with them."—Carver.

their faces, and for a long time deny themselves every amusement.*

The deceased is buried with his arms and ornaments, and a supply of provisions for his long journey; the face is painted, and the body arrayed in the richest robes that can be obtained; it is then laid in the grave in an upright posture, and skins are carefully placed around, that it may not touch the earth. At stated intervals of eight, ten, or twelve years, the Indians celebrate the singular ceremony of the Festival of the Dead; till this has been performed, the souls of the deceased are supposed still to hover round their earthly remains. At this solemn festival, the people march in procession to the burial-ground, open the tombs, and continue for a time gazing on the moldering relics in mournful silence. Then, while the women raise a loud wailing, the bones of the dead are carefully collected, wrapped in fresh and valuable robes, and conveyed to the family cabin.† A feast is then held for several days, with dances, games, and prize combats. The relics are next carried to the council-house of the nation, where they are publicly displayed, with the

* Captain Franklin says of the Chippewyans, "No article is spared by these unhappy men when a near relative dies; their clothes and tents are cut to pieces, their guns broken, and every other weapon rendered useless if some person do not remove these articles from their sight."

"When the French missionaries asked the Indians why they deprived themselves of their most necessary articles in favor of the dead, they answered, 'that it was not only to evidence their love for their departed relatives, but that they might avoid the sight of objects which, having been used by them, would continually renew their grief.' The same delicacy of feeling, so inconsistent with the coarseness of the Red Man's nature, was manifested in their custom of never uttering the names of the dead; and if these names were borne by any of the other members of the family, they laid them aside during the whole of their mourning. And it was esteemed the greatest insult that could be offered to say to any one, 'Your father is dead, your mother is dead.'"—Charlevoix, tom. vi., p. 109.

† Père Brébeuf, *Relation de la Nouvelle France;* Charlevoix; Lafitau. Catlin describes the same ceremonies.

It has been often said that the care taken by the Indians for the deceased corpses of their ancestors was in consequence of a universally received tradition that these corpses were to rise again to immortal life.

presents destined to be interred with them. Sometimes the remains are even carried on bearers from village to village. At length they are laid in a deep pit, lined with rich furs; tears and lamentations are again renewed, and for some time fresh provisions are daily laid, by this simple people, upon the graves of their departed friends.

CHAPTER VIII.

In the warmer and milder climates of America, none of the rude tribes were clothed; for them there was little need of defense against the weather, and their extreme indolence indisposed them to any exertion not absolutely necessary for their subsistence. Others were satisfied with a very slight covering, but all delighted in ornaments. They dressed their hair in different forms, stained their skins, and fastened bits of gold, or shells, or bright pebbles in their noses and cheeks. They also frequently endeavored to alter their natural form and feature; as soon as an infant was born, it was subjected to some cruel process of compression, by which the bones of the skull while still soft, were squeezed into the shape of a cone, or flattened, or otherwise distorted.*

* "The custom of squeezing and flattening the head is still strictly adhered to among the Chinooks. The people bearing the name of Flat Heads are very numerous, but very few among them actually practice the custom. Among the Chinooks it is almost universal. The process is thus effected: The child is placed on a thick plank, to which it is lashed with thongs to a position from which it can not escape, and the back of the head supported by a sort of pillow made of moss or rabbit-skins, with an inclined piece resting on the forehead of the child. This is every day drawn down a little tighter by means of a cord, which holds it in its place, until at length it touches the nose, thus forming a straight line from the crown of the head to the end of the nose. This process is seemingly a cruel one, though I doubt whether it causes much pain, as it is done in earliest infancy, while the bones are soft and cartilaginous, and easily pressed into this distorted shape by forcing the occipital up and the frontal down, so that the skull at the top in profile will show a breadth of not more

But in all efforts to adorn or alter their persons, the great object was to inspire terror and respect. The warrior was

than an inch and a half or two inches, when in a front view it exhibits a great expansion on the sides, making it at the top nearly the width of one and a half natural heads. By this remarkable operation the brain is singularly changed from its natural state, but in all probability not in the least diminished or injured in its natural functions. This belief is drawn from the testimony of many credible witnesses who have closely scrutinized them, and ascertained that those who have the head flattened are in no way inferior in intellectual powers to those whose heads are in their natural shapes. This strange custom existed precisely the same until recently among the Choctaws and Chickasaws, who occupied a large part of the states of Mississippi and Alabama, where they have laid their bones, and hundreds of their skulls have been procured, bearing marks of a similar treatment, with similar results."—Catlin's *American Indians*, vol. ii., p. 112.

With respect to the origin of this singular custom, Humboldt is inclined to think that it may be traced from the natural inclination of each race to look upon their own personal peculiarities as the standard of beauty. He observes that the pointed form of the heads is very striking in the Mexican drawings, and continues thus: "If we examine osteologically the skulls of the natives of America, we see that there is no race on the globe in which the frontal bone is more flattened or which have less forehead.[1] (Blumenbach, *Decas Quinta Craniorum*, tab. xlvi., p. 14, 1808.) This extraordinary flattening exists among people of the copper-colored race, who have never been acquainted with the custom of producing artificial deformities, as is proved by the skulls of Mexican, Peruvian, and Aztec Indians, which M. Bonpland and myself brought to Europe, and several of which are deposited in the Museum of Natural History at Paris. The negroes prefer the thickest and most prominent lips, the Calmucks perceive the line of beauty in turned-up noses. M. Cuvier observes (*Leçons d'Anatomie Comparée*, tom. ii., p. 6) that the Grecian artists, in the statues of heroes, raised the facial line from 85° to 100°, or beyond the natural form. I am led to think that the barbarous custom, among certain savage tribes in America, of squeezing the heads of children between two planks, arises from the idea that beauty consists in this extraordinary compression of the bone by which Nature has characterized the American race. It is no doubt from following this standard of beauty that even the Aztec people, who never disfigured the heads of their children, have represented their heroes and principal divinities with heads much flatter than any of the Caribs I saw on the Lower Orinoco."—Humboldt's *Researches on the Ancient Inhabitants of America.*

[1] "L'anatomine comparée en offre une autre confirmation dans la proportion constante du volume des lobes cérébrales avec le degré d'intelligence des animaux."—Cuvier's *Report to the Institute on Flouren's Experiments in* 1822.

indifferent to the admiration of woman, whom he enslaved and despised, and it was only for war or the council that he assumed his choicest ornaments, and painted himself with unusual care. The decorations of the women were few and simple; all those that were precious and splendid were reserved for their haughty lords. In several tribes, the wives had to devote much of their time to adorning their husbands, and could bestow little attention upon themselves. The different nations remaining unclothed show considerable sagacity in anointing themselves in such a manner as to provide against the heat and moisture of the climate. Soot, the juices of herbs having a green, yellow, or vermilion tint, mixed with oil and grease, are lavishly employed upon their skin to adorn it and render it impervious. By this practice profuse perspiration is checked, and a defense is afforded against the innumerable and tormenting insects that abound every where in America.* Black and

* "Ces huiles leur sont absolument nécéssaires, et ils sont mangés de vermine quand elles leur manquent."—Lafitau, tom. i., p. 59.

It is supposed by Volney that the fatal effects of the small-pox among the Indians are to be attributed to the obstacle that a skin thus hardened opposes to the eruption.—P. 416. In the most detailed account given of the ravages of this disease, Catlin particularly mentions that no eruption was visible in any of the bodies of the dead. Forster, the English translator of Professor Kalm's *Travels in America*, held the same opinion as Volney.

"When the Kalmucks in the Russian dominions get the small-pox, it has been observed that very few escape. Of this, I believe, no other reason can be alleged than that the small-pox is always dangerous, either when the open pores of the skin are too numerous, which is caused by opening them in a warm-water bath, or when they are too much closed, which is the case with all the nations that are dirty and greasy. All the American Indians rub their body with oils; the Kalmucks rub their bodies and their fur coats with grease; the Hottentots are also, I believe, patterns of filthiness: this shuts up all the pores, hinders perspiration entirely, and makes the small-pox always fatal among these nations."—*Note* by the translator of Kalm, p. 532.

"The ravages which the small-pox made this year (1750) among their Mohawk friends was a source of deep concern to these revered philanthropists. These people having been accustomed from early childhood to anoint themselves with bear's grease, to repel the innumerable tribes of noxious insects in summer, and to exclude the

red are the favorite colors for painting the face. In war, black is profusely laid on, the other colors being only used to heighten its effect, and give a terrible expression to the countenance.* The breast, arms, and legs of the Indian are tattooed with sharp needles or pointed bones, the colors being carefully rubbed in. His Manitou, and the animal chosen as the symbol of his tribe, are first painted, then all his most remarkable exploits, and the enemies he has slain or scalped, so that his body displays a pictorial history of his life.†

In the severe climate of the north the Indian's dress is somewhat more ample. Instead of shoes he wears a strip of soft leather wrapped round the foot, called the moccasin. Upward to the middle of the thigh, a piece of leather or cloth, fitting closely, serves instead of pantaloons and stockings: it is usually sewed on to the limb, and is never removed. Two aprons, each about a foot square, are fastened to a girdle round the waist, and hang before and behind. This is their permanent dress. On occasions of ceremony, however, and in cold weather, they also wear a short shirt, and over all a loose robe, closed or held together in front. Now, an English blanket is generally used for this garment; but, before the produce of European art was known among them, the skins of wild animals furnished all their covering. The

extreme cold in winter, their pores are so completely shut up that the small-pox does not rise upon them, nor have they much chance of recovery from any acute disorder."—*Memoirs of an American Lady*, vol. i., p. 322.

* M. de Tracy, when governor of Canada, was told by his Indian allies that, with his good-humored face, he would never inspire the enemy with any degree of awe. They besought him to place himself under their brush, when they would soon make him such that his very aspect would strike terror.—Creuxius, *Nova Francia*, p. 62; Charlevoix, tom. vi., p. 40.

† St. Isidore of Seville, and Solinus, give a similar description of the manner of painting the body in use among the Picts. "The operator delineates the figures with little points made by the prick of a needle, and into these he insinuates the juice of some native plants, that their nobility, thus written, as it were, upon every limb of their body, might distinguish them from ordinary men by the number of the figures they were decorated with."—Isidor., *Origin.*, lib. xix., cap. xxiii.; Solin., *De Magnâ Britanniâ*, cap. xxv.

chiefs usually wear a sort of breast-plate, covered with shells, pebbles, and pieces of glittering metal. Those who communicate with Europeans display beads, rings, bracelets, and other gauds instead. The ear, too, is cumbrously ornamented with showy pendents, and the tuft of hair on the crown of the head is interwoven with feathers, the wings of birds, shells, and many fantastic ornaments. Sometimes the Indian warrior wears buffalo horns,* reduced in size and polished, on his head: this, however, is a distinction only for those renowned in war or in the council. The dress of the women varies but little from that of the men, except in being more simple. They wear their hair long and flowing, and richly ornamented, whenever they can procure the means.

* "These horns are made of about a third part of the horn of a buffalo bull, the horn having been split from end to end, and a third part of it taken, and shaved thin and light, and highly polished. They are attached to the top or the head-dress on each side, in the same place as they rise and stand on the head of a buffalo, rising out of a mat of ermine skins and tails, which hangs over the top of the head-dress somewhat in the form that the large and profuse locks of hair hang and fall over the head of a buffalo bull. This custom is one which belongs to all northeastern tribes, and is no doubt of very ancient origin, having purely a classic meaning. No one wears the head-dress surmounted with horns except the dignitaries who are very high in authority, and whose exceeding valor, worth, and power is admitted by all the nation. This head-dress is used only on certain occasions, and they are very seldom: when foreign chiefs, Indian agents, or other important personages visit a tribe, or at war parades. Sometimes, when a chief sees fit to send a war party to battle, he decorates his head with this symbol of power, to stimulate his men, and throws himself into the foremost of the battle, inviting the enemy to concentrate his shafts upon them. The horns upon these head-dresses are but loosely attached at the bottom, so that they easily fall backward or forward; and by an ingenious motion of the head, which is so slight as to be almost imperceptible, they are made to balance to and fro, and sometimes one backward and the other forward like a horse's ears, giving a vast deal of expression and force of character to the appearance of the chief who is wearing them. This is a remarkable instance, like hundreds of others, of a striking similarity to Jewish customs, to the kerns (or *keren*, in Hebrew), the horns worn by the Abyssinian chiefs and Hebrews as a symbol of power and command —worn at great parades and celebrations of victories."—Catlin, vol. i., p. 104.

The dwellings of the Indians usually receive much less attention than their personal appearance. Even among tribes comparatively far advanced in civilization, the structure of their houses or cabans was very rude and simple. They were generally wretched huts, of an oblong or circular form, and sometimes so low that it was always necessary to preserve a sitting or lying posture while under their shelter. There were no windows; a large hole in the center of the roof allowed the smoke to escape; and a sort of curtain of birch bark occupied the place of the door. These dwellings are sometimes 100 feet long, when they accommodate several families. Four cabans generally form a quadrangle, each open to the inside, with the fire in the center common to all. The numerous and powerful tribes formerly inhabiting Canada and its borders usually dwelt in huts of a very rude description. In their expeditions, both for war and the chase, the Indians erect temporary cabans in a remarkably short space of time. A few poles, raised in the shape of a cone, and covered with birch bark, form the roof, and the tops of pine branches make a fragrant bed. In winter the snow is cleared out of the place where the caban is to be raised, and shaped into walls, which form a shelter from the wind. The permanent dwellings were usually grouped in villages, surrounded with double and even triple rows of palisades, interlaced with branches of trees, so as to form a compact barrier, and offering a considerable difficulty to an assailing foe.

The furniture in these huts was very scanty. The use of metal being unknown, the pots or vessels for boiling their food were made of coarse earthen-ware, or of soft stone hollowed out with a hatchet. In some cases they were made of wood, and the water was boiled by throwing in a number of heated stones.

The Indian displays some skill in the construction of canoes, and they are admirably adapted for his purpose. They are usually made of the bark of a single tree, strengthened by ribs of strong wood. These light and buoyant skiffs float safely on stormy or rapid waters under the practiced guidance of the Indian, and can with ease be borne on his shoulder from one river or lake to another. Canoes formed out of the trunk of a large tree are also sometimes used, especially in winter, for the purpose of crossing rivers when there is floating ice, their great strength rendering them capable of enduring the collision with the floating masses, to which they are liable.

Even among the rudest Indian tribes a regular union between man and wife was universal, although not attended with ceremonials. The marriage contract is a matter of purchase. The man buys his wife of her parents; not with money, for its value is unknown, but with some useful and precious article, such as a robe of bear or other handsome skin, a horse, a rifle, powder and shot. When the Indian has made the bargain with his wife's parents, he takes her home to his caban, and from that time she becomes his slave. There are several singular modes of courtship among some of the tribes, but generally much reserve and consideration are exhibited.* In many respects, however, the morals and

* "When a young Indian becomes attached to a female, he does not frequent the lodge of her parents, or visit her elsewhere, oftener, perhaps, than he would provided no such attachment existed. Were he to pursue an opposite course before he had acquired either the reputation of a warrior or a hunter, and suffer his attachment to be known or suspected by any personal attention, he would become the derision of the warriors and the contempt of the squaws. On meeting, however, she is the first, excepting the elderly people, who engages his respectful and kind inquiries; after which, no conversation passes between them, except it be with the language of the eyes, which, even among savages, is eloquent, and appears to be well understood. The next indication of serious intentions on the part of the young hunter is the assumption of more industrious habits. He rises by daybreak, and, with his gun or bow, visits the woods and prairies, in search of the most rare and esteemed game. He endeavors to acquire the character of an expert and industrious hunter, and, whenever success has crowned his efforts, never fails to send the parents of the object of his affections some of the choicest he has procured. His mother is generally the bearer, and she is sure to tell from what source it comes, and to dilate largely on the merits and excellences of her son. The girl, on her part, exercises all her skill in preparing it for food, and when it is cooked, frequently sends some of the most delicious pieces, accompanied by other small presents, such as nuts, moccasins, &c., to her lover. These negotiations are usually carried on by the mothers of the respective parties, who consider them confidential, and seldom

manners of the Indians are such as might be expected in communities where the precepts of Christianity are unknown, and where even the artificial light of civilization is wanting. There are occasionally instances of a divorce being resorted to from mere caprice; but, usually, the marriage tie is regarded as a perpetual covenant. As the wife toils incessantly, and procures a great part of the subsistence, she is considered too valuable a servant to be lightly lost. Among the chiefs of the tribes to the west and south, polygamy is general, and the number of these wife-servants constitute the principal wealth; but among the northern nations this plurality is very rarely possessed. The Indian is seldom seen to bestow the slightest mark of tenderness upon his wife or children: he, however, exerts himself to the utmost for their welfare, and will sacrifice his life to avenge their wrongs. His indomitable pride prompts him to assume an apparent apathy, and to control every emotion of affection, suffering, or sorrow.

Parents perform few duties toward their children beyond procuring their daily bread. The father is by turns occupied in war and the chase, or sunk in total indolence, while the mother is oppressed by the toils of her laborious bondage, and has but little time to devote to her maternal cares. The infant is fastened to a board, cushioned with soft moss, by thongs of leather, and is generally hung on the branch of a tree, or, in traveling, carried on the mother's back.* When

divulge even to the remaining parents, except one or both of the candidates should be the offspring of a chief, when a deviation from this practice is exacted, and generally observed. After an Indian has acquired the reputation of a warrior, expert hunter, or swift runner, he has little need of minor qualifications, or of much address or formality in forming his matrimonial views. The young squaws sometimes discover their attachment to those they love by some act of tender regard, but more frequently through the kind offices of some confidante or friend. Such overtures generally succeed: but should they fail, it is by no means considered disgraceful, or in the least disadvantageous to the female; on the contrary, should the object of her affections have distinguished himself especially in battle, she is the more esteemed on account of the judgment she displayed in her partiality for a respectable and brave warrior."—Hunter, p. 235–237.

* See Appendix, No. LVII.

able to move, it is freed from this confinement, and allowed to make its way about as it pleases. It soon reaches some neighboring lake or river, and sports itself in the water all day long. As the child advances in years it enjoys perfect independence; it is rarely or never reproved or chastised. The youths are early led to emulate the deeds of their fathers; they practice with the bow, and other weapons suited to a warrior's use; and, as manhood approaches, they gradually assume the dignified gravity of the elders. In some tribes the young men must pass through a dreadful ordeal when they arrive at the age of manhood, which is supposed to prepare them for the endurance of all future sufferings, and enables the chiefs to judge of their courage, and to select the bravest among them to lead in difficult enterprises.

During four days previous to this terrible torture the candidates observe a strict fast, and are denied all sleep. When the appointed day arrives, certain strange ceremonies of an allegorical description are performed, in which all the inhabitants of the village take part. The candidates then repair to a large caban, where the chiefs and elders of the tribe are assembled to witness the ordeal. The torture commences by driving splints of wood through the flesh of the back and breasts of the victim: he is next hoisted off the ground by ropes attached to these splints, and suspended by the quivering flesh, while the tormenters twist the hanging body slowly round, thus exquisitely enhancing the agony, till a death-faint comes to the relief of the candidate: he is then lowered to the ground and left to the care of the Great Spirit. When he recovers animation, he rises and proceeds on his hands and feet to another part of the caban: he there lays the little finger of the left hand upon a buffalo skull, as a sacrifice to the Great Spirit, and another Indian chops it off. The fore-finger is also frequently offered up in the same manner: this mutilation does not interfere with the use of the bow, the only weapon for which the left hand is required. Other cruel tortures are inflicted for some time, and at length the wretched victim, reeling and staggering from the intensity of his suffering, reaches his own dwelling, where he is placed under the care of his friends. Some of the famous warriors of the tribe pass through this horrible ordeal repeatedly, and the oftener it is endured, the greater is their estimation among their people. No bandages are applied to the wounds thus inflicted, nor is any attention paid to their cure; but, from the extreme exhaustion and debility caused by want of sustenance and sleep, circulation is checked, and sensibility diminished; the bleeding and inflammation are very slight, and the results are seldom injurious.

The native tribes are engaged in almost perpetual hostility against each other. War is the great occupation of savage life, the measure of merit, the high road of ambition, and the source of its intensest joy—revenge.* In war the Indian character presents the darkest aspect; the finer and gentler qualities are vailed or dormant, and a fiendish ferocity assumes full sway. It is waged to exterminate, not to reduce. The enemy is assailed with treachery, and, if conquered, treated with revolting cruelty. The glory and excitement of war are dear to the Indian, but when the first drop of blood is shed, revenge is dearer still. He thirsts to offer up the life of an enemy to appease the departed spirit of a slaughtered friend. Thus each contest generates another even more embittered than itself. The extension or defense of the hunting-grounds is often a primary cause of hostility among the native nations, and the increase of the power of their tribe by incorporating with them such of the vanquished as they may spare from a cruel death is another frequent motive. The savage pines and chafes in long-continued peace, and the prudence of the aged can with difficulty restrain the fierce impetuosity of the young. Individual quarrels and a thirst for fame often lead a single savage to invade a hostile territory against the counsels of his tribe;

* "They firmly believe that the spirits of those who are killed by the enemy without equal revenge of blood, find no rest, and at night haunt the houses of the tribe to which they belonged; but when that kindred duty of retaliation is justly executed, they immediately get ease and power to fly away."—Adair's *Account of the American Indians.*

but, when war is determined by the general voice, more enlarged views, and a desire of aggrandizement guide the proceedings.

As soon as the determination of declaring war is formed, he who is chosen by the nation as the chief enters on a course of solemn preparation, entreating the aid and guidance of the Great Spirit. As a signal of the approaching strife, he marches three times round his winter dwelling, bearing a large blood-red flag, variegated with deep tints of black. When this terrible emblem is seen, the young warriors crowd around to hearken to the words of their chief. He then addresses them in a strain of impassioned, but rude and ferocious eloquence, calling upon them to follow him to glory and revenge. When he concludes his oration, he throws a wampum belt on the ground, which is respectfully lifted up by some warrior of high renown, who is judged worthy of being second in command. The chief now paints himself black, and commences a strict fast, only tasting a decoction of consecrated herbs to assist his dreams, which are strictly noted and interpreted by the elders. He then washes off the black paint. A huge fire is lighted in a public place in the village, and the great war-caldron set to boil : each warrior throws something into this vessel, and the allies who are to join the expedition also send offerings for the same purpose. Lastly, the sacred dog is sacrificed to the God of War, and boiled in the caldron to form the chief dish at a festival, to which only the warriors and men great in council are admitted.

During these ceremonies the elders watch the omens with deep anxiety, and if the promise be favorable, they prepare for immediate departure. The chief then paints himself in bright and varied colors, to render his appearance terrible, and sings his war song, announcing the nature of the projected enterprise. His example is followed by all the warriors, who join a war-dance, while they proclaim with a loud voice the glory of their former deeds, and their determination to destroy their enemies. Each Indian now seizes his arms : the bow and quiver hang over the left shoulder, the tomahawk from the left hand, and the scalping-knife* is stuck in the girdle. A distinguished chief is appointed to take charge of the Manitous or guardian powers of each warrior; they are collected, carefully placed in a box, and accompany the expedition as the ark of safety. Meanwhile the women incite the warriors to vengeance, and eagerly demand captives for the torture, to appease the spirits of their slaughtered relatives, or sometimes, indeed, to supply their place. When the war party are prepared to start, the chief addresses his followers in a short harangue; they then commence the march, singing, and shouting the terrible war-whoop. The women proceed with the expedition for some distance; and when they must return, exchange endearing names with their husbands and relations, and express ardent wishes for victory. Some little gift of affection is usually exchanged at parting.

Before striking the first blow the Indians make open declaration of war. A herald, painted black, is sent, bearing a red tomahawk, on one side of which are inscribed figures representing the causes of hostilities. He reaches the enemy's principal village at midnight, throws down the tomahawk in some conspicuous place, and disappears silently. When once warning is thus given, every stratagem that cunning can suggest is employed for the enemy's destruction.

* "The modern scalping-knife is of civilized manufacture made expressly for Indian use, and carried into the Indian country by thousands and tens of thousands, and sold at an enormous price. In the native simplicity of the Indian, he shapes out his rude hatchet from a piece of stone, heads his arrows and spears with flints, and his knife is a sharpened bone or the edge of a broken silex. His untutored mind has not been ingenious enough to design or execute any thing so savage or destructive as these civilized refinements on Indian barbarity. The scalping-knife, in a beautiful scabbard which is carried under the belt, is generally used in all Indian countries where knives have been introduced. It is the size and shape of a butcher's knife with one edge, manufactured at Sheffield perhaps for sixpence, and sold to the poor Indians in these wild regions for a horse. If I should ever cross the Atlantic, with my collection, a curious enigma would be solved for the English people who may inquire for a scalping-knife, when they find that every one in my collection (and hear, also, that nearly every one that is to be seen in the Indian country, to the Rocky Mountains and the Pacific Ocean) bears on its blade, the impress of G. R."—Catlin's *American Indians*, vol. i., p. 236.

As long as the expedition continues in friendly countries, the warriors wander about in small parties for the convenience of hunting, still, however, keeping up communication by means of sounds imitating the cries of birds and beasts. None ever fail to appear at the appointed place of meeting upon the frontier, where they again hold high festival, and consult the omens of their dreams. When they enter the hostile territory a close array is observed, and a deep silence reigns. They creep on all fours, walk through water, or upon the stumps of trees, to avoid leaving any trace of their route. To conceal their numbers they sometimes march in a long single file, each stepping on the foot-print of the man before him. They sometimes even wear the hoofs of the buffalo or the paws of the bear, and run for miles in a winding course to imitate the track of those animals. Every effort is made to surprise the foe, and they frequently lure him to destruction by imitating from the depths of the forest the cries of animals of the chase.

If the expedition meet with no straggling party of the enemy, it advances with cautious stealth toward some principal village; the warriors creep on their hands and feet through the deep woods, and often even paint themselves the color of dried leaves to avoid being perceived by their intended victims. On approaching the doomed hamlet, they examine it carefully, but rapidly, from some tree-top or elevated ground, and again conceal themselves till nightfall in the thickest covert. Strange to say, these subtle warriors neglect altogether the security of sentinels, and are satisfied with searching the surrounding neighborhood for hidden foes; if none be discovered, they sleep in confidence, even when hostile forces are not far off. They weakly trust to the protecting power of their Manitous. When they have succeeded in reaching the village, and concealing themselves unobserved, they wait silently, keeping close watch till the hour before dawn, when the inhabitants are in the deepest sleep. Then crawling noiselessly, like snakes, through the grass and underwood, till they are upon the foe, the chief raises a shrill cry, and the massacre begins. Discharging a shower of arrows, they finish the deadly work with the club and tomahawk. The great object, however, of the conquerors is to take the enemy alive, and reserve him to grace their triumph and rejoice their eyes by his torture. When resistance is attempted, this is often impossible, and an instant death saves the victim from the far greater horrors of captivity and protracted torment. When an enemy is struck down, the victor places his foot upon the neck of the dead or dying man, and with a horrible celerity and skill tears off the bleeding scalp.* This trophy is ever preserved with jealous care by the Indian warriors.

After any great success the war party always return to their villages, more eager to celebrate the victory than to improve its advantages. Their women and old men await their return in longing expectation. The fate of the war is announced from afar off by well-known signs; the bad tidings are first told. A herald advances to the front of the returning party, and sounds a death-whoop for each of their warriors who has fallen in the fray. Then, after a little time, the tale of victory is told, and the number of prisoners and of the slain declared. All lamentations are soon hushed, and congratulations and rejoicing succeed. During the retreat, if the war party be not hard pressed by the enemy, prisoners are treated with some degree of humanity, but are very closely guarded. When the expedition has returned to the village, the old men, women, and children form themselves into two lines; the prisoners are compelled to pass between them, and are cruelly bruised with sticks and stones, but not vitally injured by their tormentors.

A council is usually held to decide the fate of the prisoners: the alternatives are, to be adopted into the conquering nation, and received as brothers, or to be put to death in the most horrible torments, thus either to supply the place of warriors fallen in battle, or to appease the spirits of the departed by their miserable end. The older warriors among the captives usually meet the hardest fate; the younger are most frequently adopted by the women, their wounds are cured, and they are thenceforth received in every respect as if they belonged to the tribe. The adopted prisoners go out

* See Appendix, No. LVIII.

to war against their former countrymen, and the new tie is held even more binding than the old.

The veteran warrior, whose tattooed skin bears record of slaughtered enemies, meets with no mercy: his face is painted, his head crowned with flowers as if for a festival, black moccasins are put upon his feet, and a flaming torch is placed above him as the signal of condemnation. The women take the lead in the diabolical tortures to which he is subjected, and rage around their victim with horrible cries. He is, however, allowed a brief interval to sing his death-song, and he often continues it even through the whole of the terrible ordeal. He boasts of his great deeds, insults his tormentors, laughing at their feeble efforts, exults in the vengeance that his nation will take for his death, and pours forth insulting reproaches and threats. The song is then taken up by the woman to whose particular revenge he has been devoted. She calls upon the spirit of her husband or son to come and witness the sufferings of his foe. After tortures too various and horrible to be particularized, some kind wound closes the scene in death, and the victim's scalp is lodged among the trophies of the tribe. To endure with unshaken fortitude* is the greatest triumph of an Indian warrior, and the highest confusion to his enemies, but often the proud spirit breaks under the pangs that rack the quivering flesh, and shouts of intolerable agony reward the demoniac ingenuity of the tormentors.

Many early writers considered that the charge of cannibalism† against the Indians was well founded: doubtless,

* The savage Cantabrians and the first inhabitants of Spain sang songs of triumph as they were led to death and while they hung on the cross. Strabo mentions this as a mark of their ferocity and barbarism.—Strabo, lib. iii., p. 114.

† The American word "cannibal," of a somewhat doubtful signification, is probably derived from the language of Hayti or that of Porto Rico. It has passed into the languages of Europe, since the end of the fifteenth century, as synonymous with that of Anthropophagi. "Edaces humanarum carnium novi heluones Anthropophagi, Caribes, alias Canibales appellati," says Peter Martyr of Anghiera, in the third decade of his *Oceanics*, dedicated to Pope Leo X. "We were assured by all the missionaries whom we had an opportunity of consulting, that the Caribbees are perhaps the least anthropophagous

in moments of fury, portions of an enemy's flesh have been rent off and eaten. To devour a foeman's heart is held by them to be an exquisite vengeance. They have been known to drink draughts of human blood, and, in circumstances of scarcity, they do not hesitate to eat their captives. It is certain that all the terms used by them in describing the torture of prisoners relate to this horrible practice; yet, as they are so figurative in every expression, these may simply mean the fullest gratification of revenge. The evidence upon this point is obscure and contradictory; the Indian can not be altogether acquitted or found guilty of this foul imputation.

The brief peace that affords respite amid the continual wars of the Indian tribes is scarcely more than a truce. Nevertheless, it is concluded with considerable form and ceremony. The first advance toward a cessation of hostilities is usually made through the chief of a neutral power. The nation proposing the first overture dispatches some men of note as embassadors, accompanied by an orator, to contract the negotiation. They bear with them the calumet* of

nation of the New Continent. We may conceive that the fury and despair with which the unhappy Caribbees defended themselves against the Spaniards when, in 1704, a royal decree declared them slaves, may have contributed to the reputation they have acquired of ferocity. The licendiado Rodrigo de Figuera was appointed by the court in 1520 to decide which of the tribes of South America might be regarded as of Caribbee race, or as *Cannibals*, and which were Guatiaos, that is, Indians of peace, and friends of the Castilians. Every nation that could be accused of having devoured a prisoner after a battle was arbitrarily declared of Caribbee race. All the tribes designated by Figuera as Caribbees were condemned to slavery, and might at will be sold or exterminated in war."—Humboldt's *Personal Narrative*, vol. vi., p. 35.

Charlevoix and Lafitau speak of the cannibalism of the North American Indians as a generally acknowledged fact: Lafitau mentions the Abenaquis as the only tribe who held it in detestation.—Lafitau, vol. ii., p. 307.

* "On ne peut guères douter que les sauvages en faisant fumer dans le calumet ceux dont ils recherchent l'alliance ou le commerce, n'ayent intention de prendre le soleil pour témoin et en quelque façon pour garant de leurs traités, car ils ne manquent jamais de pousser la fumée vers cette astre: . . . Fumer donc dans la même pipe, en signe d'alliance, est la même chose que de boire dans la même coupe, comme il s'est de tout tems pratiqué dans plusieurs nations."—Charlevoix, tom. v., p. 313.

peace as the symbol of their purpose, and a certain number of wampum belts* to note the objects and conditions of the

Calumet in general signifies a pipe, being a Norman word, derived from *chalumeau.* The savages do not understand this word, for it was introduced into Canada by the Normans when they first settled there, and has still continued in use among the French planters. The calumet, or pipe, is called in the Iroquois language *ganondaoe*, and by the other savage natives, *poagau.*

Embassadors were never safe among any of the savage tribes who do not smoke the calumet.—Lafitau, vol. ii., p. 313. At the time of the early French writers on Indian customs, the calumet, since almost universally in use, was only known among the tribes inhabiting Louisiana, who in many respects were more advanced in civilization than those of the cold northern regions.

* Wampum is the Indian name of ornaments manufactured by the Indians from vari-colored shells[1] which they get on the shore of the fresh-water streams, and file or cut into bits of half an inch, or an inch in length, and perforate, giving them the shape of pieces of broken pipe-stems, which they string on deer's sinews, or weave them ingeniously into war-belts for the waist. The wampum is evidently meant in the description of the *esurgny* or *cornibolz*, given by Verazzano in Ramusio, which has so much puzzled translators and commentators. Lafitau and Charlevoix both describe it under the name of *porcelaine.*

"La porcelaine dont nous parlons ici, est bien differente de ces ouvrages de porcelaine qu'on apporte de la Chine ou du Japan[2] dont

1 "Among the numerous shells which are found on the sea-shore, there are some which by the English here are called clams, and which bear some resemblance to the numan ear. They have a considerable thickness, and are chiefly white, excepting the pointed end, which both within and without hath a blue color, between purple and violet. The shells contain a large animal, which is eaten both by Indians and Europeans. The shells of these clams are used by the Indians as money, and make what they call their wampum; they likewise serve their women for an ornament when they intend to appear in full dress. These wampums are properly made of the purple part of the shells, which the Indians value more than the white parts. A traveler who goes to trade with the Indians, and is well stocked with them, may become a considerable gainer, but if he take gold coin or bullion he will undoubtedly be a loser; for the Iudians who live farther up the country put little or no value on the metals which we reckon so precious, as I have frequently observed in the course of my travels. The Indians formerly made their own wampums, though not without a great deal of trouble; but at present the Europeans employ themselves in that way, and get considerable profit by it."—Kalm in Pinkerton, vol. xiii., p. 455.

2 "Marsden et la Comte Baldelli ont rappellé, dans leur savans commentaires du Milione de Marco Polo, que c'est le nom de la coquille du genere Cypræa à dos bombé (porcellanor, de porcello, en latin porcellus, pourcelaine du perè Trigault) qui a donné lieu à la dénomination de *porcelaine* par laquelle les peuples occidentaux ont désigné les *Vasa Sinica.* Marco Polo se sert du mot porcellane, et pour les coquilles *karis*, ou *couries*, employées comme monnaie dans l'Inde, et pour la poterie fine de la Chine,

negotiation. The orator explains the meaning of the belts

la matière est une terre beluttée et préparée. Celle ci est tirée de certains coquillages de mer, connues en générale sous le nom de porcelaines—celles dont nos sauvages se servent sont canelées, et semblable pour leur figure aux coquilles de St. Jacques. Il y a de porcelaine de deux sortes, l'une est blanche, et c'est la plus commune. L'autre est d'un violet obscur; plus elle tire sur le noir plus elle est estimée. La porcelaine qui sert pour les affaires d'état est toute travaillée au petits cylindres de la longueur d'un quart de pouce et gros à proportion. On les distribue en deux manières, en branches et en colliers. Les branches sont composées de cylindres enfilés sans ordre, à la suite les uns des autres comme des grains de chapelet. La porcelaine en est ordinairement toute blanche, et on ne s'en sert que pour des affaires d'une legère conséquence. Les colliers sont de larges ceintures, où les petits cylindres blancs et pourpre sont disposés par rangs et assujettès par de petites bandelettes de cuir, dont on fait un tissu assez propre. Leur longeur, leur largueur et les grains de couleur se proportionnent à l'importance de l'affaire. Les colliers communs et ordinaires sont de onze rangs de cent quatre-vingt grains chacun. Le fisc, ou le tresor public consiste principalement en ces sortes de colliers. . . . . . Les sauvages n'ont rien de plus précieux que leur Porcelaine; ce sont leurs bijoux, leurs pierreries. Ils en comptent jusqu' aux grains, et cela leur tient lieu de toute richesse." —Lafitau, 1720.

Catlin writes thus in 1842: "Among the numerous tribes who have formerly inhabited the Atlantic coast, wampum has been invariably manufactured and highly valued as a circulating medium (instead of coins, of which the Indians have no knowledge), so many strings, or so many hands' breadth, being the fixed value of a horse, a gun, a robe, &c. It is a remarkable fact, that after I passed the Mississippi I saw but very little wampum used, and on ascending the Missouri, I do not recollect to have seen it worn at all by the Upper Missouri Indians, although the same materials for its manufacture are found in abundance in those regions. Below the Lions and along the whole of our western frontier, the different tribes are found loaded and beautifully ornamented with it, which they can now afford to do, for they consider it of little value, as the fur traders have ingeniously introduced an imitation of it, manufactured by steam or otherwise, of porcelain or some composition closely resembling it, with which they have flooded the whole Indian country, and sold at so reduced a price as to cheapen, and consequently destroy, the value and meaning of the original wampum, a string of which can now but very rarely be found in any part of the country."—Catlin, vol. i., p. 223.

. . . . . La blancheur lustrée de plusieurs espèces de la famille des Buccinoides, appellées de pourcelaines au moien âge, a sans doute suffi pour faire donner aux beaux vases céramiques de la Chine une denomination analogue. Ces coquilles ne sont pas entrées dans la composition de la porcelaine."—Humboldt, *Géog. du Nouveau Continent*, tom. v., p. 106.

to the hostile chiefs, and if the proposition be received, the opposite party accept the proffered symbols, and the next day present others of a similar import. The calumet is then solemnly smoked, and the burial of a war hatchet for each party and for each ally concludes the treaty. The negotiations consist more in presents, speeches, and ceremonies, than in any demands upon each other; there is no property to provide tribute, and the victors rarely or never require the formal cession of any of the hunting-grounds of the vanquished. The unrestrained passions of individuals, and the satiety of long continued peace, intolerable to the Indian, soon again lead to the renewal of hostility.

The successful hunter ranks next to the brave warrior in the estimation of the savage. Before starting on his grand expeditions, he prepares himself by a course of fasting, dreaming, and religious observances, as if for war. He hunts with astonishing dexterity and skill, and regards this pursuit rather as an object of adventure and glory than as an industrious occupation.

With regard to cultivation and the useful arts, the Indians are in the very infancy of progress.* Their villages are usually not less than eighteen miles apart, and are surrounded by a narrow circle of imperfectly-cleared land, slightly turned up with a hoe, or scraped with pointed sticks, † scarcely interrupting the continuous expanse of the

* "Avant d'avoir l'usage des moulins, ils brisaient leurs grains dans les piles, ou des mortiers de bois, avec des pilons de même matière. Hésiode nous donne la mesure de la pile et du pilon des anciens, et de nos sauvages, dans ces paroles, 'Coupez moi une pile de trois pieds de haut, et un pilon de la longueur de trois coudées.' (Hesiod, *Opera et Dies*, lib. v., 411; Servius in lib. ix., Æneid. Init.) Caton met aussi la pile et le pilon, au nombre des meubles rustiques de son temps. Les Pisons prirent leur nom de cette manière de piler le bled."—Lafitau.

† "Il leur suffit d'un morceau de bois recourbé de trois doigts de largeur, attaché à un long mouche qui leur sert à sarcler la terre, et à la remuer legèrement."—Lafitau, tom. ii., p. 76.

Catlin says that the tribe of Mandans raise a great deal of corn. This is all done by the women, who make their hoes of the shoulder-blades of the buffalo or elk, and dig the ground over instead of plowing it, which is consequently done with a vast deal of labor.—Vol. i., p. 121.

forest. They are only acquainted with the rudest sorts of clay manufactures, and the use of the metals (except by European introduction) is altogether unknown.* Their women, however, display considerable skill in weaving fine mats, in staining the hair of animals, and working it into brilliant colored embroideries. The wampum belts are made with great care and some taste. The calumet is also elaborately carved and ornamented; and the painting and tattooing of their bodies sometimes presents well-executed and highly descriptive pictures and hieroglyphics. They construct light and elegant baskets from the swamp cane, and are very skillful in making bows and arrows; some tribes, indeed, were so rude as not to have attained even to the use of this primitive weapon, and the sling was by no means generally known.

Most of the American nations are without any fixed form of government whatever. The complete independence of every man is fully recognized. He may do what he pleases of good or evil, useful or destructive, no constituted power interferes to thwart his will. If he even take away the life of another, the by-standers do not interpose. The kindred of the slain, however, will make any sacrifice for vengeance. And yet, in the communities of these children of nature there usually reigns a wonderful tranquillity. A deadly hostility exists between the different tribes, but among the

* "Nothing so distinctly marks the uncivilized condition of the North American Indian as his total ignorance of the art of metallurgy. Forged iron has been in use among the inhabitants of our hemisphere from time immemorial; for, though the process employed for obtaining the malleability of a metal in its malleable state is very complicated, yet M. de Marian has clearly proved that the several eras at which writers have pretended to fix the discovery are entirely fabulous."—*Lettres sur la Chine.*

Consequently the weapons of brass and other instruments of metal found in the dikes of Upper Canada, Florida, &c., are among the strongest indications of the superiority of those ancient races of America who have now entirely passed away.

"Know, then," says Cotton Mather, "that these doleful creatures are the veriest ruins of mankind. They live in a country full of metals, but the Indians were never owners of so much as a knife till we came among them. Their name for an Englishman was 'knife-man.'"

members comprising each the strictest union exists. The honor and prosperity of his nation is the leading object of the Indian. This national feeling forms a link to draw him closely to his neighbor, and he rarely or never uses violence or evil speech against a countryman. Where there is scarcely such a thing as individual property, government and justice are necessarily very much simplified. There exists almost a community of goods. No man wants while another has enough and to spare. Their generosity knows no bounds. Whole tribes, when ruined by disasters in war, find unlimited hospitality among their neighbors; habitations and hunting-grounds are allotted to them, and they are received in every respect as if they were members of the nation that protects them.

As there is generally no wealth or hereditary distinction among this people, the sole claim to eminence is founded on such personal qualities as can only be conspicuous in war, council, or the chase. During times of tranquillity and inaction all superiority ceases. Every man is clothed and fares alike. Relations of patronage and dependence are unknown. All are free and equal, and they perish rather than submit to control or endure correction. During war, indeed, or in the chase, they render a sort of obedience to those who excel in character and conduct, but at other times no form of government whatever exists. The names of magistrate and subject are not in their language. If the elders interpose between man and man, it is to advise, not to decide. Authority is only tolerated in foreign, not in domestic affairs.

Music and dancing express the emotions of the Indian's mind. He has his songs of war and death, and particular moments of his life are appointed for their recital. His great deeds and the vengeance he has inflicted upon his enemies are his subjects; the language and music express his passions rudely but forcibly. The dance* is still more im-

* Chateaubriand, vol. i., p. 233; Charlevoix.

"The dances of the Red Indians form a singular and important feature throughout the customs of the aborigines of the New World. In these are typified, by signs well understood by the initiated, and, as it were, by hieroglyphic action, their historical events, their pro-

portant: it is the grand celebration at every festival, and alternately the exponent of their triumph, anger, or devotion. It is usually pantomimic, and highly descriptive of the subject to which it is appropriate.

The Indians are immoderately fond of play as a means of excitement and agitation. While gaming, they, who are usually so taciturn and indifferent, become loquacious and eager. Their guns, arms, and all that they possess are freely staked, and at times where all else is lost, they will trust even their personal safety to the hazard of the die.* The most barbarous of the tribes have unhappily succeeded in inventing some species of intoxicating liquor: that from the root of the maize was in general use; it is not disagreeable to the taste, and is very powerful. When the accursed fire-water is placed before the Indians, none can resist the temptation. The wisest, best, and bravest succumb alike to this odious temptation: and when their unrestrained passions are excited by drinking, they are at times guilty of enormous outrages, and the scenes of their festivities often become stained with kindred blood. The women are not permitted to partake of this fatal pleasure; their duty is to serve the guests, and take care of their husbands and friends when overpowered by the debauch. This exclusion from a favorite enjoyment is evidence of the contempt in which females are held among the Indians.

In the present day, he who would study the character and habits of these children of Nature must travel far away

jected enterprises, their hunting, their ambuscades, and their battles, resembling in some respects the Pyrrhic dances of the ancients."—Washington Irving's *Columbus*, vol. ii., p. 122.

"In the province of Pasto, on the ridge of the Cordillera, I have seen masked Indians, armed with rattles, performing savage dances around the altar, while a Franciscan monk elevated the host."—Humboldt's *Nouveau Espagne*, vol. i., p. 411.

See, also, Lafitau's *Mœurs des Sauvages Amériquains comparés aux mœurs des premiers temps*, tom. i., p. 526. He refers to Plutarch, *in Lycurgo*, for an account of similar Spartan dances.

* Charlevoix; Lafitau; Boucher, *Histoire du Canada*.

"The players prepare for their ruin by religious observances; they fast, they watch, they pray."—Chateaubriand, vol. i., p. 240. See Appendix, No. LIX.

beyond the Rocky Mountains, where the murrain of perverted civilization has not yet spread. There he may still find the virtues and vices of the savage, and lead among those wild tribes that fascinating life of liberty which few have ever been known to abandon willingly for the restraints and luxuries of civilization and refinement.

CHAPTER IX.

WHILE the French were busied in establishing themselves upon the banks of the St. Lawrence, their ancient rivals steadily progressed in the occupation of the Atlantic coasts of North America.

Generally speaking, the oldest colonies of England were founded by private adventurers, at their own expense and risk. In most cases, the soil of the new settlements was granted to powerful individuals or companies of merchants, and by them made over in detail to the actual emigrants for certain considerations. Where, however, as often occurred, the emigrants had settled prior to the grant, or were in a condition to disregard it, they divided the land according to their own interests and convenience. These unrecognized proprietors prospered more rapidly than those who were trammeled by engagements with non-resident authorities. The right of government, as well as the nominal possession of the soil, was usually granted in the first instance, and the new colonies were connected with the crown of Great Britain by little more than a formal recognition of sovereignty. But the disputes invariably arising between the nominal proprietors and the actual settlers speedily caused, in most cases, a dissolution of the proprietary government, and threw the colonies one by one under royal authority.

The system then usually adopted was to place the colony under the rule of an English governor, assisted by an upper House of Parliament, or Council, appointed by himself, and a Lower House, possessing the power of taxation, elected by the people. All laws, however, enacted by these local authorities were subject to the approbation of the British crown. This was the outline of colonial constitutions in every North American settlement, except in those established under peculiar charters. The habit of self-government bore its fruit of sturdy independence and self-reliance among our transatlantic brethren, and the prospect of political privileges offered a special temptation to the English emigrant to embark his fortunes in the New World. At their commencement trade was free in all, and religion in most of the new colonies ; and it was only by slow degrees that their fiscal regulations were brought under the subordination of the mother country.

Although a general sketch of British colonization in North America is essential to the illustration of Canadian history, it is unnecessary to detail more than a few of the leading features of its nature and progress, and of the causes which placed its interests in almost perpetual antagonism with those of French settlement. This subject is rendered not a little obscure and complicated by the contradictory claims and statements of proprietors, merchant adventurers, and settlers ; the separation of provinces ; the abandonment of old, and the foundation of new settlements.*

Sir Humphrey Gilbert,† of Compton, in Devonshire, formed the first plan of British colonization in America. Queen Elizabeth, who then wore the crown, willingly granted a patent conveying most ample gifts and powers to her worthy and distinguished subject. He was given forever all such "heathen and barbarous countries" as he might discover, with absolute authority therein, both by sea and land. Only homage, and a fifth part of the gold and silver that might be obtained, was reserved for the crown.

The first expedition of Sir Humphrey Gilbert failed in

* See Preface to Bancroft's *History of the United States.*

† "Sir Humphrey had published, in 1576, a treatise concerning a northwest passage to the East Indies, which, although tinctured with the pedantry of the age, is full of practical sense and judicious argument."—P. F. Tytler's *Life of Sir Walter Raleigh*, p. 26.

the very commencement. The adventurers were unfortunately selected; many deserted the cause, and others engaged in disastrous quarrels among themselves. The chief was ultimately obliged to set out with only a few of his own tried friends.* He encountered very adverse weather, and was driven back with the loss of a ship and one of his trustiest companions† [1580]. This disaster was a severe blow to Sir Humphrey Gilbert, as most of his property was embarked in the undertaking. However, with unshaken determination, and aided by Sir George Peckham, Sir Walter Raleigh,‡ and other distinguished men, he again equipped an expedition, and put to sea in the year 1583.

* "Sir Walter Raleigh, step-brother to Sir Humphrey Gilbert, was one of his companions in this enterprise, and, although it proved unsuccessful, the instructions of Sir Humphrey could not fail to be of service to Raleigh, who at this time was not much above twenty-five, while the admiral must have been in the maturity of his years and abilities."—Tytler, p. 27.

† "On its homeward passage, the small squadron of Gilbert was dispersed and disabled by a Spanish fleet, and many of the company were slain; but, perhaps owing to the disastrous issue of the fight, it has been slightly noticed by the English historians."—Oldy's *Life of Raleigh*, p. 28, 29.

‡ Raleigh, who had by this time risen into favor with the queen, did not embark on the expedition, but he induced his royal mistress to take so deep an interest in its success, that, on the eve of its sailing from Plymouth, she commissioned him to convey to Sir H. Gilbert her earnest wishes for his success, with a special token of regard—a little trinket representing an anchor guided by a lady. The following was Raleigh's letter, written from the court: "Brother—I have sent you a token from her majesty, an anchor guided by a lady, as you see; and, further, her highness willed me to send you word that she wished you as great good hap and safety to your ship as if she herself were there in person, desiring you to have care of yourself as of that which she tendereth; and therefore, for her sake, you must provide for it accordingly. Farther, she commandeth that you leave your picture with me. For the rest, I leave till our meeting, or to the report of this bearer, who would needs be the messenger of this good news. So I commit you to the will and protection of God, who sends us such life and death as he shall please or hath appointed. Richmond, this Friday morning. Your true brother, WALTER RALEIGH."—This letter is indorsed as having been received March 18, 1582–3, and it may be remarked that it settles the doubt as to the truth of Prince's story of the golden anchor, questioned by Campbell in his *Lives of the Admirals*. In the *Heroologia Angliæ*, p. 65, there is a fine print of Sir

The force with which this bold adventurer undertook to gain possession of a new continent was miserably small. The largest vessel was but of 200 tons burden: the Delight, in which he himself sailed, was only 120 tons, and the three others composing the little fleet were even much smaller. The crew and adventurers numbered altogether 260 men, most of them tradesmen, mechanics, and refiners of metal. There was such difficulty in completing even this small equipment, that some captured pirates were taken into the service.

The expedition sailed from Concert Bay on the 11th of May, 1583. Three days afterward, the Raleigh,* the largest ship of the fleet, put back to land, under the plea that a violent sickness had broken out on board, but, in reality, from the indisposition of the crew to risk the enterprise. The loss of this vessel was a heavy discouragement to the brave leaders. After many delays and difficulties from the weather and the misconduct of his followers, Sir Humphrey Gilbert reached the shores of Newfoundland, where he found thirty-six vessels engaged in the fisheries. He, in virtue of his royal patent, immediately assumed authority over them, demanding and obtaining all the supplies of which he stood in need: he also proclaimed his own and the queen's possession of the country. Soon, however, becoming sensible that this rocky and dreary wilderness offered little prospect of wealth, he proceeded with three vessels, and a crew diminished by sickness and desertion, to the

Humphrey Gilbert, taken evidently from an original picture; but, unlike the portrait mentioned by Granger, it doos not bear the device mentioned in the text. Raleigh's letter explains this difference. When Sir Humphrey was at Plymouth, on the eve of sailing, the queen commands him, we see, to leave his picture with Raleigh. This must allude to a portrait already painted; and, of course, the golden anchor then sent could not be seen in it. Now, he perished on the voyage. The picture at Devonshire House, mentioned by Granger, which bears this honorable badge, must, therefore have been painted *after* his death.—Tytler's *Raleigh*, p. 45; Granger's *Biographical History*, vol. i., p. 246; Cayley, vol. i., p. 31; Prince's *Worthies of Devonshire*.

* "This ship was of 200 tons burden: it had been built under Raleigh's own eye, equipped at his expense, and commanded by Captain Butler, her master being Thomas Davis, of Bristol."—Tytler, p. 44.

American coast. Owing to his imprudence in approaching the foggy and dangerous shore too closely, the largest vessel* struck, and went to pieces. The captain and many of the crew were lost; some of the remainder reached Newfoundland in an open boat, after having endured great hardships.

Sir Humphrey Gilbert altogether failed in reaching any part of the main land of America. The weather became very bad, the winter approached, and provisions began to fail: there was no alternative but to return, and with bitter regret and disappointment he adopted that course. The two remaining vessels proceeded in safety as far as the meridian of the Azores; there, however, a terrible tempest assailed them. On the afternoon of the 9th of September the smaller of the two boats was observed to labor dangerously. Sir Humphrey Gilbert stood upon her deck, holding a book in his hand, encouraging the crew. "We are as near to heaven by sea as by land," he called out to those on board the other vessel, as it drifted past just before nightfall. Darkness soon concealed his little bark from sight; but for hours one small light was seen to rise and fall, and plunge about among the furious waves. Shortly after midnight it suddenly disappeared, and with it all trace of the brave chief and his crew. One maimed and storm-tossed ship returned to England of that armament which so short a time before had been sent forth to take possession of a New World.†

The English nation was not diverted from the pursuit of colonial aggrandizement by even this disastrous failure. The queen, however, was more ready to assist by grants and patents than by pecuniary supplies. Many plausible schemes of settlement were put forward; but the difficulty of obtain-

* The *Delight*. The *Swallow* had, a short time before, been sent home with some of the crew, who were sick. The remaining barks were the *Golden Hind* and the *Squirrel*, the first of forty, the last of ten tons burden. For what reason does not appear, the admiral insisted, against the remonstrances of his officers and crew, in having his flag in the *Squirrel*. It was a fatal resolution. The larger vessel, the *Golden Hind*, arrived at Falmouth on the 22d September, 1583.

† See Captain Edward Haies's *Narrative of the Expedition of Sir Humphrey Gilbert*; Hakluyt, vol. iii., p. 143–159.

ing sufficient means of carrying them into effect, prevented their being adopted. At length the illustrious Sir Walter Raleigh undertook the task of colonization at his own sole charge, and easily obtained a patent similar to that conferred upon Sir Humphrey Gilbert. He soon sent out two small vessels, under skillful naval officers, to search for his new government. Warned by the disasters of their predecessors, they steered a more southerly course. When soundings indicated an approach to land, they already observed that the breeze from the shore was rich with delicious odors of fruits and flowers. They proceeded very cautiously, and presently found that they had reached a long, low coast, without harbors. The shore was flat and sandy; but softly undulating green hills were seen in the interior, covered with a great profusion of rich grapes. This discovery proved to be the island of Okakoke, off North Carolina. [1584.] The English were well received by the natives, and obtained from them many valuable skins in exchange for trinkets. Some limited explorations were made, after which the expedition returned to England, bearing very favorable accounts of the new country,* which filled Raleigh with joy, and raised the expectations of the whole kingdom. In honor of England's maiden queen, the name of Virginia was given to this land of promise.

Sir Walter Raleigh now embarked nearly all his fortune in another expedition, consisting of seven small ships, which he placed under the able command of Sir Richard Greenville, surnamed "the Brave." The little fleet reached Virginia on the 29th of June, 1585, and the colony was at once landed. The principal duties of settlement were intrusted to Mr. Ralph Lane, who proved unequal to the charge. The coast, however, was explored for a considerable distance, and the magnificent Bay of Chesapeake discovered.

Lane penetrated to the head of Roanoke Sound; there,

* Oldy's *Life of Raleigh*, p. 58. The description given of Virginia by the two captains in command of the expedition (Captains Philip Amadas and Walter Barlow) was, that "the soil is the most plentiful, sweet, fruitful, and wholesome of all the world. We found the people most gentle, loving, faithful, void of all guile and treason, and such as lived after the manner of the Golden Age."

without provocation, he seized a powerful Indian chief and his son, and retained the latter a close prisoner, in the hope, through him, of ruling the father. The natives, exasperated at this injury, deceived the English with false reports of great riches to be found in the interior. Lane proceeded up the river for several days with forty men, but, suffering much from the want of provisions, and having been once openly attacked by the savages, he returned disheartened to the coast, where he found that the Indians were prepared for a general rising against him, in a confederacy formed of the surrounding tribes, headed by a subtle chief called Pemisapan. In the mean time, however, the captive became attached to the English, warning them of the coming danger, and naming the day for the attack. Lane, resolving to strike the first blow, suddenly assailed the Indians and dispersed them; afterward, at a parley, he destroyed all the chiefs with disgraceful treachery. Henceforth the hatred of the savages to the English became intense, and they ceased to sow any of the lands near the settlement, with the view of starving their dangerous visitors.

The colonists were much embarrassed by the hostilities of the Indians; the time appointed by Raleigh and Greenville for sending them supplies had passed; a heavy despondency fell upon their minds, and they began earnestly to wish for a means of returning home. But, suddenly, notice was given that a fleet of twenty-three sail was at hand, whether friendly or hostile no one could tell: to their great joy, it proved to be the armament of Sir Francis Drake. Lane and his followers immediately availed themselves of this opportunity, and with the utmost haste embarked for England, totally abandoning the settlement. [1586.] A few days after this unworthy flight, a vessel of 100 tons, amply provided with aid for the colony, arrived upon its deserted shores; the crew in vain searched the coast and neighborhood for their fellow-countrymen, and then steered for England. A fortnight after Sir Richard Greenville arrived with three well-appointed ships, and found a lonely desert where he had expected a flourishing colony: he also returned to England in deep disappointment, leaving, however, a small party to hold possession of the country till he should return with ampler resources.

The noble Raleigh was not discouraged by this unhappy complication of errors and disasters; he immediately dispatched another expedition, with three ships under the command of John White. But a terrible sight presented itself on their arrival: the fort razed to the ground, the houses ruined and overgrown with grass, and a few scattered bones, told the fate of their countrymen. The little settlement had been assailed by 300 Indians, and all the colonists destroyed or driven into the interior to an unknown fate. By an unfortunate error, White attacked one of the few tribes that were friendly to the English, in the attempt to revenge the cruel massacre. After this unhappy exploit, he was compelled, by the discontent of his followers, to return to England, for the purpose of procuring them supplies.* From various delays, it was not till 1590 that another expedition reached Virginia. But again silence and desolation reigned upon that fatal shore. The colony left by White had been destroyed like its predecessor. Raleigh at last abandoned the scheme of settlement that had proved ruinously disastrous to him and all concerned, and the brave Sir Richard Greenville was soon after slain. [1591.]†

* Unfortunately, on White's arrival in England, the nation was wholly engrossed by the expected invasion of the Spanish Armada, and Sir Richard Greenville, who was preparing to sail for Virginia, received notice that his services were wanted at home. Raleigh, however, contrived to send out White with two more vessels; but they were attacked by a Spanish ship of war, and so severely shattered that they were obliged to return. Another expedition could not be undertaken until 1590; and no trace could then, or ever after, be found of the unfortunate colony left by White.

"Robertson reproaches Raleigh with levity in now throwing up his scheme of a Virginian colony. But, really, when we consider that in the course of four years he had sent out seven successive expeditions, each more unfortunate than the other, and had spent £40,000—nearly his whole fortune—without the least prospect of a return, it can not be viewed as a very unaccountable caprice that he should get sick of the business, and be glad to transfer it into other hands."—Murray, vol. i., p. 254.

† For an account of Sir Richard Greenville's death, see Appendix, No. LX.

The interest of the public in Virginia remained suspended till the year 1602, when Captain Bartholomew Gosnold undertook a voyage thither, and brought back such brilliant reports of the beauty and fertility of the country, that the dormant attention of the English toward this part of the world was again aroused. In 1606, Arundel, Lord Wardour, sent out a vessel under the command of Captain Weymouth, to make further discoveries. The report of this voyage more than confirmed that of the preceding.

The English nation were now at length prepared to make an efficient attempt to colonize the New World. In London, and at Plymouth and Bristol, the principal maritime cities of the kingdom, the scheme found numerous and ardent supporters. James I., however, only granted such powers to the adventurers as suited his own narrow and arbitrary views: he refused to sanction any sort of representative government in the colony, and vested all power in a council appointed by himself.* Virginia was, about that time, divided somewhat

* "The fundamental idea of the older British colonial policy appears to have been, that wherever a man went, he carried with him the rights of an Englishman, whatever these were supposed to be. In the reign of James I., the state doctrine was, that most popular rights were usurpations; and the colonists of Virginia, sent out under the protection of government, were therefore placed under that degree of control which the state believed itself authorized to exercise at home. The Puritans exalted civil franchise to a republican pitch; their colonies were therefore republican; there was no such notion as that of an intermediate state of tutelage or semi-liberty. Hence the entire absence of solicitude on the part of the mother country to interfere with the internal government of the colonies arose not altogether from neglect, but partly from principle. This is remarkably proved by the fact that representative government was seldom expressly granted in the early charters; *it was assumed by the colonists as a matter of right*. Thus, to use the odd expression of the historian of Massachusetts, 'A house of burgesses broke out in Virginia,' in 1619,[1] almost immediately after its second settlement; and although the constitution of James contained no such element, it was at once acceded to by the mother country as a thing of course. No thought was ever seriously entertained of supplying the colonies with the elements of an aristocracy. Virginia was the only province of old foundation in which the Church of England was established; and there it was abandoned, with very little help, to the caprice or prejudices of the colonists, under which it speedily de-

[1] Hutchinson's *History of Massachusetts*, p. 94.

capriciously into two parts: the southern portion was given to a merchant company of London, the northern to a merchant company of Bristol and Plymouth.*

The southern, or London Company, were the first to commence the work of colonization with energy. On the

cayed. The Puritans enjoyed, undisturbed, their peculiar notions of ecclesiastical government. 'It concerneth New England always to remember that they were originally a plantation religious, not a plantation of trade. And if any man among us make religion as twelve, and the world as thirteen, such an one hath not the spirit of a true New Englandman.' And when they chose to illustrate this noble principle by decimating their own numbers by persecution, and expelling from their limits all dissenters from their own establishment, the mother country never exerted herself to protect or prohibit. The only ambition of the state was to regulate the trade of its colonies: in this respect, and this only, they were fenced round with restrictions, and watched with the most diligent jealousy. They had a right to self-government and self-taxation; a right to religious freedom, in the sense which they chose themselves to put upon the word; a right to construct their municipal polity as they pleased; but no right to control or amend the slightest fiscal regulation of the imperial authority, however oppressively it might bear upon them.

"Such, I say, were the general notions prevailing in England on the subject of colonial government during the period of the foundation and early development of our transatlantic colonies—the notions by which the practice of government was regulated—although I do not assert that they were framed into a consistent and logical theory. Perhaps we shall not be far wrong in regarding Lord Chatham as the last distinguished assertor of these principles, in an age when they had begun to be partially superseded by newer speculations."—Merivale *On Colonization*, vol. i., p. 102.

* "In the spring of 1606, James I. by patent divided Virginia into two colonies. The *southern* included all lands between the 34th and 41st degrees of north latitude. This was granted to the London Company. The *northern* included all lands between the 38th and 45th degrees of north latitude, and was granted to the Plymouth Company. To prevent disputes about territory, the colonies were forbidden to plant within a hundred miles of each other. There appears an inconsistency in these grants, as the lands lying between the 38th and 41st degrees are covered by both patents.

"In the month of August, 1615, Captain John Smith arrived in England, where he drew a map of the northern part of Virginia, and called it New England. From this time the name of Virginia was confined to the southern part of the colony."—Winterbottom's *History of America*, vol. iv., p. 165. See Bancroft's *History of the United States*, vol. i., p. 120.

19th of December, 1606, they dispatched an expedition of three vessels, commanded by Captain Newport, comprising a number of people of rank and distinction. Among these was Captain John Smith, whose admirable qualities were afterward so conspicuously and usefully displayed. The expedition met with such delays and difficulties that it was at one time on the point of returning to England. At length, however, they descried an unknown cape, and soon afterward entered Chesapeake Bay, where the beauty and fertility of the shores even surpassed their expectations.* On first landing, they met the determined hostility of the savages, but when the fleet proceeded to Cape Comfort, they there received a more friendly reception, and were invited ashore. The Indians spread their simple stores of dainties before the strangers, smoked with them the calumet of peace, and entertained them with songs and dances. As the expedition moved higher up the bay, where no English had been before seen, it met with a still more cordial welcome.

Jamestown was the first permanent English settlement established in America, although it has not since risen to very great importance. The site was chosen by this expedition about forty miles above the entrance, upon the banks of James River, where the emigrants at once proceeded to establish themselves. They suffered great distress from the commencement on account of the bad quality of the provisions, furnished under contract by Sir Thomas Smith, one of the leading members of the company. Disease soon followed want, and in a short time fifty of the settlers died. Under these difficult circumstances, the energy and ability of Captain John Smith pointed him out as the only person to command, and by the consent of all he was invested with absolute authority. He arranged the internal affairs of the colony as he best could, and then set out to collect supplies in the neighboring country. The Indians met him with derision, and refused to trade with him; he therefore, urged by necessity, drove them away, and took possession of a village well stocked with provisions. The Indians soon returned in force and attacked him furiously, but were easily repulsed. After

* Percy, in Purchas, iv., 1687.

their defeat they opened a friendly intercourse, and furnished the required supplies. Smith made several further excursions. On returning to the colony, he found that a conspiracy had been formed among his turbulent followers to break up the settlement and sail for England; this he managed to suppress, and soon again started to explore the country. In this expedition he rashly exposed himself unprotected to the assaults of the Indians, and was taken prisoner after a most gallant attempt at escape. He was led about in triumph for some time from village to village, and at length sentenced to die. His head was laid upon a stone, and the executioner stood over him with a club, awaiting the signal to slay, when Pocahontas, daughter of the Indian chief, implored her father's mercy for the white man. He was inexorable, and ordered the execution to proceed; but the generous girl laid her head upon that of the intended victim, and vowed that the death blow should strike her first. The savage chief moved by his daughter's devotion, spared the prisoner's life.* Smith was soon afterward escorted in safety to Jamestown, and given up on a small ransom being paid to the Indians.† [1608.]

Smith found, on his arrival, that the colonists were fitting out a pinnace to return to England. He, with ready decision, declared that the preparations should be discontinued immediately, or he would sink the little vessel. His prompt determination was successful, and the people agreed to remain. Through the generous kindness of Pocahontas, supplies of provisions were furnished to the settlement, till the arrival of a vessel from England, replenished its stores. Soon after

* "This celebrated scene is preserved in a beautiful piece of sculpture over the western door of the Rotundo of the Capitol at Washington. The group consists of five figures, representing the precise moment when Pocahontas, by her interposition, saved Smith from being executed. It is the work of Capellano, a pupil of Canova's."—Thatcher's *Indian Biography*, vol. i., p. 22. See Appendix, No. LXI., for the History of Pocahontas.

† Smith, in Pinkerton, xiii., 51–55. "The account is fully contained in the oldest book printed in Virginia, in our Cambridge library. It is a thin quarto, in black letter, by John Smith, printed in 1608."—Bancroft's *Hist. of the United States*, vol. i., p. 132.

his happy escape from the hands of the savages, Smith again started fearlessly upon an expedition to explore the remainder of Chesapeake Bay. He sailed in a small barge, accompanied only by twelve men, and with this slender force completed a voyage of 3000 miles along an unknown coast, among a fierce and generally hostile people, and depending on accident and his own ingenuity for supplies. During several years Pocahontas continued to visit the English, but her father was still hostile, and once endeavored to surprise Smith and slay him in the woods; but again the generous Indian girl saved his life at the hazard of her own: in a dark night she ran for many miles through the forest, evading the vigilance of her fierce countrymen, and warned him of the threatened danger. An open war now ensued between the English and the Indians, and was continued with great mutual injury, till a worthy gentleman named Thomas Rolfe, deeply interested by the person and character of Pocahontas, made her his wife; a treaty was then concluded with the Indian chief, which was henceforth religiously observed. [1613.]

The colony* meanwhile proceeded with varied fortunes. The emigrants had been very badly selected for their task: "poor gentlemen, tradesmen, serving-men, libertines, and such like, ten times more fit to spoil a commonwealth than either to begin or maintain one." These men were tempted into the undertaking by hopes of sudden wealth, and were altogether disinclined to even the slight labor of tilling that exuberant soil, when only a subsistence was to be their reward. In 1619 James commenced the system of transporting malefactors, by sending 100 "dissolute persons" to Virginia. These men were used as laborers, or rather slaves, but tended seriously to lower the character of the

* In the year 1610, the South Virginian or London Company sealed a patent to Lord Delawarr, constituting him Governor and Captain-General of South Virginia. His name was given to a bay and river, and to the Indians who dwelt in the surrounding country, called in their own tongue Lenni-Lenape, which name signifies THE ORIGINAL PEOPLE. Lord Delawarr's health was ruined by the hardships and anxieties he was exposed to in Virginia, and he was obliged to return to England in little more than a year.

voluntary emigration.* In 1625 only 1800 convicts remained alive out of 9000 who had been transported at a cost of £15,000.† The contracted and arbitrary system of the exclusive company was felt as a great evil in the colony.‡ This body was at length superseded by the forfeiture of its charter, and the crown assumed the direction of affairs. Many years of alternate anarchy and tyranny followed. During the rebellion of Bacon in 1676, the most remarkable event in this early period of Virginian history, English troops were first introduced into the American colonies. Sir William Berkeley, who was appointed governor in 1642, visited the insurrectionists with a terrible vengeance, when the death of the leader, Bacon, left them defenseless. "The old fool," said Charles II. (with truth), "has taken away more lives in that naked country than I for the murder of my father." But, though the complaints of the oppressed were heard in England with impartiality, and Berkeley was hunted to death by public opinion on his return there to defend himself, the permanent results of Bacon's rebellion were disastrous to Virginia: all the meas-

* Captain Smith says of Virginia, "that the number of felons and vagabonds did bring such evil character on the place, that some did choose to be hanged rather than go there, and *were*."—Graham's *Rise and Progress of the United States*, vol. i., p. 71.

"England adopted in the seventeenth century the system of transportation to her North American plantations, and the example was propagated by Cromwell, who introduced the practice of selling his political captives as slaves to the West Indians. But the number of regular convicts was too small, and that of free laborers too large, in the old provinces of North America, to have allowed this infusion of a convict population to produce much effect on the development of those communities, either in respect of their morals or their health.[1] Our own times are the first which have witnessed the phenomena of communities, in which the bulk of the working people consists of felons serving out the period of their punishment."—Merrivale, vol. ii., p. 3.

† Stith's *Hist. of Virginia*, p. 167, 168; Chalmers's *Annals of the United Colonies*, p. 69.

‡ Stith's *Hist. of Virginia*, p. 307.

[1] It must be remembered that the crimes of the convicts were chiefly political. The number transported to Virginia for social crimes was never considerable—scarcely enough to sustain the sentiment of pride in its scorn of the laboring population—certainly not enough to affect its character.—Bancroft, vol. ii., p. 191

ures of reform which had been attempted during its brief success were held void, and every restrictive feature that had been introduced into legislation by the detested governor was perpetuated.

Among the first settlers in Virginia, gold was the great object, it was every where eagerly sought, but in vain. Several ships were loaded with a sort of yellow clay, and sent to England under the belief that it contained the most precious of metals, but it was found to be utterly worthless. The colonists next turned their attention to the cultivation of tobacco.* This speedily became so profitable that it was pursued even to the exclusion of all other industry.

* It is asserted by Camden that tobacco was first brought into England by Mr. Ralph Lane, who went out as chief governor of Virginia in the first expedition commanded by Sir Richard Greenville. There can be little doubt that Lane was desired to import it by his master, Sir Walter Raleigh, who had seen it used in France during his residence there.—Camden, in Kennet, vol. ii., p. 509.

"There is a well-known tradition that Sir Walter first began to smoke it privately in his study, and the servant coming in with his tankard of ale and nutmeg, as he was intent upon his book, seeing the smoke issuing from his mouth, threw all the liquor in his face by way of extinguishing the fire, and, running down stairs, alarmed the family with piercing cries that his master, before they could get up, would be burned to ashes."—Oldy's *Life of Raleigh*, p. 74.

"King James declared himself the enemy of tobacco, and drew against it his royal pen. In the work which he entitled 'Counterblast to Tobacco,' he poured the most bitter reproaches on this 'vile and nauseous weed.' He followed it up by a proclamation to restrain 'the disorderly trading in tobacco,' as tending to a general and new corruption of both men's bodies and minds. Parliament also took the fate of this weed into their most solemn deliberation. Various members inveighed against it, as a mania which infested the whole nation; that plowmen took it at the plow; that it 'hindered' the health of the whole nation, and that thousands had died of it. Its warmest friends ventured only to plead that, before the final anathema was pronounced against it, a little pause might be granted to the inhabitants of Virginia and the Somer's Isles to find some other means of existence and trade. James's enmity did not prevent him from endeavoring to fill his coffers by the most enormous imposts laid upon tobacco, insomuch that the colonists were obliged for some time to send the whole into the ports of Holland. The government of New England, more consistently, passed a complete interdict against tobacco, the smoke of which they compared to that of the bottomless pit. Yet tobacco, like other proscribed objects, throve under persecution, and achieved a

There yet remains to be told one terrible incident in the earlier story of Virginia, an incident that resulted in the total destruction of the Indian race. The successor to the father of Pocahontas had conceived a deadly enmity against the English: this was embittered from day to day, as he saw the hated white men multiplying and spreading over the hunting grounds of his fathers. Then a fierce determination took possession of his savage heart. For years he matured his plans, and watched the favorable moment to crush every living stranger at a blow. He took all his people into counsel, and such was their fidelity, and so deep the wile of the Indian chief, that, during four years of preparation, no warning reached the intended victims. To the last fatal moment, a studied semblance of cordial friendship was observed; some Englishmen, who had lost their way in the woods were kindly and carefully guided back again.

One Friday morning (March 22d, 1622) the Indians came to the town in great numbers, bearing presents, and finding their way into every house. Suddenly the fierce shout of the savages broke the peaceful silence, and the death-shriek of their victims followed. In little more than a minute, three hundred and forty-seven, of all ages and sexes, were struck down in this horrid massacre. The warning of an Indian converted to Christianity saved Jamestown. The surviving English assembled there, and began a war of extermination against the savages. By united

final triumph over all its enemies. Indeed, the enmity against it was in some respects beneficial to Virginia, as drawing forth the most strict prohibitions against 'abusing and misemploying the soil of this fruitful kingdom' to the production of so odious an article. After all, as the impost for an average of seven years did not reach a hundred and fifty thousand pounds, it could not have that mighty influence, either for good or evil, which was ascribed to it by the fears and passions of the age."—Chalmers, b. i., ch. iii., with notes. Massaire, p. 210. Wives, p. 197, quoted by Murray.

"Frenchmen they call those tobacco plants whose leaves do not spread and grow large, but rather spire upward and grow tall; these plants they do not tend, not being worth their labor."—Mr. Clayton's *Letter to the Royal Society*, 1688. *Miscellanea Curiosa*, vol. iii., p. 303–310.

force, superior arms, and, it must be added, by treachery as black as that of their enemies, the white men soon swept away the Indian race forever from the Virginian soil.*

As has been before mentioned, the northern part of Virginia was bestowed by royal grant upon a Merchant Company of Plymouth, and other southern and western sea-ports. The first effort to take possession of the new territory was feeble and disastrous. Twenty-nine Englishmen and two Indians were sent out in a little bark of only fifty-five tons burden [1606]; they were taken by the Spaniards off the coast of Hispaniola, who treated them with great cruelty. Some time after this ill-fated expedition had failed, another colony of 100 men, led by Captains Popham and Gilbert, settled on the River Sagadahock, and built a fort called by them St. George. [1607.] They abandoned the settlement, however, the following year, and returned to England. The next project of British North American colonization was set on foot by Captain John Smith, already so highly distinguished in transatlantic history. [1614.] After much difficulty, he effëcted the equipment of two vessels, and sailed for the Virginian shore; but, although successful as a trading speculation, the only permanent fruits of the voyage was a map of the coast, which he presented to Charles I. The king, always interested in maritime affairs, listened favorably to Smith's accounts of the New World, but proved either unable or unwilling to render him any useful assistance. The next year this brave adventurer again crossed the seas in a small vessel containing only sixteen emigrants. The little expedition was captured by the French, and the leader, with great difficulty, effected his return to England.

* The colonists of Virginia, in a kind of manifesto published in 1622, expressed their satisfaction at some late warlike excursions of the Indians as a pretext for robbing and subjugating them. "Now these cleared grounds in all their villages, which are situated in the fruitfullest parts of the land, shall be inhabited by us, whereas heretofore the grubbing of woods was the greatest labor. The way of conquering them is much more easy than that of civilizing them by fair means; for they are a rude, barbarous, and naked people, scattered in small companies, which are helps to victory, but hinderances to civility."—*Tracts relating to Virginia in the British Museum*, quoted by Merrivale. See Appendix, No. LXII.

Meanwhile, a man named Hunt, who had been left in charge of one of the ships in Smith's first expedition, committed an outrage upon the natives that led to deplorable results [1616]; he inveigled thirty of them on board, carried them suddenly away, and sold them into slavery. The savages rose against the next English party that landed upon their coast, and killed and wounded several in revenge. Captain Dormer, a prudent and conciliatory person, with one of the betrayed natives, was sent by the company to explain to the furious Indians that Hunt's crime was the act of an individual, and not of the nation: this commission was well and wisely executed. For about two years Dormer frequently repeated his visits with advantage to his employers, but finally was attacked by strange savages and wounded fatally.

But still, through all these difficulties and disasters, adventurers pressed on to the fertile Western desert, allured by liberal grants of land from the chartered companies. The undefined limits of these concessions led to constant and mischievous quarrels among the settlers, often attended with violence and bloodshed: from these causes the early progress of the colony was very slow. One hundred and twenty years after England had discovered North America, she only possessed a few scattered fishing huts along the shore. But events were now at hand which at once stamped a peculiar character upon the colonization of this part of the New World,* and which were destined to exercise an influ-

* "Il faut envisager surtout l'influence qu'a exercée le Nouveau Continent sur les destinées du genre humain sous le rapport des institutions sociales. La tourmente religieuse du seizième siècle, en favorisant l'essor d'une libre reflexion, a préludé à la tourmente politique des temps dans lesquels nous vivons. Le premier de ces mouvemens a coincidé avec l'époque de l'etablissement des colonies Européennes en Amérique; le second s'est fait sentir vers la fin du dix-huitième siècle, et a fini par briser les liens de dépendance qui unissaient les deux mondes. Une circonstance sur laquelle on n'a peut-être pas assez fixé l'attention publique et qui tient à ces causes mystérieuses dont a dépendu la distribution inégale du genre humain sur le globe, a favorisée, on pourroit dire, à rendre possible l'influence politique que je viens de signaler. Une moitié du globe est restée si faiblement peuplée que, malgré le long travail d'une civilisation

ence upon the human race of an importance even yet incalculable.

indigène, qui a eu lieu entre les decouvertes de Lief et de Colomb, sur les côtes Américaines opposées à l'Asie, d'immenses pays dans la partie orientale n'offroient au quinzième siècle que des tribus éparses de peuples chasseurs. Cet état de depopulation dans des pays fertiles et éminemment aptes à la culture de nos céreales, a permis aux Européens d'y fonder des établissemens sur une échelle qu'aucune colonisation de l'Asie et de l'Afrique n'a pu atteindre. Les peuples chasseurs ont été refoulés des côtes orientales vers l'interieur, et dans le nord de l'Amérique, sous des climats et des aspects de végétation très analogues à ceux des îles Britanniques, il s'est formé par émigration, dès la fin de l'année 1620, des communautés dont les institutions se présentent comme le reflet des institutions libres de la mère patrie. La Nouvelle Angleterre n'étoit pas primitivement un établissement d'industrie et de commerce, comme le sont encore les factoreries de l'Afrique; ce n'étoit pas une domination sur les peuples agricoles d'une race différente, comme l'empire Britannique dans l'Inde, et pendant longtemps, l'empire Espagnole au Mexique et au Pérou. La Nouvelle Angleterre, qui a reçu une première colonisation de quatre mille familles de puritains, dont descend aujourd'hui un tiers de la population blanche des Etats Unis, étoit un établissement religieux. La liberté civile s'y montrait dès l'origine inséparable de la liberté du culte. Or l'histoire nous revèle que les institutions libres de l'Angleterre, de la Hollande, et de la Suisse, malgré leur proximité, n'ont pas réagi sur les peuples de l'Europe latine, comme ce reflet de formes de gouvernemens entièrement democratiques qui, loin de tout ennemi extérieur, favorisés par une tendance uniforme et constante de souvenirs et de vielles mœurs, ont pris dans un calme long-temps prolongé, des développemens inconnus aux temps modernes. C'est ainsi que le manque de population dans des régions des Nouveau Continent opposées à l'Europe, et le libre et prodigieux accroissement d'une colonisation Anglaise audelà de la grande vallée de l'Atlantique, a puissamment contribué à changer la face politique et les destinées de l'ancien continent. On a affirmé que si Colomb n'avoit pas changé, selon les conseils d'Alonzo Pinzon,[1] le 7 Octobre, 1492, la direction de sa route, qui étoit de l'est à l'ouest, et gouverné vers le sud-ouest, il seroit entré dans le courant d'eau chaude ou Gulf Stream, et auroit été porté vers la Floride, et de là peut-être vers le cap Hatteras et la Virginie, incident d'une immense importance, puisqu'il auroit pu donner aux Etats Unis, en lieu d'une population Protestante Anglaise, une population Catholique Espagnole."—Humboldt's *Géog. du Nouveau Continent*, tom. iii., p. 163.

[1] Alonzo s'étoit écrié "que son cœur lui disoit que pour trouver la terre, il falloit gouverner vers le sud-ouest." L'inspiration d'Alonzo étoit moins mystérieuse qu'elle peut le paraître au premier abord. Pinzon avoit vu dans la soirée passer des perroquets, et il savoit que ces oiseaux n'alloient pas sans motif du côte du sud. Jamais vol d'oiseau n'a eu des suites plus graves.

CHAPTER X.

The Protestant Reformation was eminently suited to the spirit of the English people, although forced upon them in the first instance by the absolute power of a capricious king, and unaccompanied by any acknowledgment of those rights of toleration and individual judgment upon which its strength seemed mainly to depend. The monarch, when constituted the head of the Church, exacted the same spiritual obedience from his subjects as they had formerly rendered to the Pope of Rome. Queen Elizabeth adopted her father's principles: she favored the power of the hierarchy, and the pomp and ceremony of external religious observances. But the English people, shocked by the horrors of Mary's reign, and terrified by the papal persecutions on the Continent, were generally inclined to favor the extremes of Calvinistic simplicity, as a supposed security against another reaction to the Romish faith. The stern and despotic queen, encouraged by the counsels of Archbishop Whitgift, assumed the groundless right of putting down the opinions of the Puritans by force. [1583.] Various severities were exercised against those who held the obnoxious doctrines; but, despite the storm of persecution, the spirit of religious independence spread rapidly among the sturdy people of England. At length a statute was passed of a nature now almost incredible—secession from the Church was punishable by banishment, and by death in case of refusal on return.* [1593.]

The Puritans were thus driven to extremity.† The fol-

* 35 Eliz., c. 1, stat. 4, p. 841–843; *Parl. Hist.*, p. 863; Strype's *Whitgift*, p. 414, &c.; Neale's *Puritans*, vol. i., p. 526, 527, quoted by Bancroft, vol. i., p. 290.

† "The *Gospel Advocate* asserts that 'the judicial law of Moses being still in force, no prince or law ought to save the lives of (*inter*

lowers of an enthusiastic seceder named Brown* formed the first example of an independent system: each congregation was in itself a Church, and the spiritual power was wholly vested in its members. This sect was persecuted to the uttermost: the leader was imprisoned in no less than thirty-two different places, and many of his followers suffered death itself for conscience' sake. Some of the Brownists took refuge in Holland† [1598]; but, impelled by a longing for an independent home, or perhaps urged by the mysterious impulse of their great destiny, they cast their eyes upon that stern Western shore, where the untrodden wilderness offered them at least the "freedom to worship God." They applied to the London Company for a grant of land, declaring that they were "weaned from the delicate milk of their native country, and knit together in a strict and sacred band,

alios) heretics, willful breakers of the Sabbath, neglecters of the sacrament without just reason.' Well may the historian of the Puritans (Neale) say, 'Both parties agreed in asserting the necessity of a uniformity of public worship, *and of using the sword of the magistrate in support of their respective principles.*' It should never be forgotten by those who are inclined to blame the severe laws passed against these Nonconformists, that the English government was dealing with men whose avowed wish and object it was not simply to be tolerated, but to subvert existing institutions in Church and State, and set up in their place those approved by themselves."—Godley's *Letters from America*, vol. ii., p. 135.

* "The most noisy advocate of the new opinions was Brown, a man of rashness, possessing neither true courage nor constancy. He has acquired historical notoriety because his hot-headed indiscretion urged him to undertake the defense of separation. . . . . Brown eventually purchased a living in the English Church by conformity."—Bancroft's *History of the United States*, vol. i., p. 287.

† "But, although Holland is a country of the greatest religious freedom, they were not better satisfied there than in England. They were tolerated, indeed, but watched. Their zeal began to have dangerous languor for want of opposition, and being without power and influence, they grew tired of the indolent security of their sanctuary. They were desirous of removing to a country where they should see no superior."—Russell's *Modern Europe*, vol. ii., p. 427.

"They were restless from the consciousness of ability to act a more important part on the theater of the world . . . . they were moved by an enlightened desire of improving their condition . . . . the honorable ambition of becoming the founders of a state."—Bancroft's *History of the United States*, vol. i., p. 303.

whom small things could not discourage, nor small discontents cause to wish themselves home again." After some delay they accomplished their object ; however, the only security they could obtain for religious independence was a promise that, as long they demeaned themselves quietly, no inquiry should be made.*

Much of the history of nations may be traced through the foundation and progress of their colonies. Each particular era has shown, in the settlements of the time, types of the several mother countries, examples of their systems, and the results of their exigencies. At one time this type is of an adventurous, at another of a religious character; now formed by political, again by social influences. The depth and durability of this impress may be measured by the strength of the first motives, and the genius of the people from whom the emigration flows.† The ancient colonies of Asia Minor

* This was a promise from James I., who had now succeeded to the throne of England.

† "A strongly-marked distinction exists between the Southern and Northern Americans. The two extremes are formed by the New Englanders[1] and the Virginians. The former are certainly the more respectable. They are industrious, frugal, enterprising, regular in their habits, pure in their manners, and strongly impressed with sentiments of religion. The name Yankee, which we apply as one of reproach and derision to Americans in general, is assumed by them as their natural and appropriate designation.[2] It is a common proverb in America, that a Yankee will live where another would starve. Their very prosperity, however, with a certain reserve in their character, and supposed steady attention to small gains, renders them not excessively popular with those among whom they settle. They are charged with a peculiar species of finesse, called 'Yankee tricks,' and the character of being 'up to every thing' is applied to them, we know not exactly how, in a sense of reproach. The Virginian planter, on the contrary, is lax in principle, destitute of industry, eager in the pursuit of rough pleasures, and demoralized by the system of negro slavery, which exists in almost a West Indian form. Yet, with all the Americans who attempt to draw the parallel, he seems rather the favorite. He is frank, open-hearted, and exercising a splendid hospitality. Both Cooper and Judge Hall report him as a complete gen-

1 Descendants of the Puritans.

2 "The word Yankees (which is the Indian corruption of English *Yengeese*) is both offensive and incorrect as applied to any but New Englanders."—Godley's *Letters from America*.

displayed the original characteristics of the mother country long after her states had become utterly changed. The Roman settlements in Italy raised upon the ruins of a subjugated nation a fabric of civilization and power that can never be forgotten. The proud and adventurous, but ruthless spirit that distinguished the Spanish nation at the time of their wonderful conquests in the New World, is still exhibited in the haughty tyranny of Cuba, and the sanguinary struggles of the South American republics. The French Canadian of to-day retains most or many of the national sentiments of those who crossed the Atlantic to extend the power of France and of her proudest king. And still, in that great Anglo-Saxon nation of the West, through the strife of democratic ambition, and amid the toils and successes of an enormous commerce, we trace the foundations, overgrown perhaps, but all unshaken, of that stern edifice of civil and religious liberty* which the Pilgrim fathers raised with their untiring labor, and cemented with their blood.

The peculiar nature of the first New England emigration was the result of those strong tendencies of the British people soon afterward strengthened into a determination sufficiently

tleman; by which they evidently mean, not the finished courtier, but the English country gentleman or squire, though the opening afforded by the political constitution of his country causes him to cultivate his mind more by reading and inquiry. A large proportion of the most eminent and ruling statesmen in America—Washington, Jefferson, Madison—were Virginians. Surrounded from their infancy with ease and wealth, accustomed to despise, and to see despised, money on a small scale, and no laborious exertions made for its attainment, they imbibe from youth the habits and ideas of the higher classes. Luxurious living, gaming, horse-racing, cock-fighting, and other rough, turbulent amusements, absorb a great portion of their life. Although, therefore, the leisure enjoyed by them, when well improved, may have produced some very elevated and accomplished characters, they can not, taken at the highest, be considered so respectable a class as their somewhat despised northern brethren; and the lower ranks are decidedly in a state of comparative moral debasement."—Murray, vol. ii., p. 394.

* "James I. ranked among their party, as much as he was able by severe usage, all those who stood up in defense even of civil liberty."—Bolingbroke's *Remarks upon English History*, p. 283.

powerful to sacrifice the monarch and subvert the Church and State.

The Brownists, or, as they are more happily called, the Pilgrim fathers, set sail on the 12th of July, 1620, in two small vessels. There were in all 120 souls, with a moderate supply of provisions and goods. On the 9th of November they reached Cape Cod, after a rough voyage; they had been obliged to send one of their ships back to England. From ignorance of the coast and from the lateness of the season, they could not find any very advantageous place of settlement; they finally fixed upon New Plymouth,* where they landed on the 21st of December. During the remainder of the winter they suffered terribly from cold, want, and sickness; no more than fifty remained alive when spring came to mitigate their sufferings. The after progress of the little colony was for some time slow and painful. The system of common property† had excited grievous discontent; this tended to create an aversion to labor that was to be productive of no more benefit to the industrious than to the idle; in a short time it became necessary to enforce a certain degree of exertion by the punishment of whipping. They intrusted all religious matters to the gifted among their brethren, and would not allow of the formation of any regular ministry. However, the unsuitableness of these systems to men subject to the usual impulses and weakness of human nature soon became obvious, and the first errors

* "In memory of the hospitalities which the company had received at the last English port from which they had sailed, this oldest New England colony obtained the name of Plymouth. The two vessels which conveyed the Pilgrim fathers from Delft Haven were the *Mayflower* and the *Speedwell.* The Mayflower alone proceeded to America."—Bancroft, vol. i., p. 313.

† "Under the influence of this wild notion, the colonists of New Plymouth, in imitation of the primitive Christians, threw all their property into a common stock."—Robertson's *America*, book x. One of the many errors with which the volume of Robertson teems. There was no attempt at imitating the primitive Christians; the partnership was a consequence of negotiation with British merchants; the colonists preferred the system of private property, and acted upon it, as far and as soon as was possible.—Bancroft's *History of the United States*, vol. i., p. 306.

were gradually corrected. In the course of ten years the population reached to 300, and the settlement prospered considerably.

King James was not satisfied with the slow progress of American colonization. [1620.] In the same year that the Pilgrim fathers landed at Plymouth, he formed a new company under the title of the Grand Council of Plymouth,* and appointed many people of rank and influence to its direction. Little good, however, resulted from this step. Though the council itself was incapable of the generous project of planting colonies, it was ever ready to make sale of patents, which sales, owing to Parliamentary opposition to their claims, soon became their only source of revenue.† They sold to some gentlemen of Dorchester a belt of land stretching from the Atlantic to the Pacific, and extending three miles south of the River Charles, and three miles north of *every* part of the River Merrimac. Other associates in the enterprise were sought and found in and about London: Winthrop, Johnson, Pinchon, Eaton, Saltonstall, Billingham, famous in colonial annals. Endicott, the first governor of the new colony, was one of the original purchasers of the patent. They were all kindred spirits, men of religious

* "The remonstrances of the Virginia corporation and a transient regard for the rights of the country could delay, but could not defeat, a measure that was sustained by the personal favorites of the monarch. King James issued to forty of his subjects, some of them members of his household and his government, the most wealthy and powerful of the English nobility, a patent, which in American annals, and even in the history of the world, has but one parallel. The territory conferred on the patentees in absolute property, with unlimited jurisdiction, the sole powers of legislation, the appointment of all officers and all forms of government, comprised, and at the time was believed to comprise, much more than a million of square miles: it was, by a single signature of King James, given away to a corporation within the realm, composed of but forty individuals."—Bancroft, vol. i., p. 273.

† "The very extent of the grant rendered it of little value. The results which grew out of the concession of this charter form a new proof, if any were wanting, of that mysterious connection of events by which Providence leads to ends that human councils had not conceived."—Bancroft, vol. i., p. 273.

The Grand Council of Plymouth resigned their charter in 1635.

fervor, uniting the emotions of enthusiasm with unbending resolution in action.

The first winter brought to these colonists the usual privation, suffering, and death, but a now rapidly-increasing emigration more than filled up the places of all casualties. From this period, many men of respectability and talent,* especially ministers of the Gospel, sought that religious freedom† in America which was denied them at home. A

* "The circumstance which threw a greater luster on the colony than any other was the arrival of Mr. John Cotton, the most esteemed of all the Puritan ministers in England. He was equally distinguished for his learning, and for a brilliant and figurative eloquence. He was so generally beloved that his nonconformity to the ritual of the Established Church, of which he was a minister, was for a considerable time disregarded. At last, however, he was called before the ecclesiastical commission, and he determined upon emigration. 'Some reverend and renowned ministers of our Lord' endeavored to persuade him that the forms to which he refused obedience were 'sufferable trifles,' and did not actually amount to a breach of the second commandment. Mr. Cotton, however, argued so forcibly on the opposite side, that several of the most eminent became all that he was, and afterward followed his example. There went out with him Mr. Hooker and Mr. Stone, who were esteemed to make 'a glorious triumvirate,' and were received in New England with the utmost exultation. It was doubtless a severe trial to these ministers, who appear really to have been, as they say, 'faithful, watchful, painful, serving their flock daily with prayers and tears,' who possessed such a reputation at home and over Europe, to find that no sooner did any half-crazed enthusiast spring up or arrive in the colony, that the people could be prevented only by the most odious compulsion from deserting their churches and flocking to him in a mass. Vainly did Mr. John Cotton strive to persuade Roger Williams, the sectary, that the red cross on the English banner, or his wife's being in the room while he said grace, were 'sufferable trifles,' and 'Mrs. Hutchinson and her ladies' treated his advice and exhortations with equal disregard and contempt. One of them sent him a pound of candles to intimate his need of more spiritual light. This was then the freedom for which his church and his country had been deserted." —Mather; Neale; Hutchinson.

† "Robertson is astonished that Neale (see Neale, p. 56) should assert that freedom of religious worship was granted, when the charter expressly asserts the king's supremacy. But this, in fact, was never the article at which they demurred; for the spirit of loyalty was still very strong. It seems quite clear, from the confidence with which they went, and the manner in which they acted when there, that, though there was no formal or written stipulation, the most full understanding existed that very ample latitude was to be allowed in this

general impulse was given among the commercial and industrious classes; vessels constantly crowded from the English ports across the Atlantic, till at length the court took the alarm. A proclamation was issued "to restrain the disorderly transportation of his majesty's subjects, because of the many idle and refractory humors, 'whose only or principal end is to live beyond the reach of authority.'" It has long been a popular story that eight emigrant ships were seized when on the point of sailing for America, and the passengers forced to land; among whom were John Hampden,* Sir Arthur Hazlerig, and Oliver Cromwell. This tale has, however, been proved untrue by modern historians.†

respect. We have seen on every occasion the vast sacrifices which kings were willing to make in order to people their distant possessions; and the necessity was increased by the backwardness hitherto visible."—Murray's *America*, vol. i., p. 249.

* During the year 1635 we find the name of John Hampden joined with those of six other gentlemen of family and fortune, who united with the Lords Say and Brooke in making a purchase from the Earl of Warwick of an extensive grant of land in a wide wilderness then called Virginia, but which now forms a part of the State of Connecticut. That these transatlantic possessions were designed by the associates ultimately, or under certain contingencies, to serve as an asylum to themselves and a home to their posterity, there is no room to doubt; but it is evident that nothing short of circumstances constituting a moral necessity would have urged persons of their rank, fortunes, and habits of life to encounter the perils, privations, and hardships attendant upon the pioneers of civilization in that inhospitable clime. Accordingly, they for the present contented themselves with sending out an agent to take possession of these territories and to build a fort. This was done, and the town called Saybrook, from the united names of the two noble proprietors, still preserves the memory of the enterprise. They finally abandoned the whole design, and sold the land in 1636, probably.—Miss Aikin's *Life of Charles I.*, p. 471. Bancroft, vol. i., p. 384.

† "In one of these embargoed ships had actually embarked for their voyage across the Atlantic two no less considerable personages than John Hampden and his kinsman, Oliver Cromwell."—*Life of Hampden*, by Lord Nugent, vol. i., p. 254. London, 1832.

Lord Nugent has fallen into the vulgar error, an invention, probably, of the Puritan historian, and unanswerably disproved by a reference to Parliamentary records. See Miss Aikin's *Life of Charles I.*, vol. i., p. 472; Bancroft's *History of the United States*, vol. i., p. 411. The exultation of the Puritan writers on the subject is excessive. They ascribe all the subsequent misfortunes of Charles I. in connection

Notwithstanding these unjust and mischievous prohibitions, a considerable number of emigrants still found their way across the Atlantic. But when the outburst of popular indignation swept away all the barriers raised by a short-sighted tyranny against English freedom, many flocked back again to their native country to enjoy its newly-acquired liberty. [1648.] The odious and iniquitous persecution of the Puritans resulted in a great benefit to the human race, and gave the first strong impulse to the spirit of resistance that ultimately overthrew oppression. It caused, also, the colonization of New England to be effected by a class of men far superior in industry, energy, principle, and character to those who usually left their English homes to seek their fortunes in new countries. That religion, for which they had made so great a sacrifice, was the main-spring of all their social and political systems. They were, however, too blindly zealous to discriminate between the peculiar administration of a theocracy and the catholic and abiding principles of the Gospel. If they did not openly profess that the judicial law of Moses was still in force, they at any rate openly practiced its stern enactments.

The intolerance of these martyrs of intolerance is a sad

with the scheme of Providence to this tyrannical edict, as they call it. —Russell's *Modern Europe*, vol. ii., p. 237. See Bancroft's *History of the United States*, vol. i., p. 412.

"Nothing could be more barbarous than this! To impose laws on men which in conscience they thought they could not comply with, to punish them for their noncompliance, and continually revile them as undutiful and disobedient subjects by reason thereof, and yet not permit them peaceably to depart and enjoy their own opinions in a distant part of the world, yet dependent on the sovereign: to do all this was base, barbarous, and inhuman. But persecutors of all ages and nations are near the same; they are without the feelings and the understandings of men. Cromwell or Hampden could have given little opposition to the measures of Charles in the wilds of North America. In England they engaged with spirit against him, and he had reason to repent his hindering their voyage. May such at all times be the reward of those who attempt to rule over their fellowmen with rigor: may they find that they will not be slaves to kings or priests, but that they know the rights by nature conferred on them, and will assert them! This will make princes cautious how they give themselves up to arbitrary counsels, and dread the consequences of them."—Harris's *Life of Cromwell*, p. 56.

example of human waywardness.* In their little commonwealth, seceders from the established forms of faith were persecuted with an unholy zeal. Imprisonment, banishment, and even death itself, were inflicted for that free exercise of religious opinions which the Pilgrim fathers had sacrificed all earthly interests to win for themselves. In those dark days of fanatic faith or vicious skepticism, the softening influence of true Christianity was but little felt. The stern denunciations and terrible punishments of the Old Testament were more suited to the iron temper of the age than the gentle dispensations of the New—the fiery zeal of Joshua than the loving persuasiveness of St. John.

As the tenets of each successive sect rose into popularity and influenced the majority, they became state questions,† distracted the Church, and threatened the very existence of the colony. The first schism that disturbed the peace of the settlements was raised by Roger Williams at Salem. [1635.] This worthy and sincere enthusiast held many just and sound views among others that were wild and injurious: he stoutly upheld freedom of conscience, and inconveniently contested the right of the British crown to bestow Indian lands upon Englishmen. On the other hand, he contrived to raise a storm of fanatic hatred against the red cross in the

* "Mr. Dudley, one of the most respectable of the governors, was found, at his death, with a copy of verses in his pocket, which included the following couplet:

> "'Let men of God in court and churches watch
> O'er such as do a toleration hatch." —CHALMERS.

† "The cutting the hair very close, which seemed supported by St. Paul's authority, was the chief outward symbol of a Puritan. In the case of a minister, it was considered essential that the ear should be thoroughly uncovered. Even after the example of Dr. Owen and other eminent divines had given a sanction to letting the hair grow, and even to periwigs, a numerous association was formed at Boston (where Mr. John Cotton was pastor), with Mr. Endicot, the governor, at their head, the members of which bound themselves to stand by each other in resisting long hair to the last extremity. Vane, a young man of birth and fashion, continued for some time a recusant against the uncouth test of his principles, but at last we find a letter congratulating him on having 'glorified God by cutting his hair.'"—Hutchinson's *Massachusetts*, quoted by Murray.

banner of St. George, which seriously disturbed the state,* and led to violent writings and altercations. At length Williams was banished as a distractor of the public peace, but a popular uproar attended his departure, and the greater part of the inhabitants were with difficulty dissuaded from following him. He retired to Providence, Rhode Island† [1636], where a little colony soon settled round him, and he there lived and died in general esteem and regard.‡

The Antinomian sect shortly after excited a still more dangerous commotion in the colony. [1637.] Mrs. Hutchinson, a Lincolnshire lady of great zeal and determination, joined by nearly the whole female population, adopted these views in the strongest manner. The ministers of the church, although decided Calvinists, and firmly opposed to the Romish doctrines of salvation by works, earnestly pressed the reformation of heart and conduct as a test of religion. Mrs. Hutchinson and her followers held that to inculcate any rule of life or manners was a crime against the Holy Spirit; in their actual deportment, however, it must be confessed that their bitterest enemies could not find grounds of censure. With the powerful advocacy of female zeal, these doctrines spread rapidly, and the whole colony was soon divided between "the covenant of works and the covenant of grace;" the ardor and obstinacy of the disputants being by no means proportioned to their full understanding of the point§ in dispute. Sir Harry Vane,‖ whose rank and character had

* One of Williams's disciples, who held some command, cut the cross out, and trampled it under foot. This red cross had nearly subverted the colony. One part of the trained bands would not march with, another would not march without it.—Mather, Neale, &c., quoted by Murray.

† "The town of Providence, now the capital of Rhode Island, was founded by Williams. The Indian name was Mooshausick, but he changed it to Providence in commemoration of his wonderful escape from persecution.—Arfwedson, vol. i., p. 224.

‡ Mather, vol. vii., ch. ii.; Neale, ch. i., p. 138; Hutchinson, p. 37, 39.

§ *Ibid.*

‖ "Mr. Controller, Sir Harry Vane's eldest son, hath left his father, his mother, his country, and that fortune which his father would have left him here, and is for conscience' sake gone into New England, there to lead the rest of his days, being about twenty years of age.

caused him to be elected governor in spite of his youth, zealously adopted Antinomian opinions, and, in consequence, was ejected from office by the opposite party at the ensuing election, Mrs. Hutchinson having failed to secure in the country districts that superiority which she possessed in the town of Boston.* After some ineffectual efforts to reconcile

He had abstained two years from taking the sacrament in England, because he could get nobody to administer it to him standing."—*Strafford Letters*, September, 1635, quoted by Miss Aikin, *Life of Charles I.*, vol. i., p. 479.

"Sir Harry Vane returned to England immediately after the loss of his election. His personal experience of the uncharitableness and intolerance exercised upon one another by men who had themselves been the victims of a similar spirit at home, seems to have produced for some time a tranquilizing effect upon the mind of Vane. He was reconciled to his father, married by his direction a lady of family, obtained the place of joint treasurer of the navy, and exhibited for some time no hostility to the measures of the government. But his fire was smothered only, not extinguished."—Miss Aikin's *Life of Charles I.*, vol. i., p. 481.

"After the Restoration of Charles II., Sir Harry Vane suffered death upon the block. (See Hallam, vol. ii., p. 443.) The manner of his death was the admiration of his times."—Bancroft, vol. ii., p. 40.

* Boston was the capital of Massachusetts, and the center of the most fervent Puritanism.

"Boston may be ranked as the seat of the Unitarians, as Baltimore is that of the Roman Catholics, and Philadelphia that of the Quakers. . . . . . No axiom is more applicable to the pensive, serious, scrutinizing inhabitant of the New England States than this: 'What I do not understand, I reject as worthless and false;' so said one of the most learned men of Boston to me. 'Why occupy the mind with that which is incomprehensible? Have we not enough of that which appears clear and plain around us?' . . . . . The greater part of the Bostonians, including every one of wealth, talents, and learning, have adopted this doctrine."—Arfwedson, vol. i., p. 179.

"In Boston all the leading men are Unitarians, a creed peculiarly acceptable to the pride and self-sufficiency of our nature, asserting, as it does, the independence and perfectibility of man, and denying the necessity of atonement or sanctification by supernatural influences.

"Though every where in New England the greatest possible decency and respect with regard to morals and religion is still observed, I have no hesitation in saying that I do not think the New Englanders a *religious* people. The assertion, I know, is paradoxical, but it is nevertheless true, that is, if a strong and earnest belief be a necessary element in a religious character: to me it seems to be its very essence and foundation. I am not now speaking of belief in *the*

the seceders to the Church, the new governor and the ministers summoned a general synod of the colonial clergy to meet at Cambridge, where, after some very turbulent proceedings, the whole of the Antinomian doctrines were condemned.

As might have been supposed, this condemnation had but little effect. The obnoxious principles were preached as widely and zealously as before, till the civil authority resorted to the rude argument of force, banished Mr. Wheelwright, one of the leaders, with two of his followers, from the colony, and fined and disfranchised others. Mrs. Hutchinson was ultimately accused, condemned, and ordered to leave the colony in six months. Although she made a sort of recantation of her errors, her inexorable judges insisted in carrying out the sentence.* The unhappy lady removed to Rhode Island, where her husband, through her influence, was elected governor, and where she was followed by many of her devoted adherents. [1638.] Thus the persecutions in the old settlement of Massachusetts had the same effect as those in England —of elevating a few stubborn recusants into the founders of

truth, but belief in something or any thing which is removed from the action of the senses. . . . . . I am not trusting to my own limited observation in arriving at this conclusion; I find in M. de Tocqueville's work an assertion of the same fact. He accounts for it, indeed, in a different way. . . . . . What I complain of is, not the absence of nominal, but of real, heartfelt, unearthly religion, such as led the Puritan Nonconformists to sacrifice country and kindred, and brave the dangers of the ocean and the wilderness for the sake of what they believed God's truth. In my opinion, those men were prejudiced and mistaken, and committed great and grievous faults; but there was, at least, a redeeming element in their character—that of high conscientiousness. There was no compromise of truth, no sacrifice to expediency about them; they believed in the invisible, and they acted on that belief. Every where the tone of religious feeling, since that time, has been altered and relaxed, but perhaps nowhere so much as in the land where the descendants of those Pilgrims lived."—Godley's *Letters from America*, vol. ii., p. 90, 133.

* "The arbitrary will of the single tyrant, the excesses of the prerogative, seem light when compared with their (the Puritans') more intolerant, more arbitrary, and more absolute power."—*Commentaries on the Life and Reign of Charles I.*, vol. iii., p. 28, by I. D'Israeli. London, 1830.

states and nations. After her husband's death Mrs. Hutchinson removed into a neighboring Dutch settlement, where she and all her family met with a dreadful fate; they were surprised by the Indians, and every one destroyed. [1643.]

Although by these violent and unjust punishments, and by disarming the disaffected, the Antinomian spirit was for a time put down, unity was by no means restored. Pride and the love of novelty continually gave birth to new sects. Ministers, who had possessed the highest reputation in England, saw with sorrow that their colonial churches were neglected for the sake of ignorant and mischievous enthusiasts. Even common profligates and rogues, when other lesser villainies had failed, assumed the hypocritical semblance of some peculiar religion, and enjoyed their day of popularity.

The Anabaptists next carried away the fickle affections of the multitude, and excited the enmity of their rulers. [1643.] This schism first became perceptible by people leaving the church when the rites of baptism were being administered; but at length private meetings for worship were held, attended by large congregations. The magistrates, as usual, practiced great severities against these seceders, first by fine, imprisonment, and even whipping; finally by banishment. The Anabaptists were, however, not put down by the arm of power, but were speedily forgotten in the sudden appearance of a stranger sect than any that had hitherto appeared even in New England.

The people called Quakers had lately made their appearance in the north of England. [1648.] They soon found their way to America, where they were received with bitter hostility from the commencement. [1656.] The dangerous enthusiasts who first went forth to preach the doctrines of this strange sect were very different men from those who now command the respect and good will of all classes by their industry, benevolence, and love of order. The original propagandists believed that the divine government was still administered on earth by direct and special communication, as in the times chronicled by Holy Writ; they therefore despised and disregarded all human authorities. To actual force, indeed, they only opposed a passive resistance; and their patience and obstinacy in carrying out this principle must excite astonishment, if not admiration. But their language was most violent and abusive against all priests and ministers, governors and magistrates.* The women of this novel persuasion were even more fanatic than the men. Several leaving their husbands and children in England, crossed the seas to bear witness to their inspiration at Boston. They were, however, rudely received, their books burned, and themselves either imprisoned or scourged and banished. No-wise intimidated by these severities, several other women brought upon themselves the vengeance of the law by frantic and almost incredible demonstrations; and a man named Faubord endeavored to sacrifice his first-born son under a supposed command from Heaven.

The ministers and magistrates came to the conclusion that the colony could never enjoy peace while the Quakers continued among them. These sectarians were altogether unmanageable by the means of ordinary power or reason; they would neither pay fines nor work in prison, nor, when liberated, promise to amend their conduct. The government now enacted still more violent laws against them, one, among others, rendering them liable to have their ears cut off for obstinacy; and yet this strange fanaticism increased from day to day. At length the Quakers were banished from the colony, under the threat of death in case of return.

* Mather affirms that the Quakers used to go about saying, "We deny thy Christ; we deny thy God, whom thou callest Father, Son, and Spirit; thy Bible is the word of the devil." They used to rise up suddenly in the midst of a sermon, and call upon the preacher to cease his abomination. One writer says, "For hellish reviling of the painful ministers of Christ, I know no people can match them." The following epithets bestowed by Fisher on Dr. Owen are said to be fair specimens of their usual addresses: "Thou green-headed trumpeter! thou hedgehog and grinning dog! thou tinker! thou lizard! thou whirligig! thou firebrand! thou louse! thou mooncalf! thou ragged tatterdemalion! thou livest in philosophy and logic, which are of the devil." Even Penn is said to have addressed the same respected divine as, "Thou bane of reason and beast of the earth." When the governor or any magistrate came in sight, they would call out, "Woe to thee, thou oppressor," and in the language of Scripture prophecy would announce the judgments that were about to fall upon their head.—Neale, cap. i., p. 341–345. Mather, b. vii., cap. iv. Hutchinson, p. 196–205.

They were, however, scarcely beyond the borders when a supposed inspiration prompted them to retrace their steps to Boston: scarcely had their absence been observed, when their solemn voices were again heard denouncing the city of their persecutors.

The horrible law decreeing the punishment of death against the Quakers had only been carried by a majority of thirteen to twelve in the Colonial Court of Deputies, and after a strong opposition; but, to the eternal disgrace of the local government, its atrocious provisions were carried into effect, and four of the unhappy fanatics were judicially murdered. The tidings of these executions filled England with horror. Even Charles II. was moved to interpose the royal power for the protection of at least the lives of the obnoxious sectarians. He issued a warrant on the 9th of September, 1661, absolutely prohibiting the punishment of death against Quakers, and directing that they should be sent to England for trial. In consequence of this interference, no more executions took place, but other penalties were continued with unabated severity.

While the persecution of the Quakers and Anabaptists raged in New England, an important addition to the numbers of the colonists was gained, a large body of Nonconformists having fled across the Atlantic from a fresh assault commenced against their liberties by Charles II. This Puritan emigration was regarded with great displeasure by the king. He speedily took an opportunity of arbitrarily depriving the colony of its charter, and sent out Sir Edmund Andros to administrate as absolute governor. The country soon felt painfully the despotic tyranny of their new ruler; and the establishment of an English Church, with the usual ritual, spread general consternation. When James ascended the throne, a proclamation of tolerance somewhat allayed the fears of the settlers; but the administration of temporal affairs became ruinously oppressive. On the pretense that the titles of all land obtained under the old charter had become void by its abrogation, new and exorbitant fees were exacted, heavy and injudicious taxes arbitrarily imposed, and all right of representation denied to the colonists. At length, in the year 1689, a man, named Winslow, brought from

Virginia the joyful news of the Prince of Orange's proclamation; he was immediately arrested for treason; but the people rose tumultuously, imprisoned the governor, and re-established the authority of their old magistrates. On the 26th of May, a vessel arrived with the intelligence that William and Mary had been proclaimed in England. Although the new monarch declared himself favorably disposed toward the colonists, he did not restore their beloved charter. He, however, granted them a Constitution nearly similar to that of the mother country, which rendered the people of New England tolerably contented.

The colony was now fated to suffer from a delusion more frantic and insane than any it had hitherto admitted, and which compromised its very existence. The New Englanders had brought with them the belief in witchcraft prevalent among the early reformers, and the wild and savage wilderness where their lot was now cast tended to deepen the impressions of superstition upon their minds. Two young girls, of the family of Mr. Paris, minister of Salem, were suddenly afflicted with a singular complaint, probably of an hysterical character, which baffled the united skill of the neighboring physicians; till one, more decided than the rest, declared that the sufferers were bewitched. From this time prayers and fasting were the remedies adopted, and the whole town of Salem at length joined in a day of humiliation. The patients, however, did not improve, till an Indian serving-woman denounced another, named Tituba, as the author of the evil. Mr. Paris assailed the accused, and tortured her in the view of extracting a confession of guilt, which she at length made, with many absurd particulars, hoping to appease her persecutor. From this time the mischievous folly spread wider; a respectable clergyman, Mr. Burroughs, was tried for witchcraft on the evidence of five women, and condemned to death, his only defense being that he was accused of that which had no existence, and was impossible. New charges multiplied daily; the jails of Salem were full of the accused, and prisoners were transferred to other towns, where the silly infection spread, and filled the whole colony with alarm.

Nothing could afford stronger proof of the hold which

this sad delusion had taken of the popular mind than the readiness so constantly displayed by the accused to confess the monstrous imputation, whose punishment was infamy and death. Many detailed long consultations held with Satan for the purpose of overthrowing the kingdom of heaven. In some cases these confessions were the result of distempered understandings; but, generally, they may be attributed to the hope of respite and ultimate reprieve, as none but the supposed impenitent sorcerers were executed. Thus only the truthful and conscientious suffered from the effects of this odious insanity. Some among the wretched people who had confessed witchcraft showed a subsequent disposition to retract. A man named Samuel Wardmell, having solemnly recanted his former statement, was tried, condemned, and executed. Despite this terrible warning, a few others followed the conscientious but fatal example. Every one of the sufferers during this dreadful period protested their innocence to the last. It seems difficult to discover any adequate motives for these atrocious and constant accusations. There is too much reason to believe that the confiscation of the condemned persons' property, malice against the accused, a desire to excite the public mind, and gain the notice and favor of those in power, were generally the objects of the witnesses.

The evil at length attained such a frightful magnitude that the firmest believers in witchcraft began to waver. In two months nineteen unhappy victims had been executed, eight more remained under sentence of death, 150 accused were still in prison, and there was no more room for the crowds daily brought in. No character or position was a shield against these absurd imputations; all lay at the mercy of a few mad or malignant beings. The first mitigation of the mischief was effected by the governor assembling the ministers to discuss whether what was called specter evidence should be held sufficient for the condemnation of the accused. The assembly decided against that particular sort of evidence being conclusive; but, at the same time, exhorted the governor to persevere in the vigorous prosecution of witchcraft, "according to the wholesome statutes of the English nation."* Public opinion, however, soon began to run strongly against those proceedings, and finally the governor took the bold step of pardoning all these under sentence for witchcraft, throwing open all the prisons, and turning a deaf ear to every accusation (January, 1693). From that time the troubles of the afflicted were heard of no more. Those who had confessed came forward to retract or disclaim their former statements, and the most active judges and persecutors publicly expressed contrition for the part they had taken in the fatal and almost incredible insanity. In the reaction that ensued, many urged strict inquiry into the fearful prejudices that had sacrificed innocent lives; but so general had been the crime, that it was deemed wisest to throw a vail of oblivion over the whole dreadful scene.†

* "Sir Matthew Hale burned two persons for witchcraft in 1664. Three thousand were executed in England during the Long Parliament. Two pretended witches were executed at Northampton in 1705. In 1716, Mrs. Hicks and her daughter, aged nine, were hanged at Huntingdon. The last sufferer in Scotland was in 1722, at Dornoch. The laws against witchcraft had lain dormant for many years, when an ignorant person attempting to revive them by finding a bill against a poor old woman in Surrey for the practice of witchcraft, they were repealed, 10 George II., 1736."—Viner's *Abridgment.*

† Neale, vol. ii., p. 164–170. Mather, vol. ii., p. 62–64.

Arfwedson says, "Close to the town of Salem is Beverley, a small, insignificant place, remarkable only in the annals of history as having formerly contained a superstitious population. Many lives have here been cruelly sacrificed, and the barren hill is still in existence where persons accused of witchcraft were hung upon tall trees. Tradition points out the place where the witches of old resided. Cotton Mather records in a work, truly original for that age, that the good people who lived near Massachusetts Bay were every night roused from their slumbers by the sound of a trumpet, summoning all the witches and demons."—Cotton Mather's *Magnalia;* Arfwedson, vol. i., p. 186.

"And thrice that night the trumpet rang,
And rock and hill replied;
And down the glen strange shadows sprang—
Mortal and fiend—a wizard gang,
Seen dimly, side by side.

"They gathered there from every land
That sleepeth in the sun;
They came with spell and charm in hand,
Waiting their master's high command—
Slaves to the Evil One."—*Legends of New England.*

While the settlers of New England were distracted by their own madness and intolerance, they had to contend with great external difficulties from the animosity of the Indians. The native races in this part of the continent appear to have been in some respects superior to those dwelling by the shores of the St. Lawrence and the Great Lake. They acknowledged the absolute power of a sachem or king, which gave a dangerous vigor and unity to their actions. They at first received the English with hospitality and kindness, and the colonists, on their part, passed laws to protect not only the persons of the natives, but to insure them an equitable price for their lands. The narrowed limits of their hunting-grounds, however, and the rapid advance of the white men, soon began to alarm the Indians.* When their jealousy was thus aroused, occasions of quarrel speedily presented themselves; the baneful influence of strong liquors, largely furnished in spite of the strictest prohibitions, increased their excitement. Some Englishmen were slain; the murderers were seized, tried, and executed by the colonial government, according to British law. These proceedings kindled a deep resentment among the savages, and led to measures of retaliation at their hands.

It has been an unfortunate feature of European settlement in America, that the border population, those most in contact with the natives, have been usually men of wild and desperate character, the tainted foam of the advancing tide of civilization. These reckless adventurers were little scrupulous in their dealings with the simple savage; they utterly disregarded those rights which his weakness could not defend, and by intolerable provocation excited him to a bloody but futile resistance. The Indians naturally confounded the whole English race with these contemptuous oppressors, and commenced a war that resulted in their own extermination.

* "During the war with Philip, the Indians took some English alive, and set them upright in the ground, with this sarcasm: 'You English, since you came into this country, have grown considerably above ground; let us now see how you will grow when planted into the ground.'"—*Narrative of the Wars in New England*, 1675.—*Harleian Miscellany*, vol. v., p. 400.

They did not face the English in the field, but hovered round the border, and, with sudden surprise, overwhelmed detached posts and settlements in a horrible destruction. The astute colonists soon adopted the policy of forming alliances, and taking advantage of ancient enmities to stir up hostilities among them. By this means they accomplished the destruction of the warlike Pequods,* their bitterest foes. Other enemies, however, soon came into the field, and at

* "The Pequods were a powerful nation on the Connecticut border, who could muster a thousand warriors. The English might have found it difficult to withstand them but for an alliance with the second most powerful people, the Narragansets, whose ancient enmity to the Pequods for a time prevailed over their jealousy of the foreigners. But at length, when the Pequods were nearly exterminated, the Narragansets, seeing the power of the strangers paramount, began to side with their enemies. The Indian chiefs began to imitate the English mode of fighting, and even to assume English names, with some characteristic epithet. One-eyed John, Stone-wall John, and Sagamore Sam, kept the colony in perpetual alarm. But their most deadly and formidable enemy was Philip, sachem of the Wampanoags. No Indian was ever more dreaded by civilized man. A century and a half has now elapsed since this hero of Pokanoket fell a victim to his own race, but even to this day his name is respected, and the last object supposed to have been touched by him in his lifetime is considered by every American as a valuable relic. This extraordinary man, whose real name was Metacom, succeeded his brother in the government of the Wampanoags. The wrongs and grievances suffered by this brother, added to those which he had himself experienced from the English colonists, induced him to engage in a war against them. The issue might, perhaps, have been less doubtful, had not one of his followers defeated his plans by a premature explosion before he had time to summon and concentrate his warriors and allies. From this time no smiles were seen on his face. But though he soon perceived that the great enterprise he had formed was likely to be frustrated, he never lost that elevation of soul which distinguished him to the last moments of his life. By his exertions and energy, all the Indian nations occupying the territory between Maine and the River Connecticut, a distance of nearly 200 miles, took up arms. Every where the name of King Philip was the signal for massacre and flames. But fraud and treason soon accomplished what open warfare could not effect; his followers gave way to numbers; his nearest relations and friends forsook him, and a treacherous ball at last struck his heart. His head was carried round the country in triumph, and exposed as that of a traitor; but posterity has done him justice. Patriotism was his only crime, and his death was that of a hero."—Arfwedson, vol. i., p. 229.

length, the original allies of the English, jealous of the encroaching power of the white strangers, also took arms against them. The Indian chiefs, after a time, began to adopt European tactics of war, and for many years kept the colony in alarm by their formidable attacks: they were, however, finally driven altogether from the field.

The New England settlers showed more sincerity than other adventurers in endeavoring to accomplish their principal professed object of colonization, that of teaching Christianity to the Indians.* They appointed zealous and pious ministers for the mission,† and established a seminary for

* "This was not the case in the earlier and more northern settlements, where Mather mentions a clergyman who, from the pulpit, alluded to this as the main object of his flock's coming out, when one of the principal members rose and said, 'Sir, you are mistaken; our main object was to catch fish.'"—Murray's *America*.

"To this day the Council of Massachusets, in the impress of their public seal, have an Indian engraven, with these words: 'Come over and help us,' alluding to Acts, xv., 9."—*Narrative of the Wars in New England*, 1675. *Harleian Miscellany*, vol. v., p. 400.

† "Among these was the celebrated Eliot. Notwithstanding the almost incredible hardships endured by Eliot during his missionary labors, he lived to the age of eighty-six. He expired in 1690, and has ever since been known by the well-earned title of Apostle to the Indians."—*Missionary Records*, p. 34.

Dr. Dwight says of him, "He was naturally qualified beyond almost any other man for the business of a missionary. In promoting among the Indians agriculture, health, morals, and religion, this great and good man labored with constancy, faithfulness, and benevolence which place his name not unworthily among those who are arranged immediately after the apostles of our Divine Redeemer." Eliot translated the Holy Scriptures into the Indian language. In 1661, the New Testament, dedicated to Charles II., was printed at Cambridge, in New England, and about three years afterward, it was followed by the Old Testament. This was the first Bible ever printed in America; and, though the impression consisted of 2000 copies, a second edition was required in 1685.—*Ibid.*, p. 27.

"When at Harvard College, a copy of the Bible was shown me by Mr. Jared Sparks, translated by the missionary, Father Eliot, into the Indian tongue. It is now a dead language, although preached for several generations to crowded congregations."—Lyell's *America*, vol. i., p. 260.

"Eliot had become an acute grammarian by his studies at the English university of Cambridge. Having finished his laborious and difficult work, the Indian grammar, at the close of it, under a full

the education of the natives, whence some scholars were to be selected to preach the Gospel among their savage countrymen. Great obstacles were encountered in this good work; the Indians showed a bigoted attachment to their own strange religious conceits, and their priests and conjurers used all their powerful influence against Christianity, denouncing in furious terms all who forsook their creed for the English God. Despite these difficulties, a number of savages were induced to form themselves in villages, and lead a civilized* and Christian life, under the guidance of

sense of the difficulties he had encountered, and the acquisition he had made, he said, 'Prayers and pains, through faith in Christ Jesus, do any thing.'"—*Life of Eliot*, p. 55.

"The Honorable Robert Boyle often strengthened Eliot's hands and encouraged him in his work—he who was not more admirable among philosophers for his discoveries in science, than he was beloved by Christians for his active kindness and his pious spirit."—*Ibid.*, p. 64.

"Nor was Eliot alone. In the islands round Massachusetts, and within the limits of the Plymonth patent, missionary zeal and missionary enterprise were active; and the gentle Mayhew, forgetting the pride of learning, endeavored to win the natives to a new religion. At a later day, he took passage for New England to awaken interest there, and the ship in which he sailed was never more heard of. But such had been the force of his example, that his father, though bowed down with the weight of seventy years, resolved on assuming the office of the son whom he had lost, and till beyond the age of fourscore years and twelve, continued to instruct the natives, and with the happiest results. The Indians within his influence, though twenty times more numerous than the whites in their immediate neighborhood, preserved an immutable friendship with Massachusetts."—Bancroft's *Hist of the United States*, vol. ii., p. 97. See *Missionary Records; Life of Eliot;* Mayhew's *Indian Converts;* T. Prince's *Account of English Ministers.*

* "History has no example to offer of any successful attempt, however slight, to introduce civilization among savage tribes in colonies or in their vicinity, except through the influence of religious missionaries. This is no question of a balance of advantages—no matter of comparison between opposite systems. I repeat that no instance can be shown of the reclaiming of savages by any other influence than that of religion. There are two obvious reasons why such should be the case: the first, that religion only can supply a motive to the governors, placed in obscure situations, and without the reach of responsibility, to act with zeal, perseverance, and charity; the other, that it alone can supply a motive to the governed to undergo that alteration of habits through which the reclaimed savage must pass,

ministers of ther own race.* In a few years thirty congregations of "praying Indians,"† their numbers amounting to 3000, were established in Massachusetts.

CHAPTER XI.

The principal characteristics of that colonization by which the vast republic of the West was formed, have been exhibited in the settlement of Virginia and Massachusetts. The other states were stamped with the impress of the two first, and in a great measure peopled from them. Rhode Island and the rest of the New England states were founded by those who had fled from the religious persecutions of Massachusetts, with the exception of Connecticut, which owes its origin chiefly to the spirit of adventure and the search for unoccupied lands. The first settlers divided this last-named state among themselves without the sanction of

and to which the hope of mere temporal advantage will very rarely induce him to consent. This position is well stated in the words of Southey: 'The wealth and power of governments may be vainly employed in the endeavor to conciliate and reclaim brute man, if religious zeal and Christian charity, in the true import of the word, be wanting.' "—Merivale *on Colonization*, vol. i., p. 289.

* "The attempt to organize an Indian priesthood at this period failed altogether, the converts possessing neither the steadiness nor the sobriety requisite for the holy office. The duty, therefore, devolved upon European teachers, who in many cases scarcely obtained the wages of a day laborer, and that very precariously. The formation, however, of a society in England for the propagation of the Gospel in this settlement, and pretty liberal contributions raised in the principal towns, in some degree remedied these evils. After the lapse of a few more generations, the Indian character, in its slow but steady upward progress under the teaching of devoted and enlightened Christian ministers, underwent a change so effectual, that the native teachers and preachers of the present day may well bear comparison in zeal, piety, and eloquence with their European colleagues."—Catlin's *American Indians;* Cotton's *American Lakes.*

† "The Indians about this time (1653) obtained the appellation of 'Praying Indians,' and the court appointed Major Daniel Gookin their ruler."—*Life of Eliot*, p. 53.

any authority, and then proceeded to form a constitution of unexampled liberality. They had to bear the chief burden in the Indian war, on account of their advanced and exposed position; but Connecticut prospered in spite of every obstacle. Several Puritans of distinction sought its shore from England. Charles II., on his restoration granted a most liberal charter, and it continued to enjoy the benefits of complete self-government till Massachusetts was deprived of her charter by James II., when Connecticut shared the same fate. At the Revolution, the younger state, more fortunate than her neighbor, was restored to all the privileges formerly enjoyed.

The states of New Hampshire and Maine were originally founded on Loyalist and Church of England principles. Sir Ferdinand Gorges and John Mason, the most energetic member of the Council of Plymouth, undertook the colonization of these districts, but their tyrannical and injudicious conduct stunted the growth of the infant colonies, and little progress was made till the religious dissensions of Boston swelled their population. Violent and even fatal dissensions, however, distracted this incongruous community, till the government of Massachusetts assumed the sway over it, and re-established order and prosperity. Gorges and Mason disputed for many years the rights of authority with the new rulers; nor was the question finally settled till Massachusetts was deprived of her charter, when a royal government was established in New Hampshire.

The important state of New York was founded under very different auspices from those of its neighbors. In 1609, Henry Hudson, while sailing in the service of the Dutch East India Company, discovered the magnificent stream which now bears his name. A small colony was soon sent out from Holland * to settle the new country, and a trading

* "On Hudson's return according to the English historians, he sold his title to the Dutch."—*British Encyc.*, vol. ii., p. 236. Chalmers questions, apparently on good grounds, the validity of this odd transaction. If, as Forster asserts, Hudson not only sailed from the Texel, but was equipped at the expense of the Dutch East India Company, there was no room for sale or purchase of any kind to constitute the region Dutch.—Chalmers, vol. ii., p. 568; Charlevoix, tom. i., p. 221.

post established at the mouth of the river. Sir Samuel Argall, governor of Virginia, conceived that this foreign settlement trenched upon the rights granted by the English crown to its subjects, and by a display of superior force constrained the Dutch colony to acknowledge British sovereignty [1613]; * but this submission became a dead letter some years later, when large bodies of emigrants arrived from the Low Countries [1620]; † the little trading post soon rose into a town, and a fort was erected for its defense. The site of this establishment was on the island of Manhattan; ‡ the founders called it New Amsterdam. When it fell into the possession of England, the name was changed to New York. Albany § was next built, at some distance up the Hudson, as a post for the Indian trade, and thence a communication was opened for the first time with the Northern Indian confederacy of the Iroquois, or the Five Nations.

Charles II., from hatred to the Dutch, as well as from the desire of aggrandizement, renewed the claims of England

* "The English jurists, referring to the wide grants of Elizabeth, according to which Virginia extended far to the north of this region, insist that there had long ceased to be room for any claim to it founded on discovery. But the Dutch, who are somewhat slow in comprehension, could not see the right which Elizabeth could have to bestow a vast region, of the very existence of which she was ignorant. They therefore sent out the small colony, 1613, which was soon after compelled by Argall to acknowledge the sovereignty of England."—Murray's *America*, vol. i., p. 331; *Fastes Chronologiques*, 1613.

† The Dutch West Indian Company was established in 1620, and sent out colonists on a large scale.

‡ "Juet, the traveling companion of Hudson, called the island on which New York is situated Manna Hatta, which means the island of manna; in other words, a country where milk and honey flow. The name Manhattoes is said to be derived from the great Indian god Manetho, who is stated to have made this island his favorite place of residence on account of its peculiar attractions."—Knickerbocker's *New York*, vol. v., p. 1.

§ "Albany bore the name of Orange when it was originally founded by the Dutch; and as a great number of this people remained in the city after it passed into the possession of England, they continued to call it Orange, and the French Canadians give it no other name."—Charlevoix, tom. i., p. 222.

"Albany received that name from the Scottish title of the Duke of York."—Bancroft.

upon the Hudson settlements, and in 1664 dispatched an armament of 300 men to enforce this claim. Stuyvesant, the Dutch governor,* was totally unprepared to resist the threatened attack, and after a short parley agreed to surrender. The settlers were, however, secured in property and person, and in the free exercise of their religion, and the greater part remained under their new rulers. In the long naval war subsequently carried on between England and Holland, the colony again passed for a time under the sway of the Dutch, but at the peace was finally restored to Great Britain. James, then Duke of York, had received from his brother a grant of the district which now constitutes the State of New York. On assuming authority, he appointed governors with arbitrary power, but the colonists in assertion of their rights as Englishmen, stoutly resisted, and even sent home Dyer, the collector of customs, under a charge of high treason, for attempting to levy taxes without legal authority. [1681.] The duke judged it expedient to

* Nine years before (1655), Stuyvesant had attacked the happy and contented little colony of Swedes who were settled on the banks of the Delaware, and after a sanguinary contest, the Swedish governor, John Rising, was obliged to submit to the Dutch authority. Such was the end of New Sweden, which had only maintained an independent existence for seventeen years. Thus the Swedish settlements passed into the hands of the English at the same time as those of the Dutch. The first Swedish colonization had been projected and encouraged by the great Gustavus Adolphus in 1638. They gave their settlement on the banks of the Delaware, the name of the Land of Canaan, and to the spot where they first landed that of Canaan, so inviting and delightful did this part of the New World first appear to them. The only thing now known of this terrestrial paradise is, that its situation was near Cape Henlopen, a short distance from the sea. The colonists purchased tracts of lands of the Indians, and threw up a few fortifications; of the city they founded, Christina, there is now no trace. It was situated near Wilmington, twenty-seven miles south of Philadelphia. The Dutch, whose principal city was then New Amsterdam, pretended that the country round the Delaware belonged to them, having paid it a visit before the arrival of the Swedes. This insinuation, moreover, did not prevent the latter from settling, and, according to Charlevoix, the two nations lived in amity with each other until Stuyvesant's aggression, the Dutch being wholly devoted to commerce and the Swedes to agriculture. The Swedish settlement was at first called New Sweden, afterward New Jersey.

conciliate his sturdy transatlantic subjects, and yielded them a certain form of representative government. In 1682, Mr. Dongan was sent out with a commission to assemble a council of ten, and a house of assembly of eighteen popular deputies. The new governor soon rendered himself beloved and respected by all, although at first distrusted and disliked, as professing the Romish faith. New York was not allowed to enjoy these fortunate circumstances for any length of time; the capricious and arbitrary duke, on his accession to the crown, abrogated the colonial constitution; shortly afterward the state was annexed to Massachusetts, the beloved governor recalled, and the despotic Andros established in his stead. [1686.] At the first rumor of the Revolution of 1688, the inhabitants, led by a merchant of the name of Leisler, rose in arms, proclaimed William and Mary, and elected a house of representatives. The new monarch sent out a Colonel Slaughter as governor, whose authority was disputed by Leisler; however, the bold merchant was soon overcome, and with quick severity tried and executed. [1691.] The English Parliament, more considerate of his useful services, subsequently reversed his attainder, and restored the forfeited estates to his family. [1695.] With the view of aiding the resources and progress of the colony, 3000 German Protestants, called Palatines, were subsequently conveyed to the banks of the Hudson, and subsisted for three years, at a great expense, by England. These sober and industrious men proved a most valuable addition to the population.*

New Jersey was formed from a part of the original territory of New York. Lord Berkeley and Sir George Carteret were the proprietors, by grant from James [1664]: they

* "The entire cost of this transportation amounted to £78,533, which, amid the ferments of party, was declared by a subsequent vote of Parliament to be not only an extravagant and unreasonable charge to the kingdom, but of dangerous consequence to the Church." —*Brit. Emp. Amer.*, vol. i., p. 249, 250.

"Swabia, with the old Palatinate, has contributed very largely to the present population of America. From the end of Queen Anne's reign to 1753, it is said that from 4 to 8000 went annually to Pennsylvania alone."—Sadler, b. iv., cap. v.

founded the new state with great judgment and liberality, establishing the power of self-government and taxation. The Duke of York, however, on the reconquest of the country from the Dutch, took the opportunity of abrogating the Constitution: the colonists boldly appealed against this tyranny, and with such force, that the duke was led to refer the question to the judgment of the learned and upright Sir William Jones, who gave it against him. [1681.] James was obliged to acquiesce in this decision till he ascended the throne, when he swept away all the rights of the colony, and annexed it, like its neighbors, to the government of Massachusetts. After the accession of William, New Jersey was entangled for ten years in a web of conflicting claims but was finally established under its own independent Legislature.

The State of Maryland was so named in honor of Henrietta Maria, the beautiful queen of Charles I., to whose influence the early settlers were much indebted. Religious persecution in England drove forth the founders of the colony; but in this case the Protestants were the instigators, and the cruel laws of Queen Elizabeth's reign against the Roman Catholics were the instruments. Lord Baltimore, an Irish peer, and other men of distinction in the popish body, obtained from Charles I., as an asylum in the New World, a grant of that angle of Virginia lying on both sides of the River Chesapeake, a district rich in soil, genial in climate, and admirably situated for commerce. An expedition of 200 Roman Catholics, many among them men of good birth, was sent under Mr. Calvert, Lord Baltimore's brother, to take possession of this favored tract. [1634.] Their first care was to conciliate the Indians, in which they eminently succeeded. The natives were even prevailed upon to abandon their village and their cleared lands around to the strangers, and to remove themselves contentedly to another situation.

Maryland was most honorably distinguished in the earliest times by perfect freedom of religious opinion. Many members of the Church of England, as well as Roman Catholics, fled thither from the persecutions of the Puritans. The Baltimore family at first displayed great liberality and judgment in their rule; but, as they gained confidence from the secret support of the king to their cherished faith, their wise moderation seems to have diminished. However, the principal grievance brought against them was, that they had not provided by public funds for Church of England clergymen as fully as for those of their own faith, although by far the larger portion of the population belonged to the flock of the former. The unsatisfactory state of morals, manners, and religion in the colony was attributed to this neglect. At the Revolution, the inhabitants of Maryland rose with tumultuous zeal against their Roman Catholic lords, and published a manifesto in justification of their proceedings, accusing Lord Baltimore's government of intolerable tyranny. These statements, whether true or false, afforded King William an opportunity to assume the colonial power in his own hands, 1691, and to deprive the Calverts of all rights over the country, except the receipt of some local taxes.*

For a long time but few settlers had established themselves in that part of North America now called Carolina;† of these, some were men who had fled from the persecutions of New England, and formed a little colony round Cape Fear [1661]; others were Virginians, attracted by the rich unoccupied lands. After the restoration of Charles, however, the energies of the British nation, no longer devoted to internal quarrels, turned into the fields of foreign and colonial adventure. Charles readily bestowed upon his followers vast tracts of an uncultivated wilderness which he had never seen; and Monk, duke of Albemarle, the Earl of Clarendon, Lords Berkeley and Ashley, Sir George Carteret, and a few

* "King William, impatient of judicial forms, by his own act constituted Maryland a royal government. The arbitrary act was sanctioned by a legal opinion from Lord Holt. The Church of England was established as the religion of the state. . . . . In the land which Catholics had opened to Protestants, the Catholic inhabitant was the sole victim to Anglican intolerance. Mass might not be said publicly. . . . . No Catholic might teach the young. . . . . The disfranchisement of the proprietary Lord Baltimore related to his creed, not to his family. To recover the inheritance of authority, Benedict, the son of the proprietary, renounced the Catholic Church for that of England. The persecution never crushed the faith of the humble colonists."—Bancroft, vol. iii., p. 33.

† This name was given in honor of Charles II.

others, were created absolute lords of the new province of Carolina. [1663.] Great exertions were then made to attract settlers; immunity from prosecution for debt was secured to them for five years, and, at the same time, a liberal Constitution was granted, with a popular House of Assembly. The proprietors, anxious to perfect the work of colonization, prevailed upon the celebrated Locke to draw up a system of government for the new state, which, however excellent in theory, proved practically a signal failure.* The principal characteristic of the scheme was the establishment of an aristocracy with fantastic titles of nobility,† who met with the deputies in a Parliament, where, however, the council solely possessed the power of proposing new laws. The whole colonial body was subject to the Court of Proprietors in England, which was presided over by a chief called the Palatine,‡ possessing nearly supreme power. The sturdy colonists neglected, or deferred for future consideration, every

* "The system framed by Locke was called 'the Fundamental Constitutions of Carolina.' .... Locke was undoubtedly well acquainted with human nature, and not ignorant of the world; but he had not taken a sufficiently comprehensive view of the history of man, nor were political speculators yet duly aware of the necessity of adapting constitutions to those for whom they were destined. The grand peculiarity consisted in forming a high and titled nobility, which might rival the splendor of those of the Old World. But as the dukes and earls of England would have considered their titles degraded by being shared with a Carolina planter, other titles of foreign origin were adopted. That of landgrave was drawn from Germany. (Locke himself was created a landgrave.) But these princely denominations, applied to persons who were to earn their bread by the labor of their hands, could confer no real dignity. The reverence for nobility, which can only be the result of long-continued wealth and influence, could never be inspired by mere titles, especially of such an exotic and fantastic character..... The sanction of negro slavery was a deep blot in this boasted system. ...... The colonists, who felt perfectly at ease under their rude early regulations, were struck with dismay at the arrival of this philosophical fabric of polity."—Murray's *America*, vol. i., p. 343.

† "It was insisted that there should be some landgraves and some caciques when many other parts of 'the Fundamental Constitutions' were given up; but these great nobles never struck any root in the Western soil, and have long since disappeared"—*Hist. Acc. of the Colonization of South Carolina and Georgia*, London, 1779, vol. i., p. 44–46; Chalmers, p. 326, quoted by Murray.

‡ Monk, duke of Albemarle, was constituted palatine.

portion of this new Constitution that appeared unsuitable to their condition, alleging that its provisions were in violation of the promises that had induced them to adopt the country.

Carolina for a long time progressed but slowly. The colonists had no fixed religion,* and their general morals and industry were very indifferent. They drew largely upon the resources of the proprietors without giving any return, and when at length that supply was stopped, they resorted to every idle and iniquitous mode of raising funds. They hunted the Indians, and sold them as slaves to the West Indies, and their sea-ports became the resort of pirates. These atrocious and ruinous pursuits soon reduced them to a state of miserable poverty, and the baneful influence of a series of profligate governors completed the mischief. One of these, named Sette Sothel,† was especially conspicuous for rapacity and injustice. [1683.] His misrule at length goaded the people into insurrection; they seized him, and were about to send him as a prisoner to England, but released him on a promise of renouncing the government, and leaving the colony for a time. After these and some other commotions, they succeeded in re-establishing their ancient charter in its original simplicity.

Carolina now began to improve rapidly, from the influx of a large and valuable immigration. The religious freedom that had been secured under the old charter was continued unrestricted even under Mr. Locke's complicated Constitution. Many Puritans flocked in from Britain to seek refuge

* "It is remarkable that the philosopher's colony seems to have been the only one founded before the eighteenth century, except Virginia, in which the Church of England was expressly established; but this clause is said to have been introduced against his will."—Merivale *on Colonization*, vol. i., p. 88–92.

† "Mr. Chalmers makes the very bold assertion that the annals of delegated authority do not present a name so branded with merited infamy, and that there never had taken place such an accumulation of extortion, injustice, and rapacity as during the five years that he misruled the colony. He had been made prisoner in his way out, and kept in close captivity at Algiers, where he took, it appears, not warning, but lessons. (Sette Sothel had purchased the rights of Lord Clarendon, one of the eight original proprietaries.)"—Murray, vol. i., p. 345.

from the persecutions of Charles II., and by their steadiness and industry soon attained considerable wealth. New England had also furnished her share to the new settlement of useful and energetic men who had been expelled by her Calvinistic intolerance. But the narrow-minded jealousy of the original emigrants soon interrupted the prosperity of the colony. Under the hypocritical plea of zeal for the Church of England, to which their conduct and morals were a scandal, they obtained, by violent means, a majority of one in the Assembly, and expelled all dissenters from the Legislature and government. They even passed a law to depose all sectarian clergy, and devote their churches to the services of the established religion. The oppressed Dissenters appealed to the British Parliament for protection. In the year 1705, an address was voted to the queen by the House of Commons, declaring the injustice of these acts, but nothing was done to relieve the colony till in 1721, when the people rose in insurrection, established a provisional government, and prayed that the king, George I., would himself undertake their rule. He granted their petition, and soon afterward purchased the rights of the proprietors. [1727.]*

In the year 1732 a plan was formed for relieving the distress then severely pressing upon England by colonizing the territory still remaining unoccupied to the south of the Savannah. Twenty-three trustees, men of rank and influence, were appointed for this purpose, and the sum of £15,000 was placed at their disposal by Parliament and by voluntary subscription. With the aid of these funds about 500 people were forwarded to the new country, and some others went at their own expense. In honor of the reigning king, the name of Georgia was given to the new settlement. The lands were granted to the emigrants on conditions of military service, and a large proportion of them were selected from among the hardy Scottish Highlanders and the veterans of some German regiments. Besides being the advance

* "The rights of the proprietors were sold to the king for about the sum of £20,000. Lord Carteret alone, joining in the surrender of the government, received an eighth share in the soil."—*Hist. Account*, &c., vol. i., p. 255–321.

guard of civilization in the Indian country, the colony was threatened with the rival claims of the Spaniards in Florida, the boundaries of whose territory were very vague and uncertain. Happily for Georgia, Mr. Oglethorpe, the original founder of the settlement, succeeded in establishing a lasting friendship with the powerful Creek Indians, the natives of the country; but the Spaniards never ceased to alarm and threaten the colony till British arms had won the whole Atlantic coast. Owing to this disadvantage, and still more to certain humane restrictions upon the Indian trade,* no great influx of population took place until 1763, when peace restored confidence, and men and money were freely introduced from England.

One of the most important of the great American states that declared their independence in 1783, was, with the exception of Georgia, the latest in its origin. Under the wise and gentle influence of the founders, however, it progressed more rapidly than any other. When time and reflection had cooled the ardor and softened the fanaticism of the early Quakers, the sect attracted general and just admiration by the mild and persevering philanthropy of its most distinguished members. The pure benevolence and patient courage of Willian Penn was a tower of strength to this new

* "The importation and use of negroes were prohibited; no rum was allowed to be introduced, and no one was permitted to trade with the Indians without special license. The colonists complained that without negroes it was impossible to clear the grounds and cut down the thick forests, though the honest Highlanders always reprobated the practice, and denied that any necessity for it existed." [1]—Murray, vol. i., p. 360.

[1] "Slavery," says Oglethorpe, "is against the Gospel, as well as the fundamental law of England. We refused, as trustees, to make a law permitting such a horrid crime."—*Memoirs of Sharpe*, vol. i., p. 234; *Stephen's Journal*, quoted by Bancroft. In 1751, however, after Oglethorpe had finally left Georgia, his humane restrictions were withdrawn. Whitefield, who believed that God's providence would certainly make slavery terminate for the advantage of the Africans, pleaded before the trustees in its favor. At last even the Moravians (who in a body emigrated to Georgia in 1733) began to think that negro slaves might be employed in a Christian spirit; and it was agreed that if the negroes are treated in a Christian manner, their change of country would prove to them a benefit. A message from Germany served to crush their scruples: "If you take slaves in faith, and with the intent of conducting them to Christ, the action will not be a sin, but may prove a benediction."—Urlsperger. vol. iii., p. 479, quoted by Bancroft, vol. iii., p. 448.

creed; well born, and enjoying a competent fortune, he possessed the means as well as the will powerfully to aid in its advancement. He endured with patience, but with unflinching constancy, a continual series of legal persecutions, and even the anger of his father, until the unspotted integrity of his life and his practical wisdom at length triumphed over prejudice and hostility, and he was allowed the privilege of pleading before the British Parliament in the cause of his oppressed brethren.

William Penn inherited from his father a claim against the government for £16,000, which King Charles gladly paid by assigning to him the territory in the New World now called Pennsylvania,* in honor of the first proprietor.† This was a large and fertile expanse of inland country partly taken from New York, New Jersey, and Maryland. It was included between the 40th and 43d degrees of latitude, and bounded on the east by the Delaware River. The enlightened and benevolent proprietor bestowed upon the new state a Constitution that secured, as far as human ordinance was capable, freedom of faith, thought, and action. He formed some peculiar institutions for the promotion of peace and good will among his brethren, and for the protection of the widow and the orphan. By his wise and just dealings with the Indians,‡ he gained their important confidence and friend-

* "He accepted this grant, because it secured them against any other claimant from Europe. It gave him a title in the eyes of the Christian world, but he did not believe that it gave him any other title."—*Colonization and Civilization*, p. 358.

† "Etablissement de la Pennsylvanie, dans le pays qui avoit porté le nom de Nouvelle Suéde: Cette colonie a reçu son nom de son fondateur, le Chevalier Guillaume Penn, Anglais à qui Charles II., Roi de la Grande Bretagne, conceda ce pays en 1680 et qui cette année 1681, y mena les Quakers ou trembleurs d'Angleterre, dont il étoit le chef. Lorsqu'il y arriva, il y trouva un grand nombre de Hollandois et de Suédois. Les premiers, pour la plupart, occupoient les endroits situés le long du golphe, et les seconds, les bords de la Rivière De la Warr, ou du midi. Il paroit par une de ses lettres, qu'il n'étoit pas content des Hollandois; mais il dit que les Suédois étoient une nation simple, sans malice, industrieuse, robuste, se souciant peu de l'abondance et se contentant du nécessaire."—*Fastes Chronologiques*, 1681.

‡ "Even Penn, however, did not fully admit into his scheme of

ship: he sent commissioners to treat with them for the sale of their lands, and in the year 1682 met the assembled chiefs near the spot where Philadelphia now stands. The savages advanced to the place of meeting in great numbers and in warlike guise, but as the approach of the English was announced, they laid aside their weapons and seated themselves in quiet groups around their chiefs.* Penn came forward fearlessly with a few attendants, all unarmed, and in their usual grave and simple attire; in his hand he held a parchment on which were written the terms of the treaty. He then spoke in a few plain words of the friendship and justice that should rule the actions of all men, and guide him, and them, and their children's children. The Indians answered that they would live in peace with him and his white brothers as long as the sun and moon shall endure. And in the Quaker's parchment and the Indian's promise was accomplished the peaceful conquest of that lovely wilderness, a conquest more complete, more secure and lasting, than any that the ruthless rigor of Cortes or the stern valor of the Puritans had ever won.

colonization the notion of retaining for the Indians a property in a part of the soil they once occupied. He gave the natives free leave to settle in certain parts of his territory, but, unfortunately, he did not treat any definite tract of the soil as their property, which would rise in value along with other tracts, and thus afford a stimulus to their gradual improvement. It was the want of systematic views in this and other respects, which rendered the benevolent intentions of Penn toward the natives of little ultimate avail; so that, after all, the chief good which he effected was by setting an example of benevolence and justice in the principle of his dealings with them."—Merivale *on Colonization*, vol. ii., p. 173.

* "William Penn of course came unarmed, in his usual plain dress, without banners, or mace, or guard, or carriages, and only distinguished from his companions by wearing a blue sash of silk net-work (which, it seems, is still preserved by Mr. Kett, of Seething Hall, near Norwich), and by having in his hand a roll of parchment, on which was engrossed the confirmation of the treaty of purchase and amity."—*Edinburgh Review of Clarkson's Life of William Penn*, p. 358.

"The scene at Shachamaxon, quoted by Howitt, forms the subject of one of the pictures of West. Thus ended this famous treaty, of which Voltaire has remarked with so much truth and severity, 'That it was the only one ever concluded which was not ratified by an oath, and the only one that never was broken.'"—Howitt, p. 360.

The prosperity of Pennsylvania advanced with unexampled rapidity.* The founder took out with him two thousand well-chosen emigrants, and a considerable number had preceded him to the new country. The orderly freedom that prevailed,† and the perpetual peace with the Indians,‡ gave a great advantage to this colony; emigration flowed thither more abundantly than to any other settlement, and thus, although of such recent origin, this state soon equaled the most successful of its older neighbors.

CHAPTER XII.

HAVING noticed the principal features of the origin and progress of the English colonies—the powerful and dangerous neighbors of the French settlements in the New World—it is now time to return to the course of Canadian history subsequent to the death of the illustrious founder of Quebec.

Monsieur de Montmagny succeeded Champlain as governor, and entered with zeal into his plans, but difficulties accumulated on all sides. Men and money were wanting, trade languished, and the Associated Company in France were daily becoming more indifferent to the success of the colony. Some few merchants and inhabitants of the out-

* "In three years from its foundation, Philadelphia gained more than New York had done in half a century."—Bancroft's *History of the United States*, vol. ii., p. 394.

† "Virtue had never, perhaps, inspired a legislation better calculated to promote the fidelity of mankind. The opinions, the sentiments, and the morals corrected whatever might be deficient in it."—Raynal, vol. vii., p. 292.

"Beautiful," said the philosophic Frederick of Prussia, when he read the account of the government of Pennsylvania; "it is perfect, if it can endure."—Herder, p. 13, 116. Quoted by Bancroft, vol. ii., p. 392.

‡ "Their conduct to the Indians never altered for the worse. Pennsylvania, while under the administration of the Quakers, never became, as New England, a slaughter-house of the Indians."—Howitt, p. 366.

posts, indeed, were enriched by the profitable dealings of the fur-trade, but their suddenly-acquired wealth excited the jealousy rather than increased the general prosperity of the settlers. The work of religious institutions was alone pursued with vigor and success in those times of failure and discouragement. At Sillery, one league from Quebec, an establishment was founded for the instruction of the savages and the diffusion of Christian light. [1637.] The Hôtel Dieu owed its existence to the Duchesse d'Aiguillon two years afterward, and the Convent of the Ursulines was founded by the pious and high-born Madame de la Peltrie.*

The partial success and subsequent failure of Champlain and his Indian allies in their encounters with the Iroquois had emboldened these brave and politic savages. They now captured several canoes belonging to the Hurons, laden with furs, which that friendly people were conveying to Quebec. Montmagny's military force was too small to allow of his avenging this insult; he, however, zealousy promoted an enterprise to build a fort and effect a settlement on the island of Montreal, which he fondly hoped would curb the

* Among the Ursulines who accompanied Madame de la Peltrie to Quebec was Marie de l'Incarnation, "the Theresa of France," and Marie de St. Joseph. The sanctity of these remarkable women and the miracles they performed are the favorite theme of the Jesuit historians of Canada. Several lives of the former have been published, one of them by Charlevoix. A quarto volume of her letters was also published (à Paris, chez Louis Billaine, 1681): they are highly extolled as "worthy of her high reputation for sanctity, ability, and practical good sense in the business of life." They record many historical facts which occurred during the thirty-two years that she passed in Canada, where she arrived in 1640. When the Ursulines and the "Filles Hospitalières" landed at Quebec, they were received with enthusiasm. "It was held as a festival day; all work was forbidden; and the shops were shut. The governor received these heroines upon the shore at the head of the troops, who were under arms, the guns firing a salute. After the first greeting he led them to the church, accompanied by the acclamations of the people; here the Te Deum was chantod."—Charlevoix.

"The venerable ash tree still lives beneath which Mary of the Incarnation, so famed for chastened piety, genius, and good judgment, toiled, though in vain, for the culture of Huron children."—Bancroft's *History of the United States*, vol. iii., p. 127.

audacity of his savage foes. The Associated Company would render no aid whatever to this important plan, but the religious zeal of the Abbé Olivier overcame all difficulties. He obtained a grant of Montreal from the king, and dispatched the Sieur de Maisonneuve and others to take possession. On the 17th of May, 1641, the place destined for the settlement was consecrated by the superior of the Jesuits.*

* "Cette ville a été nommée Ville Marie par ses fondateurs, mais ce nom n'a pu passer dans l'usage ordinaire; il n'a lieu que dans les actes publics, et parmi les seigneurs, qui en sont fort jaloux."—Charlevoix. When the foundations of the city of Montreal were first laid, the name given to it was Ville Marie. Bouchette, vol. i., p. 215; La Hontan, vol. xiii., p. 266.

Charlevoix gives the following account of the formation and progress of the remarkable settlement at Montreal: "Quelques personnes puissantes, et plus recommandable encore par leur piété et par leur zèle pour la religion, formèrent donc une société, qui se proposa de faire en grand à Montréal, ce qu'on avoit fait en petit à Sillery. Il devoit y avoir dans cette isle une bourgade Françoise, bien fortifiée, et à l'abri de toute insulte. Les pauvres y devoient être reçus, et mis en état de subsister de leur travail. On projetta de faire occuper tout le reste de l'isle par des sauvages, de quelque nation qu'ils fussent, pourvû qu'ils fissent profession du Christianisme, ou qu'ils voulussent se faire instruire de nos mystères, et l'on étoit d'autant plus persuadé qu'ils y viendraient en grand nombre qu' outre un asile assuré contre les poursuites de leurs ennemis, ils pouvoient se promettre des secours toujours prompts dans leurs maladies, et contre la disette. On se proposoit même de les policer avec le tems, et de les accoûtumer à ne plus vivre que du travail de leurs mains. Le nombre de ceux qui entroient dans cette association fut de trente-cinq; dès cette année 1640, en vertu de la concession que le roi lui fit de l'isle, elle en fit prendre possession à la fin d'une messe solennelle, qui fut célébrée sous une tente. Le quinzième d'Octobre l'année suivante, M. de Maisonneuve fut déclaré gouverneur de l'isle. Le dix-septième de May suivant, le lieu destiné à l'habitation Françoise fut béni par le Supérieur des Jésuites, qui y célébra les saints mystères, dédia à la mère de Dieu une petite chapelle, qu'on avoit bâtie, et il y laissa le St. Sacrement. Cette cérémonie avoit été précédé d'une autre, trois mois auparavant, c'est à dire vers la fin de Février: tous les Associés s'etant rendus un Jeudi matin à Nôtre Dame de Paris, ceux qui étoient prêtres, y dirent la messe, les autres communièrent à l'autel de la Vierge et tous supplièrent la reine des anges de prendre l'isle de Montréal sous sa protection. Enfin le quinze d'Août, la fête de l'Assomption de la mère de Dieu fut solemnisée dans cette isle avec un concours extraordinaire de François et de sauvages. On ne négligea

At the same time the governor erected a fort at the entrance of the River Richelieu, then called the Iroquois. The workmen employed at this labor were constantly exposed to the harassing warfare of the Indians, but at length completely repulsed them. A garrison, such as could be spared from the scanty militia of the colony, was placed in the little stronghold for its defense. Although the minds of the fierce Iroquois were fixed upon the utter destruction of the French, and in their confident boastings they declared that they could drive the white men into the sea, they indicated from time to time a desire for peace. Montmagny was compelled by weakness and the difficulties of his situation, to accept overtures which he could not but dread as insidious and treacherous, and he assumed an air of confidence which he by no means felt. His native allies were also eagerly anxious for the blessings of peace, and, through their means, an opportunity for opening negotiations soon offered. The governor and the friendly native chiefs met the deputies of the Iroquois nation at Three Rivers to arrange

rien dans cette occasion pour intéresser le ciel en faveur d'un établissement si utile, et pour donner aux infidèles une haute idée de la religion Chrétienne."—Charlevoix, tom. i., p. 345.

In the year 1644 Charlevoix says, "L'isle de Montréal se peuploit insensiblement, et la piété de ces nouveaux colons disposoit peu à peu les sauvages qui les approchoient à se soûmettre au joug de la foi." In 1657, however, it was considered that "les premiers possesseurs de l'isle n'avoient pas poussé l'établissement autant qu'on avoit d'abord espéré," and it was therefore ceded to the Seminary of St. Sulpice in Paris. From that time the establishment made a rapid progress, M. de Maisonneuve still continuing its governor, after it had changed masters. He was a man of ability and piety: under his auspices the order of "Filles de la Congrégation" was established at Montreal by Margaret Bourgeois, who had accompanied the first settlers on the island from France. For the details of this admirable institution see Charlevoix, tom. ii., p. 94. He speaks of it with justice as one of the brightest ornaments of New France.

"Jusqu' en l'année 1692, la justice particulière de Montréal appartenoit à Messieurs du Séminaire de St. Sulpice, en qualité de seigneurs. Ils en donnèrent alors leur démission au roi, à condition que l'exercice leur en resteroit dans l'enclos de leur séminaire, et dans leur ferme de St. Gabriel, avec la propriété perpétuelle et incommutable du Greffe de la justice royale, qui seroit établie dans l'isle, et la nomination du premier juge."—Charlevoix, tom. ii., p. 140.

the terms of the proposed treaty. [1645.] After various orations, songs, dances, and exchanges of presents, peace was concluded to the satisfaction of both parties; and for the time at least, with apparent good faith, for the following winter the French and their new allies joined together in the chase, and mixed fearlessly in friendly intercourse.

M. de Montmagny was superseded as governor of Canada by M. d'Ailleboust in the year 1647. He had proved himself a man of judgment, courage, and virtue, and had gained the love of the settlers and Indians, as well as the approval of the court. But, in consequence of the governor of the American islands having recently refused to surrender office to a person appointed by the king, it was decreed that no one should hold the government of a colony for more than three years. M. d'Ailleboust was a man of ability and worth, and, having held the command at Three Rivers for some time, was also experienced in colonial affairs, but he received no more support from home than his predecessor; and, despite his best efforts, New France continued to languish under his rule.

The colony, however, was now free from the scourge of savage hostility. The Indians turned their subtle craft and terrible energy to the chase instead of war. From the far-distant hunting-grounds of the St. Maurice and of the gloomy Saguenay, they crowded to Three Rivers and Tadoussac with the spoils of the forest animals. At those settlements the trade went briskly on, and many of the natives became domesticated among their white neighbors. The worthy priests were not slow to take advantage of this favorable opportunity; many of the hunters from the north, who were attracted to the French villages by the fur trade, were told the great tidings of redemption; and usually, when they returned the following year, they were accompanied by others, who desired, with them, to receive the rites of baptism.*

* The kindness of the missionaries has been one of the causes that has perpetuated a kindly feeling toward the French. Among the American Indians, "a person, even in times of hostility, speaking French will find security from the attachment of the people to every thing that is French."—Imlay, p. 8.

The most numerous and pious of the proselytes were of the Huron tribe, an indolent and unwarlike race, against whom the bold and powerful Iroquois held deadly feud, which the existing peace only kept in abeyance till opportunity might arise for effective action. The little settlement of St. Joseph was the place where first an Indian congregation assembled for Christian worship; the Father Antoine Daniel was the pastor; the flock were of the Huron tribe. Faith in treaties and long-continued tranquillity had lulled this unhappy people into a fatal security, and all cautions were forgotten,* when, on the morning of the 4th of July, 1648, while the missionary was performing service, there suddenly arose a cry of terror that the Iroquois were at hand. None but old men, women, and children were in the village at the time; of this the crafty enemy were aware; they had crept silently through the woods, and lain in ambush till

"To do justice to truth, the French missionaries in general have invariably distinguished themselves every where by an exemplary life, befitting their profession. Their religious sincerity, their apostolic charity, their insinuating kindness, their heroic patience, their remoteness from austerity and fanaticism, fix in these countries memorable epochs in the annals of Christianity; and while the memory of a Del Vilde, a Vodilla, &c., will be held in everlasting execration by all truly Christian hearts, that of a Daniel, a Brebeuf, &c., will never lose any of that veneration which the history of discoveries and missions has so justly conferred upon them. Hence that predilection which the savages manifest for the French, a predilection which they naturally find in the recesses of their souls, cherished by the traditions which their fathers have left in favor of the first apostles of Canada, then called New France."—Beltrami's *Travels*, 1823. The authority of this passage, Chateaubriand observes, is the stronger, as the writer is severe in his condemnation of the modern Jesuit.

* "Ce n'étoit pas la faute de leurs missionnaires, s'ils s'endormaient de la sorte; mais ces religieux ne pouvant gagner sur leurs néophytes qu'ils prissent pour leur sûreté les précautions que la prudence exigeoit, redoublèrent leurs soins pour achever de les sanctifier, et pour les préparer à tout ce qui pourroit arriver. Ils les trouvèrent sur cet article d'une docilité parfaite; ils n'eurent aucune peine à les faire entrér dans les sentimens les plus convenables à la triste situation où ils se reduisaient euxmêmes par une indolence, et un aveuglement, qu'on ne pouvoit comprendre et qui n'a peut-être point d'exemple dans l'histoire. Ce qui consoloit les pasteurs, c'est qu'ils les voyoient dans l'occasion braver la mort avec un courage, qui les animoit euxmêmes à mourir en héros Chrétiens."—Charlevoix.

morning gave them light for the foul massacre. Not one of the inhabitants escaped, and last of all, the good priest was likewise slain.

During this year the first communication passed between the French and British North American colonies. An envoy arrived at Quebec from New England, bearing proposals for a lasting peace with Canada, not to be interrupted even by the wars of the mother countries. M. d'Ailleboust gladly entertained the wise proposition, and sent a deputy to Boston with full powers to treat, providing only that the English would consent to aid him against the Iroquois. But the cautious Puritans would not compromise themselves by this stipulation. They were sufficiently remote from the fierce and formidable savages of the Five Nations to be free from present apprehension, and to their steady and industrious habits the plow was more suitable than the sword. The negotiation, therefore, totally failed, which was probably of little consequence, for it is difficult to perceive how these remote and feeble colonies could have preserved a neutrality in the contentions of England and France, which was impossible even to powerful states.

After a treacherous calm of some six months' duration, the unhappy Hurons again relapsed into a fatal security; the terrible lessons of the past were forgotten in the apparent tranquillity of the present. Watch and ward were relaxed, and again they lay at the mercy of their ruthless enemies. When least expected, 1000 Iroquois warriors started up from the thick coverts of a neighboring forest, and fell fiercely upon the defenseless Hurons, burned two of their villages, exterminated the inhabitants, and put two French missionaries to death with horrible tortures. Then the remnant of the defeated tribe despaired; the alliance of the French had only embittered the hostility of their enemies without affording protection; therefore they arose and deserted their villages and hunting grounds, wandering away, some into the northern forests, others as suppliants among neighboring nations.

The greater body of the Hurons, however, attached themselves to the fortunes of the missionaries, and under them formed a settlement on the island of St. Joseph, but they neglected to cultivate the land. As the autumn advanced, the resources of the chase became exhausted, and the horrors of famine commenced. They were shortly reduced to the most dreadful extremities of suffering; every direst expedient that starvation could prompt and despair execute was resorted to for a few days' prolonging of life. Then came the scourge of contagious fever, sweeping numbers away with desolating fury. While these terrible calamities raged among the Hurons, the Iroquois seized the opportunity of again invading them. The village of St. John, containing nearly 3000 souls, was the first point of attack. The feeble inhabitants offered no resistance, and, with their missionary, were totally destroyed. Most of the remnant of this unhappy tribe then took the resolution of presenting themselves to their conquerors, and were received into the Iroquois nation. The few who still remained wandering in the forests were hunted down like wolves, and soon exterminated.

The terror of the Iroquois name now spread rapidly along the shores of the great lakes and rivers of the north. The fertile banks of the Ottawa, once the dwelling-place of numerous and powerful tribes, became suddenly deserted, and no one could tell whither the inhabitants had fled.

About this time was introduced among the Montagnez, and the other tribes of the Saguenay country, an evil more destructive than even the tomahawk of the Iroquois—the "accursed fire-water;" despite the most earnest efforts of the governor, the fur traders at Tadoussac supplied the Indians with this fatal luxury. In a short time, intoxication and its dreadful consequences became so frequent, that the native chiefs prayed the governor to imprison all drunkards. At Three Rivers, however, the wise precautions of the authorities preserved the infant settlement from this monstrous calamity.

In the year 1650 M. d'Ailleboust was worthily succeeded by M. de Lauson, one of the principals of the Associated Company. The new governor found affairs in a very discouraging condition, the colony rapidly declining, and the Iroquois, flushed by their sanguinary triumphs, more audacious than ever. These fierce savages intruded fearlessly among the French settlements, despising forts and intrenchments, and insulting the inhabitants with impunity. The island of Montreal suffered so much from their incursions, that M. de Maisonneuve, the governor, was obliged to repair to France to seek succors, for which he had vainly applied by letter. He returned in the year 1653 with a timely re-enforcement of 100 men.

Although the Iroquois had now overcome or destroyed all their native enemies, and proved their strength even against the Europeans, some of their tribes were more than ever disposed to a union with the white men. The Onnontagués dispatched an embassy to Quebec to request that the governor would send a colony of Frenchmen among them. He readily acceded to the proposition, and fifty men were chosen for the establishment, with the Sieur Dupuys for their commander. Four missionaries were appointed to found the first Iroquois church; and to supply temporal wants, provisions for a year, and sufficient seed to sow the lands about to be appropriated, were sent with the expedition. This design excited the jealousy of the other Iroquois tribes; the Agniers even tried to intercept the colonists with a force of 400 warriors; they, however, only succeeded in pillaging a few of the canoes that had fallen behind. The same war party soon after made an onslaught upon ninety Hurons, working on the Isle of Orleans under French protection, slew six, and carried off the rest into captivity. As they passed before Quebec they made their unhappy prisoners sing aloud, insultingly attracting the attention of the garrison. The marauders were not pursued; they dragged the prisoners to their villages, burned the chiefs, and condemned the rest to a cruel bondage. M. de Lauson can hardly be excused for thus suffering his allies to be torn from under his protection without an effort to save them from their merciless enemies. These unfortunates had been converted to Christianity, which increased the rage and ferocity of the captors against them. One brave chief, whose tortures had been prolonged for three days as a worshiper of the God of the white men, bore himself faithfully to the last, and died with the Saviour's blessed name upon his quivering lip.

In the mean time the expedition to the country of the Onnontagués suffered great privations, and only escaped starvation by the generosity of the natives. Their spiritual mission was, however, at first eminently successful, the whole nation seeming disposed to adopt the Christian faith. But the allied tribes having carried their insolence to an intolerable degree, and massacred three Frenchmen near Montreal, the commandant at Quebec seized all the Iroquois within his reach, and demanded redress. The answer of the haughty savages was, to prepare for war. Dupuys and his little colony were now in a most perilous position: there was no hope of aid from Quebec, and but little chance of being able to escape from among their dangerous neighbors. They labored diligently and secretly to construct a sufficient number of canoes to carry them away in case some happy opportunity might arise, and found means to warn the people of Quebec of the coming danger. By great industry and skill the canoes were completed, and stored with the necessary provisions; through an ingenious stratagem, the French escaped in safety, while the savages slept soundly after one of their solemn feasts. In fifteen days the fugitives arrived at Montreal, where they found alarm on every countenance. The Iroquois swarmed over the island, and committed great disorders, although still professing a treacherous peace. The savages soon, however, threw off the mask, and broke into open war.

On the 11th of July, 1658, the Viscompte d'Argenson landed at Quebec as governor. The next morning the cry "to arms" echoed through the town. The Iroquois had made a sudden onslaught upon some Algonquins under the very guns of the fortress, and massacred them without mercy. Two hundred men were instantly dispatched to avenge this insult, but they could not overtake the wily marauders. In the same year, however, a party of the Agniers met with a severe check in a treacherous attempt to surprise Three Rivers. The lesson was not lost, and the colony for some time enjoyed a much-needed repose. The missionaries seized this interval of tranquillity to recommence their sacred labors: they penetrated into many remote districts where Europeans had never before reached, and discovered several routes to the dreary shores of Hudson's Bay. In the year 1659, the exemplary François de Laval, abbé de Montigny, arrived at Quebec to preside over the Canadian Church as the first American bishop.*

The temporal affairs of the colony were falling into a lamentable condition; no supplies arrived from France, and the local production was far from sufficient. Terror of the Indians kept the settlers almost blockaded in the forts, and cultivation was necessarily neglected. It was proposed by many that all the settlements should be abandoned, and that they should again seek the peaceful shores of their native country. Many individuals were massacred by the savages, and two armed parties, one of thirty and the other of twenty-six men, were totally destroyed. But some of the Indians, too, began to weary of this murderous war, and to long again for Christian instruction and peaceful commerce. The new governor was at first little inclined to negotiate with his

* The Abbé de Montigny was titular Bishop of Petræa, and had received from the pope a brief as vicar apostolic. The Church of Quebec was not erected into a bishop's see until 1670, when its bishop was no longer called titular Bishop of Petræa, but Bishop of Quebec. "Ce qui avoit fait traîner la cause si fort en longueur, c'est qu'il y eut de grandes contestations sur la dépendance immédiate du Saint Siège, dont le pape ne voulut point se relâcher. Cela n'empêche pourtant pas que l'Evêché de Quebec ne soit en quelque façon uni au clergé de France, en la manière de celui du Puy, lequel relève aussi immédiatement de Rome."—Charlevoix, tom. ii., p. 189; *Petits Droits*, &c., tom. ii., p. 492.

"When the bishopric of Quebec was erected, Louis XIV. endowed it with the revenue of two abbacies, those of Benevent and L'Estrio. About thirty years ago, the then bishop, finding it difficult, considering the distance, to recover the revenues of them, by consent of Louis XV., resigned the same to the clergy of France, to be united to a particular revenue of theirs, styled the economats, applied to the augmentation of small livings, in consideration of which, the bishop of this see has ever since received yearly 8000 livres out of the said revenues. A few years before the late bishop's death, the clergy of France granted him, for his life only, a further pension of 2000 livres; the bishop had no estate whatever, except his palace at Quebec, destroyed by our artillery, a garden, and the ground-rent of two or three houses adjoining it, and built on some part of the lands."—Governor Murray's *Report on the Ancient Government and Actual State of the Province of Quebec in* 1762.

fierce and capricious enemies; but, influenced by the miserable state of the colony, which even a brief truce might improve, he at length agreed to an exchange of prisoners and a peace.

In 1662 the King of France was at last induced to hearken to the prayers of his Canadian subjects. M. de Monts* was sent out to inquire into the condition of the country, and 400 troops added to the strength of the garrison. But these encouraging circumstances were more than neutralized on account of the permission then granted by the new governor, Baron d'Avaugour, for the sale of ardent spirits.† The disorder soon rose to a lamentable height, and the clergy in vain opposed their utmost influence to its pernicious progress. At length the worthy bishop hastened to France, and represented to the king the dreadful evil that afflicted the colony. His remonstrances were effectual; he succeeded in obtaining such powers as he deemed necessary to stop the ruinous commerce.

The year 1663 was rendered memorable by a tremendous earthquake, spoken of in a preceding chapter. In the same year the Associated Company remitted to the crown all their rights over New France, which the king again

* Charlevoix, tom. ii., p. 120.

† "Jusques-là, les gouverneurs généraux avoient assez tenue la main à faire exécuter les ordres, qu'ils avoient eux-mêmes donnés, de ne point vendre d'eau de vie aux sauvages; et le baron d'Avaugour avoit décerné des peines très sévères contre ceux qui contreviendroient à ses ordonnances sur ce point capital. Il arriva qu'une femme de Quebec fut surprise en y contrevenant, et, sur le champ, conduite en prison. Le P. Lallemant, à la prière de ses amis, crut pouvoir sans conséquence intercéder pour elle. Il alla trouver le général, qui le reçut très mal, et qui sans faire réflexion qu'il n'y a point d'inconséquence dans les ministres d'un Dieu qui a donné sa vie pour détruire le pêché et sauver le pécheur, à agir avec zèle pour réprimer le vice, et à demander grace pour le criminel, lui répondit brusquement, que puisque la traité de l'eau de vie n'étoit pas une faute punissable pour cette femme, elle ne le seroit désormais pour personne . . . . il ne consulta que sa mauvaise humeur et sa droiture mal entendue; et ce qu'il y eut de pis, c'est qu'il se fit un point d'honneur de ne point retracter l'indiscrète parole qui lui étoit echappée. Le peuple en fut bientôt instruit et le desordre devint extrême."—Charlevoix, tom. ii., p. 121.

transferred to the West India Company.* Courts of law were for the first time established, and many families of valuable settlers found their way to the colony. Up to this period extreme simplicity and honesty seems to have prevailed in the little community, and it was not till then that a Council of State was appointed by the crown to co-operate with the governor in the conduct of affairs.† The king sent

* Petit, vol. i., p. 24. *Colony Records.* There are no books of record in the secretary's office before this period. The old records were either carried to France, or destroyed at the fire, when the intendant's palace was burned down in 1725.

"The company, 'des Cents Associés,' formed in 1628, though one of the most powerful, according to Charlevoix, that had ever existed, with respect to the number, the rank, and the accorded privileges of its members, had allowed the colony to fall into a deplorable state of weakness. In 1662, when it relinquished its rights to Louis XIV., the original number of 100 had diminished to 45."—Charlevoix, ii., p. 149.

The East India Company was erected by the great Colbert in 1664. This company, having fallen into decay, was united with the West Indian Company, which was founded by law in 1718, and survived the ruin of its projector.

† "Jusques-là il n'y avoit point eu proprement de cour de justice en Canada; les gouverneurs généraux jugeant les affaires d'une manière assez souveraine; on ne s'avisoit point d'appeller de leurs sentences; mais ils ne rendoient ordinairement des arrêts, qu'apres avoir inutilement tentés les voies de l'arbitrage, et l'on convient que leurs décisions étoient toujours, dictées par le bon sens, et selon les regles de la loi naturelle, qui est audessus de toutes les autres. D'ailleurs les Créoles du Canada, quoique de race Normande, pour la plupart n'avoient seulement l'esprit processif, et aimoient mieux pour l'ordinaire céder quelque chose de leur bon droit, que de perdre le tems à plaider. Il sembloit même que tous les biens fussent communes dans cette colonie, du moins on fut assez long tems sans rien fermée sous la clef, et il étoit inoui qu'on s'en abusât. Il est bien étrange et bien humiliant pour l'homme que les précautions qu'un prince sage prit pour éviter la chicane et faire regner la justice, aient presque été l'époque de la naissance de l'une, et de l'affoiblissement de l'autre. . . . . . La justice est rendue selon les ordonnances du royaume et la coutume de Paris. Au mois de Juin, 1679, le roi autorisa par un édit quelques réglemens du conseil de Quebec, et c'est ce qu'on appelle dans le pays la réduction du Code. . . . . . par un autre edit en 1685 le conseil fut autorisé à juger les causes criminelles au nombre de cinq juges. . . . . . c'est sur le modèle du conseil supérieur à Quebec, qu'on a depuis etabli ceux de la Martinique, de St. Domingue, et de Louisiane. Tous ses conseils sont d'epée."—Charlevoix, vol. ii., p. 140.

out the Sieur Gaudais to inquire into the state of his newly-acquired dependency, and to investigate certain complaints preferred against the Baron d'Avaugour, who had himself prayed to be recalled. The sieur performed his invidious task to the satisfaction of all parties: he made valuable reports as to the general character of the colonial clergy, of the advantages and disadvantages of the local administration of government, and imputed no fault to to the Baron d'Avaugour, but a somewhat too rigid and stern adherence to the letter of the law, and the severity of justice. The baron then joyfully returned to France, but soon afterward fell in the defense of the fort of Serin against the Turks, while, with the permission of the French king, serving the emperor.

M. de Mésy succeeded as governor, upon the recommendation of the Bishop of Canada, whose complaints on the subject of the sale of spirituous liquors had been the principal cause of the Baron d'Avaugour's recall. The new appointment proved far from satisfactory to those by whose influence it was made. M. de Mésy at once raised up a host of enemies by his haughty and despotic bearing. He thwarted the Jesuits to the utmost extent of his power; the council supported them, alleging that their influence over the native race was essential to the well-being of the colony. Various representations of these matters were made to the court of France, and the final result was, that the governor was recalled.

Alexandre de Prouville, marquis de Tracy, was next appointed viceroy in America by the king, with ample powers to establish, destroy, or alter the institutions of the Canadian colony. Daniel de Remi, seigneur de Courcelles, the new governor, and M. Talon, the intendant, were conjoined with the viceroy in a commission to examine into the charges against M. de Mésy. [1665,] M. de Tracy was the first to arrive at Quebec; he bore with him the welcome re-enforcement of some companies of the veteran regiment of Carignan-Salières.* He sent a portion of this force at once

* "The regiment de Carignan-Salières was just arrived from Hungary, where it had distinguished itself greatly in the war against the Turks."—Charlevoix, tom. ii., p. 150.

against the Iroquois, accompanied by the allied savages. The country was speedily cleared of every enemy, and the harvest gathered in security. The remaining part of the regiment arrived soon after, with the viceroy's colleagues; a large number of families, artisans, and laborers; the first horses that had ever been sent to New France; cattle, sheep; and, in short, a far more complete colony than that which they came to aid.

Being now established in security, and confident in strength, the viceroy led a sufficient force to the mouth of Richelieu River, where he erected three forts* to overawe the turbulent Iroquois.† These works were rapidly and skillfully executed, and for a time answered their purpose; but the wily savages soon perceived that there were other routes by which they could enter the settlements. In the mean time M. Talon remained at Quebec, collecting much valuable information concerning the country and its native inhabitants. He was spared, however, the task of inquiring into the conduct of M. de Mésy, for that gentleman died before the news of his recall reached Canada.

* "M. de Sorel, a captain in the Regiment De Carignan, was employed on the erection of the first fort, on the same site as the fort De Richelieu, built by M. de Montmagny, now quite in ruins. De Sorel gave his own name to the fort, and in time the river Richelieu, or Iroquois, acquired it also.

"The second fort was called St. Louis; but, as M. de Chambly, captain in the same regiment, had superintended the erection, and afterward acquired the land on which it was situated, the whole district, and the stone fort, which has been erected since upon the ruins of the former one, have acquired and retained the name of Chambly. This was a very important fortress, as it protected the colony on the side of New York, and the lower Iroquois.

"The third fort was built under the direction of M. de Salières, the colonel of the regiment De Carignan. He named it St. Theresa, because it was finished on that saint's day."—Charlevoix, tom. ii., p. 152.

† "Every omen was now favorable, except the conquest of New Netherlands (New York) by the English in 1664. That conquest eventually made the Five Nations (Iroquois) a dependance on the English nation; and if for twenty-five years England and France sued for their friendship with unequal success, yet afterward, in the grand division of parties throughout the world, the Bourbons found in them implacable opponents."—Bancroft's *History of the United States*, vol. ii., p. 149.

Toward the end of December, 1665, three tribes of the Iroquois nation dispatched envoys to the viceroy at Quebec with proposals for peace and for an exchange of prisoners. The terms were readily complied with. M. de Tracy received the Indians with politic kindness and attention, and sent them back with valuable presents. But the formidable tribes of the Agniers and Onneyouths still kept sullenly apart from the French alliance; it was, therefore, determined to give them a severe lesson for their former insolence and treachery, and make them feel the supremacy of France. M. de Courcelles and M. de Sorel were sent with two corps to humble the haughty savages. The hostile Indians, alarmed at the preparations for their destruction, now sent deputies to Quebec to avert the threatening storm, although some of their war parties still infested the settlements, and had lately put to death three French officers, among them M. de Chasy, the viceroy's nephew. One of the Indian deputies boasted at M. de Tracy's table that he had slain the French officers with his own hands. He was immediately seized and strangled, and the negotiations broken off.

The two French expeditions found the hostile country altogether deserted, and returned without effecting any thing, having suffered great fatigue and hardship. M. de Tracy then took the field in person, at the head of 1200 French and 600 friendly Indians, with two pieces of cannon. As he was setting out on the march, chiefs again came from the Agniers and Onneyouths to pray for peace; but he would hear of no accommodation, and even imprisoned the deputies. The French army marched on the 14th of September, 1666; provisions soon failed in the solitary desert through which they had to pass; in their greatest necessity, however, they entered a wood abounding in chestnut-trees, whose fruit supplied them with sustenance till they gained the first village of the enemy. The warriors had abandoned the old men, women, and children, and ample stores of food, and retired through the forest. The French found the Indian cabans larger and better than any they had seen elsewhere, and in ingeniously contrived magazines, sunk under the ground, sufficient grain was discovered to supply the whole colony for two years. The invaders burned and utterly destroyed all the villages, and carried away, as captives, all the inhabitants that remained, but they could not succeed in overtaking the warriors to force them to action. They then retraced their steps, strengthening the settlements on the River St. Lawrence as they passed. When M. de Tracy reached Quebec, he caused some of the prisoners to be put to death as a warning, and dismissed the remainder. Having established the authority of the West India Company instead of that of "The Hundred Associates," he returned to France the following spring.

The humiliation of the Iroquois restored profound peace to New France. Then the wisdom and energy of M. Talon were directed to the development of the resources of the country. Scientific men were sent to examine the mineral resources of several districts where promising indications had been observed. The clearing of land proceeded rapidly, and invariably discovered a rich and productive soil. The population increased in numbers, and enjoyed abundant plenty: all were in a condition to live in comfort. According to the perhaps partial authority of the Jesuit missionaries, the progress in morality and attention to religious observances kept pace with the temporal prosperity of this happy colony.

Although M. de Courcelles showed little activity in conducting the internal government of the colony, which was principally directed by M. Talon, he was highly energetic and vigorous in his relations with the Indians. Having learned that the Iroquois were intriguing with the Ottawas to direct their fur trade to the English colonies, thus probably to ruin the commerce of New France, he resolved to visit the Iroquois, and impress them with an idea of his power. For this purpose he took the route of the deep and rapid St. Lawrence, making his way in bateaux for 130 miles above Montreal. His health, however, suffered so much in this difficult expedition that he was obliged to demand his recall.

On his return to Quebec he found that several atrocious murders and robberies had been committed upon Iroquois and Mahingan Indians by Frenchmen, which filled the savages with indignation, and roused them to a fury of revenge. They attacked and burned a house in open day, and a woman perished in the flames. Numbers of the two injured nations and their savage allies hovered round Montreal, awaiting an opportunity for vengeance. M. de Courcelles, with his wonted vigor in emergencies, hastened to the threatened settlement, and called upon the Indian chiefs to hold parley. They assembled, and hearkened with attention while he enumerated the advantages that both parties derived from the existing peace. He then caused those among the murderers who had been convicted of the crime to be led out and executed on the spot. The Indians were at once appeased by this prompt administration of justice, and even lamented over the malefactors' wretched fate; they were also fully indemnified for the stolen property. The assembly then broke up with mutual satisfaction.

But soon again the repose of the country was threatened by the Iroquois and Ottawas, who had begun to make incursions upon each other. M. de Courcelles promptly interfered to quell this growing animosity, declaring that he would punish with the greatest severity either party that would not submit to reasonable conditions. He required them to send deputies to state their wrongs, and the grounds of dispute, and took upon himself to do justice to both parties. He was obeyed: the chiefs of the contending tribes repaired to Quebec, and by the firmness and judgment of the governor, the breach was healed, and peace secured.

At this time a scourge more terrible than even savage war visited the red race of Canada. The small-pox first appeared among the northern tribe of the Attikamegues, and swept them totally away: many of their neighbors shared the same fate. Tadoussac, where 1200 Indians usually assembled to barter their rich furs at the end of the hunting season, was deserted. Three Rivers, once crowded with the friendly Algonquins, was now never visited by a red man, and a few years after the frightful plague first appeared, the settlement of Sillery, near Quebec, was attacked; 1500 savages took the fatal contagion, and not one survived. The Hurons, who had been always most intimately associated with the French, suffered least among the native nations from the malady. In 1670 Father Chaumonat assembled the remnant of this once powerful tribe in the neighborhood of Quebec, and established them in the village of Lorette,* where a mixed race of their descendants remains to this day.

Even the presence of the dreadful infliction of the small-pox and the fear of French power could not long restrain the savage impulse for war. The most distant tribe of the Iroquois became engaged in a sanguinary quarrel with a neighboring nation, and took a number of prisoners. The governor immediately sent to warn these turbulent savages that if they did not desist from war, and return their prisoners, he would destroy their villages as he had those of the Agniers. This peremptory message raised the indignation of the Iroquois, they at first proudly disclaimed the right of the French to dictate to the free people of the forest, and vowed that they would perish rather than bow down to the strangers' will; but, finally, the wisdom of the old men prevailed in the council: they knew that they were not prepared to meet the power of the Europeans; it was therefore decided that they should send a portion of their prisoners to the governor. He either believed, or pretended to believe, that they had fully complied with his demands, deeming it prudent not to drive the Indians to extremities.

CHAPTER XIII.

TAKING advantage of the profound peace which now blessed New France,† M. Talon, the intendant, dispatched

* "La chapelle à Lorette est bâtie sur le modèle et avec toutes les dimensions de la Santa Case d'Italie, d'où l'on a envoyé à nos néophytes une image de la vierge, semblable à celle, que l'on voit dans ce célébre sanctuaire. On ne pouvoit guère choisir pour placer cette mission, un lieu plus sauvage."—Charlevoix.

† "On espéroit beaucoup de la Compagnie des Indes Occidentales, mais elle ne prit guère plus à cœur les intérêts de la Nouvelle France, que n'avoit fait la précédente, ainsi que M. Talon avoit prévu. Ce-

an experienced traveler, named Nicholas Perrot, to the distant northern and western tribes, for the purpose of inducing them to fix a meeting at some convenient place with a view of discussing the rights of the French crown. This bold adventurer penetrated among the nations dwelling by the great lakes, and with admirable address induced them all to send deputies to the Falls of St. Mary, where the waters of Lake Superior pour into Lake Huron. The Sieur de St. Lusson met the assembled Indian chiefs at this place in May, 1671; he persuaded them to acknowledge the sovereignty of his king, and erected a cross bearing the arms of France.

M. de Courcelles was succeeded by the able and chivalrous Louis de Buade, comte de Frontenac. The new governor was a soldier of high rank, and a trusty follower of the great Henry of Navarre; his many high qualities were, however, obscured by a capricious and despotic temper. His plans for the advancement of the colony were bold and judicious, his representations to the government of France fearless and effectual, his personal conduct and piety unimpeachable, but he exhibited a bitterness and asperity to those who did not enter into his views little suited to the better points of his character, and it is said that ambition and the love of authority at times overcame his zeal for the public good.*

M. Talon, the intendant, was at this time recalled by his own wish, but before he departed from the scenes of his useful labors he planned a scheme of exploration more extensive than any that had yet been accomplished in New France. From the rumors and traditions among the savages of the far West, with which the meeting at St. Mary's had made the French acquainted, it was believed that to the

pendant comme les secours que le Canada avait reçus les dernières années, l'avoient mis sur un assez bon pied, il s'y conserva quelque tems, et il n'est pas même retombé depuis dans l'état de foiblesse et d'épuisement dont le roi venoit de le tirer."—Charlevoix, tom. ii., p. 161.

* "Le peuple adoroit Frontenac à cause de sa bonté."—La Potherie, tom. iv., p. 110; Charlevoix, tom. ii., p. 246.

southwest of New France there flowed a vast river, called by the natives Mechasèpè, whose course was neither toward the great lakes to the north, nor the Atlantic to the east. It was therefore surmised that this unknown flood must pour its waters either into the Gulf of Mexico or the Pacific Ocean. The wise intendant was impressed with the importance of possessing a channel of navigation to the waters of the south and west, and before his departure from America made arrangements to have the course of the mysterious stream* explored. He intrusted the arduous duty to Father Marquette, a pious priest, who was experienced in Indian travel, and an adventurous and able merchant of Quebec, named Jolyet. [1673.] The Comte de Frontenac gave hearty aid to this expedition, and in the mean time he himself extended the line of French settlement to the shores of Lake Ontario,† built there the fort that still bears his name, and opened communication with the numerous tribes westward of the Allegany Mountains.

The exploring party, led by Marquette‡ and Jolyet, con-

* The Mississippi.

† "Ce lac a porté quelque tems le nom de St. Louis, ou lui donna ensuite celui de Frontenac, aussi bien qu'au fort de Catarocoui dont le Comte de Frontenac fut le fondateur, mais insensiblement le lac a repris son ancien nom, qui est Huron ou Iroquois, et le fort celui du lieu où il est bâti (1721)."—Charlevoix, tom. v., p. 287.

‡ "Le Père J. Marquette, natif de Laon en Picardie, a été un des plus illustres missionnaires de la Nouvelle France; il en a parcouru presque toutes les contrées, et il y a fait plusieurs découvertes dont la dernière est celle du Micissipi. Deux ans après cette découverte, comme il alloit à Michillimackinac, il entra le 18me de May, 1675, dans la rivière dont il s'agit; il dressa son autel sur le terrein bas, qu'on lassia à droite en y entrant, et il y dit la messe. Il s'éloigna, ensuite un peu pour faire son action de graces, et pria les hommes qui conduisoient son canot, de le laisser seul pendant une demie heure. Ce tems passé, ils allèrent le chercher, et furent très surpris de le trouver mort, ils se souvinrent néanmoins qu'en entrant dans la rivière, il lui étoit échappé de dire qu'il finiroit la son voyage. Aujourd'hui les sauvages n'appellent cette rivière autrement que la rivière de la robe noire;[1] les François lui ont donné le nom du Père Marquette, et ne manquent jamais de l'invoquer, quand ils se trouvent en quelque danger sur le Lac Michigan. Plusieurs ont assûré qu'ils

[1] "Les sauvages appellent ainsi les Jésuites. Ils nomment les Prêtres, les Collets blancs, et les Recollets, les Robes grises."

sisted of only six men, in two little bark canoes: at the very outset the Indians of the lakes told them that great and terrible dangers would beset their path, and recounted strange tales of supernatural difficulties and perils for those who had ventured to explore the mysterious regions of the West. Hearkening carefully to whatever useful information the natives could bestow, but despising their timid warnings, these adventurous men hastened on over the great lakes to the northwestern extremity of the deep and stormy Michigan, now called Green Bay. Numerous Indian tribes wandered over the surrounding country; among others, the Miamis, the most civilized and intelligent of the native race that they had yet seen. Two hunters of this nation undertook to guide the expedition to one of the tributaries of the great river of which they were in search. The French were struck with wonder at the vast prairies that lay around their route on every side, monotonous, and apparently boundless as the ocean.

The Fox River was the stream to which the Miamis first led them. Although it was broad at its entrance into the lake the upper portion was divided by marshes into a labyrinth of narrow channels; as they passed up the river, the wild oats grew so thickly in the water that the adventurers appeared to row through fields of corn. After a portage of a mile and a half, they launched their canoes in the Wisconsin River, a tributary of the Mississippi, and the guides left them to find their way into the unknown solitudes of the West. Their voyage down the tributary was easy and prosperous, and at length, to their great joy, they reached the magnificent stream of the Mississippi. The banks were rich and beautiful, the trees the loftiest they had yet seen, and wild bulls and other animals roamed in vast herds over the flowery meadows.*

For more than 200 miles Marquette and his companions continued their course through verdant and majestic solitudes, where no sign of human life appeared. At length the foot-

se croyoient redevables à son intercession, d'avoir echappé à de très grands perils."—Charlevoix, tom. vi., p. 21.

* Relation de Marquette: Recueil de Thevenot, tom. i.

prints of men rejoiced their sight, and, by following up the track, they arrived at a cluster of inhabited villages, where they were kindly and hospitably received. Their hosts called themselves Illinois, which means "men" in the native tongue, and is designed to express their supposed superiority over their neighbors. Marquette considered them the most civilized of the native American nations.

Neither fear for the future nor the enjoyment of present comfort could damp the ardor of the French adventurers; they soon again launched their little canoes on the Father of Waters, and followed the course of the stream. They passed a number of bold rocks that rose straight up from the water's edge; on one of these, strange monsters were curiously painted in brilliant colors. Soon after they came to the place where the great Missouri pours its turbid and noisy flood into the Mississippi; and next they reached a lofty range of cliffs, that stretched nearly across from bank to bank, breasting the mighty stream. With great difficulty and danger they guided their little canoes through these turbulent waters. They passed the entrance of the Ohio,* and were again astonished at the vast size of the tributaries which fed the flood of the mysterious river. The inhabitants of the villages on the banks accepted the calumet of peace, and held friendly intercourse with the adventurers; and although, after passing the mouth of the Arkansas River, a proposition was made in the council of one tribe to slay and rob them, the chief indignantly overruled the cruel suggestion, and presented them with the sacred pipe.

At the village where they were threatened with this great danger they were inaccurately informed that the sea was only distant five days' voyage. From this the travelers concluded that the waters of the Mississippi poured into the Gulf of Mexico, and not, as they had fondly hoped, into the Pacific Ocean. Fearing, therefore, that by venturing further they might fall into the hands of the Spaniards, and lose all the fruits of their toils and dangers, they determined

* The signification of the word Ohio is "Beautiful River." According to Bancroft, it was called the Wabash in La Salle's time, and long afterward.

to reascend the stream and return to Canada. After a long and dreary voyage, they reached Chicago, on Lake Michigan, where the adventurers separated. Father Marquette remained among the friendly Miamis, and Jolyet hastened to Quebec to announce their discoveries. Unfortunately, their enlightened patron, M. Talon, had already departed for France.

There chanced, however, to be at Quebec at that time a young Frenchman, of some birth and fortune, named Robert Cavalier, sieur de la Salle, ambitious, brave, and energetic. He had emigrated to America with a hope of gaining fame and wealth in the untrodden paths of a new world. The first project that occupied his active mind was the discovery of a route to China* and Japan, by the unexplored regions of the west of Canada. The information brought by Jolyet to Quebec excited his sanguine expectations. Impressed with the strange idea that the Missouri would lead to the Northern Ocean, he determined to explore its course, and having gained the sanction of the governor, sailed for France to seek the means of fitting out an expedition. In this he succeeded by the favor of the Prince of Conti. The Chevalier de Tonti, a brave officer, who had lost an arm in the Sicilian wars, was associated with him in the enterprise.

On the 14th of July, 1678, La Salle and Tonti embarked at Rochelle with thirty men, and in two months arrived at Quebec. They took Father Hennepin with them, and hastened on to the great lakes,† where they spent two years in

* "La Chine is a fine village three French miles to the southeast of Montreal, but on the same side, close to the River St. Lawrence. Here is a church of stone, with a small steeple, and the whole place has a very agreeable situation. Its name is said to have had the following origin: As the unfortunate M. de Sales was here, who was afterward murdered by his own countrymen further up the country, he was very intent on discovering a shorter road to China by means of the River St. Lawrence. He talked of nothing at that time but his new short way to China; but, as his project of undertaking this journey in order to make this discovery was stopped by an accident which happened to him here, and he did not at that time come any nearer China, this place got its name, as it were, by way of joke."—Kalm, in Pinkerton, vol. xiii., p. 699.

† See Appendix, No. LXIV.

raising forts and building vessels of forty or fifty tons burden, and carrying on the fur trade with the natives. The party then pushed forward to the extremity of Michigan. Their friendly relations with the Indians were here interrupted by a party of the Outagamis having robbed them of a coat. The French held a council to devise means of deterring the savages from such depredations, and it was somewhat hastily determined to demand restitution of the coat under the threat of putting the offending chief to death. The Outagamis, having divided the stolen garment into a number of small pieces for general distribution, found it impossible to comply with this requisition, and thinking that no resource remained, presented themselves to the French in battle array. However, through the wise mediation of Father Hennepin, the quarrel was arranged, and a good understanding restored.

La Salle now set out with a party of forty-four men and three Recollets, top ursue his cherished object of exploring the course of the Mississippi. He descended the stream of the Illinois, and was charmed with the beauty and fertility of the banks: large villages rose on each side; the first, containing 500 wooden huts, they found deserted, but in descending the river they suddenly perceived that two large bodies of Indians were assembled on opposite banks, in order of battle. After a parley, however, the Indians presented the calumet of peace, and entertained the strangers at a great feast.

The discontents among his own followers proved far more dangerous to La Salle than the caprice or hostility of the savages. They murmured at being led into unknown regions, among barbarous tribes, to gratify the ambition of an adventurer, and determined to destroy him and return to France. They were base enough to tell the natives that La Salle was a spy of the Iroquois, their ancient enemies, and it required all his genius and courage to remove this idea from the minds of the ignorant savages. Failing in this scheme, they endeavored to poison him and all his faithful adherents at a Christmas dinner; by the use of timely remedies, however, the intended victims recovered, and the villains, having fled, were in vain pursued over the trackless deserts.

La Salle was obliged to return to the forts for aid, on account of the desertion of so many of his followers; but he sent Father Hennepin, with Dacan and three other Frenchmen, to explore the sources of the Mississippi, and left Tonti in the command of a small fort, erected on the Illinois, which he, however, was soon obliged to desert, in consequence of the hostility of the Iroquois. La Salle collected twenty men, with the necessary arms and provisions, and, unshaken by accumulated disasters, determined at once to make his way to the Gulf of Mexico down the course of the Mississippi. He passed the entrance of the swollen and muddy Missouri, and the beautiful Ohio, and, still descending, traversed countries where dwelt the numerous and friendly Chickasaw and Arkansaw Indians. Next he came to the Taencas, a people far advanced beyond their savage neighbors in civilization, and obeying an absolute prince. Farther on, the Natchez received him with hospitality; but the Quinipissas, who inhabited the shores more to the south, assailed him with showers of arrows. He wisely pursued his important journey without seeking to avenge the insult. Tangibao, still lower down the stream, had just been desolated by one of the terrible irruptions of savage war: the bodies of the dead lay piled in heaps among the ruins of their former habitations. For leagues beyond, the channel began to widen, and at length became so vast that one shore was no longer visible from the other. The water was now brackish, and beautiful sea-shells were seen strewn along the shore. They had reached the mouth of the Mississippi, the Father of Rivers.

La Salle celebrated the successful end of his adventurous voyage with great rejoicings. Te Deum was sung, a cross was suspended from the top of a lofty tree, and a shield, bearing the arms of France, was erected close at hand. They attempted to determine the latitude by an observation of the sun, but the result was altogether erroneous.

The country immediately around the outlet of this vast stream was desolate and uninteresting. Far as the eye could reach, swampy flats and inundated morasses filled the dreary prospect. Under the ardent rays of the tropical sun, noisome vapors exhaled from the rank soil and sluggish waters, poisoning the breezes from the southern seas, and corrupting them into the breath of pestilence. Masses of floating trees, whose large branches were scathed by months of alternate immersion and exposure, during hundreds of leagues of travel, choked up many of the numerous outlets of the river, and, cemented together by the alluvial deposits of the muddy stream, gradually became fixed and solid, throwing up a rank vegetation.* Above this dreary delta, however, the country was rich and beautiful, and graceful undulations succeeded to the monotonous level of the lower banks.

After a brief repose, La Salle proceeded to re-ascend the river toward Canada, eager to carry the important tidings of his success to France. His journey was beset with difficulties and dangers. The course of the stream, though not rapid, perpetually impeded his progress. Provisions began to fail, and dire necessity drove him to perilous measures for obtaining supplies. Having met with four women of the hostile tribe of the Quinipissas, he treated them with great kindness, loading them with such gifts as might most win their favor. The chief of the savages then came forward and invited the French to his village, offering them the much-needed refreshments which they sought. But a cruel treachery lurked under this friendly seeming, and the adventurers were only saved from destruction by the careful vigi-

* "This is the site of New Orleans. New Orleans, holding, from its position, the command of all the immense navigable river-courses of interior America, is making the most rapid progress of any American city, and will doubtless one day become the greatest in that continent—perhaps even in the world. A formidable evil, however, exists in the insalubrity of the air, arising from the extensive marshes and inundated grounds which border the lower part of the Mississippi. The terrible malady that bears the name of the yellow fever, makes its first appearance in the early days of August, and continues till October. During that era New Orleans appears like a deserted city; all who possibly can, fly to the north or the upper country; most of the shops are shut; and the silence of the streets is only interrupted by the sound of the hearse passing through them. In one year two thousand died of this fever. Since the morasses have been partially cleared, its ravages have been less destructive; and, as this work is going on, the city may hope, in time, to be almost free from this terrible scourge."—Murray's *America*, vol. ii., p. 428.

lance of their leader. At daybreak the following morning, the Indians made a sudden attack upon their guests; the French, however, being thoroughly on the alert, repulsed the assailants, and slew several of the bravest warriors. Infuriated by the treachery of the savages, the victors followed the customs of Indian warfare, and scalped those of the enemy who fell into their power.

As they ascended the river they were again endangered by the secret hostility of the Natchez,* from the effects of which a constant front of preparation alone preserved them. After several months of unceasing toil and watchfulness, with many strange and romantic adventures, but no other serious obstruction, the hardy travelers at length joyfully beheld the headland of Quebec.

Immediately after his arrival, La Salle hastened to France to announce his great discovery,† and reap the distinction justly due to his eminent merits. [1682.] He was received with every honor, and all his plans and suggestions were approved by the court. Under his direction and command, an expedition was fitted out, consisting of four vessels and 280 men, for the purpose of forming a settlement at the mouth of the Mississippi, and thence establishing a regular communication with Canada, along the course of the Great River. At the same time, he received the commission of governor over the whole of the vast country extending between the lakes and the Gulf of Mexico. The little squadron sailed from La Rochelle on the 24th of July, 1684, along with the West India fleet, and having touched at St. Domingo and Cuba by the way, arrived in safety on the coast of Florida.

La Salle was involved in great perplexity by ignorance of the longitude of the river's mouth. Not having descended so far in his former expedition as to be able to judge of its

* "Garcilasso de la Vega parle de cette nation comme d'un peuple puissant, et il n'y a pas six ans qu'on y comptoit quatre mille guerriers. Aujourd'hui les Natchez ne pourroient pas mettre sur pied deux mille combattans (1714)."—Charlevoix, tom. vi., p. 177.

† "La Louisiane est le nom que M. de la Sale a donné au pays qu'arrose le Mississippi audessous de la Rivière des Illinois et qu'il a conservé jusqu'à present. C'étoit en l'honneur de Louis XIV., qui regnoit alors en France."—Charlevoix, tom. ii., p. 436.

appearance from the sea, he passed the main entrance of the Mississippi unawares, and proceeded 200 miles to the westward, where he found himself in a bay, since called St. Bernard's. Attracted by the favorable appearance of the surrounding country, La Salle here founded the fort which was to be the basis of his future establishment. But difficulties and misfortunes crowded upon him; the vessel containing his stores and utensils was sunk through the negligence or treachery of her commander, and a great portion of the cargo lost or seized by the Indians. The violent measures he adopted to compel restitution of the plundered goods kindled a deep resentment in the minds of this fierce and haughty tribe, the Clamcoets by name. They made a sudden midnight attack upon the settlement, slew two of the French, and wounded several, and whenever opportunity offered afterward, repeated their assaults. The tropical climate, however, proved a far deadlier foe than even the savage, and at length the spirit of the colonists gave way under accumulated difficulties.

Meanwhile Tonti, who had descended the Mississippi to join La Salle, sought him in vain at the mouth of the river, and along the coast for twenty leagues at either side. Having found no trace or tidings of the expedition, he relinquished the search in despair, and sailed upward again to the Canadian Lakes.

La Salle bore up with noble courage and energy against the difficulties that surrounded him. His subordinates thwarted him on every occasion, and at length broke out into a violent mutiny, which he, however, vigorously suppressed. But when he discovered that the settlement founded and sustained by his unceasing labors was not, as he had fondly supposed, at the mouth of the Great River, he experienced the bitterest disappointment. The surrounding country, though fertile, offered no brilliant prospect of sudden wealth or hopes of future commerce. He determined, therefore, once again to explore the vast streams of the Mississippi and Illinois, and to endeavor to gain a greater knowledge of the interior of the continent. He took with him on this expedition his nephew, a worthy but impetuous youth, named Moranger, and about twenty men. This young man's haughty spirit excited a savage thirst of vengeance in the minds of his uncle's lawless followers; they watched their opportunity, and in a remote and dreary solitude in the depths of the new continent, La Salle and Moranger were both slain by their murderous hands. Thus sadly perished, in a nameless wilderness, one of the most daring and gifted among those wonderful men to whom the discovery of the New World had opened a field of glory. His temper was, doubtless, at times, violent and overbearing,* but he was dearly loved by his friends, respected by his dependents, and fondly revered by those among the Indians who came within his influence. His greatest difficulties arose from those who were placed under his command, abandoned and ungovernable men, the very refuse of society, and amenable to no laws, human or divine.

It has been already mentioned that La Salle had sent Dacan and Father Hennepin to explore the Mississippi, on his first return from the Illinois to Lake Michigan. They descended that great river almost to the sea; but their followers, becoming alarmed at the idea of falling into the hands of the Spaniards, compelled them to return without having perfected their expedition. They re-ascended the stream, and passed the mouths of the Illinois and Wisconsin, and even reached beyond those magnificent falls to which the adventurous priest has given the name of St. Anthony. Continual danger threatened these travelers, from the caprice or hostility of the Indians; they were held for a long time in a cruel captivity, forced to accompany their captors through the most difficult countries, at a pace of almost incredible rapidity, till, with their feet and limbs cut and bleeding,

* Charlevoix thus speaks of the selection of M. de la Sale by M. de Seignelay: "Il n'est point de vertu qui ne soit melée de quelque défaut: c'est le sort ordinaire de l'humanité. Ce qui met le comble a notre humiliation, c'est que les plus grands défauts accompagnent souvent les plus éminentes qualités, et que la jalousie que celles-ci inspirent trouve presque toujours dans ceux-là un spécieux prétexte pour couvrir ce que cette passion a de bas et d'injuste. C'est à ceux qui sont établis pour gouverner les hommes à se faire jour pour sortir de cette labyrinthe, à dégager le vrai des ténébres dont la passion veut l'offusquer, et à connoître si bien ceux dont ils veulent se servir, qu'en leur donnent lieu de faire usage de ce qu'ils ont de bon, ils se précautionnent sur ce qu'ils ont de mauvais."—Charlevoix, tom. ii., p. 2.

they were well-nigh incapable of moving any further. After some time Hennepin was adopted by a chief as his son, and treated with much kindness; when winter came on, however, and a great scarcity of provisions arose, the Indians, being unable any longer to support their captives, allowed them to depart. The father and his companions used this liberty to continue their explorations down the Mississippi. After many other perils and adventures, they at length met the Sieur de Luth, who commanded a party sent in search of them, and with further instructions to form a settlement on the Great River. Hennepin at first turned back with the sieur, but found so many obstacles and difficulties that he determined for the present to return to Canada.

The disasters attending the expeditions of La Salle and Hennepin for some time deterred others from venturing to explore the dangerous regions of the West, and the government totally neglected to occupy the splendid field which the adventure of those men had opened to French enterprise. It was left to the love of gain or glory, or the religious zeal of individuals, to continue the explorations of this savage but magnificent country. The Baron la Hontan was one of the first and most conspicuous of these dauntless travelers.* He had gone to Canada in early life with a view of retrieving the broken fortunes of his ancient family, and had obtained employment upon the lakes under the French government. While thus occupied, he became intimately acquainted with the life and customs of the savages, and, from his intercourse with them, formed the idea of penetrating into the interior of their country, where the white man's foot had never before trodden. His actual discoveries were probably not very important, and his record of them is confused and imperfect; but he was the first to learn the existence of the Rocky Mountains, and of that vast ocean which separates the western coast of North America from the continent of Asia.†

* *Mémoires de l'Amérique Septentrionale par M. le Baron de la Hontan:* à Amsterdam, 1705. For the character of these memoirs, see Charlevoix, tom. vi., p. 408. They are translated in Pinkerton, vol. xiii.

† The North Pacific Ocean. The South Pacific Ocean had been discovered by the Spaniard Balboa in 1513.

CHAPTER XIV.

An embittered disagreement between the governor general, Comte de Frontenac, and the intendant, M. de Cheneau, M. Talon's successor, rendered it necessary to recall both those officers from the colony. The French court attributed the greater share of blame to the governor, but the haughty and unbending disposition of the intendant was probably a principal cause of those untoward disputes. M. le Févre de la Barre and M. de Meules succeeded them in their respective offices, with special recommendation from the king to cultivate friendly relations with each other, and with M. de Blénac, the governor general of the French American islands.

New France had for many years remained in a state of great confusion, and had made but little progress in prosperity or population, and now the prospects of a disastrous war darkened the future of the colonists. Various causes had united to revive the hostility of the Iroquois, their ancient and powerful foes. Since New York had fallen into English hands, the savages found it more advantageous to carry their trade thither than to barter their furs with the privileged company of France. The falling off of commercial intercourse soon led to further alienation, which the death of an Iroquois chief by the hands of an Illinois, in the territory of the Ottawas, then allies of the white men, soon turned into open hostility. The Comte de Frontenac had failed in his attempts to negotiate with the savages; and on the arrival of his successor, an invasion of the colony was hourly expected. M. de la Barre at once perceived the dangerous state of affairs; he therefore summoned an assembly of all the leading men in the country, ecclesiastical, civil, and military, and demanded counsel from them in the emergency.

The assembly was of opinion that the Iroquois aimed at the monopoly of all the trade of Canada, by the instigation of the English and Dutch of New York, who were also supposed to incite them to enmity against the French, and that, consequently, those nations should be held hostile. It was also believed that the savages had only endeavored to gain time by their negotiations, while they either destroyed the tribes friendly to the colonists, or seduced them from their alliance. With this view they had already assailed the Illinois, and it was therefore the duty of the French to save that nation from this attack, whatever might be the cost or danger of the enterprise. For that purpose the colony could only furnish 1000 men; and to procure even this number, it was necessary that the labors of husbandry should be suspended. Re-enforcements of troops and a supply of laborers were therefore urgently required for the very existence of the settlements; and an earnest appeal for such assistance was forwarded to the king, as the result of the deliberations of the assembly. This application was immediately answered by the dispatch of 200 soldiers to New France, and by a remonstrance addressed to the King of Great Britain, who instructed Colonel Dongan, the English governor of New York, to encourage more friendly relations with his French neighbors.

While M. de la Barre pushed on his preparations for war against the Iroquois, he still kept up the hope of treating with them for peace in such a manner as not to forfeit the dignity of his position. In the mean time, however, he received intimation that a formidable expedition of 1500 warriors had assembled, ostensibly to wage war with the Illinois, but in reality for the destruction of the Miamis and Ottawas, both allies of the French. The governor promptly dispatched an envoy, who arrived at the village where the Iroquois had mustered on the evening of the day appointed for the beginning of their campaign. The envoy was received with dignity and kindness; and he succeeded in obtaining a promise that the expedition should be deferred, and that they would send deputies to Montreal to negotiate with the French chief. But the wily savages had promised only to deceive; and in the month of May following, the governor received intelligence that 700 of these fierce warriors were on their march to attack his Miami and Ottawa allies, while another force was prepared to assail the settlements of the French themselves. He attributed these dangerous hostilities to the instigation of the English.

The governor made urgent representations to the minister at home as to the necessity of crushing two of the Iroquois tribes, the most hostile and the most powerful. For this purpose, he demanded that a re-enforcement of 400 men should be sent to him from France as soon as possible, and that an order should be obtained from the Duke of York, to whom New York then belonged, to prevent the English from interfering with or thwarting the expedition.

The Iroquois found the free trade with the English and Dutch more advantageous than that with the French, which was paralyzed by an injudicious monopoly; but they were still unwilling to come to an open rupture with their powerful neighbors. They therefore sent deputies to Montreal to make great but vague professions of attachment and good will. For many reasons, De la Barre placed but little confidence in these addresses: their object was obviously to gain time, and to throw the French off their guard. He, however, received the deputies with great distinction, and sent them back enriched with presents. But a few months after this, however, a small detachment of Frenchmen was assailed by the Iroquois, and plundered of merchandize which they were bearing to traffic with the Illinois.

After this flagrant outrage, nothing remained for M. de la Barre but war. He had received intelligence that the Iroquois were making great preparations for an onslaught upon the French settlements, and that they had sent embassadors to the Indians of the south for the purpose of insuring peace in that quarter, while they threw all their power into the struggle with the hated pale faces. The governor promptly determined to adopt the bolder but safer course of striking the first blow, and making the cantons of his savage enemies the field of battle. As yet, few and small were the aids he had received from France, and a considerable time must elapse ere the further supplies he anticipated could arrive: he was, therefore, unwillingly compelled to avail himself of the assistance of his Indian allies. The native tribes dwelling around the shores of Lake Michigan entertained a deep and ancient jealousy of the powerful confederacy of the Iroquois or Five Nations, who aspired to universal dominion over the Northern Continent; they, therefore, held themselves equally interested with the French in the destruction of those formidable warriors. M. de la Durantaye, who commanded the fort on the far-distant shores of Lake Michigan, announced to his Indian neighbors that his countrymen were about to march against the Iroquois, and requested that all the native warriors friendly to the white men should meet them in the middle of August at Niagara. He was not, however, very successful in making levies, and with difficulty led 500 warriors to the place of meeting, where, to his dismay, he found that the French had not arrived: his followers were not easily reconciled to this disappointment.

In the mean time, M. de la Barre had, on the 9th of July, 1683, marched from Quebec to Montreal, where he appointed the troops to assemble for the expedition. No precautions to insure success were neglected. He dispatched a message to the English governor of New York to invite him to join in the attack, or, at least, to secure his neutrality. He also sent belts and presents to three of the Iroquois tribes, to induce them to refrain from joining in the quarrel of those among their confederates who alone had injured him and his nation. He arrived at Montreal on the 21st, with 700 Canadians, 130 soldiers, and 200 Indians: his force was organized in three divisions. After a brief stay he continued his march westward.

The governor had not proceeded far when he received intelligence that the other Iroquois tribes had obliged the Tsonnonthouans, his especial enemies, to accept of their mediation with the French, and that they demanded the Sieur le Moyne, in whom they placed much confidence, to conduct the negotiation. At the same time, he learned that the tribe he proposed to assail had put all their provisions into a place of security, and were prepared for a protracted and harassing resistance. His appeals both to the remaining Iroquois tribes and to the English had also failed, for the former would assuredly make common cause against him in case of his refusing their mediation, and the latter had actually offered to aid his enemies with 400 horse, and a like force of infantry. Influenced by these untoward circumstances, he dispatched M. le Moyne to treat, and agreed to await the Iroquois deputies on the shores of Lake Ontario. In the mean time, M. de la Barre and his army underwent great privations from the scarcity and bad quality of their provisions; they could with difficulty hold their ground till the arrival of the savages, and such was their extremity that the name of the Bay of Famine was given to the scene of their sufferings.

The savage deputies met the French chief with great dignity, and, well aware of the advantage given them by the starvation and sickness of the white men, carried their negotiations with a high hand. They guaranteed that the Tsonnonthouans should make reparation for the injuries inflicted on the French, but at the same time insisted that the governor and his army should retire the very next day. With this ignoble stipulation M. de la Barre was fain to agree. On his return to Quebec, he found, to his chagrin, that considerable re-enforcements had just arrived from France, which would have enabled him to dictate instead of submitting to dictation. The new detachment was commanded by MM. Monterlier and Desnos, captains of marine, who were commissioned by the king to proceed to the most advanced and important posts, and to act independently of the governor's authority. They were further instructed to capture as many of the Iroquois as possible, and to send them to France to labor in the galleys. In this same year the Chevalier de Callières, an officer of great merit, was sent from France to assume the duties of governor of the Montreal district, as successor to M. Perrot, who had embroiled himself with the members of the powerful Order of St. Sulpicius.

In the year 1685, the Marquis de Dénonville arrived at Quebec as governor general in succession to M. de la Barre, whose advanced age and failing health unfitted him for the arduous duties of the office. The new governor was selected by the king for his known valor and prudence; a re-enforcement of troops was placed at his disposal, and it was determined to spare no effort to establish the colony in security and peace. Dénonville lost not a moment in proceeding to the advanced posts on the lakes, and, at the same time, he devoted himself to a diligent study of the affairs of Canada and the character of the Indians. His keen perception promptly discovered the impossibility of the Iroquois being reconciled and assimilated to the French, and he at once saw the necessity of extirpating, or at least thoroughly humbling, these haughty savages. But beyond the present dangers and difficulties of Indian hostility, this clear-sighted politician discerned the far more formidable evils that threatened the power of his country from the advancing encroachments of the hardy traders and fearless adventurers of the English colonies. He urged upon the king the advantage of building and garrisoning a fort at Niagara to exclude the British from the traffic of the lakes, and interrupt their communications with the Iroquois, and also to check the desertion of the French, who usually escaped by that route, and transferred the benefits of their experience and knowledge of the country to the rival colonies. The Northwest Company of merchants at Quebec earnestly desired this establishment, and engaged to pay an annual rent of 30,000 livres to the crown for the privilege of exclusive trade at the proposed station.

The suspicions of the Marquis de Dénonville as to English encroachments were soon confirmed. He received a letter from the governor of New York, dated 29th of May, 1686, demanding explanations of the preparations which were being made against the Iroquois—the subjects of England—as any attack upon them would be a breach of the peace then existing between England and France. The British governor also expressed surprise that the French should contemplate erecting a fort at Niagara, "because it should be known in Canada that all that country was a dependency of New York." M. de Dénonville, in reply, denied the pretensions of the English to sovereignty in New France, and pointed out the impropriety of hostile communications between inferiors, while the kings whom they served remained on amicable terms. He rendered, however, some sort of evasive explanation on the subject of his preparations against the Iroquois.

The following year the governor general received from the court the notification of a most important agreement between England and France, that, "notwithstanding any rupture between the mother countries, the colonies on the American continent should remain at peace." Unfortunately, however, the force of national prejudice, and the clashing of mutual interests, rendered this wise and enlightened provision totally fruitless.

In the summer of 1687, M. de Dénonville marched toward Lake Ontario with a force of 2000 French and 600 Indians, having already received all the supplies and re-enforcements which he had expected from France. His first act of aggression was one that no casuistry can excuse, no necessity justify—one alike dishonorable and impolitic. He employed two missionaries, men of influence among the savages, to induce the principal Iroquois chiefs to meet him at the fort of Cataracouy, under various pretenses; he there treacherously seized the unsuspecting savages, and instantly dispatched them to Quebec, with orders that they should be forwarded to France to labor in the galleys. The missionaries who had been instrumental in bringing the native chiefs into this unworthy snare were altogether innocent of participation in the outrage, never for a moment doubting the honorable intentions of their countrymen toward the Indian deputies. One, who dwelt among the Onneyouths, was immediately seized by the exasperated tribe, and condemned to expiate the treachery of his nation, and his own supposed guilt, in the flames. He was, however, saved at the last moment by the intervention of an Indian matron, who adopted him as her son. The other—Lamberville by name—was held in great esteem among the Onnontagués, to whose instruction he had devoted himself. On the first accounts of the outrage at Cataracouy, the ancients assembled and called the missionary before them. They then declared their deep indignation at the wrong which they had suffered; but, at the moment when their prisoner expected to feel the terrible effects of their wrath, a chief arose, and with a noble dignity addressed him:

"Thou art now our enemy—thou and thy race. We have held counsel, and can not resolve to treat thee as an enemy. We know thy heart had no share in this treason, though thou wert its tool. We are not unjust; we will not punish thee, being innocent, and hating the crime as much as we do ourselves. But depart from among us; there are some who might seek thy blood; and when our young men sing the war-song, we may be no longer able to protect thee." The magnanimous savages then furnished him with guides, who were enjoined to convey him to a place of safety.

M. de Dénonville halted for some time at Cataracouy, and sent orders to the commanders of the distant western posts to meet him on the 10th of July at the River Des Sables, to the eastward of the country of the Tsonnonthouans, against whom they were first to act. The governor marched upon this point with his army, and, by an accident of favorable presage, he and the other detachments arrived at the same time. They immediately constructed an intrenchment, defended by palisades, in a commanding situation over the river, where their stores and provisions were safely deposited. M. d'Orvilliers, with a force of 400 men, was left for the protection of this dépôt, and to insure the rear of the advancing army.

On the 13th the French pushed into the hostile country, and passed two deep and dangerous defiles without opposition, but at a third they were suddenly assailed by 800 of the Iroquois, who, after the first volley, dispatched 200 of their number to outflank the invaders, while they continued the front attack with persevering courage. The French were at first thrown into some confusion by this fierce and unexpected onslaught; but the allied savages, accustomed to the forest warfare, boldly held their ground, and effectually covered the rallying of the troops. The Iroquois, having failed in overpowering their enemies by surprise, and conscious of their inferiority in numbers and arms, after a time broke their array and dispersed among the woods. The

French lost five men killed and twenty wounded; the Iroquois suffered far more—forty-five were left dead upon the field, and sixty more disabled in the conflict. The Ottawas, serving under M. de Dénonville, who had been by no means forward in the strife, with savage ferocity mangled and devoured the bodies of the slain. The Hurons, and the Iroquois Christians following the French standard, fought with determined bravery.

The army encamped in one of the four great villages of the Tsonnonthouans, about eight leagues from the fort at the River Des Sables: they found it totally deserted by the inhabitants, and left it in ashes. For ten days they marched through the dense forest with great hardship and difficulty, and met with no traces of the enemy, but they marked their progress with ruin: they burned about 400,000 bushels of corn, and destroyed a vast number of hogs. The general, fearing that his savage allies would desert him if he continued longer in the field, was then constrained to limit his enterprise. He, however, took this opportunity of erecting a fort at Niagara, and left the Chevalier de la Troye with 100 men in garrison. Unfortunately, a deadly malady soon after nearly destroyed the detachment, and the post was abandoned and dismantled. The constant and harassing enmity of the savages combined with the bad state of the provisions left in the fort, to render the disease which had broken out so fatal in its results.

The French had erected a fort called Chambly,* in a strong position on the left bank of the important River Richelieu.† This little stronghold effectually commanded

* Afterward called Sorel.

† The River Iroquois, or Sorel. "Dans les premières années de notre établissement en Canada les Iroquois, pour faire des courses jusque dans le centre de nos habitations, descendèrent cette rivière à laquelle pour cette raison on donna le nom de rivière des Iroquois. On l'a depuis appellé la Rivière de Richelieu, à cause d'un fort qui portoit ce nom et qu'on avoit construit à son embouchure. Ce fort ayant été ruine, M. de Sorel en fit construire un autre auquel on donna son nom; ce nom s'est communiqué à la rivière qui le conserve encore aujourd'hui, quoique le fort ne subsiste plus depuis longtems (1721)."—Charlevoix, tom. v., p. 221.

"There is another Iroquois river marked on the French maps, fall-

the navigation of the stream, and through it, the communication between Lake Champlain and the southern districts with the waters of the St. Lawrence. On the 13th of November, 1687, a formidable party of the Iroquois suddenly attacked the fort; the little garrison made a stout defense, and the assailants abandoned the field with the morning light; the settlement which had grown up in the neighborhood was, however, ravaged by the fierce Indians, and several of the inhabitants carried away into captivity. The French attributed this unexpected invasion to the instigation of their English neighbors, and it would appear with reason, for, on the failure of the assault, the governor of New York put his nearest town into a state of defense, as if in expectation of reprisals.

In this same year there fell upon Canada an evil more severe than Indian aggression or English hostility. Toward the end of the summer a deadly malady visited the colony, and carried mourning into almost every household. So great was the mortality, that M. de Dénonville was constrained to abandon, or rather defer, his project of humbling the pride and power of the Tsonnonthouans. He had also reason to doubt the faith of his Indian allies; even the Hurons of the far West, who had fought so stoutly by his side on the shores of Lake Ontario, were discovered to have been at the time in treacherous correspondence with the Iroquois.

While doubt and disease paralyzed the power of the French, their dangerous enemies were not idle. Twelve hundred Iroquois warriors assembled at Lake St. Francis, within two days' march of Montreal, and haughtily demanded audience of the governor, which was immediately granted. Their orator proclaimed the power of his race and the weakness of the white men with all the emphasis and striking illustration of Indian eloquence. He offered peace on terms proposed by the governor of New York, but only allowed the French four days for deliberation.

This high-handed diplomacy was backed by formidable

ing into the Teakiki. It received this name from a defeat experienced by the Iroquois from the Illinois, a race whom they had always despised."—Charlevoix, vol. vi., p. 118.

demonstrations. The whole country west of the River Sorel, or Richelieu, was occupied by a savage host, and the distant fort of Cataracouy, on the Ontario shore, was with difficulty held against 800 Iroquois, who had burned the farm stores with flaming arrows, and slain the cattle of the settlers. The French bowed before the storm they could not resist, and peace was concluded on conditions that war should cease in the land, and all the allies should share in the blessings of repose. M. de Dénonville further agreed to restore the Indian chiefs who had been so treacherously torn from their native wilds, and sent to labor in the galleys of France.

But, in the mean time, some of the savage allies, disdaining the peaceful conclusions of negotiation, waged a merciless war. The Abenaquis, always the fiercest foes of the Iroquois confederacy, took the field while yet the conferences pended, and fell suddenly upon the enemy by the banks of the Sorel. They left death behind them on their path, and pushed on even into the English settlements, where they slew some of the defenseless inhabitants, and carried away their scalps in savage triumph. On the other hand, the Iroquois of the Rapids of St. Louis and the Mountain, made a deadly raid into the invaders' territories.

The Hurons of Michillimakinac were those among the French allies who most dreaded the conclusion of a treaty of which they feared to become the first victims. Through the extraordinary machinations and cunning of their chief, Kondiaronk, or the Rat, they continued to reawaken the suspicions of the Iroquois against the French, and again strove to stir up the desolating flames of war.

In the midst of these renewed difficulties M. de Dénonville was recalled to Europe, his valuable services being required in the armies of his king. In colonial administration he had shown an ardent zeal for the interests of the sovereign and the country under his charge, and his plans for the improvement of Canada were just, sound, and comprehensive, but he was deficient in tenacity of purpose, and not fortunate or judicious in the selection of those who enjoyed his confidence. His otherwise honorable and useful career can, however, never be cleansed from the fatal blot of one dark act of treachery. From the day when that evil deed was done, the rude but magnanimous Indian scorned as a broken reed the sullied honor of the French.

The Comte de Frontenac was once again selected for the important post of governor of New France, and arrived at Montreal on the 27th of October, 1689, where his predecessor handed over the arduous duties of office. The state of New France was such as to demand the highest qualities in the man to whose rule it was intrusted : trade languished, agriculture was interrupted by savage aggression, and the very existence of the colony threatened by the growing power of the formidable Iroquois confederacy. At the same time, a plan for the reduction of New York was being organized in Paris, which would inevitably call for the cooperation of the colonial subjects of France, and, in the event of failure, leave them to bear the brunt of the dangerous quarrel. M. de Frontenac was happily selected in this time of need.

Impelled by the treacherous machinations of the Huron chief Kondiaronk, the Iroquois approached the colony in very different guise from that expected. While M. de Dénonville remained in daily hopes of receiving a deputation of ten or twelve of the Indians to treat for peace, he was astounded by the sudden descent of 1200 warriors upon the island of Montreal.* Terrible indeed was the devastation they

* Charlevoix says of Montreal in 1721, "Elle n'est point fortifiée, une simple palisade bastionnée et assez mal entretenue fait toute sa défence, avec une assez mauvaise redoute sur un petit tertre, qui sert de boulevard, et va se terminer en douce pente à une petite place quarrée. C'est ce qu'on rencontre d'abord en arrivant de Quebec. Il n'y a pas même quarante ans, que la ville étoit toute ouverte, et tous les jours exposée à être brulée par les sauvages ou par les Anglois. Ce fut le Chevalier de Callières, frère du plénipotentiaire de Riswick, qui la fit fermer, tandis qu'il en étoit gouverneur. On projette depuis quelques années de l'environner de murailles,[1] mais il ne sera pas aisé d'engager les habitans à y contribuer. Ils sont braves et ils ne sont pas riches : on les a dejà trouvé difficiles à persuader de la nécessité de cette dépense, et fort convaincus que leur valeur est plus que suffisante pour défendre leur ville contre quiconque osoit l'attaquer."

[1] "Ce projet est presentement executé. 1740."

caused; blood and ashes marked their path to within three leagues of the territory, where they blockaded two forts, after having burned the neighboring houses. A small force of 100 soldiers and 50 Indians, imprudently sent against these fierce marauders, was instantly overpowered, and taken or destroyed. When the work of destruction was completed, the Iroquois re-embarked for the Western lakes, their canoes laden with plunder, and 200 prisoners in their train.

This disastrous incursion filled the French with panic and astonishment. They at once blew up the forts of Cataracouy and Niagara, burned two vessels built under their protection, and altogether abandoned the shores of the Western lakes. The year was not, however, equally unfortunate in all parts of New France. While the island of Montreal was swept by the storm of savage invasion, M. d'Iberville supported in the north the cause of his country, and the warlike Abenaquis avenged upon the English settlers the evils which their Iroquois allies had inflicted upon Canada. Upon his arrival, the Comte de Frontenac determined to restore the falling fortunes of his people by means of his great personal influence among the triumphant Iroquois, backed as he was with the presence of those prisoners who had been so treacherously seized by his predecessor, but whose entire confidence and good-will he had acquired while bringing them back to their native country. A chief named Oureouharé, the most distinguished among the captives, undertook to negotiate with his countrymen—a duty which was performed more honestly than efficiently: an exchange of prisoners took place, but nothing further was accomplished.

The Northern Indians, allies of the French, had long desired to share the benefits of English commerce with the Iroquois; it had, however, been the policy of the Canadian government to keep these red tribes continually at war, with the view of interrupting the communications of traffic through their country. But the allied savages soon began to see the necessity of making peace with the Iroquois, in order to establish relations with the traders of the British settlements. With this view the Ottawas sent embassadors to the cantons of the Five Nations, restoring the prisoners captured in the war, and proffering peace and amity. The agents and missionaries of the French strongly remonstrated against these proceedings, but in vain; their former allies replied by insulting declarations of independence, and contemptuous scoffs at their want of power and courage to meet the enemy in the field; their commerce, too, was spoken of as unjust, injurious, and inferior to that of the English, of which they had endeavored to deprive those whom they could not protect in war; the French were also accused of endeavoring to shelter themselves under a dishonorable treaty, regardless of the safety and interests of the Indians who had fought and bled in their cause.

When M. de Frontenac became aware of this formidable disaffection, he boldly determined to strike a blow at the English power that should restore the military character of France among the savages, and deprive the recreant Indians of their expected succor. He therefore organized three expeditions to invade the British settlements by different avenues. The first, consisting of 110 men, marched from Montreal, destined for New York, but only resulted in the surprise and destruction of the village of Corlar,* or Schenectady, and the massacre and capture of some of the inhabitants. They retreated at noon the following day, bearing with them forty prisoners; after much suffering from want of provisions, they were obliged to separate into small parties, when they were attacked by their exasperated enemies, and sustained some loss. Many would have perished from hunger in this retreat, but that they found a resource in living upon horse flesh: their cavalry, from fifty, was re-

* "Corlar was the name of a Dutchman of consideration, who founded the village of Schenectady. This man enjoyed great influence with the Indians, who, after his death, always addressed the governor of New York with the title of Corlar, as the name most expressive of respect with which they were acquainted."—Graham, vol. ii., p. 288.

"Au-dessus de la ville d'Orange il y a un fort avec une bourgade, qui confinent avec les cantons Iroquois, et qu'on appelle Corlar, d'où ces sauvages se sont accoûtumés à donner le nom de Corlar au gouverneur de New York."—Charlevoix, tom. i., p. 222.

duced to six by the time they regained the shelter of Montreal.

The second invading division was mustered at Three Rivers, and only numbered fifty men, half being Indians. They reached an English settlement, called Sementels (Salmon Falls), after a long and difficult march and succeeded in surprising and destroying the village, with most of its defenders. In their retreat they were sharply attacked, but succeeded in escaping, through the aid of an advantageous post, which enabled them to check the pursuers at a narrow bridge. They soon after fell in with M. de Mamerval, governor of Acadia, with the third party, and, thus re-enforced, assailed the fortified village of Kaskebé upon the sea-coast, which surrendered after a heavy loss of the defenders.

To regain the confidence of his Indian allies, M. de Frontenac saw the necessity of rendering them independent of English commerce, and safe from the hostility of the Iroquois. To accomplish these objects, he dispatched a large convoy to the west, escorted by 143 men, and bearing presents to the savage chiefs. On the way they encountered a party of the Five Nations, and defeated them after a sanguinary engagement.

All these vigorous measures produced a marked effect: the convoy arrived at Michillimakinac at the time when the embassadors of the French allies were on the point of departing to conclude a treaty with the Iroquois. When, however, the strength of the detachment was seen, and the valuable presents and merchandise were displayed, the French interests again revived with the politic savages, and they hastened to give proofs of their renewed attachment: 110 canoes, bearing furs to the value of 100,000 crowns, and manned by 300 Indians, were dispatched soon after for Montreal, to be laid before the governor general. He dismissed the escort with presents, and exhorted them and their nation to join with him in humbling their mutual and deadly foe. They departed well pleased with their reception, and renewed professions of friendship for the French.

In the mean time the terrible war-cry of the Iroquois was

never silent in the Canadian settlements. Bands of these fierce and merciless warriors suddenly emerged from the dense forests when least expected, and burst upon isolated posts and villages with more or less success, but always with great loss of life to the assailants and assailed,* and with great destruction of the fruits of industry. These disastrous events caused much disquietude to the governor. He called to his counsels the Iroquois chief Oureouharé, who still remained attached to him by the closest bonds of friendship and esteem, and complained of the bitter hostility of his nation: "You must either not be a true friend," said M. de Frontenac, "or you must be powerless in your nation, to permit them to wage this bitter war against me." The generous chief was mortified at this discourse, and answered that his remaining with the French, instead of returning to his own hunting grounds, where he was ardently beloved, was a proof of his fidelity, and that he was ready to do any thing that might be required of him, but that it would certainly need time and the course of circumstances to allay the fury of his people against those who had treacherously injured them. The governor could not but acknowledge the justice of Oureouharé's reply; he gave him new marks of esteem and friendship, and determined more than before to confide in this wise and important ally.†

* "Colden relates that, during the war between the French and Iroquois, two old men were cut to pieces, and put into the war-kettle for the Christian Indians to feast on."—Colden, vol. i., p. 81.

"Frontenac stands conspicuous among all his nation for deeds of cruelty to the Indians. Nothing was more common than for his Indian prisoners to be given up to his Indian allies to be tormented. One of the most horrible of these scenes on record was perpetrated under his own eye at Montreal in 1691."—Colden, vol. i., p. 441, quoted by Howitt.

"Les habitans en firent brûler, persuadés que le seul moyen de corriger ces barbares de leurs cruautés, étoit de les traiter eux-même comme ils traitoient les autres."—Charlevoix, *Jésuite*, tom. iii., p. 139.

† "Oureouharé mourut en vrai Chrétien, l'an 1697. Le missionnaire qui l'assista pendant sa maladie, lui parlant un jour des opprobres et des ignominies de la passion du Sauveur des hommes; il entra dans un si grand mouvement d'indignation contre les Juifs, qu'il s'écria, 'Que n'étois-je là? je les aurois bien empêché de traiter ainsi mon Dieu.' The similar exclamation of the Frank monarch, Clovis, is well known."—Charlevoix, tom. iii., p. 332.

But now the greatest danger that had ever yet menaced the power of France upon the American continent hung over the Canadian shores. The men of New England were at last aroused to activity by the constant inroads and cruel depredations of their northern neighbors, and in April, 1690, dispatched a small squadron from Boston, which took possession of Port Royal and all the province of Acadia. In a month the expedition returned, with sufficient plunder to repay its cost. Meanwhile the British settlers deputed six commissioners to meet at New York in council for their defense. On the first of May, 1690, these deputies assembled, and promptly determined to set an expedition on foot for the invasion of Canada. Levies of 800 men were ordered for the purpose, the contingents of the several states fixed, and general rules appointed for the organization of their army. A fast-sailing vessel was dispatched to England with strong representations of the defenseless state of the British colonies, and with an earnest appeal for aid in the projected invasion of New France; they desired that ammunition and other warlike stores might be supplied to their militia for the attempt by land, and that a fleet of English frigates should be directed up the River St. Lawrence to co-operate with the colonial force. But at that time England was still too much weakened by the unhealed wounds of domestic strife to afford any assistance to her American children, and they were thrown altogether on their own resources.

New York and New England boldly determined, unaided, to prosecute their original plans against Canada. General Winthrop, with 800 men, was marched by the way of Lake Champlain, on the shores of which he was to have met 500 of the Iroquois warriors; but, through some unaccountable jealousy, only a small portion of the politic savages came to the place of muster. Other disappointments also combined to paralyze the British force: the Indians had failed to provide more than half the number of canoes necessary for the transport of the troops across the lake, and the contractor of the army had imprudently neglected to supply sufficient provisions. No alternative remained for Winthrop but to fall back upon Albany for subsistence.

In the mean time, Major Schuyler, who had before crossed Lake Champlain with a smaller British force, pushed on against the French post of La Prairie de la Madeleine, and attacked it with spirit. He soon overcame the handful of Canadian militia and Indians who formed the garrison, and compelled them to fall back upon Chambly, a fort further to the north. Having met M. de Sanermes and a considerable force advancing to their relief, they turned and faced their pursuers. Schuyler rashly ventured to attack this now superior enemy; he was soon forced to retire, with the loss of nearly thirty men. The French, however, suffered much more severely in this affair, no less than thirteen officers and nearly seventy of their men having been killed and wounded.

The naval expedition against Quebec was assembled in Nantasket Road, near Boston, and consisted of thirty-five vessels of various size, the largest being a 44-gun frigate. Nearly 2000 troops were embarked in this squadron, and the chief command was confided by the people of New England to their distinguished countryman, Sir William Phipps, a man of humble birth, whose own genius and merit had won for him honor, power, and universal esteem. The direction of the fleet was given to Captain Gregory Sugars. The necessary preparations were not completed, and the fleet did not get under way till the season was far advanced; contrary winds caused a still further delay; however, several French posts on the shores of Newfoundland and of the Lower St. Lawrence were captured without opposition, and the British force arrived at Tadoussac, on the Saguenay, before authentic tidings of the approaching danger had reached Quebec.

When the brave old Frontenac learned from his scouts that Winthrop's corps had retreated, and that Canada was no longer threatened by an enemy from the landward side, he hastened to the post of honor at Quebec, while by his orders M. de Ramsey and M. de Callières assembled the hardy militia of Three Rivers and the adjoining settlements to re-enforce him with all possible dispatch. The governor found that Major Provost, who commanded at Quebec before his arrival, had made vigorous preparation to receive the invaders;* it was only necessary, therefore, to continue the works, and confirm the orders given by his worthy deputy. A party, under the command of M. de Longueuil, was sent down the river to observe the motions of the British, and, if possible, to prevent their landing. At the same time, two canoes were dispatched by the shallow channel north of the island of Orleans to seek for some ships with supplies, which were daily expected from France, and to warn them of the presence of the hostile fleet.

The Comte de Frontenac continued the preparations for defense with unwearied industry. The regular soldiers and militia were alike constantly employed upon the works, till in a short time Quebec was tolerably secure from the chances of a sudden assault. Lines of strong palisades, here and there armed with small batteries, were formed round the crown of the lofty headland, and the gates of the city were barricaded with massive beams of timber and casks filled with earth. A number of cannon were mounted on advantageous positions, and a large wind-mill of solid masonry was fitted up as a cavalier. The lower town was protected by two batteries each of three guns, and the streets leading up the steep, rocky face of the height were embarrassed with several intrenchments and rows of "chevaux de frise." Subsequently during the siege two other batteries were erected a little above the level of the river. The commanding natural position of the stronghold, however, offered far more serious obstacles to the assailants than the hasty and imperfect fortifications.

At daylight on the 5th of October the white sails of the British fleet were seen rounding the headland of Point Levi,

* "It does not appear that the fortifications of Quebec were of much importance till after the year 1690, when eleven stone redoubts which served as bastions, were erected in different parts of the heights of the Upper Town. The remains of several of these redoubts are still in existence. They were connected with each other by a strong line of cedar picketing, ten or twelve feet high, banked up with earth on the inside. This proved sufficient to resist the attacks of the hostile Indians for several years."—Lambert's *Travels*, vol. i., p. 39.

"In 1720 a more extensive system of fortification was commenced, under the direction of M. de Lery."—Smith's *Canada*, vol. i., p. 184.

and crowding to the northern shore of the river, near the village of Beauport; at about ten o'clock they dropped anchor, lowered their canvas, and swung round with the receding tide. There they remained inactive till the following morning. On the 6th, Sir William Phipps sent a haughty summons to the French chief, demanding an unconditional surrender in the name of King William of England, and concluding with this imperious sentence: "Your answer positive in an hour, returned with your own trumpet, with the return of mine, is required upon the peril that will ensue."

The British officer who bore the summons was led blindfold through the town, and ushered into the presence of Comte Frontenac in the council-room of the castle of Quebec. The bishop, the intendant, and all the principal officers of the government surrounded the proud old noble. "Read your message," said he. The Englishman read on, and when he had finished, laid his watch upon the table with these words: "It is now ten; I await your answer for one hour." The council started from their seats, surprised out of their dignity by a burst of sudden anger. The comte paused for a time ere he could restrain his rage sufficiently to speak, and then replied, "I do not acknowledge King William, and I well know that the Prince of Orange is a usurper, who has violated the most sacred rights of blood and religion . . . . . who wishes to persuade the nation that he is the saviour of England and the defender of the faith, though he has violated the laws and privileges of the kingdom, and overturned the Church of England: this conduct, the Divine Justice to which Phipps appeals will one day severely punish."

The British officer, unmoved by the storm of indignation which his message had aroused, desired that this fierce reply should be rendered to him in writing for the satisfaction of his chief. "I will answer your master by the mouth of my cannon," replied the angry Frenchman, "that he may learn that a man of my rank is not to be summoned in this manner." Thus ended the laconic conference.

On the return of the messenger, Sir William Phipps

called a council of war: it was determined at once to attack the city. At noon, on the 8th, 1300 men were embarked in the boats of the squadron, under the command of Major Walley, and landed without opposition at La Canardière, a little to the east of the River St. Charles. While the main body was being formed on the muddy shore, four companies pushed on toward the town, in skirmishing order, to clear the front; they had scarcely begun the ascent of the sloping banks when a sharp fire was poured upon them by 300 of the Canadian militia, posted among the rocks and bushes on either flank, and in a small hamlet to the right. Some of the British winced under this unexpected volley, fired, and fell back; but the officers, with prompt resolution, gave the order to charge, and themselves gallantly led the way; the soldiers followed at a rapid pace, and speedily cleared the ground. Major Walley then advanced with his whole force to the St. Charles River, still, however, severely harassed by dropping shots from the active light troops of the French: there he bivouacked for the night, while the enemy retreated into the garrison.

Toward evening of the same day the four largest vessels of Phipps's squadron moved boldly up the river, and anchored close against the town. They opened a spirited but ineffectual fire; their shot, directed principally against the lofty eminence of the Upper Town, fell almost harmless, while a vigorous cannonade from the numerous guns of the fortress replied with overwhelming power. When night interrupted the strife, the British ships had suffered severely, their rigging was torn by the hostile shot, and the crews had lost many of their best men. By the first light of morning, however, Phipps renewed the action with pertinacious courage, but with no better success. About noon the contest became evidently hopeless to the stubborn assailants; they weighed anchor, and, with the receding tide, floated their crippled vessels down the stream, beyond the reach of the enemy's fire.*

* The flag of the rear admiral was shot away, and, drifting toward the shore, a Canadian swam out into the stream and brought it in triumphantly. For many years the precious trophy was hung up in the parish church of Quebec.

The British troops, under Major Walley, although placed in battle array at daylight, remained inactive, through some unaccountable delay, while the enemy's attention was diverted by the combat with Phipps's squadron. At length, about noon, they moved upon the formidable stronghold along the left bank of the River St. Charles. Some allied savages plunged into the bush in front to clear the advance, a line of skirmishers protected either flank, and six field-pieces accompanied the march of the main body. After having proceeded for some time without molestation, they were suddenly and fiercely assailed by 200 Canadian volunteers under M. de Longueuil; the Indians were at once swept away, the skirmishers overpowered, and the British column itself was forced back by their gallant charge. Walley, however, drew up his reserve in some brushwood a little in the rear, and finally compelled the enemy to retreat. During this smart action, M. de Frontenac, with three battalions, placed himself upon the opposite bank of the river, in support of the volunteers, but showed no disposition to cross the stream. That night, the English troops, harassed, depressed, diminished in numbers, and scantily supplied, again bivouacked upon the marshy banks of the stream: a severe frost, for which they were but ill prepared, chilled the weary limbs of the soldiers and enhanced their sufferings.

On the 10th, Walley once more advanced upon the French positions, in the hope of breaching their palisades by the fire of his field pieces; but this attempt was altogether unsuccessful. His flanking parties fell into ambuscades, and were very severely handled, and his main body was checked and finally repulsed by a heavy fire from a fortified house on a commanding position which he had ventured to attack. Utterly dispirited by this failure, the British fell back in some confusion to the landing-place, yielding up in one hour what they had so hardly won. That night many of the soldiers strove to force their way into the boats, and order was with great difficulty restored; the next day they were harassed by a continual skirmish. Had it not been for the gallant conduct of "Captain March, who had a good company, and made the enemy give back," the confusion would probably have been irretrievable. When darkness put an end to the fire on both sides, the English troops received orders to embark in the boats, half a regiment at a time. But all order was soon lost; four times as many as the boats could sustain crowded down at once to the beach, rushed into the water, and pressed on board. The sailors were even forced to throw some of these panic-stricken men into the river, lest all should sink together. The noise and confusion increased every moment, despite the utmost exertions of the officers, and daylight had nearly revealed the dangerous posture of affairs before the embarkation was completed. The guns were abandoned, with some valuable stores and ammunition. Had the French displayed, in following up their advantages, any portion of the energy and skill which had been so conspicuous in their successful defense, the British detachment must infallibly have been either captured or totally destroyed.

Sir William Phipps, having failed by sea and land, resolved to withdraw from the disastrous conflict. After several ineffectual attempts to recover the guns and stores which Major Walley had been forced to abandon, he weighed anchor and descended the St. Lawrence to a place about nine miles distant from Quebec, whence he sent to the Comte de Frontenac to negotiate for an exchange of prisoners. Humbled and disappointed, damaged in fortune and reputation, the English chief sailed from the scene of his defeat; but misfortune had not yet ceased to follow him, for he left the shattered wrecks of no less than nine of his ships among the dangerous shoals of the St. Lawrence. The government of Massachusetts was dismayed at the disastrous news of which Phipps was himself the bearer. He arrived at Boston on the 19th of November, with the remains of his fleet and army, his ships damaged and weather beaten, and his men almost in a state of mutiny from having received no pay. In these straits the colonial government found it impracticable to raise money, and resorted to "bills of credit," the first paper money which had ever been issued on the American continent.

Great indeed was the joy and triumph of the French

when the British fleet disappeared from the beautiful basin of Quebec. With a proud heart the gallant old Comte de Frontenac penned the dispatch which told his royal master of the victory. He failed not to dwell upon the distinguished merit of the colonial militia, by whose loyalty and courage the arms of France had been crowned with success. In grateful memory of this brave defense, the French king caused a medal to be struck, bearing the inscription, "FRANCIA IN NOVO ORBE VICTRIX: KEBECA LIBERATA.—A.D., M.D.C.X.C." In the lower town a church was built by the inhabitants to celebrate their deliverance from the British invaders, and dedicated to "Nôtre Dame de la Victoire."

On the 12th of November, the vessels, long expected from France, arrived in safety at Quebec, having escaped the observation of the English fleet by ascending for some distance the land-locked waters of the Saguenay. Their presence, however, only tended to increase a scarcity then pressing upon the colony, the labor of the fields in the preceding spring having been greatly interrupted by the harassing incursions of the Iroquois. The troops were distributed into those parts of the country where supplies could most easily be obtained, and were cheerfully received by those who had through their valor been protected from the hated dominion of the stranger.

CHAPTER XV.

In May, 1691, the Iroquois, to the number of about 1000 warriors, again poured down upon the settlements near Montreal, and marked their course with massacre and ruin. Other bands, less numerous, spread themselves over the fertile and beautiful banks of the Richelieu River, burning the happy homesteads and rich store-yards of the settlers. At length, the Sieur de la Mine, with a detachment of militia, surprised a party of these fierce marauders at Saint Sulpice, and slew them without mercy. Twelve of the

Iroquois escaped into a ruinous house, where they held out for a time with courage and success; but the French set fire to the building, and they were obliged to abandon it: some were killed in their efforts to escape, but five fell alive into the hands of their exasperated enemies, and were burned, with a savage cruelty such as they themselves would have exhibited.

Intelligence now arrived that a formidable force of English, Iroquois, and Mahingan Indians were advancing upon Montreal by the River Richelieu or Sorel; 800 men led by the Chevalier de Callères, were sent to oppose their progress, and encamped on the Prairie de la Madeleine,* by the borders of the St. Lawrence. Before daylight, the following morning, the invaders carried an important position by surprise, slaying several of the defenders, and finally retreated in good order and with little loss. On falling back into the woods, they met and destroyed a small French detachment, and boldly faced a more considerable force under M. de Valrenes. For an hour and half these formidable warriors withstood the fire, and repelled the charges of the Canadian troops; but at length they were overpowered and dispersed, not, however, before inflicting a loss of no less than 120 men upon their conquerors. An Englishman captured in the engagement declared that the invaders had purposed to destroy the harvest, which would have reduced the colony to the last extremity. The design, in a great measure, failed, and an abundant crop repaid the industry and successful courage of the French.

At the first news of this alarming inroad, M. de Frontenac hastened to the post of danger, but tranquillity had already been restored, and the toils of the husbandman were again plied upon the scene of strife. At Montreal he found a dispatch from the governor of New England, proposing an exchange of prisoners and a treaty of neutrality with Canada,

"* Vis à vis de Montreal, du côté du sud est un endroit qu' on appelle la Prairie de la Madeleine."—Charlevoix, tom. ii., p. 233.

"Le Cap de la Madeleine a eu son nom de l'Abbé de la Madeleine, un des membres de la Compagnie des cent Associés." The name of the Prairie had probably the same origin.—Charlevoix, tom. v., p. 167.

notwithstanding the war then carried on between the mother countries. The Canadian governor mistrusted the sincerity of the English proposals, and they were not productive of any result. During the remainder of the year the Iroquois continued to disturb the repose of the colony by frequent and mischievous irruptions, and many valuable lives were lost in repelling those implacable savages.

The war continued with checkered results and heavy losses on both sides in the two following years. An invasion of the canton of the Agniers, by the French, was at first successful, but in the retreat the colonists suffered great privation, and most of their prisoners escaped, while any of their number that strayed or fell in the rear were immediately cut off by their fierce pursuers. The fur trade was also much injured by these long-continued hostilities, for the vigilant enmity of the Iroquois closed up the communication with the Western country by the waters of the St. Lawrence and its magnificent tributaries.

We have seen that for a long period the history of the colony is a mere chronicle of savage and resultless combats, and treacherous truces between the French and the formidable Iroquois confederacy. This almost perpetual warfare gave a preponderance to the military interests among the settlers, not a little injurious to their advance in material prosperity. The Comte de Frontenac had, by his vigorous administration, and haughty and unbending character, rendered himself alike respected and feared by his allies and enemies. But, while all acknowledged his courage and ability, his system of internal government bore upon the civil inhabitants with almost intolerable severity; upon them fell all the burden and labor of the wars; they were ruined by unprofitable toil, while the soldiers worked the lands for the benefit of the military officers whom he desired to conciliate. He also countenanced, or at least tolerated, the fatal trade in spirituous liquors, which his authority alone could have suppressed. Owing to these causes, the colony made but little progress, commerce languished, and depression and discontent fell upon the hearts of the Canadian people.

In the year 1695, M. de Frontenac re-established the

fort of Catarocouy, despite the universal disapprobation of the settlers and the positive commands of the king. The object was, however, happily and ably accomplished by M. de Crisasy in a very short time, and without the loss of a man. This brave and active officer made good use of his powerful position. He dispatched scouts in all directions, and, by a judicious arrangement of his small forces, checked the hostilities of the Iroquois upon the Canadian settlements.

The Sieur de Révérin, a man of enlightened and enterprising mind, had long desired to develop the resources of the Canadian waters, and in 1697 at length succeeded in associating several merchants with himself, and establishing a fishery at the harbor of Mount Louis, among the mountains of Nôtre Dame, half way between Quebec and the extremity of the Gulf of St. Lawrence on the southern side. The situation was well chosen, the neighboring soil fertile, and the waters abounded in fish. But, where nature had provided every thing that industry could require, the hand of man interfered to counteract her bounty. The hostility of the English embarrassed the infant settlement and alarmed its founders. Despite of these difficulties, a plentiful harvest and successful fishing at first rewarded the adventurers; subsequently, however, they were less fortunate, and the place was for some time neglected and almost forgotten.*

Louis de Buade, comte de Frontenac, died in the seventy-eighth year of his age, 1698, having to the last preserved that astonishing energy of character which had enabled him to overcome the difficulties and dangers of his adventurous career. He died as he had lived, beloved by many, respected by all; with the unaided resources of his own strong mind, he had preserved the power of France on the American continent undiminished, if not increased, through years of famine, disaster, and depression. He loved patronage and power, but disdained the considerations of selfish interest. It must, however, be acknowledged that a jealous, sullen, and even vindictive temper obscured in some degree the luster of his success, and detracted from the dignity of his nature. The

* There was a flourishing settlement at Mount Louis in 1758, which was destroyed by General Wolfe.

Chevalier de Callières, governor of Montreal, was appointed his successor, to the satisfaction of all classes in the colony.

The new governor* applied himself vigorously to the difficult task of establishing the tranquillity of his territories. He endeavored to procure the alliance of all the Indian tribes within reach of French intercourse or commerce, but the high price charged by the Canadian merchants for their goods proved a constant difficulty in the way of negotiation, and ever afforded the savages a pretext for disaffection and complaint. In the midst of his useful labors, this excellent chief was suddenly cut off by death; his upright and judicious administration won the esteem of all the colonists, and the truth and honesty of his dealings with the native tribes gave him an influence over them which none of his predecessors had ever won. On the petition of the inhabitants of Canada, the king willingly appointed the Marquis de Vaudreuil to the vacant government. Soon after his accession a deputation of the Iroquois arrived at Quebec, and for the first time formally acknowledged the sovereignty of France, and claimed the protection of her flag.

M. de Raudot, the intendant, introduced various important judicial and fiscal improvements in the affairs of the colony at this time; by his influence and mediation he effectually checked a litigious spirit which had infused itself among the Canadians to a ruinous extent, and by strong representations induced the king to remove the cruel restrictions placed upon colonial industry by the jealousy of the mother country.

* "Sans avoir le brilliant de son prédécesseur, il en avait tout le solide; des vûës droites et désinteressés, sans préjuge et sans passion; une fermeté toujours d'accord avec la raison, une valeur, que le flegme sçavoit modérer et rendre utile: un grand sens, beaucoup de probité et d'honneur, et une pénétration d'esprit, à laquelle une grande application et une longue expérience avoient ajouté tout ce que l'expérience peut donner de lumières. Il avoit pris dès les commencemens un grand empire sur les sauvages, qui le connoisoient exacte à tenir sa parole, et ferme à vouloir qu' on lui gardât celles qu' on lui avoient données. Les François de leur côté étaient convaincus qu'il n' exigeroient jamais rien d'eux, que de raisonnable; que pour n' avoir ni la naissance, ni les grandes alliances du Comte de Frontenac, ni le rang de lieutenant général des armées du roi, il ne sçauroit pas moins se faire obéir que lui."—Charlevoix, tom. iii., p. 353.

In the spring of 1708 a council was held at Montreal to deliberate upon the course to be pursued in checking the intrigues of the English among the allied savages: the chiefs of all the Christian Indians and the faithful and warlike Abenaquis were present on the occasion. It was resolved that a blow should be struck against the British colonies, and a body of 400 men, including Indians, was formed for the expedition, the object of which was kept secret. After a march of 150 leagues across an almost impracticable country, the French attacked the little fort and village of Haverhill, garrisoned by thirty New Englandmen, and carried them after a sharp struggle; many of the defenders were killed or captured, and the settlement destroyed. The neighboring country was, however, soon aroused, and the assailants with difficulty effected a retreat, losing thirty of their men.

Intelligence reached the French in the following year that Colonel Vetch, who, during a residence of several years at Quebec, had contrived to sound all the difficult passages of the River St. Lawrence, had successfully instigated the Queen of England to attempt the conquest of New France; that a fleet of twenty ships was being prepared for the expedition, and a force of 6000 regular troops were to sail under its protection, while 2000 English and as many Indians, under the command of General Nicholson, were to march upon Montreal by the way of Lake Champlain. M. de Vaudreuil immediately assembled a council of war to meet the emergency, where some bold measures were planned, but a misunderstanding between the governor general and one of his principal officers paralyzed their execution. Finally, indeed, a considerable force was marched to anticipate the British attack; but the dissensions of the leaders, the insubordination of the troops, and the want of correct intelligence, embarrassed their movements, and drove them to an inglorious retreat. On the other hand, the English, mistrusting the faith of their Indian allies, and suffering from a frightful mortality, burned their canoes and advanced posts, and retreated from the frontier. The perfidious Iroquois, while professing the closest friendship, had poisoned the stream hard by the British camp, and thus caused the fatal malady which decimated their unsuspecting allies. The fleet destined for the attack of Quebec never crossed the Atlantic: it was sent to Lisbon instead, to support the falling fortunes of Portugal against the triumphant arms of Castile.

In the following year, another abortive expedition was undertaken by the English against Canada. Intelligence was brought to M. de Vaudreuil that ten ships of war of 50 guns each and upward had arrived from England, and were assembled at Boston, together with 35 transports capable of conveying 3000 men, while a force of provincial militia and Indians of New York, nearly 2000 strong, were collected in that state to assail him by land. The French governor immediately called together the Iroquois deputies, and successfully urged their neutrality in the approaching struggle. He also secured the somewhat doubtful allegiance of the allied tribes, but only accepted the proffered services of a few warriors of each nation, and this more as hostages than for the purpose of increasing his strength.

M. de Vaudreuil then hastened from Montreal to Quebec, where he found that his lieutenant, M. de Boucourt, had effectually executed his orders to strengthen the defenses. The settlements along the coast below that important stronghold were sufficiently guarded to render a hostile debarkation difficult and dangerous. The governor immediately reascended the St. Lawrence, and formed a corps of 3000 men under M. de Longueiul, at Chambly, to await the approach of the English. The invading army, however, retreated without coming to action, having received information of a great disaster which had befallen their fleet. The British admiral had neglected the warnings of an experienced French navigator, named Paradis, who accompanied him, and approached too near a small island in the narrow and dangerous channel of the Traverse; a sudden squall from the southeast burst upon him at that critical moment, and his own, with seven other ships of the fleet, were driven on the rocky shore, and utterly destroyed: very few men escaped from these ill-fated vessels.*

* "Enfin la retraite des deux armées Anglaises qui devaient attaquer en même tems la Nouvelle France par terre et par mer, et diviser ses forces en les occupant aux deux extremités de la colonie,

The generosity and loyalty of the merchants of Quebec furnished the governor with 50,000 crowns, to strengthen the fortifications of their town, on the occasion of a rumor that the English were again preparing an invasion of Canada, in 1712, aided by the Iroquois, to whom they had become reconciled. At the same time, a new enemy entered the field—the fiercest and bravest of the native tribes; this people, called Outagamis or Foxes, joined in a confederacy with the Five Nations, and undertook to burn the French fort at Detroit,* and destroy the inhabitants. A large force

n' étant plus douteuse, et le bruit s' étant répandu que la première avait fait naufrage dans le fleuve St. Laurent vers les Sept Isles, M. de Vaudreuil y envoya plusieurs barques. Elles y trouvérent les carcasses de huit gros vaisseaux, dont on avoit enlevé les canons et les meilleurs effets, et pres de trois mille personnes noyées, dont les corps étoient étendus sur le rivage. On y reconnut deux compagnies entières des Gardes de la Reine, qu' on distingua à leurs casaques rouges, et plusieurs familles Ecossoises, destinées à peupler le Canada, mais quoique le reste de la flotte eût resté mouillé plusieurs jours au même endroit, pour enlever toute la charge des vaisseaux brisés, on ne laissa point d' y faire un assez grand butin."—Charlevoix, tom. iv., p. 82.

* The city of Detroit dates its history from July, 1701. At that time M. de la Motte Cadillac, with one hundred men, and a Jesuit, carrying with them every thing necessary for the commencement and support of the establishment meditated, reached this place. "How numerous and diversified," said a public literary document, "are the incidents compressed within the history of this settlement. No place in the United States presents such a series of events interesting in themselves and permanently affecting, as they occurred, its progress and prosperity. Five times its flag has changed; three different sovereignties have claimed its allegiance; and since it has been held by the United States, its government has been thrice transferred. Twice it has been besieged by the Indians, once captured in war, and once burned to the ground."

"Detroit has long been considered as the limit of civilization toward the northwest. This town, or commercial port, is dignified by the name, and enjoys the chartered rights of a city, although its population at present does not exceed three thousand. The banks of the river above and below the city are lined with a French population, descendants of the first European traders among the Indians in that quarter, and extending from Lake Erie to Lake St. Clair, increasing in density as they approach the town, and averaging, perhaps, one hundred per mile. This place, but a little while ago so distant, is now brought within four days of the city of New York, the track pursued being seven hundred and fifty miles. Here, at Detroit, some of the finest

of their warriors advanced upon the little stronghold, but Du Buisson, the able and gallant commandant, having summoned the neighboring allies to the assistance of his garrison of twenty Frenchmen, defeated the dangerous invaders after a series of conflicts almost unparalleled for obstinacy in Indian war, and destroyed more than a thousand of their best and bravest.*

These important successes, however, could not secure to the French an equality in trade with their English rivals; their narrow and injudicious commercial system limited the supply of European goods to be exchanged for the spoils of the Red Man's forests; the fur trade, therefore, fell almost wholly into the hands of British merchants, and even those native tribes in closest alliance with the Canadian governor obtained their scanty clothing from the looms of Yorkshire, and their weapons of the chase from the industrious hands of our colonists.

By the treaty of Utrecht in 1713, Louis the Magnificent ceded away forever, with ignorant indifference, the noble province of Acadia,† the inexhaustible fisheries of Newfoundland, and his claims to the vast but almost unknown regions of Hudson's Bay; his nominal sovereignty over the Iroquois was also thrown into the scale,‡ and thus a dearly-purchased

steamers in North America come and go every day, connecting it with the east, and have begun already to search out the distant west and north."—Colton's *Tour to the American Lakes*, vol. i., p. 46.

* "Le fruit de sa victoire (Du Buisson) fut que les Anglois désespérèrent de s' établir au Détroit, ce qui auroit été la ruine entière de la Nouvelle France, non seulement à cause de la situation de ce lieu, qui est le centre et le plus beau pays du Canada, mais encore parcequ'il ne nous auroit plus été possible d'entretenir la moindre communication avec les sauvages d'en haut ni avec la Louisiane."—Charlevoix, vol. iv., p. 105.

† "Le roi très Chrétien céde à la reine d'Angleterre à perpétuite, l'Acadie, ou Nouvelle Ecosse, en entier, conformément à ses anciennes limites, comme aussi la ville de Port Royal, maintenant appellée Annapolis Royale."—*Article XII. du Traité d'Utrecht*, 1713.

‡ "Ce dernier article ne nous ôta rien de réel, et ne donna non plus rien aux Anglais, parceque les cantons renouvellèrent les protestations, qu'ils avoient dejà faites plus d'une fois contre les prétentions réciproques de leurs voisins et ont très bien sçu se maintenir dans la possession de leur liberté et de leur indépendance."—Charlevoix.

peace restored comparative tranquillity to the remnant of his American empire.*

The fierce Outagamis, more incensed than weakened by their losses at Detroit, made savage and murderous reprisals upon all the nations allied to the French. Their vindictive vigilance rendered the routes between the distant posts of Canada, and those southward to Louisiana,† for many years almost impracticable. At one time, indeed, when over-

* "Il (Prior) étoit pareillement autorisé à traite sur les limites de l'Amerique septentrionale, et s'il plaisoit au roi, ces deux articles pouvoient être réglés en peu de tems."—*Mémoires de Torcy sur la Paix d'Utrecht*, vol. iii., p. 426.

† It is hardly remembered at the present day that the French nation once claimed, and had begun to colonize the whole region which lies at the back of the thirteen original United States, from the mouth of the St. Lawrence to that of the Mississippi, comprising both the Canadas and the vast fertile valley of the Ohio, and had actually occupied the two outlets of this whole region by its ports at Quebec and New Orleans.[1] Canada, the oldest French colony, and the only one on the continent to which that nation has sent any considerable number of settlers, was under the management of an exclusive company, from 1663 to the downfall of what was called the Mississippi Scheme, in 1720; and this circumstance, still more, perhaps, than the vicious system of granting the land to nonresident proprietors, to be held by seignorial tenure, checked its progress. Louisiana, with more sources of surplus wealth from climate and soil, was never a very thriving colony, and was surrendered to Spain with little reluctance, from which last power its dominion passed to the United States.

The French traders and hunters intermarried and mixed with the Indians at the back of our settlements, and extended their scattered posts along the whole course of the two vast rivers of that continent. Even at this day, far away on the upper waters of these mighty streams, and beyond the utmost limits reached by the backwoodsman, the traveler discovers villages in which the aspect and social usages of the people, their festivities and their solemnities, in which the white and red man mingle on equal terms, strangely contrast with the habits of the Anglo-American, and announce to him, on his first approach, their Gallic origin.—Merivale, vol. i., p. 58; Sismondi, *Etudes sur L'Ecole Politique*, vol. ii., p. 200; Latrobe.

1 "La ville de Nouvelle Orléans fut fondée dans l'anneé 1717. M. de Bienville fit choix de la situation. On a nommé cette fameuse ville la Nouvelle Orléans. Ceux qui lui ont donné ce nom croyoient qu' Orléans est du genre féminin, mais qu' importe? l' usage est établi et il est au-dessus des régles de la grammaire.. Cette ville est la première qu' un des plus grands fleuves du monde ait vu s'elever sur ses bords."—Charlevoix, vol. viii., p. 192.

whelmed by a successful invasion, these implacable savages made a formal cession of their territories to M. de Vaudreuil; but, the moment opportunity offered, they renewed hostilities, and, although beaten in repeated encounters, having united the remnant of their tribe to the powerful Sioux and Chichachas,* they continued for a long time to harass the steps of their detested conquerors.

On the 10th of April, 1725, M. de Vaudreuil closed his useful career. For one-and-twenty years he had discharged his important duties with unswerving loyalty, ability, and vigilance. Good fortune crowned him with well-merited success, and he went to rest from his earthly labors with the blessings of a grateful people, who, under his wise rule, had rapidly progressed to prosperity.

The Marquis de Beauharnois, captain of the marine, succeeded to the government of the now tranquil colony. His anxiety was aroused, however, the year after his accession, by the vigorous efforts of the English to extend their commerce even into the heart of the Canadian territories. Governor Burnet, of New York, had erected a fort and trading post at Oswego, with the view of monopolizing the rich traffic of the Western lakes. To counteract this design, M. de Beauharnois sent the Baron de Longueuil to negotiate with the Indians in the neighborhood of Niagara, for their consent to the erection of a French fort and establishment upon the banks of their magnificent river, where it enters the waters of Ontario. After many difficulties in reconciling the jealousy of the native tribes, the French succeeded in effecting their object. On the other hand, the men of New

* "Garcilasso de la Vega parle des Chichachas dans son histoire de la conquête de la Floride, et il les place à peu près au même endroit où ils sont encore présentement. . . . Ce sont encore les plus braves soldats de la Louisiane, mais ils etoient beaucoup plus nombreux du tem de Ferdinand de Soto. . . . C'est notre alliance aves les Illinois qui nous a mis en guerre avec les Chichachas et les Anglois de la Caroline attisent le feu. Notre établissement dans la Louisiane fait grand mal au cœur à ceux-ci; c'est une barrière que nous mettons entre leurs puissantes colonies de l'Amerique septentrionale, et le Mexique. . . . Les Espagnols qui nous voyent avec des yeux si jaloux nous fortifiér dans ce pays, ne sentent pas encore l'importance du service que nous leur rendons."—Charlevoix, tom. vi., p. 160.

York strengthened their defenses at Oswego, and increased the garrison. Angry communications then passed between the French and English governors in peremptory demands for its abandonment by the one, and prompt refusals by the other. Each was well aware of the importance of the position: it served as a means of diverting nearly all the Indian trade by Albany and the channel of the Hudson into the British colonies, and also formed a frontier protection to those numerous and flourishing settlements which Anglo-Saxon industry and courage were rapidly forming in the wilderness.

In the vain hope of checking the irrepressible energies of rival colonization, Beauharnois erected a fort at Crown Point, on Lake Champlain, commanding its important navigation, and also serving to hold in terror the settlers on the neighboring banks of the Hudson and Connecticut. The English remonstrated without effect against this occupation, and the French remained in peaceable possession of their establishment. The next war that broke out between the mother countries spread rapine and destruction over the colonial frontiers, without any real result beyond mutual injury and embittered hatred. From this fort at Crown Point, and other posts held by the Canadians, marauding parties poured upon the British settlements, and destroyed them with horrid barbarity. A party of French and Indians even penetrated to Saratoga, within forty miles of Albany, attacked and burned the fort, and slew or carried into captivity the unhappy defenders.

For many subsequent years the history of Canada is but a chronicle of the accession of governors and the registration of royal edicts. In comparison with her southern rivals, the progress in material prosperity was very slow. Idleness and drunkenness, with all their attendant evils, were rife to a most injurious extent. The innumerable fêtes, or holidays of the Church, afforded opportunities to the dissolute, and occasioned frequent instances of serious disorders, till the king was urged to interfere: the number of these fête-days was then very much reduced, to the great benefit of the colony. The feudal system of tenure also operated most unfavorably upon the development of agricultural resources, and the forced partition of lands tended to reduce all the landholders to a fraternity of pauperism. The court of France endeavored vainly to remedy these evils, without removing the causes, and passed various edicts to encourage the further clearance of wild land, and to stimulate settlement.

In 1745, the year when the power of France in Europe was exalted by the splendid victory of Fontenoy, a dangerous blow was struck at her sovereignty in America by the capture of Louisburg, and with it the whole island of Cape Breton,* by the New Englanders under Mr. Pepperel,†

* From the year 1706 the name of Cape Breton was changed to Ile Royale. Louisburg was called le Havre à l'Anglais.

† "The importance of the colonies[1] was too little considered until the commencement of the last war. The reduction of Cape Breton by the people of New England was an acquisition so unexpected and fortunate, that America became, on that remarkable event, a more general topic of conversation. Mr. Shirley, the governor of Massachusetts Bay, was the principal projector of that glorious enterprise; an enterprise which reduced to the obedience of his Britannic majesty the *Dunkirk* of North America. Of such consequence to the French was the possession of that important key to their American settlements, that its restitution was, in reality, the purchase of the last general peace of Europe."[2]—*A Review of the Military Operations in North America, in a Letter to a Nobleman*, p. 4 (London, 1757).

"The plan of the invasion of Cape Breton was laid at Boston, and New England[3] bore the expense of it. A merchant named Pepperel,[4]

[1] "L'ile de Cap Brêton n' étoit pas alors (at the time of the treaty of Ryswick), un objet, et l' établissement que nous y avions n'avoit rien qui put exciter la jalousie des Anglais: elle nous demeura."—Charlevoix, tom. iii., p. 349.

[2] "The island of Cape Breton, of which the French were shamefully left in possession at the treaty of Utrecht, 1713, through the negligence or corruption of the British ministry, when Great Britain had the power of giving law to her enemies."—Russell's *Modern Europe*, vol. iii., p. 223.

"Only three years after Cape Breton was taken by the New Englanders, England was obliged reluctantly to resign her favorite conquest of Cape Breton, in order to obtain the restitution of Madras. This was by the treaty of Aix-la-Chapelle in 1748. The final conquest took place in 1758, by the English, under Amherst and Wolfe."—Belsham, vol. ii., p. 333.

[3] "The sum of £235,749 was granted by the British Parliament to the provinces of New England, to reimburse them for the expense of reducing Cape Breton."—Smollett, vol. iii., p. 224.

[4] "The news of this victory being transmitted to England, Mr. Pepperel was preferred to the dignity of a baronet of Great Britain."—*Ibid.*, vol. iii., p. 154.

aided by Admiral Warren's squadron. This disaster was no sooner known in Paris* than an extensive armament was equipped under the command of the Duc d'Anville, an officer of known valor and ability. The wounded pride of the French hurried on rapidly the preparations for this ex-

who had excited, encouraged, and directed the enterprise, was intrusted with the command of the army of 6000 men, which had been levied for this expedition. Though these forces, convoyed by a squadron from Jamaica, brought the first news to Cape Breton of the danger that threatened it; though the advantage of a surprise would have secured the landing without opposition; though they had but six hundred regular troops to encounter, and eight hundred inhabitants hastily armed, the success of the undertaking was still precarious. What great exploits, indeed, could have been expected from militia suddenly assembled, who had never seen a siege or faced an enemy, and were to act under the direction of sea-officers only? These inexperienced troops stood in need of the assistance of some fortunate accident, with which they were indeed favored in a singular manner. The construction and repair of the fortifications had always been left to the care of the garrison at Louisburg. The soldiers were eager to be employed on these works, as the means of procuring a comfortable subsistence. When they found that those who were to have paid them appropriated to themselves the profits of their labors, they demanded justice: it was denied them, and they determined to assert their right. As the depredations had been shared between the chief persons of the colony and the subaltern officers, the soldiers could obtain no redress. They had, in consequence, lived in open rebellion for above six months when the English appeared before the place. This was the time to conciliate the minds of both parties; the soldiers made the first advances, but their commanders distrusted a generosity of which they themselves were incapable. It was firmly believed that the soldiers were only desirous of sallying out that they might have an opportunity of deserting, and their own officers kept them in a manner prisoners, until a defense so ill managed had reduced them to the necessity of capitulating. The whole island shared the fate of Louisburg, its only bulwark. This valuable possession, restored to France by the treaty of Aix-la-Chapelle, was again attacked by the English in 1748, and taken. The possession was confirmed to Great Britain by the peace in 1763, since which the fortifications have been blown up, and the town of Louisburg dismantled."—Winterbottom's *History of America*, vol. iv., p. 14.

* "When Marshal Belleisle was told of the taking of Cape Breton, he said he could believe that, because the ministry had no hand in it. We are making bonfires for Cape Breton, and thundering over Genoa, while our army in Flanders is running away."—Walpole's *Letters to Sir Horace Mann*, July 26, 1745.

pedition, which they confidently hoped would redeem the tarnished honor of their arms in the Western world. Early in May the fleet was already completely appointed; but the elements did not second these energetic preparations, and contrary winds detained the armament till the 22d of June. Then it at last put to sea, in the formidable strength of eleven ships of the line, thirty smaller vessels of war, and transports containing 3000 regular soldiers. Nova Scotia, the Acadia* of other days, was their destination. There it was expected that the old French settlers, who had unwillingly submitted to English conquest, would readily range themselves once more under the fleur-de-lys: Canada had already sent her contingent of 1700 men under M. de Ramsay to aid the enterprise, and M. de Conflans, with four ships of the line from the West Indies, was directed to join the squadron.

This formidable fleet was but a short time at sea when the ships separated and fell into hopeless confusion. On the 12th of September, indeed, the Duc d'Anville reached the Western continent in the Northumberland, accompanied by a few other vessels, but there no laurels awaited the gallant admiral: he was suddenly seized with apoplexy, and in four days his body was committed to the deep. The vice admiral

* "The tract of country known by the name of Nova Scotia, or New Scotland, was in 1784 divided into two provinces, viz., New Brunswick on the southwest, and Nova Scotia on the southeast. The former comprehends that part of the old province of Nova Scotia which lies to the northward and westward of a line drawn from the mouth of the River St. Croix, through the center of the Bay of Fundy to Baye Verte, and thence into the Gulf of St. Lawrence, including all lands within six leagues of the coast. The rest is the province of Nova Scotia, to which is annexed the island of St. John's, which lies north of it in the Gulf of St. Lawrence. The modern Nova Scotia is the French Acadia. The modern New Brunswick is the French Nouvelle Ecosse. This name was given by Sir William Alexander, to whom the first grant of lands was given by James I.; since then the country has frequently changed hands, from the French to the English nation, backward and forward. It was not confirmed to the English till the peace of Utrecht. Three thousand families were transported into this country in 1749, at the charge of the government, and they built and settled the town of Halifax."—Winterbottom's *History of America*, vol. iv., p. 39.

immediately proposed returning to France, on account of the absence of the greater part of his force; but other officers strongly opposed this desponding counsel, and urged a bold attack upon Nova Scotia* rather than an inglorious retreat. The more vigorous course was adopted by a council of war, which threw the vice admiral into such a state of frantic excitement that he ran himself through the body, fancying he had fallen into the hands of the enemy. De la Jonquière succeeded to the command, and, although more than three-score years of age, acted with unimpaired energy. But the elements were again hostile to France; the fleet was dispersed by a violent storm off Cape Sable, and the shattered remnant of the expedition returned ingloriously to their country, without having accomplished any of the objects for which they had been sent forth.

The government at Paris was, however, by no means cast down by these untoward occurrences, and the armament was speedily equipped to renew their efforts against the English colonies. The expedition was prepared at Brest, under the command of M. de la Jonquière, and, at the same time, a squadron under M. de St. George was armed with a view to threaten the coasts of British India.

The English ministry, early informed of all the movements of their opponents, resolved to intercept both these squadrons, which they had been apprised would sail from port at the same time. Admiral Anson and Rear-admiral Warren were ordered upon this enterprise with a formidable fleet, and, taking their departure from Plymouth, steered for Cape Finisterre, on the Gallican coast. On the third of May, 1746, they fell in with the French squadrons of six large

* "La cour de France avoit extrêmement à cœur de recouvrer cette province (Acadia); les efforts reitérés des Anglois pour l'avoir en leur puissance, et plus encore, leur triomphe après l'avoir conquise, avoit enfin ouvert les yeux aux François sur la grandeur de la perte qu'ils avoient faite. M. de Pontchartrain écrivit ainsi à M. de Beauharnois: 'Je vous ai fait assez connoître combien il est important de reprendre ce poste (le Port Royal) avant que les ennemies y soient solidement établis. La conservation de toute l'Amérique septentrionale, et le commerce des Pêches le démandent également: ce sont deux objets qui me touchent vivement.' "—Charlevoix, tom. iv., p. 90.

men-of-war, as many frigates, four armed East Indiamen, and a valuable convoy of thirty ships. The enemy's heavier vessels immediately formed in order of battle, while the merchantmen made all sail away, under the protection of the frigates. The British were also ready for action, and a severe combat ensued. Before night all the French line of battle ships were captured after a spirited defense, but two thirds of the convoy escaped through the darkness of the night. A considerable quantity of bullion fell into the hands of the victors, and their grateful sovereign rewarded the courage and good fortune of the admirals by raising Anson to the peerage, and decorating Warren with the ribbon of the Bath.

Admiral de la Jonquière, the newly-appointed governor of Canada, was among the numerous captives who graced the triumph of the British fleet. When the news of this event reached Paris, the king appointed to the vacant dignity the Comte de la Galissonière,* an officer of distinguished

* "Roland Michel Barrin, marquis de la Galissonière, remplit la poste de gouverneur comme s'il ne se fût toute sa vie occupé que de cet objet...... Il établit à Quebec un arsenal maritime, et un chantier de construction, où l'on n'employa que les bois des pays. Il conçut, proposa, et fit adopter le vasté plan dont il commenca l'éxécution, de joindre le Canada et la Louisiana par une chaine de forts et d'établissements, le long de l'Ohio et des Mississippi, à travers les régions désertes qui séparaient ces deux colonies à l'ouest des lacs. A l'avantage d'établir entre elles une communication moins pénible et moins long que par le nord, se joignoit celui de pouvoir faire parvenir les dépêches en France, en hiver par la Louisiane, tandis que l'embouchure du fleuve St. Laurent est fermeé par les glaces; enfin celui de resserrer les Anglais entre les montagnes et la mer...... Il emporta tous les regrets quand il revint en France, en 1749...... La défaite de l'amiral Anglais, Byng, et la prise de Minorque que fut le fruit de cette victoire décisive, couronnèrent sa carrière. Il avoit entrepris cette dernière expédition contre l'avis des médécins qui lui avoient annoncé sa mort comme prochaine, s'il se rembarquoit...... Il cacha ses maux tant qu'il put, mais il fut enfin obligé de se démettre du commandement. Il revint en France et se mit en route pour Fontainebleau où étoit alors le roi. Les forces lui manquèrent totalement à Nemours, où il mourut le 26 Octobre, 1756...... A ses talens éminens comme marin, la Galissonière unissoit une infinité de connaissances...... Sérieux et ferme, mais en même tems doux, modéré, affable, et intégre, il se faisito respecter et chérir de tous ceux qui servoient sous ses ordres......

merit and ability. The wisdom of this selection was speedily displayed; the new governor no sooner entered upon the duties of office than his active zeal found employment in endeavoring to develop the magnificent resources of his province. He made himself thoroughly acquainted with the face of the country, the climate, population, agriculture, and commerce, and then presented an able statement to the French court of the great importance of the colony, and a system which, had it been adopted in time, might have secured it against English aggression.

The Comte de la Galissonière proposed that M. du Quesne, a skillful engineer, should be appointed to establish a line of fortifications through the interior of the country, and, at the same time, urged the government of France to send out 10,000 peasants to form settlements on the banks of the great lakes and southern rivers. By these means he affirmed that the English colonies would be restricted within the narrow tract lying eastward from the Allegany Mountains, and in time laid open to invasion and ruin. His advice was, however, disregarded, and the splendid province of Canada soon passed forever from under the sway of France.*

Tant de belles qualités étoient cachées sous un extérieur peu avantageux. La Galissonière étoit de petite taille et bossu. Lorsque les sauvages vinrent le saluer à son arrivée au Canada, frappés de son peu d'apparence, ils lui parlèrent en ces termes, 'Il faut que tu aies une bien belle âme, puisqu' avec un si vilain corps, le grand chef notre père t'a envoyé ici pour nous commander.' Ils ne tardèrent pas à reconnaître la justice de leur opinion, et entourèrent de leur amour et de leur vénération, en l'appellant du nom de père, l'homme qui ne se servit du pouvoir que pour améliorer leur sort."—*Biographie Universelle*, art. Galissonière.

* "In observing on old maps the extent of the ancient French colonies in America, I was haunted by one painful idea. I asked myself how the government of my country could have left colonies to perish which would now be to us a source of inexhaustible prosperity. From Acadia and Canada to Louisiana, from the mouth of the St. Lawrence to that of the Mississippi, the territories of New France surrounded what originally formed the confederation of the thirteen United States. The eleven other states, the district of Columbia, the Michigan, Northwest, Missouri, Oregon, and Arkansas territories, belonged, or would have belonged to us, as they now belong to the United States, by the cession of the English and Spaniards, our first heirs in Canada and in

Under the impression that the expected peace between the mother countries would render it important to define the boundaries of their colonial possessions, the active governor of Canada dispatched M. de Celeron de Bienville, with 300 men, to traverse the vast wilderness lying from Detroit south-east to the Apalachian Mountains. Assuming this range as the limit of the British colonies, he directed that leaden plates, engraved with the arms of France, should be buried at particular places in the western country, to mark the territories of France, and that the chief of the expedition should endeavor to secure a promise from the Indians to exclude for the future all English traders. At the same time, he gave notice to the governor of Pennsylvania that he was commanded by the King of France to seize all British merchants found in those countries, and to confiscate their goods. De Celeron fulfilled his difficult commission to the best of his powers, but the forms of possession which he executed excited the jealous apprehension of the Indians, who concluded that he designed to subject or even enslave them.

When M. de la Galissonière failed in his endeavor to obtain the aid of an extensive immigration from France, he turned his thoughts toward the Acadian settlers* (whom

Louisiana. More than two thirds of North America would acknowledge the sovereignty of France. . . . . . We possessed here vast countries which might have offered a home to the excess of our population, an important market to our commerce, a nursery to our navy. Now we are forced to confine in our prisons culprits condemned by the tribunals, for want of a spot of ground whereon to place these wretched creatures. We are excluded from the New World, where the human race is recommencing. The English and Spanish languages serve to express the thoughts of many millions of men in Africa, in Asia, in the South Sea Islands, on the continent of the two Americas; and we, disinherited of the conquests of our courage and our genius, hear the language of Racine, of Colbert, and of Louis XIV. spoken merely in a few hamlets of Louisiana and Canada, under a foreign sway. There it remains, as though but for an evidence of the reverses of our fortune and the errors of our policy. Thus, then, has France disappeared from North America, like those Indian tribes with which she sympathized, and some of the wrecks of which I have beheld."—Chateaubriand's *Travels in America*, vol. ii., p. 207.

* From the treaty of St. Germain-en-Laye, 1632, till 1654, the French had quiet possession of Acadia; then Cromwell sent Major

the treaty of Utrecht had transferred to the British crown), with the object of forming a new colony. The readiest expedient to influence this simple and pious people was, obviously, by gaining over their clergy; the Abbè le Loutre was selected as the fittest embassador to induce them to withdraw from allegiance to the English government. This politic and unscrupulous priest appealed to their interests, nationality, and religion as inducements to abandon the conquered country, and to establish themselves under the French crown in a new settlement which he proposed to form on the Canadian side of Acadia. Le Loutre's persuasions influenced many of these primitive people to proceed to the French posts, where every protection and attention was bestowed upon them.

Animated by the success of this measure, and sanguine that large numbers of the Acadians would follow the first seceders, De la Galissonière induced the home government to appoint a considerable sum yearly to carrying out his views; but, in the midst of his patriotic exertions, he was obliged to hand over the reins of government to M. de la Jonquière, who had now arrived to claim the post so ably held by another during his captivity with the English. Galissonière, however, before he sailed for France, magnanimously furnished his successor with the best information on colonial matters, and pointed out the most promising plans for the improvement of the province.* De la Jonquière un-

Sedgwick to attack it, with orders to expel all who would not acknowledge themselves subjects of England. Sedgwick executed his commission, and Cromwell passed a grant of Acadia to one De la Tour, a French refugee, who had purchased Lord Sterling's title to that country; and De la Tour soon after transferred his right to Sir William Temple.

Nova Scotia was ceded to France at the treaty of Breda, in 1670. In 1690 it was retaken by Sir William Phipps on his way to Quebec. It was given back to France by the treaty of Ryswick; retaken by General Nicholson (who gave the name of Annapolis to Port Royal) in 1710, during the War of the Succession. It was formally and finally ceded to England at the peace of Utrecht. The undefined limits of Nova Scotia were a constant source of dispute between the French and English nations.

* Professor Kalm thus speaks of La Galissonière, who was the

wisely rejected such as related to the Acadian settlements; but the King of France disapproved of his inaction, and reprimanded him for not having continued the course of his predecessor. Instructions were given him to take immediate possession of the neighboring country, to build new forts for

governor of Quebec at the time of his travels through Canada. "He was of a low stature and somewhat hump-backed. He has a surprising knowledge in all branches of science, and especially in natural history, in which he is so well versed, that, when he began to speak to me about it, I imagined I saw our great Linnæus under a new form. When he spoke of the use of natural history, of the method of learning, and employing it to raise the state of a country, I was astonished to see him take his reasons from politics, as well as natural philosophy, mathematics, and other sciences. I own that my conversation with this nobleman was very instructive to me, and I always drew a great deal of useful knowledge from it. He told me several ways of employing natural history to the purposes of politics, and to make a country powerful in order to depress its envious neighbors. Never has natural history had a greater promotion in this country, and it is very doubtful whether it will ever have its equal here. As soon as he got the place of governor general, he began to take those measures for getting information in natural history which I have mentioned before. When he saw people who had for some time been in a settled place of the country, especially in the more remote parts, he always questioned them about the trees, plants, earths, stones, ores, animals, &c., of the place. Those who seemed to have clearer notions than the rest were obliged to give him circumstantial descriptions of what they had seen. He himself wrote down all the accounts he received, and by this great appreciation, so uncommon among persons of his rank, he soon acquired a knowledge of the most distant parts of America. The priests, commandants of forts and of several distant places, are often surprised by his questions, and wonder at his knowledge when they come to Quebec to pay their visits to him, for he often tells them that near such a mountain, or on such a shore, &c., where they often went a hunting, there are some particular plants, trees, earths, ores, &c., for he had got a knowledge of these things before. From hence it happened that some of the inhabitants believed he had a preternatural knowledge of things, as he was able to mention all the curiosities of places, sometimes near 200 Swedish miles from Quebec, though he never was there himself. Never was there a better statesman than he, and nobody can take better measures, and choose more proper means for improving a country and increasing its welfare. Canada was scarcely acquainted with the treasure it possessed in the person of this nobleman when it lost him again; the king wanted his services at home, and could not have him so far off."—Kalm, in Pinkerton, vol. xiii., p. 679.